# Ernest Thompson Seton's
# America

AMERICAN NATURALISTS SERIES

Farida A. Wiley, General Editor

*Published*

JOHN BURROUGHS' AMERICA
ERNEST THOMPSON SETON'S AMERICA

*In Preparation*

WILLIAM BARTRAM'S AMERICA
WASHINGTON IRVING'S AMERICA

*Ernest Thompson Seton in 1941*

# Ernest Thompson Seton's America

## SELECTIONS FROM THE WRITINGS OF
## THE ARTIST - NATURALIST

*Edited with an Introduction by*
### FARIDA A. WILEY

*With Contributions by*
### JULIA M. SETON

*And Drawings by Ernest Thompson Seton*

1962

## THE DEVIN-ADAIR COMPANY
*New York*

# IMPRESSIONS

### by Julia M. Seton

I SEE myself as I was that day, one of a large audience in a New England woodland. I had no particular interest in the announced speaker or his subject; I had merely accompanied some friends who had asked me to go.

My own work was along other lines, and in anticipation of the program, I experienced no feeling of pleasure.

The speaker appeared. He was a tall, handsome, robust man with a vigorous, aggressive personality. His shock of heavy black hair was worn conspicuously long. His piercing black eyes darted swiftly this way and that as he gauged his audience before he began to speak.

Even his unusual appearance did not arouse my interest.

But when the first words came from his lips, a thrill went through me. The depth of tone, the roundness of enunciation, the clarity of diction, the sheer magic of speech gripped the whole assembly. The children, who had been fussing and fidgeting in their seats, sat still, enthralled, long before the sense of the story could have had any message for them.

He told a simple tale which lasted for perhaps ten minutes. At the beginning, I was engrossed in his technique, but soon fell under the spell of the narrative. Yet, when the speaker ceased, I realized that I had not taken in the end of the story—I had been wholly lost in the cadence of his voice.

Many times in the next few years I was to have the opportunity of listening to public addresses by the same speaker. Some were fairy tales told to little children, some were scientific discourses to learned societies, some were animal stories with the mimicry of voice and action in which he was so proficient; but it was only after a long time, and by a direct effort of will, that I finally became able to listen with my mind to the end of what he had to say. Each time, at the close, I found myself floating in a sea of resonance, a rhythmic ebb and flow of modulated sound.

That first afternoon in the woodland, I was introduced to him after the conference. From that day onward, and for nearly a third of a century, we were associated not only in our personal lives but —in what to the world is more important—in our work. It soon became a twenty-four-hour-a-day companionship.

It is difficult to say what Seton's real *métier* was. Perhaps he is best known to the world as the writer of animal stories. He was the originator of his type of natural history tale—a type in which the animals were never humanized. Yet they live in his books as perhaps no other wild creatures ever have, each an individual, living his own life, dying his own death, but preserved forever in the memory of all who can read.

Rudyard Kipling once wrote Seton that it was the reading of *Molly Cottontail* that got him started writing his *Jungle Tales.* Yet Kipling never achieved the same effect with his own animal stories; somehow, the animal that talks like a person and thinks like a person loses its hold when the audience is grown up.

Seton's stories, on the other hand, mean even more to the adult than to the child. The philosophy between the lines, though rarely expressed in words, concerns human as well as animal life; and the mature reader comes away from one of Seton's stories with a conviction that living is a matter of heroic purpose and high enthusiasm, with flashes of insight into an infallible System.

Perhaps another reason that his stories appeal to everyone is the fact that he never was concerned with writing "literature." He had something to tell, and he went at it simply and sincerely. Style, so called, was not his aim; he achieved it through an innate talent for writing rather than by a studied attempt at creating a masterpiece.

If Seton had done no more than write the forty-odd volumes that line the shelves of nature-lovers' libraries all over the world, he would surely have won lasting fame. Many have won it on less. But he did more: he also illustrated all of his own books, as well as the scientific articles and treatises that are standard in every museum and zoo.

To Seton belongs the credit for the modern method of field identification popularized by Roger Tory Peterson in his series of field guides. It was he who in his drawings first used that device of emphasizing the definitive characteristics of a species which can be observed from a distance.

Now at Seton Village, in New Mexico, we have almost seven thousand of his drawings and paintings, counting small sketches. And this in addition to the hundreds that have been placed in public collections, both here and abroad, as well as those bought for private homes and museums. He is considered by those whose business it is to appraise such things as probably the best animal artist that ever lived.

At times, when he worked on the illustrations for a story that brought back thoughts of some unhappy occurrence, I would read to him, in order to keep his mind off the memories that were distasteful. This became a custom all through our life together, whenever I found him engaged with brush or crayon.

Writing, on the other hand, did not bother him at all. His manuscripts were all done in longhand; he never had any desire to use a typewriter, in fact never had any experience with one. He never even used a fountain pen, declaring that such contraptions never worked when one needed them. He used an old-fashioned pen and regular ink.

Seton was devoid of temperament in the ordinary meaning of the word, unconsciously demonstrating the validity of the dictum that temperament is temper in the world of art. I have seen him many times concentratedly writing a story or an important article, when a group of casual visitors was announced. With not even a trace of impatience, he would always rise to greet them, spend sometimes a couple of hours with them in conversation. Then, upon their departure, he would quietly return to his desk, pick up his pen, and go on with the thought he had been engaged on before the interruption.

He liked people, crowds of people, and had a most friendly and considerate manner, but abhorred back-slapping familiarity. There was not much temptation to treat him in that way, but I saw him on two occasions jump up from his chair ready to fight when some thoughtless young man patted his shoulder.

There is no doubt that Seton had a one-track mind—that is, one track at a time. While he was engaged in any project, be it writing, painting, building or conversation, nothing else in the world could compete for his attention. This quality undoubtedly accounts for his tremendous output of work. A shining example was the writing of his *magnum opus, Lives of Game Animals*. The preliminary notes had been accumulated through nearly sixty years of indefatigable research, accurate observation, and daily notation in his fifty-odd volumes of *Journals*.

But when the time came for the actual writing of what turned out to be three thousand pages of most careful scientific natural history, we practically went into retreat. For seven years, we worked seven days a week from eight o'clock in the morning till late each night. We did no other writing during that period; we stopped our annual lecture tours and accepted almost no social engagements. In those years, there was but one focal point in our lives, a definite goal to attain, a concise pattern for purposeful living. And the joy we had in the doing could never be equaled by the high degree of success which the book achieved, or by the signal honors it brought him.

Seton's achievements were indeed many and great: a writer who in his own field has never been excelled, if equaled; an artist acclaimed as at least among the best in the line of his own work; an architect and builder whose ideas have been copied by many a professional; a deep student of American Indian life; a lecturer and storyteller *par excellence;* the founder and projector of the first of all the outdoor youth movements. In all of these rôles, he was master beyond dispute.

But to me who worked with him in all these fields, he stands out above all else not as writer, artist, or student, but as a man. It is the lovable trivia which come to mind—the intangible foibles, the frailties, the misbehaviors, the peccadilloes—all the insignificant things that constituted the warm human quality in him, the wholesome spirit that was the foundation of his charm and his greatness.

Our dream of a home in the West had been postponed for many years. But it finally came to pass, and the joy we had in building it in all its ramifications was supreme.

We laid great store by the little rituals and ceremonies we performed at home through the years. Every hearth fire was blessed on its first lighting, each of our rooms carried on the door the totem of the occupant, no birthday ever passed without its joyous celebration. There were a number of meaningful customs which we used at the table—on the face of them trifling perhaps, but wondrously powerful in establishing and perpetuating an atmosphere of love.

The driveways, the bridle trails, the gates and the paths throughout our place here at Seton Village still carry the laugh-provoking signs and carvings that he rejoiced in nailing up to surprise me at my next passing. One which still perplexes transient visitors is a wooden placard on a bridge over a dry river bed, which says: NO FISHING. The day he placed it there, he explained to me as I gazed questioningly, "That is not an order—it is a mere statement of fact."

In recalling our experiences together, I am always struck by the diversity of interests in Seton's life. And it comes to me very forcefully that all of these interests were deep-laid, not superficial veneers of endeavor; each was a field in which he not only worked sincerely and well, but excelled beyond the common run.

Perhaps this was the secret of his lifelong vitality, in physical health as well as in mental accomplishment. He never could have settled into a rut, for the whole world was his to deal with and to make his own.

Julia M. Seton

*Seton Village,*
*New Mexico*

# INTRODUCTION

### by Farida A. Wiley

Ernest Thompson Seton, artist, naturalist, author, architect, un-excelled teller of stories, student of Indian life, and scientist of world renown, was born of Scottish parentage in the seaside city of South Shields, England, on August 14, 1860. He died at Santa Fe, New Mexico, October 23, 1946.

Seton's great-grandfather, Lord Seton, was Earl of Winton. His father was the legal heir to that title but never used it, choosing Thompson—an assumed name taken by a Scottish ancestor—instead. In telling of the various forms his own name took during his lifetime, Seton explains (in his autobiography) that Seton-Thompson was a *nom de plume* and Seton his real family name; but due to a promise made to his mother, he used Seton-Thompson throughout the duration of her life. His earlier works appear under that name.

The tenth son, born to a mother who wanted only girls, was christened Ernest Evan; the Evan in memory of a famous wolf-hunting relative who helped rid Scotland of some of the fierce wolves of his day. It was bestowed, so his mother said, in the hope that Ernest would inherit the courage, fortitude, and renown of his Cameron ancestor.

It is interesting to note that throughout his career Seton used for his insignia the imprint of a wolf track, and that the wolf became one of the animal heroes about which he wrote many stories and on whose life history he did much scientific research.

His most famous wolf story, *Lobo,* was about an animal that lived in the Currumpaw Valley near Clayton, New Mexico. This area, in the 1880's, was one of the finest cattle-ranch territories of the West, but the wolves were so destructive to young cattle that Seton accepted a ranch owner's challenge to go to Clayton and try to rid the area of them. Two of these wolves became so adept in avoiding traps, poison, dogs, and man that they became well-known figures and were immortalized by Seton in his stories "Lobo, the King of the Currumpaw" and "Badlands Billy," both of which are included in this volume.

Ernest was only six when his family lost their money and left England for Quebec, Canada. From Quebec they traveled some five hundred miles inland to an area about three miles from Lindsay, Ontario, where they purchased a one-hundred-acre tract of forest land and settled down in the wilderness to live the life of pioneers. The family consisted of the ten sons, one adopted daughter, a father who knew little about farming, and a mother who had been used to a large house and many servants.

For Ernest, this wilderness area was to furnish a perfect stage for the actors that were to influence his whole career. Even when he was only six, the natural world held an intense interest for him— an interest which his father deplored and continued to frown on for many a year, fearing it would not prove remunerative.

Pioneering had many compensations, and the Seton family learned by experience. These learning-experiences included clearing land, building a house and barn, taking care of sheep, cattle, and chickens, cutting firewood, planting gardens, inventing forms of amusement, and making toys. The Seton youngsters soon learned to be self-reliant and to develop their own abilities, and it was here that Ernest learned the lessons that were to be of such inestimable value to him throughout his life.

After four years of pioneering, the family moved to Toronto.

It soon became evident that in addition to Ernest's way with birds and animals, he had artistic ability, and when he was eighteen, his art won for him a Gold Medal in the Ontario Art School of Toronto. Using this as a talking point, he persuaded his father to allow him to go to London to study art. His father agreed to supply $25.00 a month "if he could possibly spare it, and it must be considered merely a loan to be repaid later." Trying to live in London on $25.00 a month almost wrecked Seton's health.

At that time the Royal Academy of Arts and Sciences was *the* school of schools, and Seton's great desire was to gain entrance to the Academy art class. Entrance was acquired on a merit basis and competition was keen. Seton's first trial entry was rejected but his second, a copy of Michelangelo's "Satyr," got him a seven-year scholarship.

Soon after his arrival in London he heard of the fabulously large natural-history library housed in the British Museum. To his disappointment, he found that eighteen-year-olds were not allowed access to this treasure house. Not being willing to take the no of library officials, he asked if they had the final word and was told that the directors made the rules. He asked who the directors were and was given the names of the Prince of Wales, the Archbishop of Canterbury, and Lord Beaconsfield. Letters to these men brought a prompt reply from each and a life-membership card which gave the budding artist-naturalist access to the reading room and to hundreds of books on natural history, of whose existence he had been unaware up to that time.

Getting acquainted with the writings of such American naturalists as Audubon, Wilson, Brewster, Ridgway, Burroughs, and Thoreau was a thrilling experience for young Seton. No doubt some of the inspiration to continue his research in the natural-history field came from the realization that many men had made a success in that field. This great "urge," which he later referred to as "The Buffalo Wind," sent him back to the prairies of Canada to observe, sketch, and record natural-history data, and several years later it sent him to New York City to find an outlet for his work.

Seton's travels took him the length and breadth of Canada and the United States, as well as to several foreign countries. He tramped, camped, hunted, and recorded observations made on these trips in words, measurements, and sketches that became voluminous. From these records he compiled his many books—books which have been enjoyed by young and old, which have been translated into many languages, and some of which have become classics.

One trip with his brother Arthur took him to the prairies of Western Canada where, at Carberry, Manitoba, he spent several happy and scientifically fruitful years. It was here, in 1882, that he started the habit of keeping daily scientific records, a habit he maintained throughout his life.

In those days, that section of Canada possessed a plentiful wildlife and had not yet been changed to any great degree. Some species were present that are rare or extinct today, thus making Seton's records doubly valuable. In his book *Arctic Prairies* he reports on the remnants of the wild herds of bison and caribou as they existed in the upper regions of the Mackenzie River as late as 1907.

In 1883, Seton—with $3.00 in his pocket—arrived in New York. He quickly met a number of influential people who helped him to get started as an illustrator and writer. One of these people was W. Lewis Frazer of *The Century Magazine,* who gave Seton the job of illustrating the second edition of *The Century Dictionary.* Another, C. Hart Merriam, was so thoroughly impressed by his sketching ability, after Seton had produced a fine likeness of a shrew for him, that he immediately ordered fifty other mammal sketches.

Then there was an old school friend, John T. Willing, who encouraged Seton to write for publication. As a result, he did a number of articles that were published in *St. Nicholas* and other magazines.

In June 1890 he sailed for Paris to continue his art studies. On board he met Miss Grace Gallatin of Sacramento, California, an author and a person of prominence. Two years later they were married, and for thirty years they were associated in the field of writing, but on widely different subjects. Their one daughter, Anya (Mrs. Hamilton Chase), was to become a writer, too. As the years went by, their interests and their work became more and more divergent, and they finally secured a legal separation.

While in Paris, as Seton was working on the illustrations for *The Century Dictionary*, he became aware of the great need for a book on the anatomy of birds and animals that would show "the visible forms and proportions of the *living* animal." He therefore set about planning, writing text, and making illustrations for such a book. It was published in 1896 under the title of *Art Anatomy of Animals* and became a leading textbook in the field of natural-history art.

It was in 1893 that Seton accepted the challenge of the New Mexico ranch owner to rid his ranch of wolves. He accepted, thinking that this area not only would give him a chance to study wolves, but would afford an opportunity to make further studies of such other mammals of the area as prairie dogs, kangaroo rats, coyotes, bears, and antelope. Much of the material of scientific import that he gathered during that period was published in *Lives of Game Animals*, which is used throughout the world as an authoritative reference on the life histories of North American mammals.

It is interesting to note that many men of large accomplishments have had to cope, during their lifetime, with ill-health and inadequate funds. Seton was no exception to this rule, for he experienced both ill-health and poverty. As a young boy he had lung trouble that threatened his life. His eyes, which were crossed in youth and were the butt of many an unpleasant joke, gave him much pain during his art-student days. In his twenty-ninth year he was stricken, while on a hunting trip, with acute arthritis, which for many years continued to be a great trial to him. But he overcame all these disabilities and lived to the venerable age of eighty-six.

In 1940, my friend Mrs. Inez M. Haring went with me to the Seton ranch near Santa Fe to be on hand for his eightieth-birthday celebration. This was a memorable occasion. On my desk before me is a candle, bearing the wolf insignia, that came from his birthday cake. One of the mental pictures which it revives is that of an alert, vigorous, stalwart figure standing before an Indian tepee, dressed in gay colors, an Indian conch belt about his waist, posing for me to take his picture.

To me, that picture typifies many of Seton's characteristics: his love for, and ability to use, bright color; his great interest in Indian customs and arts; his kindly manner and greatness of character.

On this 2,500-acre ranch, which Seton bought in 1930, he and his second wife, Julia Seton, planned and built their "castle." And it was there that he completed his colorful life on October 23, 1946, there in the land of wide-open spaces which he loved so well.

Seton was chairman of the committee that brought the Boy Scout movement to the United States. He served as Chief Scout for five years and wrote their first outdoor manual. Because he differed with some of the officials on such questions as militarism and what he termed the too-low standards for honors, he broke with them but continued his leadership in the Woodcraft League, which in 1934 had over 80,000 members.

At his home in Greenwich, Connecticut, he held training courses for those who aspired to be leaders of various children's groups. It was my privilege to work as an instructor in these training courses.

To those outdoors groups he was always known as "Chief," and none who ever saw him in action doubted the aptness of the title. Nor will they forget his dexterity in the use of the rubbing stick and bow to produce a spark to light the campfire. Three of the favorite stories told by Chief around these campfires are included in this book: "The Mackenzie River Ghost," "Gorm, the Giant of the Club," and "Little Burnt-All-Over."

How Seton's outdoor-group program was formulated can best be retold in his own words: "First, guided by my own preferences, I selected a hero as a model. Not Robin Hood, not Rollo the Sea King, nor King Arthur; but the ideal of Fenimore Cooper, perfectly embodied in Tecumseh, the great Shawnee—physically perfect, wise, brave, picturesque, unselfish, dignified.

"Then I framed a code of exploits, beginning with the things physical, rising through mental and spiritual, to find climax in the idea of service to one's people.

"For each exploit there was a badge, and all were earned by standards, not by competition. Competition means downing the other fellow; standards mean raising yourself."

During his lifetime Seton gave over 3,000 lectures. His own stories, illustrated with animal calls, were among the favorite topics called for in these appearances. The last lecture I heard him give was "Voices of the Night," at the Staten Island Zoo on February 15, 1942, when he was eighty-two. Before the lecture he amused a group of us by tapping out a certain rhythm on the cage of a large ape that responded each time by doing a most interesting dance. This ability to get response to rhythm made the story, told during the lecture, of how he called a moose into the open by means of a birch-bark horn, seem quite logical and possible. And I still remember how his imitation of the hunting call of a wolf made my scalp tingle. Even at eighty-two he still had that rare ability to make a story *live,* just as he did in his younger days.

The illustrations used in this book are made from original Seton sketches, line drawings and halftones, many of which have never before been published. These in a small way demonstrate his unsurpassed ability as an animal artist.

Seton's contributions to scientific literature are represented by quotes from various books and articles and include comments on the grizzly bear, gray wolf, bighorn sheep, prairie chicken, and sandhill crane.

Something of his admiration for the Indian and his ways will be caught in the excerpts from Seton's compilations of the creeds and prayers of the Indians; also in the Indian-sign-language characters (pages 168, 169) from his book *Sign Talk.*

Chief's first book of animal stories, *Wild Animals I Have Known,* published in October 1898, brought him quick fame and fortune. Three editions were published before the end of the year. The story of the immortal Lobo, included in this volume, is from that book.

Seton was at times criticized for ending his stories so tragically. To this criticism he would reply, "There is only one way to make an animal's history untragic, and that is to stop before the last chapter."

To the frequently asked question, "Are the stories true?" Seton had the following to say: "Lobo lived his wild romantic life from 1889 to 1894 in the Currumpaw region, as the ranchmen know too well, and died, precisely as related, on January 31, 1894. . . . The Mustang lived not far from Lobo in the early nineties. The story is given strictly as it occurred, excepting that there is a dispute as to the manner of his death. . . . Of course, we know nothing of the lamb days of Krag. I have constructed them out of fragments from the lives of many mountain lambs. But the latter parts, the long hunt and the death of Scotty MacDougall, are purely historical.

"I have been bitterly denounced, first, for killing Lobo; second, and chiefly, for telling of it to the distress of many tender hearts.

"To this I reply: In what frame of mind are my readers left with regard to the animal? Are their sympathies quickened toward the man who killed him, or toward the noble creature who, superior to every trial, died as he had lived, dignified, fearless, and steadfast?

"I have tried to stop the stupid and brutal work of destruction by an appeal—not to reason, that has failed hitherto—but to sympathy, and especially the sympathies of the coming generation.

"Men have spent millions of dollars each year on pictures. Why not? It is money well spent; good pictures give lasting elevating pleasure to all who see them. At the same time, men spend much labor and ingenuity in destroying harmless wild animals. No good, but great mischief, comes of this extermination. The main reason for preserving good pictures applies to the preservation of most animals. There will always be wild land not required for settlement; and how can we better use it than by making it a sanctuary for living wild things that afford pleasure to all who see them?"

In making these selections from some twenty different books, pamphlets and periodicals—almost all out of print—I have endeavored to give the reader an impression of Ernest Thompson Seton's diversified abilities, as well as an opportunity to enjoy his great understanding of the world of natural science.

If the book serves to keep alive the memory of a great man and to inspire some of its readers with a love of the out-of-doors, it will have fulfilled its purpose.

Farida A. Wiley

*American Museum of Natural History*
*New York*

# CONTENTS

# LIST OF ILLUSTRATIONS

# Ernest Thompson Seton's
# America

# 1.

# BOYHOOD DAYS IN CANADA

**I** WAS not quite six when we left England. I can clearly see yet the bustle of preparation in that summer of 1866—Father, Mother, ten sons (for two came after I did), and my cousin Polly Burfield, then eighteen years old, adopted as a sister; I see yet the piles and piles of boxes all lashed with strong, tarry rope that told of the ship tradition. I can still smell the cats in that cheap lodging in Glasgow where we spent a day and a night before going aboard the *St. Patrick,* a steamer bound for Quebec.

The strongest impression of this three-weeks' voyage is of rats.*

Quebec lives in my memory as a big rock that blocked the back window of the hotel, where we had sour bread to eat. There was talk of a wonderful pet bear kept by the blacksmith, but I did not see it—which left a tinge of regret.

Of the long, five-hundred-mile journey through interminable swamps of spruce and tamarack to Lindsay, Ontario, I remember only one night. As we were preparing to sleep in the train, Father told us to look out, and we saw an amazing sight—the woods full of shooting stars. They were everywhere, some close to the train, blazing, twinkling, sailing about. When the wonder had sunk in, Father told us they were not shooting stars, but little insects called "fire-flies," each of which carried a lantern. It was one of those delicious rare moments when your dream fairy comes to you, and you know it is really true.

July and August of 1866 we spent in Lindsay town. I can realize

*The sources of material in this book are indicated in the Appendix, to which the numbers at the end of each section refer. See page 399.

it now—wooden sidewalks, huge pine stumps everywhere with vigorous young cedars growing about their roots; barefooted, bareheaded boys and girls scoffing at our un-Canadian accent. Apple trees laden with fruit to which we soon learned to help ourselves; tall rank weeds with swarms of grasshoppers everywhere; the coffee-colored river with its screaming, roaring sawmills; cows and pigs on the main street; great, hulking, heaving oxen drawing loads of hay, with heavy breathing that was wonderfully meadowlike and fragrant; and over and above all, in memory as in place, the far-pervading, sweet, sanctifying smell of new-cut boards of pine. . . .

We moved out to our backwoods farm that September. It had a small house—the usual pioneer log shanty—and a few ramshackle outbuildings, the handiwork of Bill McKenna, who first had staked the claim.

The house was very small for us, very badly prepared for winter, and swarming with rats. . . .

The log schoolhouse was a mile away; but I was six years old and, with my eight-year-old brother, was sent every morning to nine-o'clock school, to sit for six hours at the feet of a tremendous person. So she seemed to me, for she was grown up; she knew everything; she was the schoolmistress. She had been only a bright young girl of sixteen then; oftentimes in winter, she had scholars older than herself.

The little log cabin was warmed by a box stove, for which the bigger boys had to cut woods at recess (pronounced *ree*-cess in those days). During school hours, it was fed by anyone the teacher selected for the honor.

One epoch-marking day, as the fire got low, Miss O'Leary said: "Ernest, put a stick of wood in the stove." Proud, but awe-stricken, I marched across the floor with a stick, opened the door, and threw it in.

"No," said the teacher, "that is not the way. Johnny Blackwell, show how it should be done."

With the swagger that was justified by superior knowledge and superior years (for he was six and a half), Johnny pulled out my stick. With the poker he raked the glowing coals to the front, set the stick on them, closed the doors, opened the dampers with a bang; then, giving me a withering glance of pity and contempt, marched haughtily to his seat.

I never forgot that lesson in woodcraft, especially as the fire began to roar immediately.

Mother had been used to an ample house and a staff of competent servants. Now she and my cousin Polly were doing all the housework, as well as milking some of the cows; and the whole of us roughing it in one log shanty, composed of a big living room, with a little box room for Father and Mother in a corner, one for my cousin in another; and the rest of us in hammocks, or upstairs in a big loft through which the wind and weather romped as out of doors, and snow drifted across our bedclothes.

Father had planned to build a convenient house with part of his remaining capital. "It must be roomy; is it not to be our home for life?" was the oft-repeated phrase.

The new house, a plain, substantial, two-story, eleven-room brick barn, forty by sixty feet, was begun in August 1866 and finished in January 1867, for the amazing sum of $1,000. Yes, that was how we reckoned in those days. Seventy-five dollars per room for a plain-built house. But laborers worked from 7 a.m. till 6 p.m. and got seventy-five cents; skilled labor, $1.25 for a ten-hour day. Butter was ten cents a pound; eggs, six to eight cents a dozen; pork, four cents, and the best beef, eight to ten cents a pound. Board and lodging was $1.50 a week. A good hired man got ten dollars a month and his keep; he worked from dawn until after dark—and was happy. We have changed things now, and have not improved them much, except in shortening the hours. . . .

As I look back on the experiences of that place, I rate them among the very best of my life training.

One of the first lessons I learned was to hold up on the end of a plank which my big brother was sawing in two. I, naturally, wanted to bear down, so as to hasten the operation; and was surprised to hear him say: "No, no, don't press down! That would break it off, and leave a long splinter, maybe split both pieces. Hold it up level, so I can saw it quite through." I never forgot that little lesson. . . .

There I learned why nails must be set zigzag in the wood, for if two are set in the same line of grain, it is likely to split. I remember to this day the shock I got when, years later, I saw a green hand nail up a board with all the nails in one line of grain.

I learned that a small hole in a piece of hardwood, burnt bigger with a red-hot iron, is a better, stronger hole than one bored the full size at the outset. I learned to love the strong look of the seared wood and the delicious incense of the wood smoke.

I learned to tie a square or reef knot, and to make a blind lashing.

I learned that window glass, held under cold water, may be cut by a pair of strong, sharp scissors; that this, indeed, was the method of the monks in making their stained-glass windows.

I learned to make molds for rifle balls, for anchors, for wheels, for ship keels; then melt the lead—of which we had a store—and pour it into them with success.

Our youngest brother was a mere baby; but we all learned to do simple carpentering; to use, or abuse, the standard tools. We were taught the difference between a rip- and a crosscut saw, and why; between center bit, auger bit, and shell bit. The differences between adze and axe, awl and scratch awl, plane and jack plane,

hewing axe and splitting axe, were part of our routine lives. . . .

I learned the grain and merits of the common woods about: that basswood was easy cutting and splitting, but miserable as timber and worthless as fuel, yet delightful to carve into animals, or to make troughs for catching maple sap. I learned that beech and maple were our best firewood (hickory was too scarce for such use) ; that cedar, though the weakest and lightest of timber, perfectly useless where strength was needed, was wonderful for shingles, everlasting as a post, and inflammable as oiled rags when used for kindling wood. . . .

I learned that hickory is the strongest wood in the forest, and yet rots in three years if set in the ground.

I learned that hemlock knots are the hardest things that grow, and would break the face of an axe as a stone would; and the better the axe, the surer its ruin in such an encounter. . . .

I learned to fly to a balsam tree when I cut a finger, and cover the wound with the crystal-clear balsam from a bark bladder.

I learned to make little treasure boxes out of solid white pine, each with a sliding lid well fitted. Basswood whistles and elderberry squirts came early.

With the help of my bigger brother, I built a small stone house, that is, two feet square; embodying the methods I saw used in our own house, for we lived with it while it grew.

I wish I now had some of the things we made—many picture frames and wood carvings of birds and beasts. At last, we evolved what we called "landskips," miniature woodland scenes constructed in a candy box with moss, twigs, lichen, and dry grass. In seeking materials for these, I was led to note the marvelous beauty of the little fairy things that were squandered in woods and swamps.

One of the earliest of my wildlife thrills was given by the king-

bird. I had heard of the feathered monarch—his prowess, and the fact that, though little larger than a sparrow, he would assail and drive off any hawk—yes, even an eagle.

But the authorities all made it so far away. The wonderful bird was found in Africa, or South America, or some vague tropical place, whose name was strange, or maybe it inhabited only "the books."

One day, as I went for the cows with my older brother George and a neighbor, Jim Parker, a couple of crows flew high across. Then, from a low tree, there launched out a small bird that uttered a shrill war cry; and dashed first at one, then another of the big black fellows. They dodged and swooped in evident fear, and flew as fast as possible into the woods.

"What is that?" I asked eagerly.

"That's a kingbird," said my brother, for he had been learning from the woodsmen.

"An' he can lick anything that flies," was added by the neighbor.

"A kingbird!" I gasped. Yes, and gulped a cup of joy. I had dreamed of it. I thought it a rare bird of far countries. Now I had seen it in our own land, with my own eyes; it had all become real. It lived and fought right here among *our* crows. The fact was glorious, stunning, in its magnitude. That man never knew how much he was giving me.

This was really a historic day for me, for the event focused my attention on the brave little kingbird. Always a hero worshiper and a wildlife idolator, I took the kingbird into my list of nobles. Each year I learned more about him and at last (in 1876) wrote a heroic poem, "The Kingbird."

In its final shape, I did not put it out until 1879, but in previous attempts and in illustrations I tried it on many of my friends in the years between. I consider it the beginning and foundation of all my work as a wild-animal-story writer.

The cowshed was of logs, capped with a huge yellow roof of straw. This was a thrillsome hunting ground for hens' eggs; and more, a safe and heavenly place in which to lie and dream. Flat on my back I lay one day, as the spring possessed the land; straight up into the intense blue sky I gazed. Huge white clouds were rolling by, their rounded bulks of sculptured purity sometimes blocking out the blue, or silently bumping together, then opening again to show the bottomless abyss of blue between. Suddenly, across one of these glimpses of eternity, there floated the forms of two majestic birds; and from them came a far, loud, croaking trumpet sound. By their long wings, long necks, long legs, and snowy plumes I later knew that they were two white cranes, the noblest thing that flies, sailing on to their northern home; and the ring triumphant of that stirring trumpet call still echoes in my heart.

What would I not give to hear it now as I heard it then, and see it with those same young eyes! Alas, I am old now, and that glorious bird is gone—gone the way of the golden West—gone forever!

With the springtime dawned a new era. We were really farmers now; and work aplenty there was for all, except the baby, who was only three years old. But five, seven, nine, thirteen years old and up had chores in abundance, if even they were no harder than feeding the pigs, guarding the gaps in the fence, or driving the cows to pasture.

We did not fit well into the neighborhood. Father and Mother were too evidently gentlefolk to attract the rude pioneers. But the elder brothers soon learned the ways and speech of the woods. I have given of it all as true a picture as I could in *Two Little Savages.*

Of course, we found birds' nests, and reveled in each thrillsome discovery. I remember how it used to send a prickling through the roots of my hair each time I found one of those wonderful treasures; and as I now analyze the emotion of the time, we got far more thrill out of a nest full of eggs than from a nest full of young birds; and of course the more eggs the tenser the thrill.

There were a few birds that everyone could name—the robin, the crow, the hen hawk, the hoot owl, the red-headed woodpecker, the flicker, the partridge, the bluebird, and the hummingbird; and sounding in hollow, far-reaching notes in the tops of the summer trees was a delightful, invisible mystery that some of the farmers called a rain crow.

All my nature craved for knowledge of these things, but there were neither books nor birdmen to help me. I wonder if other boys suffer so from that heart hunger. When I glimpsed some new bird, some wonderful unknown kind, I got a curious prickling in my scalp. Something clutched my throat; and when the bird flew off, leaving me dark as ever, it was like a swift blackness with a vague sense of sorrow and of loss.

Then I heard that a man named Charlie Foley, a hardware man in town, had a collection of stuffed birds. Much scheming and many pleadings it cost before I was taken to town to see the great man. Into his room over the store I followed, awe silenced, and there on a few board shelves were forty or fifty birds stuffed by himself. He talked little with me, as a sporting friend was present who discoursed volubly on his dogs. But he told me the names of many—the tanager, the wood duck, the blue crane, the gull, the barn swallow.

My visit to Charlie Foley that day solved one problem which had troubled me. On the past Christmas Day my brothers had celebrated by putting up a target on a tree in the beaver meadow, and shooting till their numbed fingers drove them home.

An owl flew by. One of them fired with a shotgun. The bird fell with a broken wing, and was brought home. I remember so well the fluffy form and yellow eyes; I can recall the menacing hiss, the snapping of his bill, and the awe with which he inspired me as I gazed from a safe distance. He was said to be frightfully dangerous. Now I recognized the creature among Foley's stuffed birds and learned its name, that it was a hawk owl, and so far from being dangerous it was one of the gentlest and most harmless songsters in the gloomy woods.

All of these names and bird portraits were precious truths to me; they sank deep into my memory. I wonder if Charlie Foley is alive now, and if he had any idea of the joy he gave me, or the seeds he planted, on that day so long ago.

There was one problem in woodcraft that we youngsters solved for ourselves. The magnitude of the principle involved I did not realize till long after I had grown up.

Part of the forest around us had been swept by fire many years agone. Thus, there were large areas with dead trees standing— huge, blackened masts, usually with the top half and all limbs gone, gone, leaving nothing but a black monument called a stub or rampike, some twenty-odd feet high. Such dead trees furnished a happy land to woodpeckers galore, chiefly redheads and flickers. These energetic birds dug prospect holes and nesting dens without number. The holes, others than the few needed to house the makers, furnished most acceptable nesting quarters for many other birds, such as blackbirds, sparrow hawks, jays, nuthatches, wrens, chickadees, etc.; as well as sundry fur-clad beasties such as red squirrels, flying squirrels, tree mice, and bats.

Our hunter instincts sent us bird-nesting and beast-hunting as soon as the season came round. The great rampikes of the burned stretch offered sure rewards.

But how were we to reach them? They were unclimbable. It would take a strong man hours with an axe to cut one down. But we found a way.

Two of us would get a long pole, usually a light fence rail, and push with it as high up as we could reach—push and pause, push and pause. The third boy would watch the top of the stub for signs of vibration, calling out: "Faster—slower—now, that's it!" when we struck the exact rhythm of the stub. Then we continued to push, pause, push, pause. The stub top swayed more and more. An ominous crackling of the roots began. Farther each time went the top then, at last, crash, it came down, and we rushed like a pack of bloodhounds to capture or gloat over young squirrels, mice, birdlings, or eggs, whose home and citadel we had wrecked.

Of course, there were trees too sound to be so approached. A pine tree's big roots never rot. Therefore, it was beyond our power. So was oak, or cedar; but a basswood or a beech was usually an easy prey. A team of horses with a chain around the stump could not have moved it; but we youngsters with our fifty-pound pushes up high, in exact rhythm guided by knowledge, were usually able to send it crashing to earth.

I often wondered why the wind had not sent such down before. The only answer I see is that the wind did not strike the rhythm of the stub.

In one of these raids on the wild land we saw a red squirrel run up a stub and into a woodpecker hole near the top. At once we were filled with hunter fire, and determined to get that squirrel.

We pounded on the trunk with clubs, and once or twice made the squirrel pop out for a moment. But soon it went back in. Then we got a long pole, and proceeded to apply the push-and-pause method. After ten minutes the stub went down with a crack, and we rushed to the top to find our prey.

The crash had shattered the top of the stub; and lying among the rotten wood and nesting trash were five blind and naked little squirrels. A few feet off lay the mother, quite still, and seemingly unhurt, except that she had a drop of blood on her nose. One of the little ones also had a bloody nose.

We grabbed our prize, and then set out, not very triumphantly, for the barn. When we got there, we realized that the mother squirrel was dead, as also was the little one with the bloody nose.

Now we experienced a surge of remorse. Why had we done it? What was the use? Why kill a helpless, harmless, beautiful wild thing for mere sport? Kill the mother while she was protecting her young! We were all of us ashamed, shocked.

And here were the four living young ones, squirming in our hands. We did not know what to do.

Then the oldest boy said impatiently: "Might just as well give them to the cat right now."

The cat had had a litter of kittens in an adjoining manger. She was there now with the one remaining kit; the other four had been drowned. And it really seemed the merciful way to end the sufferings of the four little squirrels—to let the cat devour them.

I leaned forward and laid the four little squirrels on the hay near the cat's nose. She reached out slowly, sniffed, licked the little orphans, and gently drew them to her, and suckled them with her own. Her heart must have been sore at the loss of her own that had been taken away, for she at once accepted the foundlings.

For several days she mothered and suckled them; but, for reasons we never knew, they died, one by one. We found them flattened out under the cat and her kit. The last one lived for a week.

Our overwhelming impulse had been to hunt and murder the escaping wild things. The cat's sole prompting had been one of sympathy and pity. The tears stood in my eyes as I lifted out the flattened little bodies. I felt rebuked, I had received a stinging rebuke from that kind old mother cat.

To most young folk, and to me in my childhood, the word "rat" conjures up a sinister ogre, an evil, terrible beast that comes in the night to destroy, destroy, destroy. My earliest rat impressions were formed on the steamer that brought us to America; I heard the rats every night, rasping, gnawing, shrieking, but never saw them.

In the log house on the farm they became real. At night they came out in dozens, they played on the shanty floor or in the shadows near the shanty. They gnawed and gnawed and shrieked. One or two we caught in a steel trap, but our real protection was the noble little terrier Snap, who mounted guard at night, and after some horrid midnight brawls came proudly forth each morning with a big brown rat in his teeth. In Toronto we had no terrier for the front line of defense; and, in spite of cats, the rats abounded and left their impress on our lives.

My hunter-naturalist instincts were roused to action heat when I saw big rats scurrying away in the gloom each time we entered the woodshed by lantern light. Steel rattraps of two or more kinds were on the market, but they cost money; besides that, they killed or mangled the victims. I wanted a "ketch-alive," so I invented one. The idea was not wholly original, but called for much ingenuity.

An empty nail keg was secured for groundwork. The bottom was intact, so in that I cut a window two inches by eight, and then guarded this with bars of number-nine wire one inch apart. But the other end was my special problem and triumph. I cut a stout inch board twenty by fourteen inches; in the middle, four inches from the long edge, I sawed a round three-inch hole; around this at half-inch intervals I set a dozen stout wires, each sharply pointed, nine inches long and pointed inward, making a tunnel that narrowed as it neared the sharp tips.

This board was the lid; it was fastened on with hooks so that it could be easily removed. With a few scraps of meat for bait inside, my trap was ready. I placed it in the woodshed, where I knew rats frolicked every night.

Next morning Father came in from the garden at breakfast time and said rather casually, "What animal is that you have in that barrel, my son?"

At once I was ablaze. I rushed out, and there, sure enough, gnawing fiercely at the crossbars of the window in the keg, was a large brown rat. My trap was a perfect success. As I gloated over the ferocious prisoner, the question was raised, now what shall we do with him? There were many easy ways of killing him in the keg, but these were not favored. Then someone suggested, "Doesn't your friend Doctor William Brodie have some live rattlesnakes in a pen and doesn't he continually seek live food for them?"

Surely this had in it the spirit of sport and adventure; it would be like an arena fight at Rome.

So on a wheelbarrow I trundled my cage and captive to Brodie's house. Brodie made a poor living as a dentist, but his real interests were in natural history, in the wild things from bugs to flowers, crawlers to crinkle weeds—a strange, wild soul. But I think his favorite pets were his rattlesnakes. His usual request was "Bring me some live food for my rattlers."

So I took my captive to the grizzly old naturalist's home. His eyes gleamed with animal joy as he saw what I had brought. He was about to tumble the rat into the rattlers' cage, as though it was an ordinary meal. But that insistent gnawing at the wires, that fierce defiance, that desperate fighting courage, were too full of warning. The rat might kill the pets before they could master him. So the old snake man dumped the rat into a bin in which was an old boot. The rat raced around, found the boot, and dodged in.

Brodie teased him with a stick till he turned in the boot, savagely fighting the stick; then, as expected, his tail appeared out of the hole at the toe. Brodie seized the tail, and thus had the rat firmly in his grasp and helpless.

"He might hurt my darlings," said the grim old snake man. "That I couldn't stand." He took a pair of dentist's pliers and snipped off at their roots the four great tusks that are the rat's main fighting tools. Then the rat was flung into the big square pit in which the rattlers dwelt.

We hung around the rim and gazed much as Nero gazed on a deadly closing fight in the Coliseum.

The rat at once made for the darkest corner and, champing his bloody jaws, glared this way and that to make appraisal of his foes. The rattlers instinctively coiled as they heard the thud of the rat when dumped in, and they heard the low chatter that is the fighting growl of the rat.

But rats are food. The snakes were hungry, and slowly, oozily, the four great reptiles drew nigh, their heads upraised so they could note the victim's every move. Slowly, with dancing tongues, they closed in crescent form about the crouching rat; in the angle of the pen he waited; a low murmur in his chest was the single sound he made. His jaws were bloody with his broken teeth, but his eyes were ablaze with fighting light.

From four far sides the serpents came, their heads up high, dancing their tongues antennaelike in air. Cautious but certain, on they came. The rat glanced here and there, appraisal made of hazards in each move; but just as they neared within their reach of strike, he sprang. The snakes recoiled, but the rat sprang high between and over to the nearest refuge—another angle of the pit. Again the snakes concentric made approach, their heads upright, with dancing tongues that seemed to taste the breeze. Again the rat at bay let off a chesty growl, evaded all four javelin stabs, and refuged in a farther angle of the pen. It could not last for long.

The rat was wearing down, was losing speed; the serpents were not stressed.

After many repetitions of the scene, it came—the rat, leaping over the flat and baleful head of one grim snake, exposed his breast a moment, half a moment, but enough. The next long coil-spring neck flashed straight; the rat was struck fair in the flank, the foe drew back.

But now the brave rat knew the death was in his blood—the one impelling thought was to make a valiant fight and die a valiant death.

At the nearest snake he flew, on that scaly neck he clamped those toothless, bloody jaws and wrenched with all his strength till the crackle of the bones and the squirming of the tail told of a broken spine—and the snake sank shivering back to fight no more.

At the next quick-moving, spitting form now went the rat; another jab of the venom squirt deterred him not a moment—he knew that he was doomed, and had no wish but this: to make a valiant fight, a finish of his foes as far as he could make.

At the third long foe he went; he could no longer spring, his hind legs were paralyzed, but his soul was undismayed; his bloody, toothless jaws could clutch and grind, and clutching, grinding, they tore the vent of the squirming foe and ground his spine with his hinder teeth, his flat grinders; strong and unafraid.

Then at the last foul beast he made poor haste—that is, he dragged his feeble, dying legs on his strong front paws. Again the rattler struck. His blood was curdling now, but, his desperate courage undismayed, he clutched that snake around the neck and chewed and clutched. The snake fell flat, the rattle on his tail rattled, rattled, then more feebly sang; it was the death rattle, the last faint song of the last of the four great rattling poison snakes. And lying by his side was the fighting rat, quite still—dead still— dead on the field of the dead.

We had gazed in frozen horror, in a daze, not knowing what we felt. I trembled, and the dentist gasped and wrung his bony hands.

"Oh, God! Oh, God! What courage—what fighting spirit! How I love him, how I hate him! He has robbed me of my rattlers. How I worship him! How I hate him!"

About this time one of my schoolmates, of sporting instincts, said to me, "Why don't you go to the Don Flat on Saturday afternoon? The game club are having a great trapshoot, with live birds."

I didn't know just what a trapshoot was, but the "live birds" caught my attention, and I tramped to the Don Flat the next Saturday immediately after the noon meal.

I found a small crowd of men, each with a double-barreled shotgun. A one-horse wagon stood near; in it were a lot of cages containing small birds. A roped area in front was the firing ground. On this were two trap stations. A trap is a small collapsible cage, which at the pull of a string opens out flat so that the bird in it has to fly. But the bird usually was downed in a few seconds by the gunner at the firing line.

Bossing the show and dominating all things there was Bill Loane, the great bird catcher and market gunner of Toronto, a big, fine-looking man of English origin and strong personality. I went to the cages full of small birds as they laid them on the ground. The birds were striving to escape, thrusting out heads and limbs at various openings. A small boy with a stick tried to push one back. The man in charge cried. "Here, don't you do that!" "Why?" The answer shocked me. "You wound them that way and they don't fly good from the trap." That is, spare the captive, not from motives of mercy, but because a cripple gives poor sport.

I hung around the big cages, and soon got from Loane some additions to my birdlore. The captives were nearly all white snowbirds, with a few shore larks and redpolls that happened to come to baited banks while the snowbird flock was there.

Then came the shoot—a novel experience for me.

"All get back of the firing line," ordered Loane.

Then his assistant put a bird in each trap. As the man who was to shoot gave the word to pull, the string opened the trap and the startled bird sprang up to escape. Bang—it fell on the snow, a crumple, broken, bloody little body. Bang—at the other trap, and another tragedy was enacted. I saw some fifty birds so slain, and their bodies gathered into a basket. "For what?" I asked. "Oh, these go to the hospital to make tidbits and soup for the inmates. That's our best protection; but for that, the law would have ended all trapping and shooting long ago."

That day I saw some horrible brutalities perpetrated on birds that chanced to get winged in the trap rise. I was in a daze of strange feelings, horror and disgust now strongest. I asked Bill Loane what he got for the birds when captured. He said one dollar a dozen for snowbirds, sixty cents a dozen for shore larks and red-polls. I had by rare chance fifteen cents in my pocket and said, "Would you sell me three for that?"

"Sure. What kind?"

"One shore lark and two redpolls."

Quickly these were secured and caged in an old strawberry box, and off I went homeward with my precious captives.

Experience on the farm had shown me that a wild bird in a wire cage never ceases to beat against the wires—they seem so slight that they promise easy escape, but such beating always kills the captive. However, wild birds behind a slat cage, though they seek and seek to escape, do not dash against the wooden slats. So I set about making a cage of slats—that is, a box two by three feet by one foot deep. By ripping mason lath in two I made a lot of slats that served well for bars whose obvious strength would keep the wild birds from dashing against them. The cage when finished had a ground space three feet by one foot by one foot high, but in the middle the height was doubled so that it provided an upper additional space for the redpolls about one foot each way. Thus, though not separated, the shore lark had a run of three feet by one foot; the redpolls had that, but also the treelike upper story of one foot by one foot, in which were some perches.

The shore lark ran up and down the floor all day. The redpolls flew when they would. I found great joy in feeding them, in studying their choice of food. I made for them what is called nightingale's food: a mixture of pea meal, olive oil, and yolk of hard-boiled eggs. This, made into a paste with water and squeezed through a colander so as to come out like worms, was eagerly eaten by my captives along with the canary seed I supplied.

The redpolls tamed quickly; they learned to take food from my fingers, and when a specially good morsel was offered they would nibble to taste it, then pass it from one to the other. The shore lark continued wild.

Then it struck me that I could tame them more quickly if I spent more time with them. To effect this, I moved the cage into my bedroom, where I did my school studying. I was delighted with the response on the part of the redpolls. Soon they would perch on my hand, so I went a step farther and turned them loose in my room. They flew about in a flutter of excitement, but at length one alighted on my shoulder. I held as still as possible. Then the other came, and after one or two times I was able to feed them on my shoulder. They were the most lovable birds I ever knew; they tamed readily and learned to come at call. They now had the full freedom of my room.

Not so the shore lark. He ran up and down the long bottom of his cage, never perching aloft, but uttering a long, plaintive *cheep*.

The spring was nearing now. The redpolls' crimson caps were

glowing brighter and the lark was yet more wildly running up and down, to the sound of his plaintive *cheep-cheep*. I determined to give him the same freedom I had given the happy redpolls. I opened the door and retired.

He peeped out slowly, fearfully, gradually sensed that here was freedom in reach. He sprang forward, realized that the bars were gone, gave one loud, ringing *cheep-cheep-a-tooral-cheep,* sprang up as though to float into the blue as once he had done, sprang up with ever-increasing force, blindly, wildly—crashed into the ceiling and fell to the floor dead at my feet.

I sat with the little broken body in my hands and wept. I didn't mean to; I only wanted to love him, to have him near me. And as I sat, the two redpolls came and perched on my shoulder and whispered some tiny little words that I did not understand. But they had a message, they offered a thought; it spurred me to action. I opened my window, gently shooed them out; and sensing, as it seemed, that again they were free of the blue, they sped away with gentle whisperings—away and away, up and on to be lost in the distance, the northern distance that led to their home—and left me in my lonely room with a dead shore lark in my hand, the dimness of deep emotion in my eyes, and in my heart a lesson that never wholly passed away.

In the summer of 1873 there appeared an announcement that "Doctor A. M. Ross's *Birds of Canada* is now published, a great work, absolutely the first and last word on the subject, now on sale at Piddington's Book Store."

I went next day, trembling with eagerness. Yes, they had it, price one dollar. What would I not have given for that dollar or that book! Had it been a work of art I think my father would have helped me, but natural history was contraband. I dared not ask; I knew I must rely wholly on myself.

I set to work with fervent eagerness to accumulate that dollar. Never before had money seemed so precious, so holy a thing. I was ready to go any honest lengths to assemble those hundred cents.

First, by a lot of word-of-mouth advertising, I sold my rabbits, a lovely pair, for fifty cents. I was halfway now. After a week or so, I volunteered to carry a load of stovewood into a certain woman's back yard from the street, and for this I got ten cents—sixty cents now. I sold my salable marbles and dime novels, and got about twelve cents. I looked for work; I offered many things to dealers, without success; but I worked for cash whenever there was a chance.

After some weeks I got as high as ninety cents. But beyond that I could not get. My luck seemed to desert me. No one seemed to desire any more dime novels, no one had any wood to carry—the labor market seemed glutted. Yet, day after day, I would go to Piddington's window and gaze rapturously and covetously at that wonderful book, the key to all the secrets of nature, no less. It was two months before I raised that last dime, and to this day I am not sure that it was clean money.

It came in this wise. My brother Walter and I had cut so much wood each day for the kitchen stove. My quota was usually done on time, Walter's rarely. My brother was intensely vain and fond of dress, I was notoriously scornful of clothes. So my big brother Joe thought to turn these foibles to account in a scheme. He offered a brand-new twenty-five-cent necktie to the one who should have his daily quota of wood most satisfactorily delivered for a whole month.

Walter went into it with wild enthusiasm. A twenty-five-cent necktie meant much to him; to me it was little or nothing.

For a few days Walter was faultless in the matter of wood, but the pace was too hot. He weakened a little, and in spite of spurts, his record at the end was much as usual. The necktie was awarded to me.

Joe gave me the prize money in cash so I could go myself and please my own taste in the selection. As I set about it, I reasoned: "No man in his senses could ever spend twenty-five cents on a necktie; what good is it?" "But," said my conscience, "the money was given for that." Still later the tempter said: "Fifteen cents is munificent for a necktie—and besides, this would give you your long-sought dime."

I fell. For fifteen cents I got my necktie—a beautiful white four-in-hand with tiny roses sprinkled on it. But I also made up my dollar.

Jingling my silver coins, I marched boldly into Piddington's store. I had a brave look, but my heart was going pit-a-pat as I walked up to the salesman and said: "Please, sir, give me a copy of Ross's *Birds of Canada.*" He turned coldly away; I expected him to say, "Too late, all are gone." Or, "The price has gone up to one hundred dollars." But he merely said, in cold, lifeless, business tones: "Green or brown cover?"

I gasped, "Green!" He took one from the shelf, looked inside the cover, and said in his melancholy way: "One dollar, ten off for cash, ninety cents, please."

I laid down the ninety cents in a daze; in spite of my Scottish instincts I almost forgot to keep the dime. I seized my treasure before he could wrap it up; I hurried away, fearing he might call me back.

Oh, how little I knew of cash discounts. Here I had suffered two months' hunger; I had delayed my entry into paradise; at last I had shocked my conscience, to raise that last, that wholly unnecessary dime.

It was only three or four years before I found out that that much-advertised book was practically worthless.

My growing realization of its weaknesses resulted in a continuous effort to correct it and bring it up to date. The book—that very copy—is before me now; nearly every page has corrections or additions in ink, as well as color added to the illustrations. These are not historically important; but on the last leaf of the lining and on the inside of the last cover is a "Key to the Hawks and Owls" which was wholly my own invention and the first germ of the plan which I later developed into a *Key to the Birds of Canada*.[1]

# 2.

# ACROSS CANADA BY RAIL
# IN THE 1880'S

T HIS was the time of the Manitoba boom. My brother Arthur had a farm up there. So I resolved to go to him. It promised outdooi life, health, opportunity to see the birds and beasts—all that I craved. My sixty dollars would take me there and set me going.

A letter from my brother mentioned that "all kinds of cattle and stock were bringing fancy prices in Manitoba just now. It would be well to invest in some."

Cattle were out of the question with me, but hens were within reach. I set to work, bought poultry with thirty dollars; with twenty-five I bought a railroad ticket to Manitoba. I had made another fifteen dollars by drawing a couple of lion trade marks for a collar company. This twenty dollars was all my ready cash and, so equipped, I gladly said good-bye to my father's house on March 16, 1882. Thenceforth I was a man on my own.

I left Toronto for the West—the glorious, wonderful, promiseful West. With me was a boy friend, about my own age, William G. A. Brodie. We were on a farmers' train; that is, a dozen boxcars with cattle, stock, etc., and one crude passenger coach. I had arranged with a cattleman for space in his car. Measured by cubic feet occupied, I had to pay ten dollars for my chicken coops; but he also charged me with the gangway space, so it cost me fifteen dollars for transport of my fowls to Manitoba.

25

The regular time rate to Winnipeg was three days, and we were somewhat dashed when the conductor told us we'd be lucky if we saw it in five.

This was my worldly wealth: youth—I was twenty-one; my hens (they numbered sixty), my turkeys (four), my geese (four), my provisions for five days, my cash, twenty dollars, of which fifteen dollars would go to the cattleman, and last of all, my energy, my hope, my belief in the future, and in myself, my eagerness for life, life, life in its fullest abundance.

In two days we were in Chicago. But I saw little of the great city. Our train was kept in the yards, and I was bound to my train.

We reached St. Paul the third day, and were now getting well acquainted with our fellow pioneers.

But a great change was pending. The bright spring weather of these three days gave place to dark clouds and driving snow.

For two days we were held in St. Paul, while newspapers gave ever more dreadful accounts of the awful blizzard that was raging on the Dakota Plains.

We knew nothing of time or season, so we could not leave our train or our cattle even for an hour. And two days went by in galling idleness and waiting. Our tickets were good on any train, but I had my stock to care for; so on the second day I said to Will Brodie: "You go on with the next through express; I'll stay with my hens." So away he went with half of our provisions; and at the same time went all the women of the party.

Meantime, our farmers held one indignation meeting after another. They were victualed for only five days; their stock was suffering, some of it dying in the cramped cars.

The men were so indignant that the yardmaster said: "I'll do the best I can for you. But the regular traffic is crippled with the snow. I can't give you a very good engine."

He gave us the best he had, I believe. But it was a broken-down old wreck, a derelict. It slowly wheezed us out about ten miles from St. Paul, then went dead, leaving us worse off than ever. And it snowed and snowed and snowed.

Fortunately for us, our train was on the main line, and we must be moved to permit the express train to pass. After waiting for three hours, we were invited to come out with shovels and dig out our train in readiness for the rescue engine.

It was hard and discouraging work, for the snow was drifting in nearly as fast as we could dig it up; but we kept on, and at last the rescue engine came backing into us from the north. After the usual bumping and jerking, we were coupled on, and felt something like elation to be once more headed for Winnipeg.

We had had a hard day, digging in the blizzard, chilled to the bone; and our sleeping quarters were nothing more than wooden seats in our passenger coach. Every seat was filled, so we slept as we sat. Outdoors, the blizzard wind was raving and hissing. But in the car was a pot-bellied stove, red with coal, and the air was fearfully hot and close.

I awoke at midnight, with a sense of horror and of suffocation. The train was going along about twenty miles an hour. My eyes were darkened with the foul air and heat. I stumbled over the sleepers to the back end of our car to seek a little fresh air. I opened the car door, but the snowstorm was blinding and terrific. So, in the gloom, I tried to step back on to the better protected platform of the next car. *There was no next car!* and, in an instant, I was clinging for dear life to the back rail, while my feet went bump, bump on the snowy ties below me.

Now, believe me, I was fully and wide awake. However, I was young and a lightweight. I hung on for a moment; then, by a mighty effort, drew myself up onto the back platform and into the hot car, badly scared, knowing that I had surely been face to face with death.

Months afterward, when I told Mother about it, her eyes filled with tears, and she said in her fervent way: "The Almighty arms were about my boy. God surely has work for you to do."

The train crawled on to Fergus Falls. Here the engine bumped us on to a siding, then left us.

Outside, the blizzard grew worse. The thermometer was far below zero. It snowed and snowed, and the rising gale filled all the sky and all the world with hissing, driving, stinging snow.

Our train was half snowed under; we knew that that could not move. So most of us left our coach, and went into the station. The room was large enough for us, and hot enough; but the only couch offered was the bare and dirty board floor. On this we all lay down, and slept as only worn-out bodies can.

About three in the morning there was an alarm raised. A new engine, a rescue, with a snowplow! This sent us scuttling back to our own train—only to see the snowplow go slowly by on the main line. So presently all were back again to sleep on the slimy, tobacco-juiced boards of the station-house floor.

A second false alarm aroused us about 6 a.m. But the railway employee would not, or could not, tell us anything of cheer. We were treated like a lot of undesirable cattle, and justified the jests about its being a "cattle train." We would have suffered worse than mere slights but that we were a score in number, and had among us a lot of rough lumberjacks just spoiling for a fight.

For four days we were held at Fergus Falls, sleeping on the floor of the station, but disturbed and stampeded about twenty times by rumors of rescue in the form of a snowplow and an engine.

One advantage we had in the Falls. We could wade through the snow to a grocery store, and those of us who had money could stock up with food. My five dollars was down to four dollars now.

I needed food for my hens, so got one dollar's worth of food for myself and two dollars' worth of corn for the hens.

At last, on March 25, we were called out by the station agent, to be told that an engine and plow would reach Fergus Falls that morning and take us on; would surely land us in Winnipeg the next day.

We were notified to be ready at 8 a.m., and we surely were. But not a sign of engine or plow did we see till 3 p.m. Then, after a vast amount of bumping and jolting, we were hooked on, and our cattle train once more was on the way.

In the tree-sheltered country about Fergus Falls we made good progress; but an hour later found us on the open plains of Dakota, where the blizzard, though slacking, was still in power. The limitless flat was like a snow sea, with waving drifts in endless succession. The drifts were still and stark, but racing over them were herds and herds of snow horses, tossing their white manes and speeding from wave crest to wave crest. Very pretty indeed to look at; but soon we found them a powerful enemy, for they piled the trail with snow which slowed our train, till at last, in a cut, the drift was so deep that the engine, big, black and irresistible as it seemed, was brought to a stop at the command of the frolicsome flying snow.

Once we stopped, the drift grew worse; for snow that would have passed on was now piled against the train. And we responded to a man when the conductor invited all to get shovels in the caboose and dig out our train.

After an hour's hard work we got her going again, and away we went for another mile or so, only to stick again in a drift that was longer and worse. Again we dug ourselves free, to stick a little later in a third drift. It was dark now, and we were worn out. The conductor gruffly told us we might dig ourselves out or lie there till morning. All of us said: "Let her lie. We can't be any worse off than we are. It's easier to sit still, and hope for luck in the morning."

Next morning, March 26, the storm had abated, but the snow-drifts had not. We began the day by digging out our train; then, after a quarter-mile run, another snowdrift held us up, and called all hands to the shovels. An hour's digging released us; then an open stretch of prairie gave us a fairway for nearly an hour. Again the slow-up warned us in the coach that the drifts were too deep. The conductor came through our car. I thought he had been to the front, and knew what sort of drift we were held in, so I indiscreetly asked:

"How long do we stay here?"

"How in hell do I know?" was his gracious reply.

"Well," said I, "I wonder if I have time to go to that ranch house for grub?"

"You better try it and find out," was all the satisfaction I got.

The ranch, a long, low group of buildings, two miles away on the open plain, was the only human habitation in sight. I was wholly out of food now. My only hope was getting some there; for all on the train were on starvation rations by this time.

If the train went on without me, I would be no worse off than at present; and, almost surely, I could overtake it when the outfit reached the next snowdrift. So I boldly left the coach, and struck out across the drifted plains.

There was little wind now, so I could plainly see my objective. But the snow was deep and treacherous; sometimes the slight crust bore me, but more often I was wallowing through two or three feet of soft snow. The ranch I judged to be two miles away; but I was fully an hour in covering this distance.

I arrived about noon, and went to the kitchen door. An inspiring smell of frying bacon was on the air. The door was opened by a raw-boned female cook from the Emerald Isle, evidently. She was putting on a skilletful of the most awful-looking green sow-belly that ever was fried under the name of pork. But it smelled wonderfully attractive to my famished inside.

"How much for that?" I said, indicating the whole panful.

"Thoity-foive cents," she replied. I got out the change, and she added: "What ye got ter put it in?"

"Nothing."

"Here, this'll do," she said, quickly picking up an old news-paper. I folded the paper into a big cone, and she dumped the panful into it. At once the hot grease began to ooze out on all sides; but I went forth into the air, and quickly—for it was far below zero—the whole mass turned hard.

I had no appetite to eat it then; I felt sick and weak all over.

In an hour more I was back to our train. There it was, just where I had left it. I climbed into the hot coach, expecting to enjoy my prize. But my whole nature revolted against that soggy, greasy, greenish mass of pigbelly. I retched and vomited a lot of bile, and lay sick and weak on the seat. Opposite to me was a big, rough-looking Bluenose; that is, in New Brunswick, a lumberjack. Like the rest of us, he was starving. He gazed at my greasy mess with the glare of a hungry wolf. I said feebly:

"Could you eat that?"

"You bet."

"Take it; it's yours."

He went at it like a wild animal, and gobbled the mass in a few minutes. Then he spread his long legs across the aisle, got out a book, and began painfully reading.

"What is that book?" I asked.

"The Bible," he replied with emphasis. "I never travel without one," and his moving lips showed that he was spelling out the sentences, a word at a time.

Now a small French-Canadian came heedlessly up the aisle, and stumbled over the Bluenose's shin. Up jumped the big fellow, shouting: "Damn your soul, can't you let a man read his Bible in peace?"

The Frenchman defended himself, and others joined in; a disagreeable row was on. To get away from it, I stepped out of the car; then, remembering that it was time to feed my poultry, I went forward. My ears were saluted by a loud outcry from among the hens. I quickly drew near, to learn that *one of them had laid an egg.*

I got that egg out in a moment, cracked the shell on my front teeth, and swallowed it, fresh, raw, and warm. That was my only meal that day. But each morning afterward, I was on hand to anticipate a new supply; and, in spite of the other hens, eager for the same kind of breakfast. For they themselves were suffering from sameness of diet; they craved animal food, and as soon as one of their numbers prepared to lay, the others gathered around like relatives around a dying man, hoping for legacies. As soon as the egg was ushered into the world, all made a dash for it. It usually lasted about a minute. So I learned to hang around; to join the group of eager expectants; and each day my watchfulness had some success—that is, one or two eggs each day.

On these it was that I lived till, at long last, six days later, I was landed in Winnipeg, fifteen days after leaving Toronto.

But before we got to Winnipeg, I had a thrillsome experience. The poplar woods grew more thickly as we neared Pembina. Then we passed for miles through solid forests, with here and there an open space. As we neared St. Boniface, the eastern outskirts of Winnipeg, we dashed across a little glade thirty yards wide, and there in the middle was a group that stirred me to the very soul.

In plain view was a great rabble of dogs, large and small, black, white, and yellow, wriggling and heaving this way and that way in a rude ring. To one side was a little yellow dog stretched out and quiet in the snow; on the outer part of the ring was a huge black dog bounding about and barking, but keeping ever behind the moving mob. And in the midst, the center and cause of it all, was a great, grim, grisly wolf.

Wolf? He looked like a lion. There he stood, with his back protected by a low bush, all alone—resolute—calm—with bristling mane, and legs braced firmly, glancing this way and that, to be ready for an attack in any direction. There was a curl on his lips —it looked like scorn, but I suppose it was really the fighting snarl of tooth display. Led by a wolfish-looking dog that should have been ashamed, the pack dashed in, for the twentieth time, no doubt. But the great gray form leaped here and there, and *chop, chop, chop* went those fearful jaws, no other sound from the lonely warrior; but a death yelp from more than one of his foes, as those that were able again sprang back, and left him statuesque as before, untamed, unmaimed and contemptuous of them all.

How I wished for the train to stick in a snowdrift now, as so often before, for all my heart went out to that great gray wolf; I longed to go and help him. But the snow-deep glade flashed by, the poplar trunks shut out the view, and we went on to our journey's end.

This was all that I saw, and it seemed little; but before many days had passed I knew surely that I had been favored with a view, in broad daylight, of a rare and wonderful creature, none less than the Winnipeg wolf.

His was a strange history—a wolf that preferred the city to the country, that passed by the sheep to kill the dogs, and that always hunted alone.

In telling the story of *le Garou*, as he was called by some, although I speak of these things as locally familiar, it is very sure that to many citizens of the town they were quite unknown. The smug shopkeeper on the main street had scarcely heard of him until the day after the final scene at the slaughterhouse, when he fell bullet riddled on a pile of dogs that he had slain. That day his great carcass was carried to Hine's taxidermist shop and there mounted, to be exhibited later at the Chicago World's Fair, and to be destroyed, alas! in the Winnipeg fire that reduced the Mulvey Grammar School to ashes in 1896.

Thus, on April 1, 1882, our storm-battered cattle train wheezed into the stockyards of snow-bound Winnipeg, and the first long leg of the journey was over.

That stockyard was a sad place for most of the travelers, so many of their animals had died from exposure and starvation.

I left my hens in charge of the man who owned the rest of the car space. There was a bag of feed for them, and it was a small matter to toss them some once a day.

At the railway station I was told that all lines were blocked with snow; and although De Winton, the station near my brother's farm, was only a hundred miles farther west, I might not get there for a week.

Outside the station I saw a sign up: "Snow shovelers wanted: two dollars per day." I applied at once, and was given a shovel and put on the gang with twenty more. They herded us into a cattle car, and ran us twenty miles southward toward Pembina. There we stopped, got out, and attacked the snowdrifts.

The frost was below zero, and the wind a blizzard. After shoveling an hour or more, one of my mates said: "Say, your face is froze."

Sure enough, my cheeks, nose, and ears had turned to the gray-white of frostbite, and had lost all sensation. I suspect my toes were in the same case, for my clothing was wholly inadequate, and I could feel nothing in my boots.

Then the foreman, a fine young fellow named Ryan, came, looked me over, and said: "Say, kid, you better go in the boxcar and thaw out." This I was glad to do.

At noon they gave us each a cup of coffee and a sandwich; and later we were taken in the car back to Winnipeg. There I got my two dollars like the rest, but realized that I was not cut out for snow shoveling in a blizzard.

With two dollars in my pocket I was rich. I slept on a bench in the railway station; had coffee and rolls for breakfast, then set out to learn the city.

I did not know anyone in town, but remembered that a few years ago an employee of my brother's had emigrated to Winnipeg. His name was Simon Peart. The post-office directory supplied his address; and in the afternoon I sought him out.

I found him comfortably established in a small house of his own on a city lot. He was a steady worker; and his wife a fine, thrifty, intelligent woman. They had three sons, the eldest in his teens. They had built up a dairy business, and the three sons had jobs as newsboys—a steady, prosperous family.

They were delighted to see me, and begged me to come in and spend the night. This I was glad to do. So that night, for the first time in three weeks, I slept in a bed.

The good wife told my mother some months later: "He looked all worn out, and slept like a man in a swoon."

For two nights and a day I enjoyed their hospitality. The car with my hens had wholly disappeared, but I knew it must be some-where about Winnipeg, for no trains could go out. Then, on the evening of April 3, I learned that a passenger car, the first, was leaving for the west—my route—that night.

I already had my ticket, bought in Toronto, and I boarded the train about 8 p.m.; had the usual night of travel, sitting up. At 4:30 a.m. the conductor shook me awake, took the ticket from my cap, and said: "De Winton next station."

Ten minutes later I was tumbled off in the darkness into the deep snow, with the wind, as usual, a raging blizzard.

The station, a small dark building alone on the open prairie, had a light in the window. I entered, found the agent sleeping in a chair. I waited till he looked up at me, and asked if Arthur S. Thompson lived anywhere near. His answer, in vernacular of unnecessary vigor, conveyed the idea that he did not know and did not care, and I better not waken him again.

On a chair in that waiting room I sat alone and silent till a little after six o'clock. Then there were signs of dawn in the east. I got up and went out.

I had a vague idea that my brother's farm was north of the track, and not far away, less than a mile. The wind had gone down; there was no drifting. So I set out looking for a trail in the deep snow.

I soon found a footpath leading northerly, and on it the track of a short, broad man—this might stand for my brother. So, for lack of a better guide, I followed it.

In half a mile, I sighted a fence, then a long, low mound of snow with a stovepipe sticking out of it. As I approached, the pathway dropped downward fully five feet; and here, at the side of the mound, was a wooden door, with my brother's name on it.

I knocked and entered—a common log shanty of one room; but at the far end four wooden bunks, and in these were three ferocious red Indians. The faces were red—regular redskins.

Then a general outburst of "Hello!" The red men grinned and shouted: "It's Ernest!" and each sunburnt, tanned, and ruddy face broke into a grin of salutation. For they were my brother Arthur, my brother Charlie, and Willie Brodie.

When in Toronto in 1881, preparing for this, my Western life, Doctor William Brodie, the naturalist, to whom I owe much, said to me: "Now, don't fail to keep a journal of your Western travels. You will be sorry if you omit this. And you will value it more each year."

I began this at once. It is before me now. The first entry is dated: *Toronto, Ont., Monday, 13 Nov., 1881.* Saw three robins over the White Bridge.

I wonder if anyone else ever got so much pure and subtle joy out of a simple statement as I did out of those first few words of record. They mean so little to others; but I felt instinctively that it was the beginning of what I wished to do. It was the first step into a glorious kingdom.

And I kept on doing it—still do so; and the Journal of my Travels and Doings is on my desk before me—fifty fat leather-clad volumes, most of them overfat and still increasing.

Scribbled in pencil, ink, water color, anything; smirched with the blood of victims sacrificed on the altar of the knowledge hunter; burned with sparks of the campfire; greasy with handling by unwashed, hasty, eager hands; badly written; at times badly illustrated with hasty sketches—hasty, but meaningful. A bookseller would not give a dime for the lot, and I would not part with them for a double million. They represent more than anything else those sixty years of my life and thought, my strivings and my joy.

Aspiring young naturalists come to me for advice from time to time; and I always give them the counsel that helped me: Keep a full and accurate journal; and remember always Science is measurement.

But I now add to that some things I did not then value at their true worth. "Collect specimens of all things that interest you, make drawings of those that are not easily collected, and label everything with at least the time and place.

"Write of each event on the day that it happened. Do not trust your memory.

"Let every page have place and date in full."

That first record was made in Toronto. But my real journal and my real life were begun in Manitoba when I scrambled down the snowy pathway to my brother's cabin under the drift.

Thus and there, that grimy little eight-by-twelve log shanty, with its dirt roof and its dirt floor, became the shining portal through which I entered into the land of all my dreams. Here I settled down to do my share of the work and really live the life.

Three feet of snow on the level prairie and high drifts along all fences put an embargo on farm work for some weeks. But I was free to go out with my sketchbook and gun.

Within a quarter of a mile the woods began. Already the spring flood of birds was arriving, and the big hunger of my life was gratified every hour of every day.

While in Toronto, I had secured a copy of Coues's *Key to the Birds of America;* also Jordan's *Manual of Vertebrates.* Thus equipped, I tramped laboriously through the deep snow each and every day.

Every species I collected I looked up in Coues or Jordan, labeled it, measured it, commented on its peculiarities, its food and its diseases; recording all in the big fat journal. I was wild with a kind of holy joy; all the hopes of boyhood and the dreams of manhood seemed coming true.

Willie Brodie took part in much of this; and thanks to his father's teaching, he was able to name for me many of the plants and insects that began to appear.

Three days after my arrival, the smoke of a freight train curled above the eastern woods. We hurried on to the station and there found, to my joy, my hens, alive and well, not one missing. The

man in charge had taken good care of them, and was well pleased with the extra five dollars that I gave him for his work.

There were sundry settlers from the neighborhood also at the station, looking for their stuff. When they saw my hens, they were most enthusiastic. I could have sold all on the spot.

As it was, I sold six thoroughbred hens for thirty dollars cash, which was the price originally paid for the whole sixty.

During the three years that followed, besides providing the house, I sold hens and eggs for cash and for groceries. I swapped them for little pigs and calves. These I raised and swapped or sold. So that when at last I went East for good, it was on hen money.

All of which is far ahead of the present story, but not altogether out of place. It illustrates this important idea that, although I was always the dreamer of the family, the poet, I can truly say that every business venture I went into *on my own,* and personally managed, was a financial success. And every time I think of it I give thanks to God for the good old Scottish blood that fills my veins.[1]

# 3.
# THE MANITOBA PRAIRIES
# IN CLAIM-STAKING DAYS

F<small>AR</small> to the south of my brother's farm at Carberry, Manitoba, some four miles away, the sand hills began; and two miles farther, the long black line of spruce forest. These were unexplored but most thrilling mysteries, sure to offer new kinds of life—birds and beasts. Like everything in the world about me, they were full of promise, full of joy.

One day in early spring, as I drove with my brother in that direction, we saw a flock of grouse skimming across the prairie. "There are the chickens," he said, "the prairie chickens. They are coming back from the bush now the snow is gone." We saw many of them; for they go into the timber to winter, but at this time were coming back.

Later on we saw a low mound on the prairie; and my brother, jerking his thumb toward it, said: "That's where they dance."

"Who?" I asked.

"The chickens," was the answer.

I did not know what to make of this. But my brother, taciturn and moody, made no further explanation.

On another occasion, a neighboring farmer made a similar remark about a low mound. When I asked for fuller details, he said: "Don't you know that the chickens have a regular dance in springtime? And that's one of their dancing places?"

It certainly looked like it. The mound, for a space of fifty feet across, was bare of grass, apparently trodden down hard, and strewn with feathers and droppings.

Within a few days I saw, far off on a ridge, half a dozen prairie chickens rushing about, uttering a sort of cackling or crowing sound; and finally got something like a near view. But the birds flew away.

There could be no doubt, however, that I had got a glimpse of the chicken dance. That merely piqued my curiosity. I wanted a full, close view. And this is how I managed:

A mile from our shanty I found a dancing mound. So, taking hatchet and spade, in the afternoon, I took my blankets to the place, and camped in the hide.

About dawn I heard the whirring wings of the grouse, and one of them sailed out of the sky to alight on the mound. Others came; and when it was light enough to see, there were a dozen quietly walking about or sitting still. Then one of them suddenly lowered its head, spread out its wings nearly horizontally, and its tail perpendicularly, distended its air sacs on either side of the neck, and erected its feathers. Then it rushed across the "floor," taking the shortest of steps, but stamping its feet so hard and rapidly that the sound was like that of a kettledrum. At the same time, it uttered a sort of budding crow, which seemed to come from the air sacs, beat the air with its wings, and vibrated its tail so that it produced a loud, rustling noise, and thus contrived at once to make as extraordinary a spectacle of itself and as much noise as possible.

As soon as one commenced, all joined in, rattling, stamping, drumming, crowing, and dancing together furiously; louder and louder the noise, faster and faster the dance became, until at last, as they madly whirled about, the birds were leaping over each other in their excitement. After a brief spell the energy of the dancers began to abate; and shortly afterward they ceased and sat down, or stood or moved about quietly, until they were again started by one of their number "leading off."

I lay there and watched them till sunrise. During that time they had at least a dozen set-to's. Then I came out of my hide; whereupon they scattered and flew in all directions.

Throughout May and June I found the chicken dance taking place; and later I learned that even in autumn, when feeling fat and fit, they assembled at the Dance Hall on fine days for a spiel.

But a more remarkable demonstration was in store for me.

In the summer of 1883, at Carberry, I had some fifteen baby prairie chickens hatched under a hen. When they were two weeks old, we were visited by a cold, driving storm of sleet. The chicks were in danger of perishing.

I brought the whole brood into the kitchen. Keeping the hen in a cage close by, I put the chilled and cowering little things under the stove, on the tin which protected the floor. Here, after half an hour, they were fully warmed. They recovered quickly, fluffed out their feathers, preened their wings, and began to look very perky.

Then the clouds broke. For the first time that day the sun shone brightly. It came through the window, down onto the stove, and partly under, on the assembled brood.

It seemed to stir them with some new thought and feeling of joy. One of the tiny things, no bigger than a sparrow, lowered his head nearly to the tin, with beak out level, raised high the little pimple where in time his tail should be, spread out at each side his tiny wings; then ran across the tin, crowing a little bubbling crow, beating his wings and stamping with his two pink feet so rapidly that it sounded like a small kettledrum.

The result was electrical. At once the rest of them leaped up and at it. Every one took the same position—head low, wings out,

beating, tail stump raised and violently vibrated, the feet pounding hard—leaping, bounding, stamping, exactly as is done by the old birds on the dance hill at love time.

For a minute or more it lasted; then they seemed tired, and all sat down for a rest.

In half an hour they were at it again; and did it several times that day, especially when the sun was on them, and they were warm and fed.

Then I found that I could start them, when the conditions were right, by rattling on the tin a tattoo with two fingers. They responded almost invariably; during the three days that I had them in the house, I started them dancing many times for myself or the neighborhood to see. A number of my friends made a buggy ride across country those days to come and see the tiny downlings "do their war dance," whenever I chose to start them beating the drum.

It is noteworthy that these chickens danced exactly as their parents do, without ever having seen those parents; therefore, the performance was wholly instinctive. All—and undoubtedly both sexes were represented—danced with equal spirit. It was not at the breeding season, and could not, in any sense, be said to have been sex urge. It was evidently and unquestionably nothing more or less than a true dance—a vigorous, rhythmic, athletic expression of health and joy.[1]

May 9, 1882. Three prairie chickens brought to me today by the boys; two males; one female; crops of all were filled with willow catkins, sandflowers (*Anemone patens*), and rose hips. The female was without the air sacs on the neck or the yellow over the eye. One had no pectinations on the toes, the other two had the imperfect remains of them only.

September 23, 1882. Prairie chickens were numerous today in a little grove just west of the house. Specimens shot showed the feathering of the legs and the pectinations of the toes in full development.

These eminently prairie birds in the summertime usually retire to the woods and sand hills on the approach of winter; but in spring, before the snow is gone, they again perform a partial migration and scatter over the prairies, where alone they are to be found during the summer. They are very shy at all times, but during the winter the comparatively heedless individuals have been so thoroughly weeded out by numerous enemies that it requires no slight amount of stalking to get within range of a flock in the springtime.

The advent of the grouse on the still-snow-covered plains might prove premature, but that they find a good friend in the wild prairie rose (*Rosa blanda*). It is abundant everywhere, and the ruddy hips, unlike most fruits, do not fall when ripe, but continue to hang on the stiff stems until they are dislodged by the coming of the next season's crop. On the Big Plain, stones of any kind are unknown, and in nearly all parts of Manitoba, gravel is unattainable during the winter; so that the "chicken" and other birds that require these aids to digestion would be at a loss were it not that the friendly rose also supplies this need; for the hips, besides being sweet and nutritious, contain a number of small, angular, hard seeds, which answer perfectly the purpose of gravel. To illustrate the importance of this shrub, in this regard, I append a table of observations on the crops and gizzards contents of grouse killed during various months as indicated:

> January. Rose hips, browse, and equisetum tops.
> February. Rose hips and browse.
> March. Rose hips and browse.
> April. Rose hips and browse of birch and willow.
> May. Rose hips and sandflowers (*Anemone patens*).
> June. Rose hips, grass, grasshoppers, and Proconia sp. (insect).
> July. Rose hips, grass, strawberries, and Proconia sp.
> August. Rose hips, grass, strawberries, and Proconia sp.
> September. Rose hips, grass, berries, and Proconia sp.
> October. Rose hips, grass, and various berries.
> November. Rose hips, birch and willow browse, and berries
>      of arbutus.
> December. Rose hips, juniper berries, and browse.

This is, of course, a mere list of samples, as in reality nothing of the nature of grain, fruit, leaves, or insects comes amiss to this nearly omnivorous bird, but it illustrates the importance of the rose hips, which are always obtainable, as they grow everywhere and do not fall when ripe. In the course of my experience I have examined some hundreds of gizzards of the prairie chicken, and do not recollect ever finding one devoid of the stony seeds of the wild rose. It is probable that the service is mutual, for these seeds secure a better distribution after being swallowed by the grouse; and as they were passed out with possibly increased vitality they may germinate more readily for the thinning their outer coat would receive during the grinding operation.

The nest of this species is placed in the long, rank grass under some tuft that will aid in its concealment, and is usually not far from a tract of brushland or other cover. It is little more than a slight hollow in the ground, arched over by the grass. The eggs, usually fourteen, but sometimes fifteen or sixteen in number, are no larger than those of the common pigeon, and are actually smaller than those of the upland plover, a bird which is only one eighth of the chicken's weight. Immediately before expulsion they are a delicate bluish green; on being laid they show a purplish grapelike bloom; after a few days' exposure they become of a deep chocolate brown, with a few dark spots. After a fortnight has passed, they are usually of a dirty white; this change is partly due to bleaching and partly to the scratching they receive from the mother's bill and feet.

A partial history of the young in the wild state is briefly as follows: At the age of six weeks they are fully feathered and at two months fully grown, although still under guidance of the mother at that time. There are usually not more than six or seven young ones left out of the original average brood of fifteen, which statement shows the number of chicks which fall a prey to their natural enemies, while many sets of eggs are destroyed by the fires which annually devastate the prairies. As the fall advances they gather more and more into flocks and become regular visitors to the stubble fields and, in consequence, regular articles of diet with the farmers until the first fall of snow buries their foraging grounds and drives them en masse to the woods.

During the summer the habits of the chickens are eminently terrestrial; they live, feed, and sleep almost exclusively on the ground; but the first snow makes a radical change. They now act more like a properly adapted perching bird, for they spend a large part of their time in the highest trees, flying from one to another and perching, browsing, or walking about among the branches with perfect ease, and evidently at times preferring an arboreal to a terrestrial life. When thus aloft they are not at all possessed of that feeling of security which makes the similarly situated ruffed grouse so easy a prey to the pothunter. On the contrary, their perfect grasp of the situation usually renders them shy and induces them to fly long ere yet the sportsman has come near enough to be dangerous.

Like most of the members of its family, the prairie chicken spends the winter nights in the snow, which is always soft and penetrable in the woods, although out on the plains it is beaten by the wind into drifts of icelike hardness. As the evening closes in, the birds fly down from the trees and either dive headlong into a drift or run about a little and select a place before going under. The bed is generally about six inches from the surface and a foot long from the entrance. Each individual prepares his own place, so that a flock of a dozen chickens may be scattered over a space of fifty yards square. By the morning each bird's breath has formed a solid wall of ice in front of it, so that it invariably goes out at one side. The great disadvantage of the snow bed is, that when there the birds are more likely to become the prey of foxes and other predaceous animals, whose sagacious nostrils betray the very spots beneath which the unsuspecting bird is soundly slumbering. I am inclined to think this is the only chance a fox has of securing one of the old birds, so wary are they at all other times.

As the winter wanes it is not uncommon for a snowstorm to be accompanied by sleet. The storm at once drives the chickens into the drifts and afterward levels the holes they formed in entering. The freezing of the sleet then forms a crust which resists all attempts at escape on the part of the birds, many of which, according to the account of hunters, are starved and thus perish miserably. I met with a single instance of this myself.

Before the winter is over, many of the birds, by continuously pulling off frozen browse, have so worn their bills that when closed there is a large opening right through immediately behind the hook. Early in April the few that have survived the rigors and perils of their winter life spread over the prairie once more and soon scatter to enter on their duties of reproduction.

The growth and shedding of the pectinations on the toes I have recorded at length, and not having heard of any use of them, conceived the idea which I have already published (1883), that they are intended to act as snowshoes, and the fact that they grow in the fall and continue in perfection all winter, only dropping off after the snow is gone, justifies this conclusion. The same remark applies to the similar appendages of the ruffed grouse. The tail seems to present a curious specialization, most marked in the outer feathers; its chief function in life appears to be noise. The central pair of soft, long, silent feathers stand out like monuments of what the tail used to be in the palmy days of the species, when not mere hubbub in the madding crowd on the noisy dance hill, but dainty decoration was the charm by which chiefly the *pediocaetes* wooed and won his mate.[2]


The birds are the actors, but the glorious plain itself is the stage. Could we but watch it from the moon, the vastness of its loveliness might be fully glimpsed.

As we see it from our shanty door or from a low sand hill, another feature claims our thought.

As soon as April snows had gone and winter vanished from the scene, there sprang up on the prairie everywhere the new living snow, the sandflower, the pasque flower of the books, the crocus of the farmer folk—first its bloom, and later the leaves. In tropical profusion the flowers pushed forth, and all the plain was bright again as if snow—yes, lilac snow; deepest not in the hollows, but on the sandy ridge.

On the prairies from Red River to the Rockies, and from the Platte to the Peace—a million square miles—there must be billions of these flowers, squandering their beauty on the expectant world. For this, indeed, the wild things have waited, counted on its coming. Buffalo, horses, cattle, deer, cranes, ducks, geese, prairie chickens, gophers—all creatures of the plains united to revel and to fatten on the rich and fleshy budding stems of this, the spring flower of the West.

Millions upon millions pasture on this, their rich support; and yet not the slightest diminution in the flowering hosts is seen, until their time is over, their day is done. The sandflowers fade and shrivel to the ground; and in their place are handlike leaves, uplifted to the sky; and, just a little later, hearselike plumes that signal to the wind, and for a while are markers on the bygone pasque flower's grave.

Thus the sandflower dies, and passes from the scene; and others follow in their ranks—a summer-long procession, a long and regalized parade, that follows close the sandflower's silent burst of song. They follow, these processionaires, with something like complete possession of the field, each for its time. The avens, the prairie daisies, the yarrow, the harebell, the sunflower, the vetch, and lilies like a flame.

Then, in June, comes the glory of the plains, the prairie rose, in an overwhelming of rich luxuriance, a squanderment of tint. And after its loud blast of bloom a wondrous wealth of fruit, the red, ripe hips that hang on their thorny stems, defying wind and weather, and scoffing later at the frost and snow. This is the manna food of the rolling plains, that feeds the wildlife of the open realm, when frost and snow have slammed the door on every other search for food.

The gentians and the goldenrods keep on till biting frost, but ever with them and beyond are the children of the rose, the hips

that offer help, through summer and autumn and winter—yes, and
early spring, till the offerings of the lesser ones come in to bear the
load, to fight the famine on the far plains, till the summertide return of "Bountiful" the Queen, the rose of the royal red, to deco-
rate its year-round Christmas trees with its year-round mead of
lush, abundant food.

Among the last of the long array are the goldenrods that squan-
der their living gold across the lavish plains. And, of the many
kinds, I found most pleasure in the smallest, the compass golden-
rod (*nemoralis*).

It is shaped like an elegant jeweled crozier, and its bent tip
points ever to the north. In gloomy times, or cloudy days, or darkest nights, I found it easy to locate north by going to a bed of these
flowers. There were some variations; but in general, their points
were to the north, no doubt because their array of flowering buds
was in this way guaranteed a better basking in the sun.[3]

# 4.

# BIRDS OF MANITOBA

## *The Popular Names of Birds*

To the Editors of *The Auk:* The "powers that be," I understand, are preparing a "Check List" and revising the scientific and popular names of our birds.

There is no doubt that scientific names are entirely in the hands of scientists, but it seems to be overlooked that popular names are just as completely in the hands of the people. Scientists may advise, but not dictate on this point. A short analysis of the principle of common names may place the matter in a new light.

A bird's name, to be popular, must be distinctive, and in accordance with the genius of our language. Examples of such are Thrush, Rail, Heron, Hawk, Crane, Nightjar, and many others. These are truly popular names, evolved originally out of description, handed down and condensed and changed until they have assumed their present terse, abrupt, and to a foreign ear uncouth forms, but, nevertheless, forms in accordance with the pervading spirit of the Saxon tongue; or, in other words, they are *really* popular.

On the other hand, look at the so-called popular, but really translated, scientific, spurious English names given to our birds, taking as examples the following: Baird's Bunting, Leconte's Sparrow, Wilson's Green Black-capped Flycatching Warbler, Bartram's Sandpiper, Sprague's Lark, Wilson's Thrush, Black Ptilo-gonys, Semipalmated Tattler, Fascinated Tit, Florida Gallinule.

Surely, the gentlemen whose names are applied to these birds have not so slight a hold on fame as to require such aids as these to attain it, if indeed aids they be, which I question; for such nomenclature *cannot* stand the test of time.

If you show an "out-wester" the two birds mentioned above as Baird's Bunting and Leconte's Sparrow, and tell him that these are their names, he will probably correct you, and say one is a "Scrub Sparrow," and the other a "Yellow Sparrow." Convince him he is wrong, and in a month he will have forgotten all but the names he formerly gave them; they are so thoroughly appropriate and nat-ural that they cannot be forgotten. The next name in the list above is clumsy enough to strangle itself with its own tail. A lad on the Plains once brought me a *Neocorys spraguei,* and asked its name. I replied it was Sprague's Lark. Soon afterward he came again; he could not remember that name; so I told him it was a "Skylark," and he never forgot that. On the Big Plain that seed was sown, and not all the scientists in America can make, or ever could make, the settlers there call that bird anything but "Skylark." And I consider that lad precisely represented the English-speaking race; he re-jected the false name, and readily remembered the true one, and was aided by that which was apt and natural. No better illustration could be given of the fact that phraseology may be the life or death of a cause, according as it is happy or unfortunate.

A similar instance is the case of the "Bartram's Sandpiper." Ever since Wilson's time this name has been continually thrust into the face of the public, only to be continually rejected; "Upland Plover" it continues to be in the East, and "Quaily" on the Assini-boine, in spite of Bartram and Wilson, and will continue so until some name, answering all conditions, is brought forward; for here, as elsewhere, the law of the survival of the fittest rigidly prevails.

As an example of the fit ousting the false, note how, in spite of scientists, "Veery" is supplanting "Wilson's Thrush" throughout the length and breadth of the land.

The spurious English names scarcely need comment, they so evidently contain in themselves the elements of their own destruction. Imagine a western farmer being told that a certain songster was a "Ptilogonys." In spite of the books, the three examples cannot hold ground against "Willet," "Ground Wren," and "Waterhen," respectively.

The purpose of a check list that includes English names is, I take it, not to attempt the impossible feat of dictating to our woodmen what names they should give their feathered friends, but rather to preserve and publish such names as are evolved in the natural way—names which are the outcome of circumstances. Only in cases of egregious error is a common name to be superseded; and in doing this it must be remembered that no name can be popular unless true to the principles of the English tongue. It must be short, distinctive, and, if possible, descriptive. Of this class are Veery, Junco, and Vireo. These are the only successful artificial names that I can at present recollect. Among natural English names for American birds are Bobolink, Chewink, Kingbird, and many others. Such as these not only more than hold their own, but are as great aids to the spread of knowledge as the Ptilogonys kind are hindrances; while such as Wilson's Thrush can only be accepted as provisional, until the better knowledge of the bird and its surroundings shall result in the evolution of an English name founded on true principles.

Ernest E. T. Seton
of Manitoba

*Glen Cottage, Howard Street,*
*Toronto, March 21, 1885*[1]

*Golden-eye Duck*

During the fall and winter of 1881, when associated with Bill Loane, Bill Lang, Sam Humphreys, and other gunners of Toronto Bay, I had been much struck by the remarkable way in which these men could identify their game, even when it was flying a quarter mile off.

When I exclaimed: "How do you do it?" their unsatisfactory answer usually was, "Practice."

I soon observed, however, that the first essential is to know what species are to be expected at a particular season in a particular region and environment.

The second is to know their habits of flocking and flight. Thus the geese and cranes fly high, in long lines, or sometimes in a V shape; the canvasbacks and some waders fly in lines, but keep low. The teal, stints and blackbirds, as well as all small birds, fly in irregular flocks. Briefly, all large birds that fly in flocks adhere to the line or V formation. Orderly flight is apparently a question of size; evidently a collision would be more serious to the larger birds.

Recently several of my friends in the aviation service have told me that, when flying in squadron formation, the airplanes copy the wild geese. When so marshaled, each airplane is behind the leader; and yet every pilot has a clear view of him, as well as of the course ahead. If one plane should, by accident, fall back, there is no danger of collision. And, finally, none of them is flying in "churned air." Just so, the geese.

The last secret of the gunner is to know the recognition marks, which render service as the birds come into much nearer view. Every species has its own peculiar labels.

These marks, or labels, I set to work to learn and map down on paper.* . . . On the Plains (Manitoba, Canada), in 1882, and in subsequent years, I drew hundreds of these impressions which, chiefly, are the fieldman's far-off identification.[2]

## *Sandhill Crane* (Grus maxicana)

This is a tolerably common summer resident; common along the boundary after leaving Pembina, Manitoba, Canada.

The first intimation that we usually have of the advent of the crane is the loud trumpeting or croaking that seems to shake the air for miles. But soon we begin to see the birds themselves, usually in pairs, even at this early season. Their food is chiefly rose hips, and as they stalk over the bare plains, gathering this manna of the feathered race, ample opportunity is offered for observation. At first one sees little to note beyond their excessive wariness, but as the warmer weather quickens their feelings, these majestic stalkers, these stately trumpeters, may often be seen so far forgetting their dignity as to wheel about and dance, flapping their wings and shouting as they "honor their partners," and in various ways contrive to exhibit an extraordinary combination of awkwardness and agility. This dance is no doubt one of the courting maneuvers, for I have observed it only during the pairing season.

It has been asked if these cranes breed in communities. To this

---

* An example of these "flying descriptions" is seen in the picture section. Seton published a paper on the subject, "The Directive Coloration of Birds," in *The Auk,* October 1897.—Ed.

I reply, I never saw anything to lead to such a conclusion; all cases of their nesting that have come under my notice were those of isolated pairs.

The localities they select are generally damp meadows, not necessarily near the sand hills, the chiefly desired surroundings being rank grass wherein to forage, and scrubby or undulating land for cover.

When first they enter the wide world, the two or three young ones are provided with a coat of reddish-yellow down and an apparently superfluous length of limb. I perceive by reference to authorities that the cranes are *praecoces,* which being interpreted meaneth "they are clothed and can run and feed themselves as soon as hatched." Not having seen the young cranes at this interesting period, I cannot gainsay the above statement; but know that a young one taken at the end of June, and evidently two or three weeks old, made such a poor attempt at walking that he reflected but little credit on the noble order of *praecoces* to which his family belongs. And yet I must admit that when I first came on him he ran with fair speed, and as his parents contrived to monopolize my attention for a time, he escaped into the scrub, but later on was found squatting still as death. He looked then deceptively like a red rabbit or a small fox. On being touched he sprang up, uttering a gentle peeping which contrasted strangely with the strong croaks of the parents. He ran for a few yards with the grace and celerity of a Cochin fowl, but soon weakened and was obliged to sit on his heels.

I took him home and found that he spent fully half his time in this elegant position, and that, moreover, although he ate well and seemed in good health, he was scarcely able to stand erect excepting in the heat of the day, and when he attempted to rise he was almost sure to fall once or twice through his neck getting entangled with his shanks in the most unpraecocial manner; nevertheless, he grew and fledged and became quite tame. Then came two other pets to share the building wherein he had dwelt so long; they were a peregrine falcon and a Swainson's buzzard. For a time all went well; the crane seemed to have strength enough and beak enough to take care of himself. Then I found out that he would share the falcon's food, so I offered him a sparrow; he seized it savagely and, uttering a peculiar harsh note, pinned it to the ground with his bayonetlike bill, then stabbed it again and again, and at last, having reduced it to a shapeless mass, he swallowed it. So that, although I have found only berries, grain, grass, and insects in the gizzards of old ones so far, I think it is likely that they will eat frogs, mice, or small birds.

How it came about I never could tell, but one morning after a storm I found the peregrine sitting on the dead body of the crane; I did not at once remove it, and when I came again the two bandits had nearly eaten my gentle pet.

Several of the neighbors also have tried to rear young cranes and almost always with success and satisfaction, for, although it is difficult to keep them over winter, they become so tame and are so interesting during their stay that their owners feel amply rewarded for what little trouble they have taken with them. As a game bird I am inclined to place the present species first on the Manitoba list, as the white crane and the swans are too rare for insertion on a list of species that the sportsman may pursue with regularity and success. An average specimen weighs about nine and three quarters or ten pounds, and the quality of the flesh is unsurpassed by that of any of our ordinary birds unless it be the partridge. I should strongly advocate the protection of this bird by the game law were it not that it is so thoroughly well able to take care of itself that legislation in its favor seems altogether unnecessary.

The young cranes are apparently strong on the wing in August, for at this time small bands of the species may be seen sailing high over the prairie, apparently strengthening their wings before they are compelled to journey southward for the season. As September draws nigh their numbers are increased, and the long array of the grand birds presents a most imposing spectacle as in serpentine lines they float away after the sun.

## Prairie Horned Lark, or Prairie Shore Lark (Otocoris alpestris praticola)

On May 12, 1882, at camp eight miles south of Brandon, midway between our tent and the fire ten feet away, I started a small bird from its nest. It ran away very reluctantly, and continued wistfully close at hand, running about among the tufts of grass in the glare of the fire, and returning each time as soon as it dared. At gray dawn I found her on the nest again; she slowly walked away when I approached to rekindle the fire, but returned almost immediately with her mate; and now, for the first time, I saw them plainly. They were a pair of shore larks. Encouraged, no doubt, by the presence of her mate, she once more crept up to her nest and took up her position on the eggs, although I was but five feet off. Frying our bacon over a brisk fire, I was very careful to avoid hurting the birds or their home; and breakfast being over, travelers, tent, fire, and horses all went off and left them to discharge their duties in peace. The nest contained three brown eggs; it was sunk in the ground, and was made of grass and fiber, and lined with two or three large feathers.

My first real acquaintance with the shore lark at his home was in Minnesota, in the last week in March 1882. A fearful blizzard, of course "the worst ever known in the country," had been raging for two days or more. On the third day, when it was nearly over, I was making my way out to see the cattle. All the fences and low buildings were buried in snow, but the tall form of an elevator

loomed up out of a circle of bare ground, caused by the eddying
of the blast, and here, in the very vortex of the storm, in the thickest of the fight, were three or four shore larks, bracing themselves
against the driving wind and picking up the seeds that had been
exposed by the displacement of the snow. Poor little things! I
thought, you must be nearly at death's door; but even while I
looked one of them, under the lee of the buildings, perched himself on a frozen clod and poured out his sweet, simple little song in
a way that seemed to say, "How happy am I."

But the longest night will end; and it is not always winter, even
at the Pole. The spring comes, and "the time of the singing birds"
arrives, and the brown shore lark raises his horns with sprightly
air, and those who may chance to see him are now reminded that
he is a near kinsman to the famed skylark—that indeed he is a
skylark. Thus far he has sung only while perching on some clod or
stone, but now the ardor of his devotion to the demure little Quak-
eress by his side demands a more ambitious demonstration; so,
ceasing to sing, he strenuously endeavors to associate with the
white, piling cumuli, and having soared, apparently, near enough
to be comfortably damp, while to us he appears a mere speck, he
floats on vibrating wings, singing a song composed of a single note,
oft repeated with lessening intervals; it may be suggested by the
syllables *trick, trick, trick, trick, trick, trick, t-r-r-r-r-r-r-r*, the
notes at last all running together like the drumming of a partridge.
During this performance he has lost much of his altitude, but at
once proceeds to regain it by a series of bounds before again repeating the song. This alternate soaring and singing is usually kept
up for over ten minutes, then the musician, having exhausted his
energy, suddenly stops and dashes down with one frightful headlong pitch, right into the grass. Upon going to the spot, one is surprised to find he has not been dashed to atoms by the violence of

the fall, but springs up, uttering his usual call note, and flits further off, again to settle on the ground.

The whole performance will be seen to resemble very closely the serenade of the Missouri skylark, the chief difference being that the shore lark is inferior in music and staying powers, and also in that the latter remains more nearly over one particular place. Another point of dissimilarity is, the shore lark sings chiefly on the ground, while the skylark confines his effusions almost entirely to his moments of physical elevation.

The shore lark is the earliest of the prairie singers to begin in the morning, being even a little earlier than the meadow lark; it commences before there is any sign of dawn, and at night it continues until the plains are enveloped in perfect gloom.

But singing will not multiply the species, and the two little "Quakers," as they are often called, set about nesting ere yet the snow is gone. Not seeking the shelter of bush or bank, but right out on the open prairie, on the level, they scrape a hole about an inch deep, then line it with grass and perhaps a feather or two from their mortal enemy, the hawk. In this are laid four or five brown eggs, freckled all over. This species has a curious habit, in common with the baywing bunting, of running on the road just before one and flying a little farther on when overtaken. The shore lark does not usually repeat the maneuver more than twice or thrice, and frequently it suddenly squats and remains so until nearly within reach, when it springs up, uttering its triple call note, and flies away to one side.

My observations incline me to believe that in Manitoba the species raises two broods each season.

## Green-winged Teal (Anas Carolinis)

On July 5, 1882, at Silver Creek, Manitoba, I came across a female green-winged teal traveling with her brood of ten young ones across the prairie toward a large pool. The mother bird was in great grief on finding that she was discovered, but she would not fly away; she threw herself on the ground at my feet and beat with her wings as though quite unable to escape and tried her utmost to lead me away. . . .

This species, I think, unlike the bluewing, usually nests quite close to the water, so that it is probably owing to the drying up of the pond that this newly hatched brood found themselves forced to take an overland journey of considerable extent before they could find a sufficiency of water.*[3]

* The story of "Mother Teal and the Overland Route" (Chap. 5) evidently had its origin in this observation.—Ed.

# 5.

# TWO BIRD STORIES

## *Mother Teal and the Overland Route*

A GREEN-WINGED TEAL had made her nest in the sedge by one of the grass-edged pools that fleck the sunny slope of the Riding Mountain. The passing half-breed, driving his creaking ox wagon, saw only a pond with the usual fringe of coarse grass, beyond which was a belt of willow scrub and an old poplar tree. But the little teal in the rushes, and her neighbors the flickers, on the nearby poplar, saw in the nestling pool a kingdom, a perfect paradise, for this was home. Now was the ripeness of the love moon, with the mother moon at hand in its fullness of promise. Indeed, the little flickers had almost chipped their glassy shells, and the eggs, the ten treasures of the teal, had lost the look of mere interesting things and were putting on each an air of sleeping personality, warm, sentient, pulsatory, and almost vocal.

The little teal had lost her mate early in the season. At least, he had disappeared, and as the land abounded in deadly foes, it was fair to suppose him dead. But her attention was fully taken up with her nest and her brood.

All through the latter part of June she tended them carefully, leaving but a little while each day to seek food, and then covering them carefully with a dummy foster mother that she had made of down from her own breast.

One morning, as she flew away, leaving the dummy in charge,

she heard an ominous crackling in the thick willows near at hand, but she wisely went on. When she returned, her neighbor the flicker was still uttering a note of alarm, and down by her own nest were the fresh tracks of a man. The dummy mother had been disturbed but, strange to tell, the eggs were all there and unharmed.

The enemy, though so near, had been baffled after all. As the days went by, and the grand finish of her task drew near, the little greenwing felt the mother love growing in her heart to be ready for the ten little prisoners that her devotion was to set free. They were no longer mere eggs, she felt, and sometimes she would talk to them in low, raucous tones, and they would seem to answer from within in whispered peepings, or perhaps in sounds that have no human name because too fine for human ear. So there is small wonder that when they do come out they have already learned many of the few simple words that make up teal talk.

The many hazards of the early nesting time were rapidly passed, but a new one came. The growing springtime had turned into a drought. No rain had fallen for many, many days, and as the greatest day of all drew near, the mother saw with dismay that the pond was shrinking, quickly shrinking. Already it was rimmed about by a great stretch of bare mud, and unless the rains came soon, the first experience of the little ones would be a perilous overland journey.

It was just as impossible to hurry up the hatching as it was to bring rain, and the last few days of the mother's task were, as she had feared, in view of a wide mud flat where once had been the pond.

They all came out at last. The little china tombs were broken one by one, disclosing each a little teal: ten little balls of mottled down, ten little cushions of yellow plush, ten little golden caskets with jewel eyes, enshrining each a priceless spark of life.

But fate had been so harsh. It was now a matter of life and death to reach a pond. Oh, why did not Old Sol give the downlings three days of paddling to strengthen on before enforcing this dreadful journey overland? The mother must face the problem and face it now, or lose them all.

The ducklings do not need to eat for several hours after they are hatched. Their bodies are yet sustained by the provender of their last abode. But once that is used up they must eat. The nearest pond was half a mile away. And the great questions were: Can these baby ducks hold out that long? Can they escape the countless dangers of the road? For not a harrier, falcon, hawk, fox, weasel, coyote, gopher, ground squirrel or snake but would count them his lawful prey.

All this the mother felt instinctively, even if she did not set it forth in clear expression; and as soon as the ten were warmed and lively she led them into the grass. Such a scrambling and peeping and tumbling about as they tried to get through and over the grass stalks that, like a bamboo forest, barred their way! Their mother had to watch the ten with one eye and the whole world with the other, for not a friend had she or they outside of themselves. The countless living things about were either foes or neutral.

After a long scramble through the grass they climbed a bank and got among the poplar scrub, and here sat down to rest. One little fellow that had struggled along bravely with the others was so weak that there seemed no chance of his reaching that far-away Happyland, the pond.

When they were rested, their mother gave a low, gentle *quack* that doubtless meant, "Come along, children," and they set off again, scrambling over and around the twigs, each peeping softly when he was getting along nicely, or plaintively when he found himself caught in some thicket.

At last they came to a wide open place. It was easy to travel here, but there was great danger of hawks. The mother rested long in the edge of the thicket, and scanned the sky in every direction before she ventured into the open. Then, when all was clear, she marshaled her little army for a dash over this great desert of nearly one hundred yards.

The little fellows bravely struggled after her, their small yellow bodies raised at an angle, and their tiny wings held out like arms as they pushed along after "mother."

She was anxious to finish it all at one dash, but soon saw that that was hopeless. The strongest of her brood could keep up with her, but the others dragged in order of weakness. The brood now formed a little procession over twenty feet long, and the weakling was nearly ten feet behind that again.

A dangerous rest in the open was now enforced. The peepers came panting up to their mother and, full of anxiety, she lay there beside them till they were able to go on. Then she led them as before, quacking gently, "Courage, my darlings!"

They were not halfway to the pond yet, and the journey was telling on them long before they reached this last friendly thicket. The brood strung out into another procession, with a wide gap to the runtie in the rear, when a great marsh hawk suddenly appeared, skimming low over the ground.

"Squat!" gasped the mother greenwing, and the little things all lay flat, except the last one. Too far off to hear the low warning, he struggled on. The great hawk swooped, seized him in his claws, and bore him peeping away over the bushes. All the poor mother could do was gaze in dumb sorrow as the bloodthirsty pirate bore off the downling, unresisted and unpunished. Yet, no; not entirely; for, as he flew straight to the bank of the pond where lodged his crew of young marauders, he heedlessly passed over the home bush of a kingbird, and that fearless little warrior screamed out his battle cry as he launched in air to give chase. Away went the pirate, and away went the king, the one huge, heavy, and cowardly, the other small, swift, and fearless as a hero, away and away, out of sight, the kingbird gaining at every stroke till his voice was lost in the distance.

The sorrow of the mother greenwing, if less deep than that of the human mother, was yet very real. But she had now the nine to guard. They needed her every thought. She led them as quickly as possible into the bushes, and for a time they breathed more freely.

Thenceforth she managed to have the journey lie through the cover. An hour or more passed by in slight alarms and in many rests, and the pond was very near; and well it was, for the ducklings were almost worn out, their little paddles were scratched and bleeding, and their strength was all but gone. For a time they gasped under shadow of the last tall bush before again setting out in a compact flock to cross the next bare place, a rough opening through the poplars.

And they never knew that death in another form had hovered on their track. A red fox crossed the trail of the little duck army. His keen nose told him at once that here was a feast awaiting, and all he had to do was follow it up and eat. So he sneaked softly and swiftly along their well-marked trail. He was already in sight of them. In the ordinary course he soon would have them, mother and all, but the ordinary course may go askew. He was near enough to count the little marchers, if count he could, when the wind brought something which made him stop, crouch low; then, at a surer whiff, he slunk away, fled as swiftly as he could without being seen. And the realest danger, surest death of all that had threatened, was thwarted by an unseen power, and not even the watchful mother duck had the slightest hint of it.

The little ones now toddled along after their mother, who led them quickly to cross the opening. To her delight, a long arm of the pond was quite close, just across that treeless lane. She made straight for it, joyfully calling, "Come, my darlings!"

But alas; the treeless opening was one of the man-made things called a "cart trail." On each side of it were two deep-worn, endless canyons that man calls "wheel ruts," and into the first of these fell four of her brood. Five managed to scramble across, but the other rut was yet deeper and wider, and the five were there engulfed.

Oh, dear, this was terrible! The little ones were too weak now to climb out. The ruts seemed endless in both directions, and the mother did not know how to help them. She and they were in despair, and as she ran about calling and urging them to put forth all their strength, there came up suddenly the very thing she most feared—the deadliest enemy of ducks—a great tall man.

The mother greenwing flung herself at his feet and flopped on the grass. Not begging for mercy! Oh, no! She was only trying to trick the man into thinking she was wounded, so that he would follow her, and she could lead him away.

But this man knew the trick, and he would not follow. Instead of that he looked about, and found the nine little bright-eyed downlings deep in the ruts, vainly trying to hide.

He stooped gently, and gathered them all into his hat. Poor little things, how they did *peep!* Poor little mother, how she did cry in bitterness for her brood! Now she knew that they all were to be destroyed before her very eyes, and she beat her breast on the ground before the terrible giant in agony of sorrow.

Then the heartless monster went to the edge of the pond, no doubt for a drink to wash the ducklings down his throat. He bent down, and a moment later the ducklings were spattering free over the water. The mother flew out on the glassy surface. She called, and they all came scurrying to her. She did not know that this man was really her friend; she never knew that he was the divinity whose mere presence had been enough to drive the fox away and to save them in their direst straits—his race has persecuted hers too long—and she went on hating him to the end.

She tried to lead her brood far away from him. She took them right across the open pond. This was a mistake, for it exposed them to other, to real, enemies. That great marsh hawk saw them, and he came swooping along, sure of getting one in each claw.

"Run for the rushes!" called out the mother greenwing; and run they all did, pattering over the surface as fast as their tired little legs could go.

"Run! run!" cried the mother. But the hawk was close at hand now. In spite of all their running he would be upon them in another second. They were too young to dive. There seemed no escape, when, just as he pounced, the bright little mother gave a great splash with all her strength, and using both feet and wings, dashed the water all over the hawk. He was astonished. He sprang back into the air to shake himself dry. The mother urged the little ones to "keep on." Keep on they did. But down came the hawk again, again to be repelled with a shower of spray. Three times did he pounce, three times did she drench him, till at last all the downlings were safe in the friendly rushes. The angry hawk now made a lunge at the mother; but she could dive, and giving a good-bye splash, she easily disappeared.

Far in the rushes she came up, and called a gentle *quack, quack!* The nine tired little ones came to her, and safely they rested at last.

But that was not all. Just as they began to feast on the teeming insect life, a far-away faint *peep* was heard. The mother greenwing called again her mothering *qu-a-a-a-a-a-c-c—k*. And through the sedge demurely paddling, like an old-timer, came their missing one that the hawk had carried off.

He had not been hurt by the claws. The valiant kingbird had overtaken the hawk over the pond. At the first blow of his bill the hawk had shrieked and dropped his prey; the little duck fell unharmed into the water, and escaped into the rushes till his mother and brothers came, then he rejoined them, and they lived happily in the great pond till they all grew up and flew away on wings of their own.[1]

## The Wild Geese of Wyndygoul

Who that knows the wild northland of Canada can picture that blue-and-green wilderness without hearing in his heart the trumpet *honk* of the wild geese? Who has ever known it there can fail to get again, each time he hears, the thrill it gave when first for him it sounded on the blue lake in the frame of green? Older than ourselves is the thrill of the gander clang. For without a doubt that trumpet note in the springtime was the inspiring notice to our far-back forbears in the days that were that the winter famine was at end—the wild geese come, the snow will melt, and the game again be back on the browning hills. The ice hell of the winter time is gone; the warm, bright heaven of the green and perfect land is here. This is the tidings it tells, and when I hear the honker clang from the flying wedge in the sky, that is the message it brings me with a sudden mist in the eyes and a choking in the throat, so I turn away, if another be there, unless that other chance to be like myself, a primitive, a "hark back" who, too, remembers and who understands.

So when I built my house in the woods and glorified a marshy swamp into a deep-blue, brimming lake, with muskrats in the water and intertwining boughs above, my memory, older than my brain, harked hungry for a sound that should have been. I knew not what; I tried to think by subtle searching, but it was chance in a place far off that gave the clue. I want to hear the honkers call; I long for the clang of the flying wedge, the trumpet note of the long-gone days.

So I brought a pair of blacknecks from another lake, pinioned to curb the wild roving that the seasons bring, and they nested on a little island, not hidden, but open to the world about. There in that exquisite bed of soft gray down were laid the six great ivory eggs. On them the patient mother sat four weeks unceasingly, except each afternoon she left them half an hour. And round and round that island, day and night, the gander floated, cruised, and tacked about, like a warship on patrol. Never once did the mother mount on guard. I tried to land and learn about the nest one day. The brooding goose it was that gave the danger call. A short quack, a long, sharp hiss, and before my boat could touch the shore the gander splashed between and faced me. Only over his dead body might my foot defile their isle—so he was left in peace.

The young ones came at length. The six shells broke and the six sweet golden downlings *peeped* inspiringly. Next day they quit the nest in orderly array. The mother first, the downlings closely bunched behind, and last the warrior sire. And this order they always kept, then and all other times that I had knowledge of. It gave me food for thought. The mother always leads, the father, born a fighter, follows—yes, obeys. And what a valiant guard he was; the snapping turtle, the henhawk, the blacksnake, the coon, and the vagrant dog might take their toll of duckling brood or chicken yard, but there is no thing alive the gander will not face for his little ones, and there are few things near his bulk can face him.

So the flock grew big and strong. Before three months they were big almost as the old ones, and fairly fledged; at four their wings were grown; their voices were small and thin, they had not got the trumpet note, but seemed the mother's counterparts in all things else. Then they began to feel their wings, and take short flights across the lake. As their wings grew strong their voices deepened, till the trumpet note was theirs, and the thing I dreamed of came about: a wild-goose band that flew and bugled in the air, and yet came back to their home water that was also mine. Stronger they grew, and long and high their flights. Then came the moon of falling leaves, and with it waning flocks of small birds flew, and in the higher sky the old loud clang was heard. Down from the north they came, the arrowheads of geese. All kinsmen these, and that ahead without a doubt the mother of the rest.

The wild geese on my lake turned up their eyes and answered back, and lined up on the lake. Their mother led the way and they whispered all along the line. Their mother gave the word, swimming fast and faster, then quacked, then called, and then their voices rose to give the *honk*; the broad wings spread a little, while they spattered on the glassy lake, then rose to the measured *honk, honk*; soaring away in a flock, they drifted into line, to join those other honkers in the southern sky.

*Honk, honk, honk!* they shouted as they sped. "Come on! Come on!" they inspired each other with the marching song; it set their wings aquiver. The wild blood rushed still faster in their wilding breasts. It was like a glorious trumpet. But—what! Mother is not in the line. Still splashed she on the surface of the lake, and father too—and now their strident trumpet overbore their clamorous "On, on! Come on!" with a strong "Come back! Come back!" And father, too, was bugling there. "Come back! Come back!"

So the downlings wheeled, and circled high above the woods,

came sailing, skirting, kiting, splashing down at the matriarchal call.

"What's up? What's up?" they called lowly all together, swimming nervously. "Why don't we go? What is it, mother?"

And mother could not tell. Only this she knew, that when she gave the bugle note for all to fly, she spattered with the rest, and flapped, but it seemed she could not get the needed send-off. Somehow she failed to get well under way; the youngsters rose, but the old ones, their strong leaders, had strangely failed. Such things will come to all. Not quite run enough, no doubt. So mother led them to the northernmost arm of the lake, an open stretch of water now, and long. They were lined up again, mother giving a low, short, double *honk* ahead, the rest aside and yet in line, for the long array was angling.

Then the mother passed the word, "Now, now," and nodding just a little, swam on, headed for the south, the young ones passed the word "Now, now," and nodding swam, and father at the rear gave his deep, strong "Now, now," and swam. So swam they all, then spread their wings, and spattered with their feet, as they put on speed, and as they rose, and rising bugled louder till the marching song was ringing in full chorus. Up, up, and away, above the treetops. *But again,* for some strange reason, mother was not there, and father too, was left behind on the pond, and once again the bugle of retreat was heard, "Come back! Come back!"

And the brood, obedient, wheeled on swishing wings to sail and slide and settle on the pond, while mother and father both expressed in low, short notes their deep perplexity.

Again and again this scene took place. The autumn message in the air, the flying wedges of their kin, or the impulse in themselves lined up that flock on the water. All the law of ceremony was complied with, and all went well but the climax.

When the mad moon came, the mania was at its height; not once but twenty times a day I saw them line up and rise, but ever come back to the mother's call, the bond of love and duty stronger than the annual custom of the race. It was a conflict of their laws indeed, but the strongest was, *obey,* made absolute by love.

After a while the impulse died and the flock settled down to winter on the pond. Many a long, far flight they took, but allegiance to the older folk was strong and brought them back. So the winter passed.

Again, when the springtime came, the blacknecks flying north stirred up the young, but in a less degree.

That summer came another brood of young. The older ones warned away whenever near. Snapper, coon, and ranging cur were driven off, and September saw the young ones on the lake with their brothers of the older brood.

Then came October, with the southward rushing of the feathered kinds. Again and again they lined up on the lake and the bugle sounded to "fly," and the same old scene, though now there were a dozen flyers who rose and circled when mother sounded the "retreat."

So through the moon it went. The leaves were fallen now, and a strange and unexpected thing occurred. Making unusual effort to meet this most unusual case, good Mother Nature had prolonged the feathers of the pinioned wing and held back those of the other side. It was slowly done, and the compensating balance not quite made till near October's end. Then, one day, the hundredth time at least that week, the bugle sang, and all the marchers rose. *Yes! mother, too,* and bugling louder till the chorus was complete, they soared about the trees, and mother marshaled all her brood in one great arrow flock, so they sailed and clamoring sailed away, to be lost in the southward blue—and all in vain on the limpid lake behind the gander trumpeted in agony of soul, "Come back! Come back!" His wings had failed him, and in the test, the young's allegiance bound them to their mother and the seeking of the southern home.

All that winter on the ice the gander sat alone. On days a snow-time hawk or some belated crow would pass above, and the ever-watchful eye of blackneck was turned a little to take him in and then go on unheeding. Once or twice there were sounds that stirred the lonely watcher to a bugle call, but short and soon suppressed. It was sad to see him then, and sadder still as we pondered, for this we knew: his family would never come back. Tamed, made trustful by life where men were kind, they had gone to the land of the gunners, crafty, pitiless, and numberless; they would learn too late the perils of the march. Next, he never would take another mate, for the wild goose mates for life, and mates but once: the one surviving has no choice—he finishes his journey alone.

Poor old blackneck, his very faithfulness it was that made for endless loneliness.

The bright days came with melting snow. The floods cut through the ice, and again there were buglers in the sky, and the gander swam to the open part of the lake and answered back.

> *Honk, Honk,* come back,
> Come back. Come back!

But the flyings squads passed on with a passing *honk!*

Brighter still the days, and the gander paddled with a little exultation in the open pond. How we pitied him, self-deluded, faithful, doomed to a long, lone life.

Then balmy April swished the woods with green; the lake was brimming clear. Old blackneck never ceased to cruise and watch, and answer back such sounds as touched him. Oh, sad it seemed that one so staunch should find his burden in his very staunchness.

But on a day, when the peeper and the woodwale sang, there came the great event! Old blackneck, ever waiting, was astir, and more than wont. Who can tell us whence the tidings came? With head at gaze he cruised the open pond, and the short, strong honk seemed sad, till some new excitation raised the feathers on his neck. He honked and honked with a brassy ring. Then long before we heard a sound, he was bugling the marching song, and as he bugled, answering sounds came—from the sky—and grew—then swooping, sailing from the blue, a glorious array of thirteen wild geese, to sail and skate and settle on the pond; and their loud honks gave place to softer chatter as they crowded round and bowed in grave and loving salutation.

There was no doubt of it. The young were now mature and they seemed strange, of course, but this was the missing mate: the mother had come back, and the faithful pair took up the life—and live it yet.

The autumn sends the ordered flock afar, the father stays perforce on guard, but the bond that binds them all and takes them off and brings them back is stronger than the fear of death. So I have learned to love and venerate the honker wild goose whom Mother Nature dowered with love unquenchable, constructed for her own good ends a monument of faithfulness unchanging, a creature heir of all the promises, so master of the hostile world around that he lives and spreads, defying plagues and beasts, and I wonder if this secret is not partly that the wise and patient mother leads. The long, slow test of time has given a minor place to the valiant, fearless, fighting male; his place the last of all, his mode of open fight the latest thing they try. And by a law inscrutable, inexorable, the young obey the matriarch. Wisdom their guide, not force. Their days are long on the earth and the homeland of their race grows wide while others pass away.[2]

# 6.

# MAMMALS OF MANITOBA

THE following paper consists chiefly of the field notes of the writer, although in some instances quotations have been made from Richardson's *Fauna Boreali-Americana* and other accredited sources, with a view to rendering the list as complete as possible.*

JUMPING DEER or MULE DEER (*Cariacus macrotis,* Say).
Cree: A-pi-tci-mu-sis = Small moose

This is the common deer of Manitoba. It is a little larger and heavier animal than the Virginia Deer, and it is also distinguished by its short, black-tipped tail, its very large ears, and by having a marked bifurcation in the beam of the antler. The usual form of its antlers is seen opposite page 210†, and this peculiar double fork is so commonly emphasized as a marked characteristic of the species that I was somewhat surprised to find on comparing a series of specimens of *macrotis* with a number of *virginianus* that a complete intergradation of form was exhibited. One of the mule deer sets was formed so exactly on the Virginia deer model, and likewise the animal had such small ears, that I was not surprised to hear some sportsmen pointing it out as distinct from the *macrotis,* especially as several similar heads were available to show that it was not an isolated case of variation. The ears of this specimen were

---

* Fifty-two species of mammals are included in this list, but space forbids the inclusion of all of these.—ED.
† In picture section.—Ed.

each eight inches in length, while those of a smaller, typical specimen from the same region were each ten and a half inches.

It will be seen that the ears of this species are of exceptional size, and it is from this circumstance that it derives the name of mule deer.

Its range is briefly generalized in the phrase Central North America, and in Manitoba, more specifically, all specimens observed by me were from the valleys of the Assiniboine and Red River.

The species manifests a decided preference for the dry woods and half-open country, avoiding the high sand hills and the damp bottom lands as well as the open prairie.

The doe produces two or sometimes three fawns at a birth, and these, as in most deer, are at first beautifully marked with white spots on a brownish-buff ground. Their voice is a peculiar squeal and bears no resemblance to the bleat of a sheep or lamb. After their birth the mother appears to follow the common habit of the family and hides them in some copse until they are able to follow her about.

This deer seems less shy than most of the family, for when a hunter chances on a locality where it has not been much disturbed, he may often have a herd of the species stand within easy range and gaze innocently at him for some minutes. If at length their inspection renders them suspicious, they will trot off some distance, and if further alarmed, they immediately begin to run in that remarkable bounding action that has bestowed the first mentioned of the common names. During this peculiar run the legs are rather rigidly set, and the impetus appears to be given by an effort of the feet only, and yet from five to eight yards are covered at each bound. To the eye, this pace is the perfection of ease and grace, but it is really very laborious, and a sustained run of a few miles will usually tire out the strongest jumping deer.

In hunting the mule deer, much the same means are employed as in the pursuit of the better known Virginia species, though I am disposed to believe that the latter is more wary and also more difficult of approach on account of the localities it frequents. The excellence of the venison and the value of the skins of these two species, as well as the noble sport afforded by the hunt, have all conduced to render their pursuit one of the most fascinating of field recreations. Of the lawful modes of killing them, hounding and still-hunting are most in favor. The still-hunt is the only method that I myself have seen practiced with the mule deer, but I am informed that hounding has recently been tried in our province.

To hound successfully the hunter must know the country and the runways. For when pursued, the deer usually keep to certain paths or routes, and it is the hunter's policy to lie in ambush in one of these while the hound drives the flying game. As soon as he sees it nearing his retreat, the hunter either shoots on the fly or, by giving a short whistle, causes the animal to stop and listen, and then he has himself to thank if the fatal bullet does not find its billet.

But the still-hunt is the true sportsman's method, for he must rely on himself alone, and to succeed must combine in himself no little perseverance and woodcraft, as well as pure physical endurance. He usually sets off alone on the trail of a deer; it has a fair chance; he meets its strength with strength, its cunning with cunning, and its speed with perseverance. Partly by a sort of instinct and partly by signs, he follows the trail. Guided by marks which to the tyro are unnoticeable, he accurately gauges his proximity to his prey, and when at last he knows that the animal cannot be more than a few hundred yards away, he must prove himself as keen of sense and as stealthy of movement as a veritable beast of prey—for this is the crucial moment, and a trifle may crown or crush his hopes. Slowly, cautiously, he closes in, until at length his quick ear catches the light rustle of brush and his keen eye sights the patch of hair through the branches. Now all depends on the sure, steady aim of the rifle, and another moment his prey either is won, or is flying fast and far and away beyond the reach of another messenger of lead.

COMMON or VIRGINIA DEER (*Cariacus virginianus,* Bod.).

This deer has been called fallow deer, Down East red deer, long-tailed, white-tailed deer, and common red deer. But as the last name has also been applied to the wapiti, and the first does not belong here at all, much confusion will be avoided if we drop both in the present connection.

It may be distinguished from the jumping deer by its smaller size, smaller ears, and by its tail, which is very long and pure white throughout the under surface. When bounding away in alarm, the animal usually holds the tail aloft, and it then, in conjunction with the white patch on the buttocks, becomes a very conspicuous object as it is seen dancing away among the trees. This white flag, as the hunters call it, is probably intended to assist the fawns in keeping sight of the dam when pursued and endeavoring to escape by flight.

Though the habitat of the species is comprehensively "all of North America, except the extreme north," the Virginia deer is far from being common in our province. Three specimens are all that have come under my notice, and these were taken on Pembina Mountain. They were in the possession of Mr. Hine, the well-known taxidermist of Winnipeg, and this gentleman informs me that during his six-years' residence in the country he has seen but nine or ten specimens, and all of these were brought from the country about the Pembina Mountain.

ELK or WAPITI (*Cervus canadensis.* Erx.). Cree: Wa-pi-ti

To the Hudson's Bay Company's employes the elk is known as the wapiti, red deer, or stag, but as the use of the last two names would cause considerable confusion, they will not herein appear. The wapiti or elk is probably the largest of the deer family that bear branching antlers, and in size and grandeur is second only to the moose of all the *Cervidae.* A full-grown buck will usually stand from four and a half to five feet at the shoulders, and will weigh between 500 and 600 pounds. The female is smaller than the male, but is nevertheless a magnificent animal. The general color is chestnut, darkest on the head and limbs, and on the rump suddenly changing into dull white. The antlers constitute the most striking feature of the species, for it is probable that they exceed in size those of any other living deer. As with most of the family, they are the distinguishing ornaments of the male. A good idea of the elk's general appearance and carriage may be gathered from Landseer's celebrated pictures of the Scottish red deer, a species almost exactly a miniature of the lordly animal under consideration.

At one time the elk was of general distribution in temperate North America, but its territory has been greatly diminished of late, its chief strongholds, at present, being the foothills of the Rockies and the valley of the Yellowstone. In the Northwest Territory, I am informed that it is found as far north as the Liard River, and the number of lakes, rivers, and creeks which are named Red Deer after this animal testifies to the universality of its distribution in this region.

In Manitoba it may still (1886) be considered an inhabitant of the Red and Assiniboine valleys in general, but it does not appear to exist in large numbers anywhere but in the Pembina Mountain.

A marked peculiarity of this species and one which in part induced Judge Caton to recommend it for domestication, is its ability to live on the veriest garbage. According to the authority named, any and all vegetable substance is pleasing to its palate. It eats, with apparently equal relish, hay, moss, grass, browse, twigs, sedge, or leaves; it is the most omnivorous of deer, and will subsist and even fatten amid bleak sand hills where ordinary cattle or almost any other ruminant would starve.

MOOSE (*Alce americanus,* Jardine). Cree: Mŭs. Ojibwa: Müz

This magnificent deer equals or exceeds a horse in stature, if not in weight, for an adult male is usually six feet in height at the shoulders, eight to nine feet in length from the snout to the tail, and weighs between 700 and 900 pounds. The female averages less, though it often exceeds the dimensions given. These figures, I am aware, are far below the guesses of enthusiastic sportsmen, which will often add at least 25 percent to each of the items given, but those are probably fair averages. Nevertheless, we must not brand as total untruths the stories one occasionally hears from hunters, of seven-foot, 1,000-pound moose, for the eminent authority, Judge Caton, is of the opinion that specimens have been killed weighing nearly 1,400 pounds, and such in all likelihood would be at least seven feet at the shoulders.

The largest moose head I have ever seen is in the possession of Mr. Cummings, of Winnipeg. The antlers measured 57 inches from tip to tip, each is 33 x 25 inches across the palmation, and the estimated weight of the pair is 50 pounds. I would venture the opinion that the animal they belonged to was considerably over six feet at the withers.

The neck of the moose is about a foot long, and of necessity very thick and strong to carry the weight of the antlers. This lack of attenuated grace, combined with the peculiar muzzle and long limbs, has moved many writers to a volley of railery at what they style the grotesque and ungainly appearance of the animal. But I do not hesitate to aver that no one who has studied the living moose without prejudice will for a moment champion any such sentiments. On first sight it is bound to look strange, but so does the elephant and, like that animal, the moose, though devoid of the airy grace that distinguishes our small deer, is possessed of a beauty that manifests itself in perfect adjustment that is insepara-ble from vast size and strength.

The moose was at one time an abundant species in nearly all the wooded regions of the higher latitudes, but at present its range is much less extensive, and it is found in great numbers only about the south of Hudson's Bay, and in the region north of Great Slave Lake. In Manitoba it is sparingly distributed wherever the locality is congenial. But it may be described as plentiful in the Duck and Riding Mountains, and in the low country about Lake Manitoba.

Usually the moose is found inhabiting the lowlands, where dense woods are alternated with swamp and damp thickets of birch and willow, finding in such localities at once security from its natural enemies and an abundance of the browse and tender twigs on which it principally subsists, while its great length of limb and its wide-spreading hoofs enable it to cross with safety the most treacherous of bogs, such even as would inevitably engulf and destroy any ox or horse that might venture upon them.

When the winter comes in, it usually quits the solitary roving life it led during the summer, and in company with a small num-ber of its kind settles down in some sheltered locality where browse and equisetum are sufficiently abundant to furnish proven-der for some time. In such a locality they will remain as long as the food holds out. If, however, the herd receive the slightest in-timation of approaching hunters, be it only the far-away crack of a stick, or even a suspicious taint on the wind, they immediately set off at full speed and maintain their swift trot for several miles, toward some more remote haunt, where they again settle, but are more than ever watchful and ready to fly on the slightest appearance of danger. During a retreat of this kind, according to my observations, the animals run in a line, single file, and each treads in the track of the one before, so that in many places only one trail appears.

My own notes on this species were made chiefly in the spruce bush at Carberry where, in the fall of 1884, Mr. James Duff and myself killed a bull moose that is worthy of notice on account of its rather anomalous condition. It was apparently very old, as the "bell" on the throat was sixteen and one-half inches long, including the hair, which was three inches in length; and yet the antlers were the smallest I ever saw on an adult, and one of them was curiously malformed.

The localities affected by this deer are also frequented by the Wis-ka-tjan or Whiskey Jack (*Perisoreus canadensis*) , and on the only occasion when I came near a herd of moose feeding, the warning and melancholy notes of the bird preceded the retreat of the shy browsers, and appeared to be a notification of danger to them. So that there may be some good reasons for this jay's name of moose bird.

The value of the animal's carcass for food, and the high quality of leather manufactured from its hide, combined with the great difficulty attendant on its pursuit, have rendered the moose the most celebrated object of the chase in America. Its powers of scent and hearing are unexcelled; its wariness and cunning are proverbial; so that one who is a successful moosehunter is acknowledged to have attained the acme of woodcraft.

The presence of two or three feet of snow appears to be of slight impediment to the long, thin shank of the moose; but when there is a crust the case is different, for then the hunter, mounted on snowshoes, has the poor beast at his mercy, and often, I almost say usually, yields to the temptation to kill far more than he really requires. As the chance for this sort of sport occurs only in late winter or early spring, when the meat is in very poor condition, and the beast is totally helpless, the whole affair is contemptible in the extreme.

In curious contrast to the habitual wariness of the moose, is the fact that it has frequently been approached when asleep, although the hunter was taking no precautions to make his approach noise-lessly. Mr. W. Clark, of the Hudson's Bay Company's service in Winnipeg, related to me the following: "I was crossing the wooded country between Lakes Manitoba and Winnipeg in the early spring. I had with me an Indian and a dog team with a loaded sled, besides a couple of hounds running loose. The dogs were being driven with the usual amount of shouting and noise, and this was increased as we came to a difficult hill. On the hill was a tall spruce, and as there was no trail, the Indian climbed it to ascertain the best route. When he was at the top we held a conversation in tones commensurate with the distance between us. Just after he came down, the dogs, that were beating about, chanced into a thicket close by my station, and with a great uproar put up two moose that had evidently lain there asleep through all the clamor of our traveling and shouting. Of course no gun was handy, so they got away; but we turned loose the train dogs, the whole pack taking after the bull, and afterward we succeeded in running him down and killing him."

The flesh of the moose is a staple article of diet in the Northwest Territory, and is considered quite as nutritious and palatable as ordinary beef, while the muscle or gristle of the snout, and the tongue are esteemed among the greatest delicacies. Its hide affords the best leather in use for moccasins and hunting coats, and the long bristles of the mane are dyed by the Indian squaws and worked into a variety of embroidery patterns, for moccasins, fire bags, and other articles of dress or ornament. The great strength of the moose, combined with its swiftness and tamableness, has induced several writers who have studied the subject to recommend the species as a draught animal. And as the experiment is being made by Mr. Bedson, of Stony Mountain, a brief account of a bull moose that was broken to harness will form a suitable close to this article.

The animal in question was owned by Mr. B. S. McLean of Ottawa, and the account given is from information supplied by the gentleman himself. The moose came into his possession when it was about nine months old. It fed on browse and twigs at first, but experience showed that it throve as well or better when supplied with bread for a change, and later, when thoroughly broken, it was found advisable to train it on clover and oats, when preparing it for a race or long journey. Its habitual action when traveling was a long, swinging trot, though it sometimes paced for a short distance, and on rare occasions varied the movement with a long "lope"; but at all times the action was clean, neat, and wonderfully smooth. Its speed for a short distance was almost incredible; thus, for a quarter of a mile it could beat all horse records; its best time for half a mile was one minute, five and a half seconds, but the animal lacked bottom and was not so completely under control that it could be induced to keep up its best speed for a mile or even to keep the track for that distance.

When urged to greater speed while in harness, it usually began screaming and roaring in a rather startling manner, whilst its glowing eyes and bristling mane gave evidence of a wild nature but little changed by its barnyard bringing up. Its only mode of attack appeared to be by striking with the fore feet; but the terrible force of the blows it could so deal showed that it required no other means to defend itself against its natural enemies. It was remarkably fond of playing and swimming in the water, but was very dangerous to boats or canoes if such chanced to come near, as it usually gave chase in a sportive manner, and did its utmost to injure or sink them by repeated blows from its hoofs. Compared with other moose, this one was remarkably heavy bodied and short legged, which may, in a measure, account for its lack of staying power. As it grew older it became more vicious; and when four years old it had to be killed; it then stood about seventeen hand high at the shoulder.

### WOODLAND CARIBOU (*Rangifer caribou,* Kerr). Cree: A-tik. Ojibwa: At-tik

In size, this animal is midway between the Virginia deer and the elk. Its general color is dirty white, shaded into chestnut on the head and legs, and suddenly becoming white again just above each hoof. Its chief anatomical peculiarities are the long, slender, palmated horns—often present in the female—its entirely hairy muzzle, and its large, spreading feet, which often have the "clouts," or accessory hoofs, prolonged so that they touch the ground.

The few Manitoban specimens that I have seen were brought from Lake Winnipeg and the country about Lake of the Woods. I never met with it myself, and have no original information to offer. I may, however, repeat the statement of a hunter with regard to the proportion of females that have antlers. He informed me that all the does have them after a certain age, about the fourth or fifth year, and I must say that the statement looks very like the truth.

Attention has more than once been directed toward this species as one suitable for domestication. That there is need for such an animal is sufficiently attested by the fact that in the vast region to the north the only draught animal is the dog, which, while it is more expensive to keep than the deer would be, is much less efficient, totally useless during half the year, and affords no useful product after death. As the caribou is practically the same as the reindeer of Lapland, the idea is perfectly practicable. Mr. Alexander Macarthur, of Winnipeg, brought the subject into notice some four years ago by an admirable paper. There was no one to deny that the reindeer can go twice as far in a day as a dog, and with thrice the load; besides it can feed itself, and is, dead or alive, a source of profit as food. The idea was favorably entertained, and the necessary capital subscribed to secure a few domesticated reindeer from Sweden. But it chanced that the time of year was not just then the most favorable for the importation, so that prudence dictated a few months' delay. During that time interest in the project subsided, nothing further was done in the matter, and finally the capital was redistributed.

BUFFALO (*Bison americanus,* Gmelin). Cree: Mus-tus'.
Ojibwa: Muc-kwi-té-pij-i-ki, Prairie Horned-beast

The buffalo is now to be regarded as a Manitoba species on the strength only of a herd kept by Mr. S. L. Bedson at Stony Mountain. Without wasting any time over the oft-told tale of the extermination of the wild buffalo in the Northwest, I will briefly describe the domesticated herd already mentioned.

In 1878 some Indians, returning to Winnipeg from the west, brought with them five buffalo calves. These became the property of Mr. James McKay, and were allowed to run about the outskirts of the town until 1882, when the herd, now numbering twenty-three, came into the possession of Mr. Bedson, by whose courtesy I was enabled to gather the following information.

At the present time (January, 1885), the herd numbers forty-

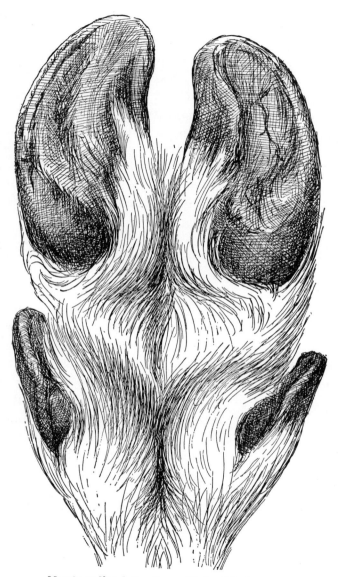

*Newfoundland Caribou: Right Hind Hoof*

one) ; of these, nine are half-breeds with the common neat cattle; six are three-quarters bred, and the rest, pure buffalo. The object of domesticating these beasts is to provide an animal better suited to the requirements of the Northwest than the common animal, for notwithstanding a story oft told to the eager immigrant, the latter species must be housed and fed during the winter, and on the ranches a number fall annually a prey to frost, famine, drought, or disease.

On the other hand, the tame buffalos referred to have never exhibited the slightest symptoms of disease. Of the number that have died, one or two have been butchered, one old bull fell from a height and broke his neck, and the rest have been shot by malicious people.

And yet this herd receives no care beyond what is necessary to prevent them wandering away or being stolen. They live on the open prairie, summer and winter, subsisting entirely on the wild grass, even when they have to dig for it through one or more feet of snow. Nor is it a mere existence that they maintain; for when I saw them late in January they were finding grass enough not merely to feed but to fatten them. When a blizzard comes on they lie down with their backs to the wind and allow the snow to drift about them, so that under the combined protection of the snow and their own woolly coats they are perfectly comfortable. In January 1884 one of the cows calved in the open prairie, and though at that time the thermometer registered thirty-eight below zero, neither cow nor calf appeared to suffer the slightest inconvenience.

In view of these facts, I think no one will deny the immensely superior hardihood of the buffalo when compared with the neat cattle; and a comparison of the material productions of each will not be seriously adverse to the former.

The hide of the common beast is worth about $1.50; as a robe it is worthless. The robe of an average buffalo is worth about $10, and we must remember that it has already established its position as an indispensable wrap in our northern climate; also that as we push our civilization farther to the north and west the demand will increase; and what is there to offer in its place if the supply gives out?

Once a year the buffalo sheds its fleece, scraping it off in great flakes against the bushes and trees. This wool is easily gathered, and readily works up into yarn that will compare favorably with that produced by the inferior breed of sheep. This it will be seen is no inconsiderable item when we are told that each animal yields from ten to twelve pounds of raw material. Many years ago there was in Winnipeg a cloth factory for the manufacture of buffalo wool, and I understand its operations were stopped only by the extirpation of the animals in the neighborhood of the town.

In one particular only is the buffalo completely inferior to its domesticated relative, and that is as a milker. But to the ranchman this very item is of no consequence whatever.

Mr. Bedson has also experimented with crosses between the buffalo and the common cattle; for the two species are perfectly interfertile in all degrees of hybridity. The hybrid animal is claimed to be a great improvement on both of its progenitors, as it is more docile and a better milker than the buffalo, but retains its hardihood, whilst the robe is finer, darker, and more even, and the general shape of the animal is improved by the reduction of the hump and increased proportion of the hindquarters.

As the scheme of domestication is now fairly well set forth as a commercial enterprise, and as its success is no longer considered problematic, it is unnecessary here to do more in the way of contending for the reasonableness and value of the experiment.

GROUND SQUIRREL (*Spermophilus richardsoni*, Sabine) .
Ojibwa: Mi-se-dji-dä-mo′ = Largest Squirrel

The ground squirrel, also known as the yellow gopher and Richardson's spermophile, is probably the most abundant member of the family in Manitoba. It is usually found on heavy clay land only, and when a locality presents an unusual number of favorable characters the ground squirrels are likely to be found there in such numbers as to present the appearance of a colony, although I do not think that the species is sociable, in the true sense of the word.

This gopher appears above ground in the spring before the snow is gone, that is, before the reappearance of the striped gopher. The yellow species appears to be much less sensitive to cold, for my caged individuals were not affected by a temperature nearly down to the freezing point, though it put all of the striped species into a state of stupor. In the fall also the present species remains above ground about a fortnight longer than the *tridecemlineatus*.

The voice of the species is a husky whistle, and each time that the sound is produced the tail is raised in a very ludicrous manner. This whistle appears to be an alarm note only.

The cheek pouches of the ground squirrel are very well developed and enable it to carry a surprising amount of grain to its hole at a single journey. A very fine specimen which I took from a hawk on the 23rd of May, 1884, weighed thirteen ounces, and its cheek pouches contained 240 grains of wheat and nearly 1,000 grains of buckwheat. Another taken July 26 had in its pouches 162 grains of oats.

My notes on the breeding season are very brief and inconclusive, but such as they are they indicate that the young are born about the middle of May. They number sometimes as high as eleven.

About the end of June they are half grown and begin to show themselves outside their burrows. The prairie about the burrows is now swarming with life and becomes a regular hunting ground for all sorts of predaceous birds and beasts.

Trapping these dull-witted creatures does not require the exercise of much ingenuity, but one is so sure of success that the interest is sustained. I have myself caught over a dozen in an hour with only two traps. My plan was to go to some thriving colony in the heat of the afternoon, at which time the proprietor of the burrow might be seen sunning himself on the mound at the entrance. I would walk gently toward one, whereupon he would disappear. I would then set my trap and leave him. If approached hastily he would be too much alarmed to come out again for a long time, but by causing him no great trepidation his return and capture were usually assured within a few seconds. Sometimes a light-weight squirrel would not spring the trap as he came out, in which case I had only to throw something at him and so make him rush for his hole when his heavier step would be the certain means of making him a prisoner. The trap never needed either bait or covering, as the little animals are so entirely without cunning that they will at once step on the pan. A simple circumstance will illustrate the superior mentalism of the striped gopher. If one walks close past one of the latter without looking at it, it watches his eye and does not stir; if, however, he turn about and face it, it disappears into its burrow. The yellow gopher, however, no matter how approached, always runs into its hole with nervous haste as soon as it sees a foe in its vicinity.

When the two gophers were kept in a cage together, the striped species bullied its larger brother mercilessly and lost no opportunity of impressing him with the superiority of mind over matter.

STRIPED GOPHER (*Spermophilus tridecemlineatus*, Michell).

This gopher is abundant all over the prairie regions of the province, where the soil is light and sandy. In the spring it begins to show itself above ground during the last week in April, and by the first week in May it is to be seen in abundance.

It is, I believe, a strictly diurnal animal and is so partial to warmth that it is not often seen above ground before the sun has attained considerable force, while on cold days it is seldom seen at all.

Its voice is exercised in the production of a number of shrill, birdlike whistles and chirps. Notwithstanding its long slender body and curious markings, it is not a pretty animal, being entirely devoid of any weasellike grace, while its harsh fur detracts from the effect of the alternate spots and stripes.

The burrows of this animal are of three kinds. First, a labyrinth of galleries with many entrances; this I take to be a mere playground. Second, the nesting burrows. The nest is usually a chamber some six inches below the surface, lined with fine grass. It is about nine inches in diameter, and is approached by many galleries and several entrances.

The third type of burrow goes nearly straight downward for six, eight, or even twelve feet. This is, I believe, the winter residence; but at one time I theorized that it was a well. However, I kept many of the animals in a state of captivity, and now think that they are almost independent of any water supply. After keeping six gophers without water for a week in hot weather, I offered them some in a saucer. Four paid no heed; two tasted, but immediately left it, and could hardly be said to have drunk.

The young are born late in May, and usually number eight or nine. They are at first blind and naked, the skin being a pale flesh color. One female that I kept in captivity brought forth her litter in time, but paid not the slightest heed to them, so that I failed of making more extensive observations on their development. I have no evidence to show that more than one litter is produced each season.

It is not to be described as a sociable species in any degree, as those that I kept in a cage never noticed each other except to fight, and in a state of nature I never saw two gophers heeding each other's presence except in the breeding season.

If the gopher on the prairie be not chased very fast, it will play with the observer and lead him about in various directions. If, however, it be really pursued, it makes for shelters; under these circumstances, when suddenly it stops and looks at its pursuer, we know it has arrived at its burrow and feels safe; and on being more nearly approached its dives down, often uttering a shrill chirrup as it disappears. But as the species is possessed of an uncontrollable curiosity, it is sure to peep out again in a few seconds, if all be still, and is then easily taken in a string noose previously placed over the hole.

It is a common sight to see a gopher sitting perfectly still and bolt upright on one of the earth mounds on the prairie. The animal's body is so long and it presses its paws so closely to its breast that under these circumstances it is often mistaken by the novice for a surveyor's stake, until a nearer approach on the part of the observer alarms the rodent and the supposed stake dives into the mound.

Although this species is supposed to be strictly terrestrial, Mr. Miller Christy and myself twice observed a gopher climb up a low spruce tree in pursuit of a baywinged bunting (*Poocaetes gramineus*) that was perched on the top.

My observations on the food of the species do not agree with the accepted accounts as, instead of being a vegetarian, it is, I find, quite omnivorous, for in a state of nature, besides all sorts of fruits, vegetables, and grains, I have known them to eat feathers, house scraps, offal, insects, small birds, and their fallen comrades, while those that I kept caged invariably manifested a preference for raw meat over any vegetable substance I could offer them.

During the latter part of August and the early part of September the gophers are seen continually running into their burrows, with cheeks distended either with grass or grain. As the days grow colder they come out less often, and by October are no more seen, but henceforth continue in darkness until the return of spring calls them into active life.

### VARYING HARE or WHITE RABBIT (*Lepus americanus,* Erxleben). Cree: Wa-pus'. Ojibwa: Wa-büs'

This is the common rabbit of Manitoba, and throughout the whole province it exists in such numbers as to entitle it to the name of being our most abundant mammal.

Many observers have remarked that during some years it is exceedingly numerous, and in others it is comparatively rare. It is said to go on multiplying for six or seven successive years, and then at length an epidemic disease regularly appears and almost exterminates the species. If this be true, there can be little doubt that 1887 is about the last year of the series of increase, as the rabbits have multiplied to such an extent as to cause uneasiness to many persons, who are aware of the trouble a kindred species has caused in Australia. In the fall of 1886 the woods about Carberry so abounded with the species that killing them ceased to be a sport. I do not think I exaggerate in saying that during the month of October I could on any one day have killed a hundred rabbits with one gun. With a view to giving a tangible illustration,

I stood at one time and counted those that I might have shot without leaving my place, and they numbered thirteen. At another time I counted six, all within a space twenty feet square. I have specified the month of October, because by an apparent seasonal miscalculation, the rabbits were then more or less white, although the snow did not come until late November. Certainly there had been a slight fall early in the month, but not sufficient to whiten the ground, and it disappeared soon after the sun arose. Thenceforth through October and part of November the weather continued bright and summerlike, and the unfortunate rabbits, in their unseasonable garb, were seen skipping silently about like ghosts, among the brown copses and bluffs of the prairie.

In making the change the largest and most robust individuals are always in advance of their smaller or sickly relatives. Out of forty examined by me at Winnipeg on October 26, five only were whitening on the body, and these five were conspicuous for their superior size and weight. On the other hand, even after the species in general were pure white I found a few puny individuals in an intermediate state of color.

During the summer the species is much subject to the attacks of the parasitic tick (*Ixodes bovis*), numbers of which may often be seen hanging on the throat and neck of the luckless rodent.

I have not yet found the nest of the hare, the nearest approach to it being a young one nestled among the leaves under a brush pile. When I seized it, it squealed lustily and very soon the mother appeared in response to the cry of her young one. This was in June 1883. On April 10 I shot a female and found two very small foeti on dissection.

At Winnipeg, in October 1886, Mr. Hine showed me an apparent albinism of this species. It was a half-grown specimen in summer pelage; instead of the usual dark-brown color, it was a pale buff above, and its eyes, as usual with such "freaks of nature," were clear pink.

## BADGER (*Taxidea americana,* Boddaert).
### Cree: Mi-ten-üsk'. Ojibwa: Mi-ten-üsk

An abundant species in the prairie regions of the south and west. The flesh diet of this omnivorous animal is, I believe, composed chiefly of gophers. I have frequently seen places where a badger, guided apparently by scent, had dug down from twenty to thirty holes at intervals, so as to strike the surface burrow of some gopher, with a view to intercepting the little miner, and the evidence went to show that ultimately the rodent fell a victim to its indefatigable foe.

The great strength of the badger is attested by the fact that, if seized by the tail just as it is disappearing into its hole, it will brace itself with its fore feet and bid defiance to all the force of a strong man. One which was so seized I tried to dislodge by pouring water down the hole, but it swelled out its body and so filled the hole that no water got past it until after a passage had been made by the insertion of a pole.

In the fall of 1884, I saw a great many badger tracks, and new earths after the first snow had fallen. In hopes of finding a specimen "denned up" for the winter, I dug to the bottom of several burrows, but in each case with the same results. The burrows all went down about six feet, and where they terminated was unmistakable evidence that the badger had dug down in search of some dormant gopher, whose hoard of grain was in each case left scattered about in the earth and all of it more or less sprouted.

Mr. Matheson, the Hudson's Bay Company's agent at Rat Portage, informed me that they received a badger skin from a point fifty miles north of Lake of the Woods.

PRAIRIE WOLF or COYOTE  (*Canis latrans,* Say) .
Cree: Mes-tca-gän-is'

Common in the prairie regions, although seldom seen in the summer.

I have had many opportunities for observing this animal, but can add very little to what is already known of it. It readily crosses with the dog, and the two species appear to be interfertile in all degrees of hybridity. Half-breeds shown me by Mr. Bedson, of Stony Mountain, partook equally of the characters of both parents. By means of a telescope I have often watched this animal when not at all alarmed by the proximity of its greatest foe. I never saw any signs of gregariousness in the species, at least during the day time. It is remarkably wary, and soon detects the presence of any but the most carefully concealed traps.

I have often observed the use to which the great bushy tail is put. In lying down for a nap, the four feet and nose of the animal, the only exposed parts, are all brought together, and the brush laid over and around them by way of a wrap. This is so invariably done that I believe a wolf would die in the winter if deprived of its tail.

The dogs, which are such a conspicuous feature of every Indian camp, are probably the domesticated descendants of this wolf, although the size and general appearance of some seem also to point out the timber wolf as their ancestor.

The Ojibwa names were given me by A-nim-i-kong (Little Thunder) , a Lake of the Woods Indian; Albert Chief, a half-breed of Rat Portage, acting as interpreter. The Cree names were given by Mr. Hector McKenzie of Winnipeg. The alphabet used in recording is that of the Bureau of Ethnology at Washington.[1]

# 7.

# BISON AND CARIBOU HERDS

In 1907 I set out to journey by canoe down the Athabaska and adjoining waters to the sole remaining forest wilds—the far north-west of Canada—and the yet more desert Arctic Plains, where still, it was said, were to be seen the caribou in their primitive con-dition.

My only companion was Edward A. Preble, of Washington, D.C., a trained naturalist, an expert canoeist and traveler, and a man of three seasons' experience in the Hudson's Bay Territory and the Mackenzie Valley. While my chief object was to see the caribou, and prove their continued abundance, I was prepared incidentally to gather natural-history material of all kinds, and to complete the shore line of the ambiguous lake called "Aylmer," as well as explore its sister, the better known Clinton-Colden.

I went for my own pleasure at my own expense, and yet I could not persuade my Hudson's Bay Company friends that I was not sent by some government, museum, or society for some secret purpose.

On the night of May 5 we left Winnipeg, and our observations began with the day at Bradon.

From that point westward to Regina we saw abundant evidence that last year had been a "rabbit year," that is, a year in which the ever-fluctuating population of northern hares (snowshoe rabbits or white rabbits) had reached its maximum, for nine tenths of the bushes in sight from the train had been barked at the snow level. But the fact that we saw not one rabbit shows that "the plague" had appeared, had run its usual drastic course, and nearly exterminated the species in this particular region. . . .

On May 11, having heard that the Athabaska was open, we left Edmonton in a livery rig, and drove ninety-four miles northward through a most promising, half-settled country, and late the next day arrived at Athabaska Landing, on the east tributary of the Mackenzie, whose waters were to bear us onward for so many weeks.

Athabaska Landing is a typical frontier town. These are hard words, but justified. We put up at the principal hotel; the other lodgers told me it was considered the worst hotel in the world. I thought I knew of two worse, but next morning accepted the prevailing view.

Our canoe and provisions arrived, but the great convoy of scows that were to take the annual supplies of trade stuff for the far north was not ready, and we needed the help and guidance of its men, so must needs wait for four days. . . .

All travelers who had preceded me into the Barren Grounds had relied on the abundant game, and in consequence suffered dreadful hardships; in some cases even starved to death. I proposed to rely on no game, but to take plenty of groceries, the best I could buy in Winnipeg, which means the best in the world; and, as will be seen later, the game, because I was not relying on it, walked into camp every day.

But one canoe could not carry all these provisions, so most of it I shipped on the Hudson's Bay Company scows, taking with us, in the canoe, food for not more than a week, which with camp outfit was just enough for ballast.

Of course I was in close touch with the Hudson's Bay people. Although nominally that great trading company parted with its autocratic power and exclusive franchise in 1870, it is still the sovereign of the north. And here let me correct an error that is sometimes found even in respectable print—the Company has at all times been ready to assist scientists to the utmost of its very ample power. Although jealous of its trading rights, everyone is free to enter the territory without taking count of the Company, but there has not yet been a *successful* scientific expedition into the region without its active cooperation.

The Hudson's Bay Company has always been the guardian angel of the north.

I suppose that there never yet was another purely commercial concern that so fully realized the moral obligations of its great power, or that has so uniformly done its best for the people it ruled.

At all times it has stood for peace, and one hears over and over again that such and such tribes were deadly enemies, but the Company insisted on their smoking the peace pipe. The Sioux and Ojibwa, Blackfoot and Assiniboine, Dogrib and Copperknife, Beaver and Chipewyan, all offer historic illustrations in point, and many others could be found for the list.

The name Peace River itself is a monument of successful effort on the part of the Company to bring about a better understanding between the Crees and the Beavers.

Besides human foes, the Company has saved the Indian from famine and plague. Many a hunger-stricken tribe owes its continued existence to the fatherly care of the Company, not simply general and indiscriminate, but minute and personal, carried into the details of their lives. For instance, when bots so pestered the caribou of one region as to render their hides useless to the natives, the Company brought in hides from a district where they still were good.

The Chipewyans were each spring the victims of snow blindness until the Company brought and succeeded in popularizing their present ugly but effectual and universal peaked hats. When their train dogs were running down in physique, the Company brought in a strain of pure Huskies or Eskimo. When the Albany River Indians were starving and unable to hunt, the Company gave the order for 5,000 lodge poles. Then, not knowing how else to turn them to account, commissioned the Indians to work them into a picket garden fence. At all times the native found a father in the Company, and it was the worst thing that ever happened to the region when the irresponsible free traders, with their demoralizing methods, were allowed to enter and traffic where or how they pleased.

At Athabaska Landing, on May 18, 1907, 10:15 a.m., we boarded the superb Petersborough canoe that I had christened the *Ann Seton.** The Athabaska River was a-flood and clear of ice; thirteen scows of freight, with sixty half-breeds and Indians to man them, left at the same time, and in spite of a strong headwind we drifted northward fully three and one half miles an hour.

The leading scow, where I spent some time, was in charge of John MacDonald himself, and his passengers comprised the Hudson's Bay Company officials, going to their posts or on tours of inspection. They were a jolly crowd, like a lot of rollicking schoolboys, full of fun and good humor, chaffing and joking all day; but when a question of business came up, the serious businessman appeared in each, and the Company's interest was cared for with their best powers. The bottle was not entirely absent in those scow fraternities, but I saw no one the worse for liquor on the trip.

That night, as the river was brimming and safe, we tied up to the scows and drifted, making thirty more miles, or sixty since embarking.

In the early morning I was much struck by the lifelessness of the

* After Seton's daughter.—ED.

scene. The great river stretched away northward, the hills rose abruptly from the water's edge, everywhere extended the superb spruce forest, here fortunately unburnt; but there seemed no sign of living creatures outside of our own numerous, noisy, and picturesque party. River, hills, and woods were calm and silent. It was impressive, if disappointing; and, when at last the fir stillness was broken by a succession of trumpet notes from the great pileated woodpecker, the sound went rolling on and on, in reverberating echoes that might well have alarmed the bird himself.

The white-spruce forest along the banks is most inspiring; magnificent here.

At night we reached the Indian village of Pelican Portage, and landed by climbing over huge blocks of ice that were piled along shore. The adult male inhabitants came down to our camp, so that the village was deserted, except for the children and a few women.

As I walked down the crooked trail along which straggle the cabins, I saw something white in a tree at the far end. Supposing it to be a white rabbit in a snare, I went near and found, to my surprise, first that it was a dead house cat, a rare species here; second, under it, eyeing it and me alternately, was a hungry-looking lynx. I had a camera, for it was near sundown and in the woods, so I went back to the boat and returned with a gun. There was the lynx still prowling, but now farther from the village. I do not believe he would have harmed the children, but a lynx is game. I fired, and he fell without a quiver or a sound. This was the first time I had used a gun in many years, and was the only time on the trip. I felt rather guilty, but the carcass was a godsend to two old Indians who were sickening on a long diet of salt pork, and that lynx furnished them tender meat for three days afterward; while its skin and skull went to the American Museum.

At Fort MacMurray we learned that there was no telling when the steamer might arrive; Major Jarvis was under orders to proceed without delay to Smith Landing; so to solve all our difficulties I bought a thirty-foot boat (sturgeonhead) of Joe Bird, and arranged to join forces with the police for the next part of the journey.

I had made several unsuccessful attempts to get an experienced native boatman to go northward with me. All seemed to fear the impending plunge into the unknown; so I was agreeably surprised when a sturdy young fellow of Scottish and Cree parentage came and volunteered for the trip. A few inquiries proved him to bear a good reputation as a riverman and worker, so William C. Loutit was added to my expedition and served me faithfully throughout.

That night we camped far down the river and on the side opposite the fort, for experience soon teaches one to give the dogs no chance of entering camp on marauding expeditions while you rest.

About ten, as I was going to sleep, Preble put his head in and said: "Come out here if you want a new sensation."

In a moment I was standing with him under the tall spruce trees, looking over the river to the dark forest, a quarter mile away, and listening intently to a new and wonderful sound. Like the slow tolling of a soft but high-pitched bell, it came. *Ting, ting, ting, ting,* and on, rising and falling with the breeze, but still keeping on about two *tings* to the second, and on, dulling as with distance, but rising again and again.

It was unlike anything I had heard, but Preble knew it of old. "That," says he, "is the love song of the Richardson owl. *She* is sitting demurely in some spruce top while he sails around, singing on wing, and when the sound sounds distant, he is on the far side of the tree."

*Ting, ting, ting, ting,* it went on and on, this soft belling of his love, this amorous music of our northern bell bird.

On June 1 the weather was so blustering and wet that we did not break camp. I put in the day examining the superb timber of this bottom land. White spruce is the prevailing conifer and is here seen in perfection. A representative specimen was one hundred eighteen feet high; eleven feet, two inches in circumference, or three feet, six and one half inches in diameter one foot from the ground, i.e., above any root spread. There was plenty of timber of similar height. Black spruce, a smaller kind, and tamarack are found farther up and back in the big country. Jack pine of fair size abounds on the sandy and gravelly parts. Balsam poplar (tulip tree) is the largest deciduous tree; its superb legions in upright ranks are crowded along all the river banks and on islands not occupied by the spruce. The large trees of this kind often have deep holes; these are the nesting sites of the whistler duck, which is found in numbers here and as far north as this tree, but not farther. White poplar is plentiful also; the hillsides are beautifully clad with its purplish masses of twigs, through which its white stems gleam like marble columns. White birch is common in impenetrable thickets to make up the rest of the forest stretches.

At this camp I had the unique experience of showing all these seasoned Westerners that it was possible to make fire by the friction of two sticks. This has long been a specialty of mine; I use a thong and a bow as the simplest way. Ordinarily I prefer balsam fir or tamarack; in this case I used a balsam block and a spruce drill, and although each kind failed when used with drill and block the same, I got fire in half a minute.

On June 3 we left this camp of tall timber. As we floated down we sighted a lynx on the bank looking contemplatively into the flood. One of the police boys seized a gun and with a charge of No. 6 killed the lynx. Poor thing, it was in a starving condition, as indeed are most meat eaters this year in the north. Though it was fully grown, it weighed but fifteen pounds. In its stomach was part of a sparrow (whitethroat?) and a piece of rawhide an inch wide and four feet long, evidently a portion of dog harness picked up somewhere along the river. I wonder what he did with the bells.

That night we decided to drift, leaving one man on guard. Next day, as we neared Lake Athabaska, the shores got lower and the spruce disappeared, giving way to dense thickets of low willow. Here the long-expected steamer *Graham* passed, going upstream. We now began to get occasional glimpses of Lake Athabaska across uncertain marshes and sand bars. It was necessary to make Fort Chipewyan while there was calm, so we pushed on. After four hours' groping among blind channels and mud banks, we reached the lake at midnight—though of course there was no night, but a sort of gloaming even at the darkest—and it took us four hours' hard rowing to cover the ten miles that separated us from Chipewyan.

It sounds very easy and commonplace when one says "hard rowing," but it takes on more significance when one is reminded that those oars were eighteen feet long, five inches through, and weighed about twenty pounds each; the boat was thirty feet long, a demasted schooner indeed, and rowing her through shallow, muddy water, where the ground suction was excessive, made labor so heavy that fifteen-minute spells were all anyone could do. We formed four relays, and all worked in turn all night through, arriving at Chipewyan 4 a.m., blistered, sore, and completely tired out. . . .

There was a long stretch of dead water before we could resume our downward drift, and worse than that, there was such a flood on the Peace River that it was backing the Athabaska, that is, the tide of the latter was reversed on the Rocher River, which extends twenty-five miles between here and Peace mouth. To meet this, I hired Colin Fraser's steamer. We left Chipewyan at 6:15; at 11:15 camped below the Peace on Great Slave River, and bade farewell to the steamer.

The reader may well be puzzled by these numerous names; the fact is the Mackenzie, the Slave, the Peace, the Rocher, and the Unchaga are all one and the same, but unfortunately the early explorers thought proper to give it a new name each time it did something, such as expand into a lake. By rights it should be the Unchaga or Unjiza, from the Rockies to the Arctic, with the Athabaska as its principal southern tributary.

The next day another lynx was collected. In its stomach were the remains of a red squirrel, a chipmunk, and a bog lemming. The last was important, as it made a new record.

A few bands of buffalo are said to exist in the country east of Great Slave Lake. Among other matters, Major Jarvis had to report on these, find out how many were left, and exactly where they were. When he invited me to join his expedition, with these questions in view, I needed no pressing.

Our first business was to get guides, and now our troubles began. Through the traders we found four natives who knew the buffalo range—they were Kiya, Sousi, Kirma, and Peter Squirrel. However, they seemed in no way desirous of guiding anyone into that country. They dodged and delayed and secured many postponements, but the Royal Mounted Police and the Hudson's Bay Company are the two mighty powers of the land, so, urged by an officer of each, these worthies sullenly assembled to meet us in Sousi's cabin.

Sousi, by the way, is Chipewyan for Joseph, and this man's name was Joseph Beaulieu. Other northern travelers have warned all that came after them to beware of the tribe of Beaulieu, so we were on guard.

Sullen silence greeted us as we entered; we could feel their covert antagonism. Jarvis is one of those affable, good-tempered individuals that most people take for "easy." In some ways he may be so, but I soon realized that he was a keen judge of men and their ways, and he whispered to me: "They mean to block us if possible." Sousi understood French and had some English, but the others professed ignorance of everything but Chipewyan. . . .

Kiya could not go nor lend his horses, because it was mostly Squirrel's country, and he was afraid Squirrel would not like it. Squirrel could not go because it would be indelicate of him to butt in after negotiations had been opened with Kiya. Kirma was not well. Sousi could not go because his wife was sick, and it preyed on his mind so that he dare not trust himself away from the settlement; at least, not without much medicine to fortify him against rheumatism, homesickness, and sadness.

Next day Kiya sent word that he had business of great moment and could not meet us, but would see that early in the morning Squirrel was notified to come and do whatever we wished. In the morning Squirrel also had disappeared, leaving word that he had quite overlooked a most important engagement to "portage some flour across the rapids," not that he loved the tump line, but he had "promised," and to keep his word was very precious to him.

Jarvis and I talked it over and reviewed the information we had. At Ottawa it was reported that the wolves were killing the calves, so the buffalo did not increase. At Winnipeg the wolves were so bad that they killed yearlings; at Edmonton the cows were not safe.

At Chipewyan the wolves, reinforced by large bands from the Barren Grounds, were killing the young buffalo, and later the cows and young bulls. At Smith Landing the wolves had even tackled an old bull, whose head was found with the large bones. Horses and dogs were now being devoured. Terrible battles were taking place between the dark wolves of Peace River and the white wolves of the Barrens for possession of the buffalo grounds. Of course the buffalo were disappearing; about a hundred were all that were left.

But no one ever sees any of the terrible wolves; the few men who know that country have plenty of pemmican,* that is, neither moose nor caribou, and the Major briefly summed up the situation: "The wolves are indeed playing havoc with the buffalo, and the ravenous leaders of the pack are called Sousi, Kiya, Kirma, and Squirrel."

Now, of all four, Sousi, being a Beaulieu and a half-breed, had the worst reputation, but of all the four he was the only one that had admitted a possibility of guiding us, and was to be found on the fifth morning. So his views were met, a substitute found to watch his fishing nets, groceries to keep his wife from pining during his absence, a present for himself, the regular rate of wages doubled, his horses hired, his rheumatism, homesickness, and sadness provided against, a present of tobacco, some more presents, a

* A ground meat with berries added and dried to preserve it.—Ed.

promise of reward for every buffalo shown, then another present, and we set out.

It's a fine thing to get started, however late in the day, and though it was 3:20 p.m. before everything was ready, we gladly set out—Sousi, Major Jarvis, and myself—all mounted, the native leading a pack horse with provisions. . . .

That night, as I sat by the fire musing, I went over my life when I was a boy in Manitoba, just too late to see the buffalo, recalling how I used to lie in some old buffalo wallow and peer out over the prairie through the fringe of anemones and long to see the big brown forms of the plains. Once in those days I got a sensation, for I did see them. They turned out to be a herd of common cattle, but still I got the thrill.

Now I was on a real buffalo hunt, some twenty-five years too late. Will it come? Am I really to see the wild buffalo on its native plains? It is too good to be true; too much like tipping back the sands of time.

We left camp on Salt River at 7:45 in the morning and traveled till 11 o'clock, covering six miles. It was all through the same level country, in which willow swamps alternated with poplar and spruce ridges. At 11:00 it began to rain, so we camped on a slope under some fine, big white spruces till it cleared, and then continued westward. The country now undulated somewhat and was varied with openings.

Sousi says that when he first saw this region, thirty years ago, it was all open prairie, with timber only in hollows and about water. This is borne out by the fact that all the large trees are in such places, and that all the level, open stretches are covered with sapling growths of aspen and fir. This will make a glorious settlement some day. In plants, trees, birds, soil, climate, and apparently all conditions, it is like Manitoba.

We found the skeleton of a cow buffalo, apparently devoured by wolves years ago, because all the big bones were there and the skull unbroken.

About 2:00 in the afternoon we came up a two-hundred-foot rise to a beautiful upland country, in which the forests were diversified with open glades, and which everywhere showed a most singular feature. The ground is pitted all over with funnel-shaped holes, from six to forty feet deep, and of equal width across the rim; none of them contained water. I saw one one hundred feet across and about fifty feet deep; some exposed limestone; in one we saw granite.

At first I took these for extinct geysers, but later I learned that the whole plateau called Salt Mountain is pitted over with them. Brine is running out of the mountain in great quantities, which means that the upper strata are being undermined as the salt washes out, and as these crack, the funnels are formed no doubt by the loose deposits settling.

In the dry woods, bear tracks became extremely numerous; the whole country, indeed, was marked with various signs. Practically every big tree has bear-claw markings on it, and every few yards there is evidence that the diet of the bears just now is chiefly berries of *Uva ursi*.*

As we rode along, Sousi prattled cheerfully in his various tongues; but his steady flow of conversation abruptly ended when, about 2 p.m., we came suddenly on some buffalo tracks, days old but still buffalo tracks. All at once and completely he was the hunter. He leaped from his horse and led away like a hound.

Ere long, of course, the trail was crossed by two fresher ones; then we found some dry wallows and several very fresh tracks. We tied up the horses in an old funnel pit and set about an elaborate hunt. Jarvis minded the stock, I set out with Sousi, after he had tried the wind by tossing up some grass. But he stopped, drew a

* Bear berry.—Ed.

fingernail sharply across my canvas coat, so that it gave a little shriek, and said, "Va pa," which is *Cela ne va pas* reduced to its bony framework. I doffed the offending coat and went forward. First we circled a little to eastward, tossing grass at intervals, but finding plenty of new sign, went northerly and westward till most of the new sign was east of us.*

Sousi then led, telling me to step in his tracks and make no noise. I did so for long, but at length a stick cracked under my foot; he turned and looked reproachfully at me. Then a stick cracked under *his* foot; I gave him a poke in the ribs. When we got to the land between the lakes Sousi pointed and said, "They are here." We sneaked with the utmost caution that way—it was impossible to follow any one trail, and in two hundred yards Sousi sank to the ground, gasping out, *"La! la! maintenant faites son portrait autant que vous voudrez."* I crawled forward and saw not one but *half a dozen* buffalo. "I must be nearer," I said, and lying flat on my breast, crawled, toes and elbows, up to a bush within seventy-five yards, where I made shot No. 1 (with camera) and saw here that there were eight or nine buffalo, one an immense bull.

Sousi now cocked his rifle. I said emphatically: "Stop! you must not fire." "No?" he said in astonished tones that were full of story and comment. "What did we come for?" Now I saw that by backing out and crawling to another bunch of herbage I could get within fifty yards.

"It is not possible," he gasped.

"Watch me and see," I replied. Gathering all the near vines and twisting them around my neck, I covered my head with leaves and creeping plants, then proceeded to show that it *was* possible, while Sousi followed. I reached the cover and found it was a bed of spring anemones on the far side of an old buffalo wallow, and there

* They were trying to keep the wind blowing across them and away from the buffalo, so the animals would not get their scent.—Ed.

in that wallow I lay for a moment reveling in the sight. All at once it came to me: now, indeed, was fulfilled the long-deferred dream of my youth, *for in shelter of those flowers of my youth, I was gazing on a herd of wild buffalo.* Then slowly I rose above the cover and took my second picture. But the watchful creatures, more shy than moose here, saw the rising mass of herbage, or may have caught the wind, rose lightly and went off. I noticed now, for the first time, a little red calf; ten buffalo in all, I counted. Sousi, standing up, counted thirteen. At the edge of the woods they stopped and looked around, but gave no third shot for the camera.

I shook Sousi's hand with all my heart, and he, good old fellow, said: "Ah! it was for this I prayed last night; without doubt it was in answer to my prayer that the good God sent me this great happiness."

Then back to camp, two hundred yards away, the old man's tongue was loosed, and he told me how the chiefs in conference, and everyone at the fort, had ridiculed him and his Englishman— "who thought they could walk up to buffalo and take their pictures."

We had not been long in camp when Sousi went off to get some water, but at once came running back, shouting excitedly, "My rifle, my rifle!" Jarvis handed it to him; he rushed off to the woods. I followed in time to see him shoot an old bear and two cubs out of a tree. She fell, sobbing like a human being, "Oh! Oh! Oh-h-h!" It was too late to stop him, and he finished her as she lay helpless. The little ones were too young to live alone, so shared her fate.

It seems, as Sousi went to the water hole, he came on an old bear and her two cubs. She gave a warning *koff, koff.* The only enemies they knew about and feared were buffalo, moose, and wolves; from these, the tree was a safe haven. The cubs scrambled up a tall poplar, then the mother followed. Sousi came shouting in apparent fear; I rushed to the place, thinking he was attacked by something, perhaps a buffalo bull, but too late to stop the tragedy that followed.

That night we roasted one of the cubs, and as I watched the old cannibal chewing the hands off that little baby bear it gave me a feeling of disgust for all flesh-eating that lasted for days. Major Jarvis felt much as I did; and old Sousi had exclusive joy in all his bear meat.

Next morning I was left at camp while Jarvis and Sousi went off to seek for more buffalo. I had a presentiment that they would find none, so kept the camera and went off to the lake a mile west, and there made drawings of some tracks, took photos, etc., and on the lake saw about twenty-five pairs of ducks, identified white-winged scoter, pintail, green-winged teal, and loon. I also watched the maneuvers of a courting peetweet.* He approached the only lady with his feathers up and his wings raised; she paid no heed (apparently), but I noticed that when he flew away she followed. I saw a large garter snake striped black and green, and with two rows of red spots, one on each side. Later I learned from Sousi and others that this snake is quite common here, and the only kind found, but in the mountains that lie not far away in the west is another kind, much thicker, fatter, and more sluggish. Its bite is fearfully poisonous, often fatal; "but the good God has marked the beast by putting a *cloche* (bell) in its tail."

About 10:00 I turned campward, but after tramping for nearly an hour I was not only not at home, I was in a totally strange kind of country, covered with a continuous poplar woods. I changed my course and tried a different direction, but soon was forced to the conclusion that (for the sixth or seventh time in my life) I was lost.

"Dear me," this is an interesting opportunity. It comes to me now that I once wrote an essay on "What to Do and What Not to

* A spotted sandpiper.—ED.

Do When Lost in the Woods." Now, what in the world did I say in it, and which are the things not to do? Yes, I remember now, these were the pieces of advice:

1. "Don't get frightened." Well, I'm not; I am simply amused.
2. "Wait for your friends to come." Can't do that; I'm too busy; they wouldn't appear till night.
3. "If you must travel, go back to a place where you were sure of the way." That means back to the lake, which I know is due west of the camp and must be west of me now.

So back I went, carefully watching the sun for guidance, and soon realized that whenever I did not, I *swung to the left*. After nearly an hour's diligent travel I did get back to the lake, and followed my own track in the margin to the point of leaving it; then, with a careful corrected bearing, made for camp and arrived in forty minutes, there to learn that on the first attempt I had swung so far to the left that I had missed camp by half a mile, and was half a mile beyond it before I knew I was wrong.

At noon, Jarvis and Sousi came back jubilant; they had seen countless buffalo trails, had followed a large bull and cow, but had left them to take the trail of a considerable band; these they discovered in a lake. There were four big bulls, four little calves, one yearling, three two-year-olds, eight cows. These allowed them to come openly within sixty yards. Then took alarm and galloped off. They saw a moose and a marten—and two buffalo skeletons. How I did curse my presentiment that prevented them having the camera and securing a really fine photograph!

At 2:00 p.m. Sousi prepared to break camp. He thought that by going back on our trail he might strike the trail of another herd off to the southeast of the mountain. Jarvis shrewdly suspected that our guide wanted to go home, having kept his promise, won the reward, and got a load of bear meat. However, the native was the guide, so we set out in a shower which continued more or less all day and into the night, so we camped in the rain.

Next day it was obvious, and Sousi no longer concealed the fact, that he was making for home as fast as he could go.

At 3:30 we reached Smith Landing, having been absent exactly three days, and having seen in that time thirty-three buffalo, four of them calves of this year, three old buffalo skeletons of ancient date, not a track or sign of a wolf, not a howl by night, or any evidence of their recent presence, for the buffalo skeletons found were obviously very old.

And our guide—the wicked one of evil ancestry and fame—he was kind, cheerful, and courteous throughout; he did exactly as he promised, did it on time, and was well pleased with the pay we gave him. Speak as you find. If ever I revisit that country I shall be glad indeed to secure the services of good old Sousi, even if he is a Beaulieu.

Reference to my Smith Landing Journal for June 17 shows the following:

"The Spring is now on in full flood, the grass is high, the trees are fully leaved, flowers are blooming, birds are nesting, *and the mosquitoes are a terror to man and beast.*" . . .

On July 9, on Nyarling River, they were much worse, and my entry was as follows:

"On the back of Billy's coat, as he sat paddling before me, I counted a round 400 mosquitoes boring away; about as many more were on the garments of his head and neck, a much less number on his arms and legs. The air about was thick with them; at least as many more, fully 1,000, stinging, singing, and filling the air with a droning hum. The rest of us were equally pestered.

"The Major, fresh, ruddy, full-blooded, far over 200 pounds in plumpness, is the best feeding ground for mosquitoes I (or they, probably) ever saw; he must be a great improvement on the smoke-dried Indians. No matter where they land on him they strike it rich, and at all times a dozen or more bloated bloodsuckers may be seen hanging like red currants on his face and neck. He maintains that they do not bother him, and scoffs at me for wearing a net. They certainly do not impair his health, good looks, or his perennial good humor, and I, for one, am thankful that his superior food quality gives us a corresponding measure of immunity."

At Salt River one could kill 100 with a stroke of the palm, and at times they obscured the color of the horses. A little later they were much worse. On six square inches of my tent I counted thirty mosquitoes, and the whole surface was similarly supplied; that is, there were 24,000 on the tent and apparently as many more flying about the door. Most of those that bite us are killed, but that makes not the slightest perceptible difference in their manners or numbers. . . .

Everyone—even the seasoned natives—agrees that they are a terror to man and beast; but, thanks to our fly-proof tents, we sleep immune. During the day I wear my net and gloves, uncomfortably hot, but a blessed relief from the torment. It is easy to get used to those coverings; it is impossible to get used to the mosquitoes.

Their natural enemies are numerous; most small birds prey on them; dragon flies also, and the latter alone inspire fear in the pest. When a dragon fly comes buzzing about one's head, the mosquitoes move away to the other side, but it makes no considerable difference.

On the Buffalo River I saw a boatman, or water spider, seize and devour a mosquito that fell within reach; which is encouraging, because, as a rule, the smaller the foe the deadlier, and the only creature that really affects the whole mosquito nation is apparently a small red parasite that became more and more numerous as the season wore on.

It appeared in red lumps on the bill and various parts of the stinger's body, and the victim became very sluggish. Specimens sent to Dr. L. O. Howard, the authority on mosquitoes, elicited the information that it was a fungus, probably new to science. But evidently it is deadly to the *Culex*. More power to it and the cause it represents; we cannot pray too much for its increase. . . .

On the morning of August 1 we launched on Artillery Lake, feeling, for the tenth time, that now we really were on the crowning stretch of our journey, and that at last we were entering the land of the caribou.

Over the deep, tranquil waters of the lake we went, scanning the painted shores with their dwindling remnants of forest. There is something inspiring about the profundity of transparency in these lakes; where they are fifteen feet deep their bottoms are no more obscured than in an ordinary eastern brook at six inches. On looking into the far-below world, one gets the sensation of flight as one skims overhead in the swift canoe. And how swift that elegant canoe was in a clear run, I was only now finding out. All my previous estimates had been too low. Here I had the absolute gauge of Tyrrell's maps and found that we four paddling could send her, not three and one half, but four and one half or five miles an hour, with a possible six when we made an effort. As we spun along the southeast coast of the lake, the country grew less rugged; the continuous steep granite hills were replaced by lower buttes with long grassy plains between; and as I took them in, I marveled at their name—the Barrens; bare of trees, yes, but the plains were covered with rich, rank grass, more like New England meadows. There were stretches where the herbage was rank as on the Indiana prairies, and the average pasture of the bleaker parts was better than the best of central Wyoming. A cattleman of the West would think himself made if he could be sure of such pastures on his range, yet these are the Barren Grounds.

At 3:00 we passed the splendid landmark of Beaver Lodge Mountain. Its rosy-red granite cliffs contrast wonderfully with its emerald cap of verdant grass and mosses, that cover it in tropical luxuriance, and the rippling lake about it was of Mediterranean hues.

We covered the last nine miles in one hour and fifty-three minutes, passed the deserted Indian village, and landed at Last Woods by 8:30 p.m.

The edge of the timber is the dividing line between the Hudsonian and the Arctic zones. It is the beginning of the country we had come to see; we were now in the land of the caribou.

At this point we were prepared to spend several days, leave a cache, gather a bundle of choice firewood, then enter on the treeless plains.

That night it stormed; all were tired; there was no reason to bestir ourselves; it was ten when we arose. Half an hour later Billy came to my tent and said, "Mr. Seton, here's some deer." I rushed to the door, and there, with my own eyes, I saw on a ridge a mile away four great caribou standing against the sky.

We made for a near hill and met Preble returning; he also had seen them. From a higher viewpoint the four proved part of a band of twenty.

Then other bands came in view, sixteen, sixty-one, three, 200, and so on; each valley had a scattering few, all traveling slowly southward or standing to enjoy the cool breeze that ended the torment of the flies. About 1,000 were in sight. These were my first caribou, the first fruits of 3,000 miles of travel.

Weeso got greatly excited; these were the forerunners of the vast herd. He said, "Plenty caribou now," and grinned like a happy child.

I went in one direction, taking only my camera. At least twenty caribou trotted within fifty feet of me.

Billy and Weeso took their rifles, intent on venison, but the caribou avoided them, and six or eight shots were heard before they got a young buck.

All that day I reveled in caribou, no enormous herds but always a few in sight.

The next day Weeso and I went to the top of the ridge eastward, he with rifle, I with camera. He has a vague idea of the camera's use, but told Billy privately that "the rifle was much better for caribou." He could not understand why I should restrain him from blazing away as long as the ammunition held out. "Didn't we come to shoot?" But he was amenable to discipline, and did as I wished when he understood.

Now on top of that windy ridge I sat with this copper-colored child of the spruce woods, to watch those cattle of the plains.

The caribou is a travelsome beast, always in a hurry going against the wind. When the wind is west, all travel west; when it veers, they veer. Now the wind was northerly, and all were going north, not walking, not galloping—the caribou rarely gallops, and then only for a moment or two; his fast gait is a steady trot, a ten-mile gait, making, with stops, about six miles an hour. But they are ever on the move; when you see a caribou that does not move, you know at once it is not a caribou; it's a rock.

We sat down on the hill at 3:00. In a few minutes a cow caribou came trotting from the south, caught the wind at fifty yards, and dashed away.

In five minutes another, in twenty minutes a young buck, in twenty minutes more a big buck, in ten minutes a great herd of about 500 appeared in the south. They came along at a full trot, lined to pass us on the southeast. At half a mile they struck our scent and all recoiled as though we were among them. They scattered in alarm, rushed south again, then, gathered in solid body, came on as before, again to spring back and scatter as they caught the taint of man. After much and various running, scattering, and massing, they once more charged the fearsome odor and went right through it. Now they passed at 500 yards and gave the chance for a far camera shot.

The sound of their trampling was heard a long way off—half a mile—but at 300 yards I could not distinguish the clicking of the feet, whereas this clicking was very plainly to be heard from the band that passed within fifty yards of me in the morning.

They snort a good deal and grunt a little, and notwithstanding their continual haste, I noticed that from time to time one or two would lie down, but at once jump up and rush on when they found they were being left behind. Many more single deer came that day, but no more large herds.

About 4:30 a fawn of this year (two and one half or three months) came rushing up from the north, all alone. It charged up a hill for 200 yards, then changed its mind and charged down again, then raced to a bunch of tempting herbage, cropped it hastily, dashed to a knoll, left at an angle, darted toward us till within forty yards, then dropped into a thick bed of grass, where it lay as though it had unlimited time.

I took one photograph, and as I crawled to get one nearer, a shot passed over my head, and the merry cackle told me that Weeso had yielded to temptation and had "collected" that fawn.

A young buck now came trotting and grunting toward us till within sixteen paces, which proved too much for Weeso, who then and there, in spite of repeated recent orders, started him on the first step toward my museum collection.

I scolded him angrily, and he looked glum and unhappy, like a naughty little boy caught in some indiscretion which he cannot understand. He said nothing to me then, but later complained to Billy, asking, "What *did* we come for?"

Next morning at dawn I dreamed I was back in New York and

that a couple of cats were wailing under my bedroom window. Their noise increased so that I awoke, and then I heard unaccounable caterwauls. They were very loud and near, at least one of the creatures was. At length I got up to see. Here on the lake a few yards from the tent was a loon swimming about, minutely inspecting the tent and uttering at intervals deep catlike mews in expression of his curiosity.

The south wind had blown for some days before we arrived, and the result was to fill the country with caribou coming from the north. The day after we came, the north wind set in, and continued for three days, so that soon there was not a caribou to be found in the region.

In the afternoon I went up the hill to where Weeso had left the offal of his deer. A large yellowish animal was there feeding. It disappeared over a rock and I could get no second view of it. It may have been a wolf, as I saw fresh wolf trail near; I did not, however, see the animal's tail.

In the evening Preble and I went again, and again the creature was there, but disappeared as mysteriously as before when we were 200 yards away. Where it went we could not guess. The country was open and we scoured it with eye and glass, but saw nothing more of the prowler. It seemed to be a young Arctic wolf, yellowish white in color, but tailless.

Next day at noon Preble and Billy returned bearing the elusive visitor; it was a large lynx. It was very thin and yet, after bleeding, weighed twenty-two pounds. But why was it so far from the forest, twenty miles or more, and a couple of miles from this little grove that formed the last woods?

This is another evidence of the straits the lynxes are put to for food, in this year of famine.

The last woods is a wonderfully interesting biological point or line; this ultimate arm of the forest does not die away gradually with uncertain edges and in steadily dwindling trees. The latter have sent their stoutest champions to the front, or produced, as by a final effort, some giants for the line of battle. And that line, with its sentinels, is so marked that one can stand with a foot on the territory of each combatant, or, as scientists call them, the Arctic Region and the cold Temperant.

And each of the embattled kings, Jack Frost and Somber Pine, has his children in abundance to possess the land as he wins it. Right up to the skirmish line are they.

The low thickets of the woods are swarming with tree sparrows, redpolls, robins, hooded sparrows; and the bare plains, a few yards away, are peopled and vocal with birds to whom a bush is an abomination. Lapland longspur, snowbird, shore lark, and pipit are here, soaring and singing, or among the barren rocks are ptarmigan in garments that are painted in the patterns of their rocks.

There is one somber fowl of ampler wing that knows no line—is at home in the open or in the woods. His sonorous voice has a human sound that is uncanny; his form is visible afar in the desert and sinister as a gibbet; his plumage fits in with nothing but the night, which he does not love. This evil genius of the land is the raven of the north. Its numbers increased as we reached the Barrens, and the morning after the first caribou was killed, no fewer than twenty-eight were assembled at its offal.

An even more interesting bird of the woods is the hooded sparrow,* interesting because so little known.

Here I found it on its breeding grounds, a little late for its vernal song, but in September we heard its autumnal renewal like the notes of its kinsmen, whitethroat and whitecrowned sparrows, but with less whistling, and more trilled. In all the woods of the Hudsonian zone we found it evidently at home. But here I was privileged to find the first nest of the species known to science. The

* Harris's Sparrow.—ED.

victory was robbed of its crown, through the nest having fledglings instead of eggs, but still it was ample reward for hours of search.

Of course it was on the ground, in the moss and creeping plants, under some bushes of dwarf birch, screened by spruces. The structure closely resembled that of the whitethroat, was lined with grass and fibrous roots; no down, feathers, or fur were observable. The young numbered four.

The last woods was the limit of other interesting creatures—the ants. Wherever one looks on the ground, in a high, dry place, throughout the forest country, from Athabaska Landing northward along our route, there is to be seen at least one ant to the square foot, usually several. Three kinds seem common—one red bodied, another a black one with brown thorax, and a third very small and black. They seemed to live chiefly in hollow logs and stumps, but are found also on marshes, where their hills are occasionally so numerous as to form dry bridges across.

On August 7 we left Camp Last Woods. Our various specimens, with stock of food, were secured, as usual, in a cache high in two trees, in this case those already used by Tyrrell seven years before, and guarded by the magic necklace of cod hooks.

By noon (in three hours) we made fifteen miles, camping far beyond Twin Buttes. All day long the boat shot through water crowded with drowned gnats. These were about ten to the square inch near shore and for about twenty yards out, after that ten to the square foot for 200 yards still farther from shore, and for a quarter mile wide they were ten to the square yard.

This morning the wind turned and blew from the south. At 2 p.m. we saw a band of some sixty caribou traveling southward; these were the first seen for two or three days. After this we saw many odd ones, and about 3 o'clock a band of 400 or 500. At night we camped on Casba River, having covered thirty-six miles in seven hours and forty-five minutes.

The place we selected for camp proved to be a caribou crossing. As we drew near, a dozen of them came from the east and swam across. A second band of eight now appeared. We gave chase. They spurted; so did we. Our canoe was going over six miles an hour, and yet was but slowly overtaking them. They made the water foam around them. Their heads, necks, shoulders, backs, rumps, and tails were out. I never before saw land animals move so fast in the water. A fawn in danger of being left behind reared up on its mother's back and hung on with forefeet. The leader was a doe or young buck, I could not be sure which; the last was a big buck. They soon struck bottom and bounded along on the shore. It was too dark for a picture.

As we were turning in for the night, thirty caribou came trotting and snorting through the camp. Half of them crossed the water, but the rest turned back when Billy shouted.

Later a band of 200 passed through and around our tents. In the morning Billy complained that he could not sleep all night for caribou traveling by his tent and stumbling over the guy ropes. From this time on we were nearly always in sight of caribou, small bands or scattering groups; one had the feeling that the whole land was like this, on and on and on, unlimited space with unlimited wild herds. . . .

I had held in my heart the wanderlust till it swept me away, and sent me afar on the back trail of the north wind; I have lived in the mighty boreal forest, with its red men, its buffalo, its moose, and its wolves; I have seen the Great Lone Land with its endless plains and prairies that do not know the face of man or the crack of a rifle; I have been with its countless lakes that reecho nothing but the wail and yodel of the loons, or the mournful music of the Arctic wolf. I have wandered on the plains of the musk ox, the home of the snowbird and the caribou. These were the things I had burned to do. *Was I content? Content!* Is a man ever content with a single sip of joy long dreamed of?

Four years have gone since then. The wanderlust was not stifled any more than a fire is stifled by giving it air. I have taken into my heart a longing, given shape to an ancient instinct. Have I not found for myself a kingdom and become a part of it? My reason and my heart say, "Go back and see it all." Grant only this, that I gather again the same brave men that manned my frail canoe, and as sure as life and strength continue I *shall go*.[1]

# 8.

# STUDIES IN THE ART ANATOMY
# OF ANIMALS

D URING the years that I was busied illustrating *The Century Dictionary* (1886), I was continually faced with the problems of animal and bird anatomy; and found that there were no books treating of the same from the artist's point of view. There were plenty of works on animal dissection and dead animals, but these had little bearing on my needs and the needs of all artists who depict animals.

I therefore planned my *Art Anatomy;* that is to say, a careful analysis of the *visible forms* and proportions of the *living* animal, which includes the feather shapes and overlaps in the birds and the fur of animals. Color does not enter in, but measurements do.

Having a clear field, I began with enthusiasm, measuring live dogs, cats, cows, horses and birds, cutting up dead ones.

I put in a couple of years' night work on this undertaking, and was still at it when I got to Paris [1894].*1

## *Art Anatomy*

We have not yet reached the point where it is no longer necessary to defend the study of anatomy for artists. Art anatomy of

* Seton studied art for two years at Boulogne, France, and at that period completed his *Studies in the Art Anatomy of Animals,* his first book, which was published in 1896.—Ed.

the human form has had many advocates; the argument that they have considered quite satisfactory being, the artist *can* draw the human form without a knowledge of its bones and muscles, but he does it much better, and much more quickly and surely, when equipped with such knowledge.

The argument for the art anatomy of animals is yet stronger, the knowledge of it is absolutely indispensable. The figure painter can always pose his models, and paint what he sees. The *animalier* must continually work with knowledge of the form, his models never pose, and, unlike those of the figure painter, they are invariably *au naturel*.

There is no more convincing argument than the practice of the masters. The advocates of human anatomy point with pride to Michelangelo, Leonardo da Vinci, and Raphael, who were profound students of surgical anatomy, as well as great lights of art. They were, in fact, pioneers in this field, entering it with a view to advancing their art.

In like manner the *animalier* may find guidance—and guidance even less equivocal—in the history of animal painters and sculptors. There have been great *genre* painters who did not study anatomy, but there has never been a famous *animalier* who did not. Bayre, Landseer, Géricault, Meñe, Cain, as well as the living men, with one voice send the student to the study of anatomy. Some of them would carry the study farther than others, but all are agreed in carrying it far, in grasping the subject thoroughly and broadly, but exactly. And yet, contradictory as it may seem, they all unite in warning the artist that he who endeavors to make a display of his anatomical knowledge is as surely lost as though he had none to display.

The question has been raised as to whether the study of anatomy is synonymous with dissection. Some writers consider that dissection is the sole means to a knowledge of the subject. I am inclined to the belief that the artist who works in the dissecting room, over ground already known, is not using his time to the best advantage. He should rather avoid the dead animal and the surgical point of view. There is no doubt that one obtains a more thorough knowledge of the construction by dissecting, but it is unnecessarily thorough. It is of much greater importance that the student should model from the living animal, using as guides the best anatomical diagrams obtainable, bearing in mind, however, that anatomy is like a virulent poison—when judiciously administered it is a powerful stimulant to art, but in an overdose it is death. This is especially true in painting; one sees but little of anatomy in the living animal except in silhouette; and he who makes it of prime importance produces mere diagrams, and loses sight of the greater essentials of light, color, and movement.

## General Considerations

Art anatomy is a scientific explanation of the *visible living form,* or, in other words, it is the study of those parts of a living animal which influence its outward form or its expression. Besides the principal bones and muscles, this includes tendons, cartilages, sinew sheaths, external veins and nerves, folds of skin, teeth, claws, beak, horns, bristles, hair, feathers, etc.; and although it has been the custom of art anatomists to treat only of the first two mentioned, it will be seen that in many animals the hair, and even the veins, are of far greater importance than many of the muscles or minor bones.

In depicting birds, also, a knowledge of the feathering is, generally speaking, of more value to the artist than familiarity with the separate muscles and bones. But a sound knowledge of the form of mammals must be founded on an acquaintance with the bony skeleton and muscular system.

All mammals are built on the same general plan; even the human form is but a slight variation of the same. All, however, are not equally good for study; some are poorly developed, some have the form obscured by wool, or by fat, some are too unwieldy or too minute, and others are not obtainable for study, through their rarity. But the greyhound will be found well adapted to the requirements of the art anatomist, in his initial study of bones and muscles. It is superbly developed, and the relation of its parts is admirably displayed through the fine skin and thin coat. It is neither too large nor too small, it is readily obtained almost anywhere, and when alive is perhaps easier to study than any other animal.

Natural sequence requires that the hairy coat be first treated or dissected. And it will be seen that this course is not entirely without justification in the importance of the subject.

## The Hair

It is remarkable that the study of the hair should have been so long and so entirely ignored. In all animals that bear it, it is of interest and value, in most it is of equal importance with the muscles, in many it is of much more consequence than these, ranking in value next to the bones as an element of form.

In the horse or the greyhound we see the hair coat at a minimum, and yet in these the hair has much to do with the appearance. In a wolf the hair masses are at least of equal importance with the muscles, and in a grizzly, or brown bear, in its winter coat, the hair masses and the bones give the clue to nearly all the visible form. In a Bayre statue of a bear now before me it is impossible to detect the form of a single muscle, except in the arm. All the rest of the detail is worked out in hair masses.

In very small mammals the turn of the hair is almost the only clue to the form, and the peculiar rounding and cracking on ham and on shoulder are the only indications of the complicated machinery of bone and muscles which lies far beneath. . . . The hair of the wolf and of most mammals is of two kinds: a fine wool next the skin, and an outer covering of long, nearly straight hairs growing through this. The first retains the heat, and the second repels the rain. The first predominates on the lower, and the second on the upper parts of the body.

The wool is better than the hair for such parts as are very supple and change much in form, consequently we see a predominance of wool in those areas of loose or sliding skin under which the body has great play.

This may be due to the wearing off of the longer, brittler hair. The wool on these sliding areas is seen to crack open when the skin is extended. These peculiar tracts are so much more the result of arrangement than of actual change in the fur, that it is impossible to distinguish them in the animal after it is skinned or long dead; but no one can look at the living, moving creature and doubt their importance from a picturesque point of view. . . .

The legs, shoulders, and the face of the wolf are covered by a variety of hair which is short, close, and very hard. This is well calculated to give to the limbs and the senses perfect freedom of action, and at the same time is readily kept clear of mud, remnants of food, etc.

In general, the direction of the hair is determined by two laws. First, the necessity of offering the least possible resistance to the air, and to grass, brushwood, and other obstacles, while the animal is in motion. (This may be illustrated by the well-known fact that the hunter can readily drag, nose first, a dead deer which, heels first, he could scarcely move, for the obvious reason that it would be "against the grain.") Second, the necessity for running off the rain, especially when the animal is lying at rest. The first law gives a backward, and the second a downward direction to the hair. . . .

The early aquatic ancestor of living mammals breathed by means of gills, which were gradually discarded as the creature became a land animal and breathed by means of the elaborated air bladder which we now call lungs. But with this conservatism so well known in organic bodies, the gill cleft in the side of the neck persisted for long afterward, and with it the accompanying circumvolution of the veins. This may be detected in the mammalian foetus, and when finally the old scar heals up, the disturbance in the surrounding hair is still to be seen, and in not a few cases the blood vessels preserve traces of the now useless circumvolutions.

The wolf illustrates the foregoing principles. The drawing* is understood to be diagrammatic, as the disposition of fur therein shown, though more or less discernible in all wolves, will but rarely be found as clear and sharp as in the drawing.

The chief masses are:

The ruff, beginning before the ears, and passing over the back of the jaw and under the throat; this is much better developed in the lynx and the lion.

The curious little cushion under each ear, a sort of central point or whorl of the several hair currents of the region.

The great thatch or mane of coarse hair; much developed in the lion.

The soft woolly part under the throat meeting the mane.

The mane along the shoulders, and the smaller crest on the top or dorsal edge of each scapula.

The patch of sliding fur behind each shoulder, and the corresponding patch on each flank, before the hind leg, showing the great play of the limbs.

The two areas of reversed hair on the breast.

The fringe of reversed hair on the back of each foreleg.

The great cushion of wool on each of the buttocks.

The tail, clad entirely in the sliding fur, except the slight thatch on the base above.

The ridges on the chest and on the belly, apparently structural scars as already defined.

* See picture section (p. 211)—Ed.

The correlation of color with this arrangement is striking. The heavy thatches are much mixed with black hair; the thatch on the base of the tail is usually ended in a dark spot; the ruff on the cheek is always paler in color than the hair on the crown and neck; the sliding fur is always paler than the hair about it; while the close fur on the limbs and face is usually darker than elsewhere.

This arrangement both of form and of color will be seen in all dogs, wolves, jackals, and foxes, and in a general sense is common to all the Carnivora; the leading features are to be found in all hairy quadrupeds, as well as in man himself. From this it will be seen that, excepting on the shoulder, the foreleg, and the hindleg below the knee, these anatomical details of the hairy coat are, in the wolf as well as in many other animals, of more importance than the anatomy of the muscles.

According to the best authorities there is no constant or reliable difference between the wolves of Europe, Northern Asia, and North America. The various terms—Russian wolf, common wolf of Europe, white wolf, timber wolf, buffalo wolf, gray wolf, etc.—are then understood either as synonyms or as names of local varieties of *Canis lupus*.

The wolf is simply a large wild dog, and differs from the domesticated species more in appearance than in anatomical details.

An ordinary male wolf is from twenty-seven to twenty-eight inches in height at the shoulder, and about three feet, nine inches in length of the head and body. When in good condition he weighs from ninety to 100 pounds. The females are smaller.

This species, however, seems to be subject to great variation, and specimens weighing as much as 150 pounds are on record.

The proportions of the bone lengths of the wolf are the same as those of the greyhound, if we add one quarter to the head and neck after constructing on the plan of the dog. Or, in other words, if we take the humerus as the unit of standard, the head equals one and one quarter, the neck equals one and one quarter, and the other proportions are as in the greyhound. The wolf, however, has the forequarters more robustly made, to correspond with the heavier head and neck; his loins are heavier, and his coat of fur is well developed.

## The Anatomy of Birds

There is a widespread idea that the bodies of birds are everywhere and equally covered with feathers. This is far from being correct. All birds, with one or two exceptions, have large naked spaces on their bodies, covered, however, by the overlap of the feathers nearest, which would in many birds show an aggregate area nearly as great as that of the feathered tracts.

The first to call attention to this arrangement of feathered tracts, or *Pterylae,* and bare tracts, or *Apteria,* was Nitsch. . . .

The importance of these tracts to the artist lies in the fact that the series of feathers which emanate from them are separately visible in the plumage of the living bird. And when drawing is made with due reference to these anatomical considerations, it wears an air of truthfulness which all recognize, even though they do not know the reason for it. Hitherto no one seems to have considered these facts to be worthy of the artist's notice, excepting the sculptors and painters of ancient Egypt, ancient Assyria, and Japan. In the last century the love of nature and truthful rendering of it has continually kept alive the study of feathers, as is abundantly attested by the exquisitely artistic and truthful representations of the Shijo, or Naturalistic School. . . .

In our time and country the bird drawings of Wolf, Keulemans, and Thorburn are among the best studies extant in this field. . . .

Common opinion has awarded to the peacock, above all birds, the palm of beauty. Many of the recently discovered hummingbirds are exquisite, as are the rare birds of paradise and some of the Asiatic pheasants brought to light by modern research; but, divested of their charm of novelty, it is found that none of the species mentioned can successfully compete with the peacock. Probably there is nothing else as beautiful in the world of zoology.

The train, or "tail" as it is commonly called, is the unique and splendid feature of this regal bird. The chromatic beauties are no less notable than the mathematical correctness with which they are displayed. It is almost unquestionably the most remarkable illustration extant of the regular arrangement of feathers. The perfect geometric design, indicated in the drawing, is not merely hypothetical, but will be seen in every peacock's "tail" when in full plumage. . . .

The true tail of the peacock, composed of eighteen ordinary feathers, is underneath the train and supports it when spread. The

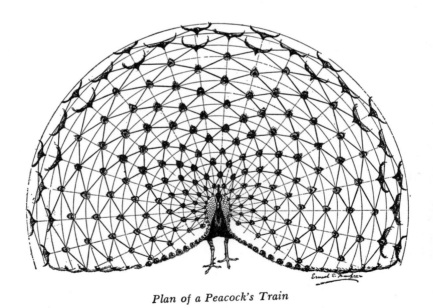

*Plan of a Peacock's Train*

train consists of 250-odd posterior feathers of the dorsal tract, which are set on in diamond pattern, as in the sparrow, and the regular lengthening of which toward the back, together with the radiation when spread, completes the mathematical figure.

A slight variation is sometimes seen when the tail is newly grown. The ends of the three outer rows, or Y feathers, are close together and separated from the true feathers by an exceptionally wide interval. They are also supplied with an embryo eye, which, however, is soon worn off.[2]

# 9.
# TRACKING AND TRAILING

Of all the feats common to hunting life and woodcraft, none seems to me half so wondrous as tracking and trailing. As practiced by man, tracking is wonderful enough; but far more marvelous is the power by which a dog or a fox can follow its prey at full speed, guided only by scent without erring or being led astray.

To us, the word scent has but little meaning; it is the name of a power with which man is, comparatively, almost unendowed. We go into the woods and see nothing but a leaf-strewn ground, thinly scattered over with herbs and thickly planted with trees; we see no quadrupeds, and find no sign of any, perhaps, save the far-away chatter of a squirrel. But our dog, merrily careering about, is possessed of a superior power. At every moment of his course he is gathering facts and reading a wonderful record of the past, the present, and even of the future. "Here," says his unseen guide, "is where a deer passed a minute ago" or "an hour ago"; "this was the course of a fox a week ago"; "that was the direction in which a rabbit flew by a few minutes ago, and, oho! there was a weasel after him!" "This track of a woodchuck leading away to yonder hole; there he lies still, and with the help of your master, you will take him home with you."

Such is the curious record of scent, revealed to the dog but hidden to man, and even inexplicable to him; for though we have a theoretical knowledge of the subject, it is too imperfect to make

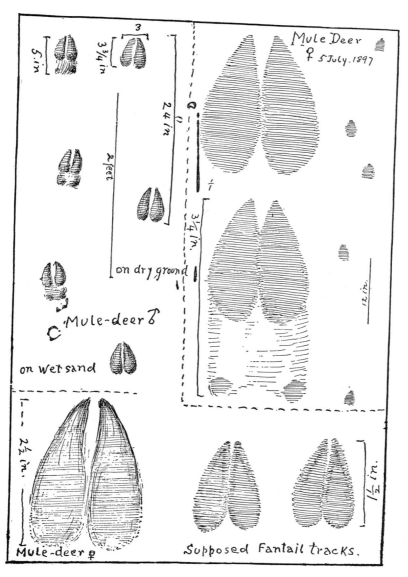

Tracks of the Mule Deer

us fully understand that not only has every kind of animal, but each individual animal, its own peculiar scent. Thus, the dog can distinguish not only the bucks, does, and fawns of the deer tribe, but can pick out of a dozen the track of the particular buck that he is following, and never leave it or lose it. Moreover, he can tell by the scent which way the animal is going, and he is never known to run backward on a trail. Now, when we compare this wonderful power with our own feeble sense of smell, we will be ready to admit that it is a faculty of which man, comparatively, has little.

Let us suppose that you were to awaken some fine morning and find that, as in the old fairy tales, a mighty genius has conferred on you a new and wonderful faculty, that enabled you to go forth and read running records with even greater accuracy and ease than can the hound—what a marvel it would be, and how interesting its exercise to a lover of nature! And yet this very miracle is what actually takes place every year in our northern country. The great genius is old Boreas, and the means by which he confers the new power is the first fall of snow.

This first snowfall marks the beginning of the real hunting season with most of the northern tribes of men; for until then it is chiefly by chance that the hunter finds his game. Now the hunter has the power of the hound, in that he can follow a track and read accurately the record of the animal's actions, its appearance, and even its very feelings.[1]

"I wish I could go West and join the Indians so that I should have no lessons to learn," said an unhappy small boy who could discover no atom of sense or purpose in any of the three R's.

"You never made a greater mistake," said the scribe. "For the young Indians have many hard lessons from their earliest days. Hard lessons and hard punishments. With them the dread penalty of failure is go hungry till you win and no harder tasks have they than their reading lesson. Not twenty-six characters are to be learned in their exercise, but a thousand; not clear straight print are they, but dim, washed-out, crooked traces; not indoors on comfortable chairs, with a patient teacher always near, but out in the forest, often alone and in every kind of weather, they slowly decipher their letters and read sentences of the oldest writing on earth—a style so old that the hieroglyphs of Egypt, the cylinders of Nippur, and the drawings of the cavemen are as things of today in comparison—a writing indeed that is older than mankind— the one universal script—*the tracks in the mud, dust, or snow.*

"These are the inscriptions that every hunter must learn to

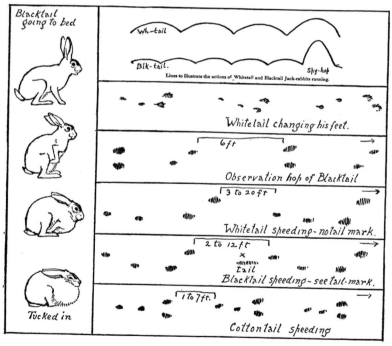

*Rabbits and Their Tracks*

read infallibly, and be they strong or faint, straight or crooked, simple or overwritten with many a puzzling diverse phrase, he must decipher and follow them swiftly, unerringly, if there is to be a successful ending to the hunt which provides his daily food.

"This is the reading of the young Indian, and it is a style that will never become superseded. The naturalist also must acquire some measure of proficiency in the ancient art. Its usefulness is perennial to the student of wildlife; without it he would know little of the people of the woods."

It is a remarkable fact that there are always more wild animals about than any but the experts has an idea of. For example, there are, within twenty miles of New York City, fully fifty different kinds—not counting birds, reptiles, or fishes—one quarter of which at least are abundant. Or, more particularly, within the limits of Greater New York there are at least a dozen species of wild beasts, half of which are quite common.

"Then how is it we never seen any?" is the first question of the incredulous. The answer is: long ago the beasts learned the dire lesson—man is your worst enemy; shun him at any price. And the simplest way to do this is to come out only at night. Man is a daytime creature; he is blind in the soft halflight that most beasts prefer.

While many animals have always limited their activity to the hours of twilight and gloom, there are not a few that were diurnal, but have given up that portion of their working day in order to avoid their archenemy.

Thus they came to flourish under our noses and eat at our tables, without our knowledge or consent. They come and go at will, and the world knows nothing of them; their presence long ago unsuspected but for one thing, well known to the hunter, the trapper, and the naturalist: wherever the wild fourfoot goes, it leaves behind it a record of its visit, its name, the direction whence it came, the time, the things it did or tried to do, with the time and direction of departure. These it puts down in the ancient script. Each of these dotted lines called a trail is a wonderful unfinished record of the creature's life during the time it made the same, and it needs only the patient work of the naturalist to decipher that record and from it learn much about the animal that made it, without that animal ever having been seen.

Savages are more skillful at it than civilized folk, because tracking is their serious lifelong pursuit and they do not injure their eyes with books. Intelligence is important here as elsewhere, yet it is a remarkable fact that the lowest race of mankind, the Australian blacks, are reputed to be by far the best trackers; not only are their eyes and attention developed and disciplined, but they have retained much of the scent power that civilized man has lost, and can follow a fresh track, partly at least, by smell.

It is hard to overvalue the powers of the clever tracker. To him, the trail of each animal is not a mere series of similar footprints: it is an accurate account of the creature's ways, habits, changing whims and emotions during the portion of life of which record is in view.

These are indeed autobiographical chapters, and differ from some other autobiographies in this—*they cannot tell a lie.* We may get wrong information from them, but it is our own fault if we do; we misread the unimpeachable document.

The ideal time for tracking, and almost the only time for most folk, is when the ground is white. After the first snow the student walks forth and begins at once to realize the wonders of the trail. A score of creatures whose existence, maybe, he did not know of, are now revealed about him, and the reading of their autographs becomes easy.

It is when snow is on the ground, indeed, that we take the fourfoot census of the woods. How often we learn with surprise

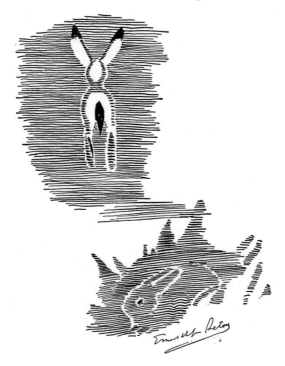

from the telltale white that a fox was around our henhouse last night, a mink is living even now under the woodpile, and a deer —yes! there is no mistaking its sharp-pointed, unsheeplike footprint—has wandered into our woods from the farther wilds.

Never lose the chance of the first snow if you wish to become a trailer. Nevertheless, remember that the first morning after a night snowfall is not so good as the second. Most creatures "lie up" during the storm; the snow hides the tracks of those that do go forth, and some actually go into a "cold sleep" for a day or two after a heavy downfall. But a calm, mild night following a storm is sure to offer abundant and ideal opportunity for beginning the study of the trail.

Here are some important facts to keep in view when you set forth to master the rudiments:

*First:* No two animals leave the same trail; not only each kind, but each individual, and each individual at each stage of its life, leaves a trail as distinctive as the creature's appearance, and it is obvious that in that they differ among themselves just as we do, because the young know their mothers, the mothers know their young, and the old ones know their mates, when scent is clearly out of the question.

Another simple evidence of this is the well-known fact that no two human beings have the same thumb mark; all living creatures have corresponding peculiarities, and all use these parts in making a trail.

*Second:* The trail was begun at the birthplace of that creature and ends only at its death. It may be recorded in visible track or peculiar odor. It may last a few hours, and may be too faint even for an expert with present equipment to follow, but evidently the trail is made, wherever the creature journeys afoot.

*Third:* It varies with every important change of impulse, action, or emotion.

*Fourth:* When we find a trail we may rest assured that, if living, the creature that made it is at the other end. And if one can follow, it is only a question of time before coming up with that animal. And be sure of its direction before setting out; many a novice has lost much time by going backward on the trail.

*Fifth:* In studying trails, one must always keep probabilities in mind. Sometimes one kind of track looks much like another; then the question is, which is the likeliest in this place?

If I saw a jaguar track in India I should know it was made by a leopard. If I found a leopard trail in Colorado I should be sure I had found the mark of a cougar or a mountain lion. A wolf track on Broadway would doubtless be the doing of a large dog, and a

St. Bernard's footmark in the Rockies, twenty miles from anywhere, would most likely turn out to be the happen-so imprint of
a gray wolf's foot. To be sure of the marks, then, one should know
all the animals that belong to the neighborhood.

These facts are well known to the hunter. Most savages are
hunters, and one of the early lessons of the Indian boy is to know
tracks of the different beasts about him. These are the *letters* of
the old, old writing.

Let us go forth into the woods in one of the Northeastern states
when there is a good tracking snow, and learn a few of those letters.

Two at least are sure to be seen—the track of the blarina* and
the deer mouse. The track of the meadow mouse is not unlike
that of the blarina, because it walks, being a ground animal,
while the deer mouse often bounds.

The meadow mouse belongs to the rank grass in the lowland
near the brook, and passing it toward the open running water
we may see the curious track of the muskrat: its five-toed hind
foot, its four-toed front, and its long-keeled tail are plainly on
record. When he goes slowly the tail mark is nearly straight; when
he goes fast it is sinuous in proportion to his pace.

The muskrat is a valiant beast; he never dies without fighting
to the last, but he is in dread of another brookland creature whose
trail is here—the mink. When bounding, the four feet are together, the hind feet track ahead, the tail mark shows, and but
four toes in each track, though the creature has five on each foot.
But why did this aquatic animal seek for a bridge to cross the
brook? Perhaps he did not: he may have been looking for food
in the water and crossed on the ice bridge where it suited him;
perhaps for the first time he scented the trail of the cottontail on
the other side. He is a dreaded enemy of poor molly, and more
than once I have seen the records of his relentless pursuit. One of

* A mole shrew.—Ed.

these fits in admirably as an illustration of our present argument.

It was in the winter of 1900. I was standing with my brother, a businessman, on Goat Island, Niagara, when he remarked, "How is it? You and I have been in the same parts of America for twenty years, yet I never see any of the curious sides of animal life that you are continually coming across."

"Largely because you do not study tracks," was my reply. "Look at your feet now. There is a whole history to be read."

"I see some marks," he replied, "that might have been made by some animal."

"That is the track of a cottontail," was the answer. "Now let us read this chapter of his life. See, he went in a general straight course as though making for some well-known haunt; his easy pace, with eight or ten inches between each set of tracks, shows unalarm. But see here, joining on is something else."

"So there is. Another cottontail."

"Not at all. This new track is smaller, the forefeet are more or less paired, showing that the creature can climb a tree; there is a suggestion of toe pads and there is a mark telling evidently of a long tail; these things combined with the size and the place identify it clearly. This is the trail of a mink. See! he also found the rabbit track, and finding it fresh, he followed it. His bounds are lengthening now, but the rabbit's are not, showing that the latter was unconscious of the pursuit."

After 100 yards the double trail led us to a great pile of wood, and into this both went. Having followed his game into dense cover, the trailer's first business is to make sure that it did not go out the other side. We went carefully around the pile; there were no tracks leading out.

"Now," I said, "if you will take the trouble to move that wood-pile you will find in it the remains of the rabbit half devoured, and the mink himself, at this moment, is no doubt curled up asleep."

As the pile was large and the conclusion more or less self-evident, my brother was content to accept my reading of the episode.

Although so much is to be read in the winter white, we cannot now make a full account of all the woodland fourfoots, for there are some kinds that do not come out in the snow; they sleep more or less all winter.

Thus, one rarely sees the track of chipmunk or woodchuck in truly wintry weather; and never, as far as I know, have the trails of jumping mouse or mud turtle been seen in the snow. These we can track only in the mud or dust. Such trails cannot be followed as far as those in snow, simply because the mud and dust do not cover the whole country, but they are usually as clear and in some respects more easy of record.

It is a most fascinating amusement to learn some creature's way of life by following its fresh track for hours in good snow. I never miss such a chance. If I cannot find a fresh track I take a stale one, knowing theoretically that it is fresher at every step, and from practical experiences that it always brings one to some track that is fresh.

How often I have wished for a perfect means of transferring these wildlife tales to paper or otherwise making a permanent collection. My earliest attempts were in free-hand drawings; which answered, but has a great disadvantage—it is a translation, a record discolored by an intervening personality, and the value of the result is likely to be limited by one's own knowledge at the time.

Casting in plaster was another means attempted; but not one track in 10,000 is fit to cast. Nearly all are blemished and imperfect in some way, and the most abundant—those in the snow—cannot be cast at all.

Then I tried spreading plastic wax where the beasts would walk on it, in pathways or before dens. How they did scoff! The simplest ground squirrel knew too much to venture on my waxen snare; around it or, if hemmed in, over it, with a mighty bound, but never a track did I secure.

Photography naturally suggested itself, but the difficulties proved as great as unexpected, almost as great as in casting. Not one track in 1,000 is fit to photograph: the essential details are almost always left out. You must have open sunlight, and even when the weather is perfect there are practically but two times each day when it is possible—in midmorning and midafternoon, when the sun is high enough for clear photographs and low enough to cast a shadow in the faint track.

Then a new method was suggested in an unexpected way. A friend of mine had a pet coon which he kept in a cage in his bachelor quarters uptown. One day, during my friend's absence, the coon got loose and set about a series of long-deferred exploring expeditions, beginning with the bachelor's bedroom. The first promising object was a writing desk. Mounting by a chair, the coon examined several uninteresting books and papers, and then noticed higher up a large stone bottle. He had several times found pleasurable stuff in bottles, so he went for it. The cork was lightly in and easily disposed of, but the smell was far from inviting, for it was merely a quart of ink. Determined to leave no stone unturned, however, the coon upset the ink to taste and try. Alas! it tasted even worse than it smelt; it was an utter failure as a beverage.

And the coon, pushing it contemptuously away, turned to a pile of fine handmade, deckle-edge, heraldry note paper—the pride of my friend's heart; and when he raised his inky little paws there were left on the paper some beautiful black prints.

This was a new idea; the coon tried it again and again. But the ink held out longer than the paper, so the fur-clad printer worked over sundry books and the adjoining walls, while the ink, dribbling over everything, formed a great pool below the desk. Something attracted the artist's attention, causing him to jump down. He landed in the pool of ink, making it splash in all directions; some of the black splotches reached the white counterpane on the bachelor's bed. Another happy idea! The coon now leaped on the bed, racing around as long as the ink on his feet gave results. As he paused to rest, or perhaps to see if any place had been neglected, the door opened, and in came the landlady. The scene which followed was too painful for description; no one present enjoyed it. My friend was sent for to come take his coon out of there forever. He came and took him away. I suppose "forever." He had only one other place for him—his office—and there it was I made the animal's acquaintance and heard of his exploits—an ink-and-paper if not a literary affair.

This gave me the hint I needed, a plan to make authentic records of animal tracks. Armed with printer's ink and paper rolls, I set about gathering a dictionary collection of imprints.

After many failures and much experiment, better methods were devised. A number of improvements were made by my wife; one was the substitution of black paint for printer's ink, as the latter dries too quickly; another was the padding of the paper, which should be light and soft for very light animals, and stronger and harder for the heavy. Printing from a mouse, for example, is much like printing a delicate etching; ink, paper, dampness, etc. must be exactly right, and furthermore you have this handicap—you cannot regulate the pressure. This is, of course, strictly a zoo method; all attempts to secure black prints from wild animals have been total failures. The paper, the smell of paint, etc. are enough to keep the wild things away.

In the zoo we spread the black pad and white paper in a narrow, temporary lane, and one by one drove, or tried to drive, the captives over them, securing a series of tracks that are life-size, properly spaced, absolutely authentic, and capable of yielding more facts as the observer learns more about the subject.

As related here, all this sounds quite easy. But no one has any idea how cross-crooked and contrary a creature can be until he wishes it to repeat for him some ordinary thing that it has hitherto done hourly. Some of them balked at the paint, some at the paper, some made a leap to clear all, and thereby wrecked the entire apparatus. Some would begin very well, but rush back when half-way over so as to destroy the print already made, and in most cases the calmest, steadiest, tamest of beasts become utterly unmanageable when approached with trackological intent.

Even domestic animals are difficult. A tame cat that was highly trained to do anything a cat could do, was selected as promising for a black track study, and her owner's two boys volunteered to get all the tracks I needed. They put down a long roll of paper in a hall, painted pussy's feet black, and proceeded to chase her up and down. Her docility vanished under the strain. She raced madly about, leaving long, useless splashes of black; then, leaping to a fanlight, she escaped upstairs to take refuge among the snowy draperies. After which the boys' troubles began.

These, however, are mere by-incidents and illustrate the many practical difficulties. After these had been conquered with patience and ingenuity, there could be no doubt of the value of the prints. They are the best of records for size, spacing and detail, but fail in giving *incidents of wildlife* or the landscape surroundings. The drawings are best for a long series and for faint features; in fact, the drawing alone can give *everything you can perceive;* but it fails in authentic size and detail.

Photography has this great advantage—it gives the essential surroundings, the essential landscape and setting and, therefore, the local reason for many changes of action on the part of the animal; also the esthetic beauties of its records are unique and will help to keep the method in high place.

Thus, each of the three means may be successful in a different way, and the best, most nearly perfect alphabet of the woods would include all three, and consist of a drawing, a pedoscript, and a photograph of each track, i.e., a simple footprint and the long series of each animal.

My practice has been to use all whenever I could, but still I find free-hand drawing is the one most practical application. When I get a photograph I treasure it as an adjunct to the sketch.

To illustrate the relative value of records, see the sketch opposite. The sign manual of a cottontail rabbit. The sketch was made on February 15, 1885, near Toronto. It is really a condensation of the facts, as the trail is shortened where uninteresting. At *A* I found a round place about five inches by eight where a cottontail had crouched during the light snowfall. At *B* he had leaped out and sat looking around; the small prints in front were made by his forefeet, the two long ones by his hind feet, and farther back is a little dimple made by the tail, showing that he was sitting on it. Something alarmed him, causing him to dart out at full speed toward *C* and *D,* and now a remarkable change is to be seen; the marks made by the front feet are behind the large marks made by the hind feet because the rabbit overreaches each time; the hind feet track ahead of the front feet; the faster he goes the farther ahead those hind feet get; and what happened if he multiplied his speed by ten I really cannot imagine. This overreach of the hind feet takes place in most bounding animals.

*A Woodland Tragedy*

Now the cottontail began a series of the most extraordinary leaps and dodgings (D, E, F), as though trying to escape from some enemy. But what enemy? There were no other tracks. I began to think the rabbit was crazy—was flying from some imaginary foe— that possibly I was on the trail of a March hare. But at G, I found for the first time some spots of blood. This told me that the rabbit was in real danger but gave no clue to its source. A few yards farther, at H, I found more blood. Twenty yards more at I, for the first time on each side of the rabbit trail were the obvious marks of a pair of broad, strong wings. Oho! Now I knew the mystery of the cottontail running from a foe, a hawk, or an owl. A few yards farther and I found the remains (J) of the cottontail partly devoured. This put the eagle out of the question; an eagle would have carried the rabbit off bodily. A hawk or an owl, then, was the assassin. I looked for something to decide which, and close by the remains found the peculiar two-paired track of an owl. A hawk's track would have been as at K, while the owl nearly always sets its feet in the ground with two toes forward and two toes back. But what owl? There were at least three in the valley that might be blamed. I looked for more proof and got it on the nearby sapling—one small feather (L), downy, as are all owl feathers, and bearing three broad bars, telling me plainly that a barred owl had been there lately and that, therefore, he was almost certainly the slayer of the cottontail. As I busied myself making notes, what should come flying up the valley but the owl himself—back to the very place of the crime, intent on completing his meal, no doubt.

He alighted on a branch ten feet above my head and just over the rabbit remains, and sat there muttering in his throat.

The proof in this case was purely circumstantial, but I think that we can come to only one conclusion, that the evidence of the track in the snow was complete and convincing. Moreover, it was all—and this is the important lesson—too long, too faint, and too

*What You Expect*

*What You See*

ill-lighted to be possible of record by the camera. . . .

A meadow-mouse autograph shows that the creature has four toes with claws on the forefeet, and five on the hind, which is evidence, though not conclusive, that it was a rodent; the absence of tail marks shows that the tail was short or wanting; the tubercules on each palm show to what group of mice the creature belongs. The alternation of the tracks shows that it was a ground animal, not a tree climber; the spacing shows the shortness of the legs; their size determines the size of the creature. Thus we come near to reconstructing the animal from its tracks, and see how, by the help of these studies, we can get much light on bygone animals whose only monuments are tracks in the sedimentary rocks about us—rocks that, when they received these imprints, were the muddy margins of these long-gone creatures' haunts.

There is another feature of trail study that gives it exceptional value—it is an account of the creature *pursuing its ordinary life*. If you succeed in getting a glimpse of a fox or hare in the woods, the chances are a hundred to one that it was aware of your presence first. They are much cleverer than we at this sort of thing, and if they do not actually sight or scent you, they observe, and are warned by, the action of some creature that *did* sense you, and so cease their occupations to steal away or hide. But the snow story will tell of the life that the animal ordinarily leads—its method of searching for food, its kind of food, the help it gets from its friends, or sometimes from its rivals—and thus offers an insight into its home ways that is scarcely to be attained in any other way. The tracker has the key to a new storehouse of nature's secrets, another of the Sybilline books is opened to his view; his fairy godmother has, indeed, conferred on him a wonderful gift in opening his eyes to the foot writ of the trail. It is like giving sight to the blind man, like the rolling away of fogs from a mountain view, and the tracker comes closer than others to the heart of the woods.[2]

# 10.

# CAN ZOO ANIMALS
# LEAD A NORMAL LIFE?

At the beginning of this century the continent of North America was one vast and teeming game range. Not only were the buffalo in millions across the Mississippi, but other large game was fully as abundant, though less conspicuous. Herds of elk, numbering 10,000 or 15,000, were commonly seen along the Upper Missouri. The antelope ranged the higher plains in herds of thousands; whitetail deer, though less gregarious, were seen in bands of hundreds; while bighorn sheep, though less disposed to gather in large flocks, were rarely out of sight in the lower parts of the eastern Rockies, and it was quite usual to see several hundred blacktail in the course of a single day's travel.

But a change set in when the pioneer Americans, with their horses, their deadly rifles, their energy, and their taste for murder, began to invade the newly found West.

The settlers increased in numbers, and the rifles became more deadly each year; but the animal did not improve his speed, cunning, or fecundity in an equal ratio, and so was defeated in the struggle for life, and started on the down grade toward extinction.

Aside from sentimental or esthetic reasons, which I shall not here discuss, the extinction of a large or highly organized animal is a serious matter.

1. It is always dangerous to disturb the balance of nature by

removing a poise. Some of the worst plagues have arisen in this way.

2. We do not know, without much and careful experiment, how vast a service that animal might have done to mankind as a domestic species.

The force of this will be more apparent if we recollect how much the few well-known domestic species have done for the advancement of our race. Who can decide which has done more for mankind, the cow or the steam engine, the horse or electricity, the sheep or the printing press, the dog or the rifle, the ass or the loom? No one, indeed, can pronounce on these, yet all on reflection feel that there is reason in the comparisons. Take away these inventions, and we are put back a century, or perhaps two; but further, take away the domestic animals, and we are reduced to absolute savagery, for it was they who first made it possible for our aboriginal forefathers to settle in one place and learn the rudiments of civilization.

It is quite possible, though of course not demonstrable, that the humble chuckie barn fowl has been a larger benefactor of our race than any mechanical invention in our possession, for there is no inhabited country on earth today where the barn fowl is not a mainstay of health. There are vast regions of South America and Europe where it is *the* mainstay, and nowhere is there known anything that can take its place, which is probably more than can be said of anything in the world of mechanics.

Now, if the early hunters of these our domestic animals had succeeded in exterminating them before their stock was domesticated, which easily might have been, for domestication succeeds only after long and persistent effort and, in effect, a remodeling of the wild animal by select breeding, the loss to the world would have been a very serious matter, probably much more serious than the loss of any invention, because an idea, being born of other ideas, can be lost temporarily, while the destruction of an organized being is irreparable.

And we today, therefore, who deliberately exterminate any large and useful, possibly domesticable, wild animal, may be doing more harm to the country than if we had robbed it of its navy.

This is the most obvious economic view of the question of extermination. But there is another, a yet higher one, which, in the end, will prove more truly more economic. We are informed, on excellent authority, that man's most important business here is to "know himself."

Evidently one cannot comprehend the nature of a wheel in a machine by study of that wheel alone; one must consider the whole machine or fail. And since it is established that man is merely a wheel in a great machine called the universe, he can never arrive at a comprehension of himself without study of the other wheels also. Therefore, to know himself, man must study not only himself but all things to which he is related. This is the motive of all scientific research.

There is no part of our environment that is not filled with precious facts bearing on the "great problem," and the nearer they are to us the more they contain for us. He who will explain the house sparrow's exemption from bacteriological infections, the white bear's freedom from trouble that we attribute to uric acid in the blood, or the buffalo's and the flamingo's immunity from the deadliest malaria, is on the way to conferring like immunities on man. Each advance of science enables us to get more facts out of the same source, so that something that is studied today may yield a hundred times the value that it could or did ten years ago; and if that source of knowledge happens to be perishable, one can do the race no greater harm than by destroying it.

The Sibylline books were supposed to contain all necessary wisdom; they were destroyed, one by one, because the natural heir to that wisdom did not realize their value. He did wake up at last, but it was too late to save anything but a fragment. What Tarquin did to the books offered by the Cumæan Sibyl, our own race in America has done to some of the most valuable books offered by nature. To illustrate: each animal is in itself an inexhaustible volume of facts that man must have, to solve the problem of knowing himself. One by one, not always deliberately, these wonderful volumes have been destroyed, and the facts that might have been read in them have been lost.

It is hard to imagine a greater injury to the world of thought, which is, after all, the real world, than the destruction of one of these wonderful unread volumes. It is possible that the study of "man" would suffer more by the extinction of some highly organized animal than it did by the burning of the Alexandrian library. This is why the men of science have striven so earnestly to save our native animals from extinction.

In 1878 there were still millions of buffalo in the West. That year the Northern Pacific Railroad opened up the Missouri region, and the annual slaughter was greatly increased. In 1882 there were still thousands of buffalo. In 1884 all were gone but for a few small, scattered bands. In 1885 there were probably fewer than five hundred buffalo alive in the United States. In 1886 an expedition fitted out by the government secured with great difficulty enough specimens to make the mounted group in the National Museum, and it was then clear that unless the authorities took immediate and vigorous steps, the buffalo, within a year or two, would cease to exist.

About this time there appeared a number of articles by well-known observers, calling attention to the fact that the buffalo's fate was also awaiting, in the near future, all our finest animals, the probable order of extinction being buffalo, elk, antelope, moose, bighorn sheep, mountain goat, mule deer, Virginia deer;

and the farthest probable date for this ruthless consummation was put at twenty years hence. It required no great argument to convince the public of the truth of these writers' main statements. It was obvious that no possible good was to be gained by exterminating these harmless animals, for the love of slaughter, not the need for their skin, flesh, or range, was the incentive; and the public, though not yet able to look on these animals as the student does, nevertheless realized that it was about to be robbed of something valuable by a few mean-spirited and selfish hunters.

Additional point was given to the obvious moral by the circumstance that, through its far-reaching system of correspondence, the Smithsonian Institution was continually receiving gifts of living animals which, for lack of space to keep them, had either to be turned into dead specimens or given away to outside zoos, or else returned to their donors.

This was the state of affairs in 1887, when the newly appointed Secretary of the Institution, Mr. S. P. Langley—who, though an astronomer and a physicist, had been very strongly impressed by the fact that our largest and most interesting native animals were rapidly approaching extinction—conceived the idea of securing a tract of country, as primitive as possible, that might be made a lasting city of refuge for the vanishing races. This was the main idea, when first Mr. Langley went to Congress to urge the establishment of a national zoological park.

In all ages it has been the custom of potentates to keep a collection of wild animals for their amusement, and the American people, being their own ruler, had numberless precedents before them when urged to make this much-needed collection of animals.

In such a case the advantage of a monarchy is that only one man must be convinced, whereas in the republic the consent of a majority of seventy millions had to be obtained.

This took time. Fierce battles had to be fought with ignorant and captious politicians. One objected that he did not see why the people should pay "to have the Nebraska elk and Florida alligators cooped up." If they had to spend money for it they would want things they could not see at home—dog-faced baboons, kangaroos, man-eating tigers, etc. Another, a fervent patriot, objected to any money being spent on exotic species, as it was contrary to the spirit of the Constitution to encourage or import foreigners!

Altogether the Secretary of the Smithsonian found it no easy bill to carry, though it was indorsed by nearly every scientist and educator in the country.

After three years of persistent effort, involving vastly more worry than the management of the whole Smithsonian Institution for three times that period, Mr. Langley succeeded in carrying both Houses of Congress over the successive stages of ridicule, toleration, and favorable consideration, to the point of accepting and providing for the scheme.

An appropriation was made for a national zoological park to be established in the District of Columbia for the "advancement of science and the instruction and amusement of the people," as well as a city refuge where those "native animals that were threatened with extinction might live and perpetuate their species in peace."

An appropriation of $200,000 was made, but it was clogged with several irksome conditions. One half of the expense was to be paid by the District of Columbia, thereby giving the commission a control which changed the plan, making the collection more like the ordinary menagerie. No animals were to be bought, which was much like a rich man building himself a picture gallery and saying, "Now, if my friends choose to present me with pictures, all right, I'll house them; but I've done enough for myself in building the gallery." And yet, though falling short of its promoter's original wish, the scheme has notably progressed, and no one who is capable of measuring the future of the institution can doubt that in founding this park, where those "native animals that were threatened with extinction might live and perpetuate their species in peace," Congress has done more for the learning, science, and amusement of the nation than it would in expending a much larger amount in a university, a theater, and a choice library combined; for the fields of the three are already well covered, but the park, by preserving the nation's heritage of wild animals, has opened important regions of biological research and zoological art.

He was a wise old farmer who said to his son, "John, make sure of your land, and everything will take care of itself." The whole appropriation was wisely expended in securing land, and although scientists have not the highest reputation for business sense, the park's projector was enough of a businessman to secure land that would now fetch at least ten times what was paid for it ten years ago.

It comprises 167 acres of land, beautifully diversified with woods and streams, in the suburbs of the city of Washington—land which the Secretary had discovered years before when on rides for recreation, and the absolute fitness of which for the purpose in hand had been helpful in developing the original plan. It included the historical grounds and buildings of the Quincy Adams mill and the classical old Holt house; but, better still, it secured a region that had always been a familiar resort of the native birds and quadrupeds of the District of Columbia, affording the best of expert testimony in favor of its salubrity. Mr. Langley recognized the merit of Mr. W. T. Hornaday, the well-known naturalist and taxidermist, and obtained his able and energetic superintendence during the earliest formative period of the park; and when he was called to duties elsewhere, Dr. Frank Baker took up the burden, and under the direction of the Secretary, whose other duties have never interfered with the attention he has given to his own creation (the park) it has been carried on with all the success that could be expected under conditions of inadequate support.

Thus the National Zoo was founded under conditions that illustrate in a curious way the adage that the onlooker sees more than the players. Goethe, the poet, surrounded by zoologists, was the first to point the true way for zoological science; it was for Franklin, the philosopher-printer, to teach his contemporaries how a perfect fireplace might be made; and so also Langley, the physicist, though surrounded by zoologists, has been the first to discern the pressing need of the study of American zoology.

The circumstances which led up to the idea were unusual, as the plan itself was unique. There have been many menageries in which the animals were confined in box cages, and there have been many game parks where the various animals inclosed have wandered at will, with no barrier but the outward wall of the grounds; but this was to be the first zoological collection in which each kind of animal was to have a park of its own, where it could live as its race should live, among natural surroundings, with as little restraint as was compatible with its safe-keeping. The available acreage was barely enough to allow of the park scheme being extended to our most important native animals, so that the foreigners, particularly those from the tropical regions, are perforce managed as in the better class menageries elsewhere. But the glory of the place is in its individual parks. The fencing used is of the invisible kind, which rarely intrudes itself on the observer, and yet is strong enough to restrain the biggest buffalo. The ample stretches of woods and hills in each inclosure are unmarred by its lines, and the effect is as nearly as possible that of seeing animals in the open.

Here they live, and no doubt enjoy their lives, and the observer has a chance to see them pretty much as they were in their native range. They group themselves naturally among the trees and rocks, while the uneven ground induces attitudes of endless variety, and the close imitation of natural conditions causes the animals to resume the habits native to their lives in the wild state, thus affording the zoologist and the artist an opportunity for study never before equaled among captive animals.

The scheme is of course in its infancy yet. Wonders have been done with small appropriations, but many of its essential divisions have not been touched.

The antelope are provided with a little plan, and the deer have a small woodland where none can harm them or make them afraid. The buffalo has its rolling prairie land, where it may bring forth its young without fear of the deadly, omnipresent rifle, and regardless of its ancient foe, the ever-near gray wolf, that used to hang on the outskirts of the herd to kill the mother at her helpless time or, failing, to sneak around, ready, like an arrow in a bent bow, watching his chance to spring and tear the tender calf.

Here, indeed, the elk can bugle his far-sounding love song in the fall, without thereby making his stand the center of a rush of ruthless hunters. But many of our forest animals are still unprovided for. The bighorn sheep, the coast blacktail, the mule deer, the moose, and the mountain goat, as well as the grizzly bear, so rapidly following the buffalo, have as yet no refuge in the National Zoo.

It is too late to talk of such species as the great auk, the Labrador duck, and the West Indies seal; and in one year, or at most two years, unless Congress is willing to devote the price, or at least half the price, of a single big gun to it, the world will have lost forever the great Alaskan bear, the largest and most wonderful of its race.

The paddock immediately to the left on entering by the west gate of the Zoological Park brings us face to face with the first game animals that met the eyes of the Pilgrim Fathers, as well as those of the first settlers of Virginia; and it is tolerably certain that General Washington himself hunted the superb creature, the Virginia deer, over this very ground where it is now protected in the city of Washington and assured a little land of lasting peace.

Of all the American game animals, the Virginia or whitetail deer is the greatest success as a species; that is, it has developed a better combination of hardiness, fecundity, speed, intelligence, keen wits, and adaptability than any of its relatives, and therefore maintains itself better in spite of the hunter. Its ancient range covered all of the United States east of the Rockies, as well as part of Canada, and today, notwithstanding guns, more numerous and deadly each year, there are whitetail deer in every part of their original range that still contains primitive woods.

In the list giving the probable order of extinction of our great game it will be seen that the Virginia deer stands last, despite the fact that it is the only one in that list whose home is in the thickly settled Eastern states. An incident will show the respect in which the hunters hold the whitetail's gift for taking care of himself.

During October of 1899 I was staying at a camp on the east side of the Rockies. One morning a miner came in to report that he had started four deer less than a mile away. Meat was scarce, and a hunter present became keenly interested.

"Whitetails or blacktails?" said he.

"Whitetails," said the miner.

"That settles it," said the hunter, resuming his seat by the fire. "If they were blacktails I'd get one within a mile, but a scared whitetail knows too much for me."

Although some of these deer in this paddock were born in the park, they show many of their wild habits. During the heat of the day they lie hidden among the bushes at the back end of their range; but early in the morning or late in the evening they come to the watering place in the open, and if alarmed there they make for the trees, raising and waving as they go the "white flag" famous in all hunting lore.

This conspicuous action might seem a mistake in an animal that is seeking to escape unnoticed; but the sum of advantage in the habit is with the deer, or he would not do it, and its main purpose will be seen in one very important and frequent situation. A mother deer has detected danger; she gives a silent but unmistakable notification to her fawns by raising the "danger flag," a white one in this case; and then, when she leads away through the woods, they are enabled to keep sight of her in the densest thickets and darkest nights by the aid of the shining beacon, which is waved in a way peculiar to this species, and is not therefore liable to be mistaken for the white patch on any other animal.

In the sign language of the Indians the gesture for the whitetail deer is made up of the general sign for a deer, and then a waving of the flat, open hand with fingers up, in imitation of the banneret as it floats away through the woods.

The form adopted for the whitetails' paddock is the result of experience. It was found that the animals became alarmed sometimes and dashed along the invisible fences, until suddenly met by another at right angles, and in this way several were hurt; but the improved plan of substituting obtuse angles, or a curve at the corners, causes them to turn aside without injury.

One cannot linger many minutes by the Virginia deer paddock without seeing some of the gorgeous Asiatics, the peacocks, walking about among the thicket or negotiating the wire fences with absolute precision whenever it suits their purpose to do so. The original half-dozen birds have increased to a hundred, and the vast stretch (several hundred acres of them) of broken, wooded country is so perfectly suited to their needs that they give us a very good imitation of life in the Indian jungle. During the winter they

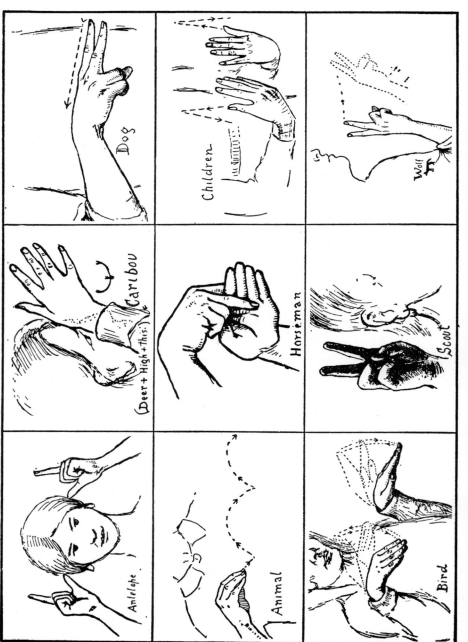

Showing Tot Row: Antelope, Caribou, Dog, Animal, Horseman, Children, Bird, Scout, Wolf.

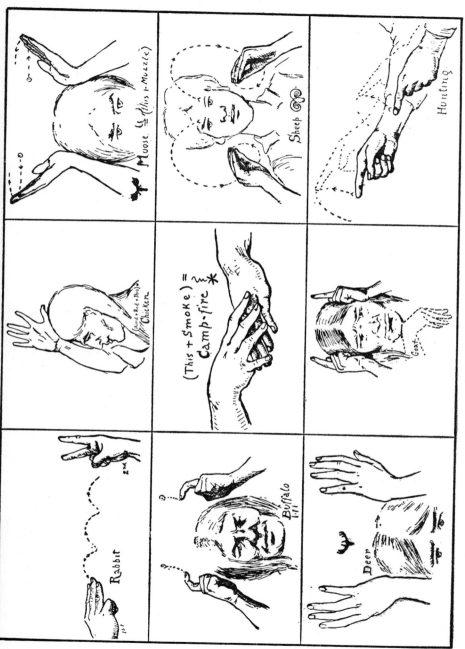

Left to Right, Starting Top Row: Rabbit, Chicken, Moose, Buffalo, Campfire, Sheep, Deer, Goat, Hunting.

roam about in promiscuous troops, but when the early spring comes and the cock is in his full regalia, the mating instinct prompts them to scatter, and each family withdraws to a part of the jungle—the park, I mean—that is understood to be theirs, and to defend which the cock is ready to do battle with all feathered intruders.

Close to the deer paddock is a sunny open glade that was for long the special domain of one particular peacock. All about it is thick shrubbery, where the soberly dressed hens might have been seen quietly moving about, paying no obvious heed to their gorgeous partner, who mounted habitually on a little sand bank and spread and quivered his splendid jewelry in the sun, turning this way and that way to get the best effect, occasionally answering the far-away call of some rival with a defiant *qua,* or replying to the dynamic explosions in a near quarry with a peculiar *bizz,* the exact meaning of which I have failed to discover.

The daily display here and in many parts of the park gives the observer a chance to see the geometric perfection of the pattern made by the "eyes" when the peacock's train is raised. I reproduced a diagram of this, made and published some years ago, when first I discovered the mathematics of this miracle in feathers.*

On crossing the road from the deer paddock toward the middle and more open part of the park, the stranger is likely to come suddenly on a band of antelope. They seem to be grazing along their native upland prairie, not far from timber, and the visitor, if he have any of the feeling of the hunter-naturalist, is sure to feel the same little thrill that would come if he met them thus in the Wild West. He has ample time to admire and watch their changing and picturesque grouping before he realizes that between him and them is the slight but necessary wire fence. The effect of this invisible fence is seen on the animals if they have been undisturbed for some hours, as well as on the onlooker; for the sudden appear-

* See p. 136—Ed.

ance of a human being close at hand, with no massive screening barrier between, causes them to behave for a moment much as they did when wild and free, and their startlement is expressed in pose and act exactly as it might have been in their native wilds; but they soon realize that they are safe and no harm is done. The erect mane and rump patch sink, and the animals resume their feeding, leaving, nevertheless, on the air a peculiar musky odor that is quite strong when one is on their lee side.

Some years ago, while riding across the upland prairie of the Yellowstone, not very far from where these very antelope had been captured, I noticed certain white specks in the far distance. They showed and disappeared several times, and then began moving southward. Then, in another direction, I discovered other white specks, which also seemed to flash and disappear. A glass showed them to be antelope, but it did not wholly explain the flashing or moving which ultimately united the two bands. I made note of the fact, but found no explanation until the opportunity came to study the antelope in the Washington Zoo. I had been quietly watching the grazing herd on their hillside for some time; in fact I was sketching, which is quite the best way to watch an animal minutely. I was so quiet that the antelope seemed to have forgotten me, when, contrary to rules, a dog chanced into the park. The wild antelope habit is to raise its head every few moments while grazing, to keep a sharp lookout for danger, and these captives kept up the practice of their race. The first that did so saw the dog. It uttered no sound, but gazed at the wolfish-looking intruder, and all the long white hairs of the rump patch were raised with a jerk that made the patch flash in the sun like a tin pan. Every one of the grazing antelope saw the flash, repeated it instantly, and raised his head to gaze in the direction where the first was gazing. At the same time I noticed on the wind a peculiar musky smell—a smell that certainly came from the antelope.

Some time later the opportunity came to make a careful dissection of the antelope's rump patch, and the keystone of the arch of facts was supplied. My specimen, taken in Jackson Hole, was a male under six months old, so that all the proportions, and indeed the character, are much less developed than in an adult.

The fresh skin was laid flat on a board, and then the pattern and mechanism of the rump patch were clearly seen. The hairs at the upper part of the patch were three and three quarter inches long, grading to the center and lower parts, where they were only one and seven eighths inches long, all snowy white and normally lying down flat, pointing toward the rear. Among the roots of the hair was a gland secreting a strong musk. On the under side of the skin was a broad sheet of muscular fibers, which have power to change the direction of the hair. As soon, therefore, as an antelope sees some strange or thrilling object, this muscle acts, and the rump patch is changed in a flash into a great double disk or twin chrysanthemum of white, that shines afar like a patch of snow; but in the middle of each bloom a dark spot, the musk gland, is exposed, a great quantity of the odor is set free, and the message is read by all those that have noses to read.

Of all the animals, man has the poorest nose; he has virtually lost the sense of smell, while among the next animals in the scale, scent is their best faculty; yet even man can distinguish this danger scent for many yards down wind, and there is no reason to doubt that another antelope can detect it a mile away.

Thus the observations on the captive animals living under normal conditions prove the key to those made on the plains, and I know now that the changing flecks in the Yellowstone uplands were made by this antelope heliograph while the two bands signaled each other, and the smaller band, on getting the musky message, "Friends," laid aside all precaution and fearlessly joined their relations.

This animal has five different sets of glands about it, each exuding a different kind of musk for use in its daily life, as a means of getting and giving intelligence to its kind. These are situated one on each foot between the toes, one on each angle of the jaw, one on the back of each hock, one on the middle of each disk on the rump, and one at the base of the tail.

Those on the jaw seem related to the sexual system, as they are largest in the buck; those on the rump, as seen, have a place in their heliographic code; and the purpose of the others, though not yet fully worked out, is almost certainly to serve in conveying news. To illustrate: an antelope passes along a certain plain, eats at one place, drinks at another, lies down at a third, is pursued by a wolf for half a mile, when the wolf gives up the unequal race, and the antelope escapes at his ease. A second antelope comes along. The foot scent from the interdigital glands marks the course of his relative as clearly for him as the track in the snow would for us. Its strength tells him somewhat of the time elapsed since it was made, and its individuality tells him whether his predecessor was a stranger or a personal friend, just as surely as a dog can tell his master's track. The frequency of the tracks shows that the first one was not in haste, and the hock scent, exuded on the plants or ground where he lay down, informs the second one of the action. At the place where the wolf was sighted, the sudden diffusion of the rump musk on the surrounding sagebrush will be perceptible to the newcomer for hours afterward. The wide gaps between the traces of foot scent now attest the speed of the fugitive, and the cause of it is clearly read when the wolf trail joins on. This may sound a far-fetched tale of Sherlock Holmes among the animals, but not so if we remember that the scent faculty is better than the sight faculty in these animals, while their sight faculty is at least as good as ours, and that, finally, if this had been in the snow we also could have read it with absolute precision.

The pronghorned antelope, or prongbuck of books, is the only horned ruminant in North America that has only two hoofs on each foot. Nature's economic plan has been to remove all parts that cease to be of use, and so save the expense of growing and maintaining them. Thus, man is losing his back wisdom teeth, since civilized diet is rendering them useless. The ancestors of the antelope had four hoofs on each foot, like a deer or a pig, but the back pair on each foot has been dropped. At an earlier step the common ancestor of antelope and deer had five well-developed toes on each extremity, but it seems that while this makes an admirable foot for wading in treacherous swamps, it is for mechanical reasons a slow foot; the fewer the toes the greater the speed. The deer still living in swamps could not afford to dispense entirely with the useful little hind or mud hoof. There they are still for bog use, though much modified from the original equal-toed types, more nearly shown in the pig. But the antelope, living on the hard, dry uplands, had no use for bogtrotters, and exchanged them for a higher rate of speed, so that it now has only two toes on each foot.

The horse family went yet further, for they lived in a region where evolution went faster. They shunned the very neighborhood of swamps; all their life was spent on the firm, dry, level country; speed and sound feet were their very hold on life, and these they maintained at their highest pitch by adopting a foot with a single, hoof-clad toe.

There is one other remarkable peculiarity of the antelope to note, and that is its horns. The ox and sheep tribes of the world have simple horns of true horny material permanently growing on a bony core which is part of the skull. The deer have horns of branched form and of bony material sprouting from the head, but dropping off to be renewed each year. Our antelope is the only animal in the world whose weapons are of true horn growing on a bony core, as in the ox tribes, yet branched and dropping off each year, as in the deer.

It is now an axiom of science that not the smallest detail is without a distinct purpose, for which it has been carefully adapted after ages of experiment; yet long ago Darwin, the apostle of the belief, confessed himself puzzled by the form of the antelope's horns. It seemed as though a simple, straight spike would be so much more effective. If the great philosopher had been with me in the Washington Zoological Park that day, his puzzle would have been solved for him by two of the antelopes themselves. They were having one of their periodical fights for the mastery; they approached with noses to the ground, and after fencing for an opening they closed with a clash, and as they thrust and parried the purpose of the prong was clear. It served the antelope exactly as the guard on a bowie knife does a Mexican or that on a foil does a swordsman, for countless thrusts that would have skipped up the horn and reached the head were caught with admirable adroitness in this fork.

And the inturned, harmless-looking points! I had to watch long before I saw how dangerous they might be when the right moment arrived. After several moments of fencing, one of the bucks got under the other one's guard, and making a sudden thrust, which the other failed to catch in the fork, he brought his inturned left point to bear on the unprotected throat of his opponent, who saved himself from injury by rearing quickly, though it seemed to me that such a move could not have stopped a fatal thrust if they had really been fighting a deadly duel.

It is a common saying among keepers that, averaging one animal with another, a menagerie must be renewed every three years. Yet I know of one manager who has kept most of his animals, those of Woodward's Gardens, San Francisco, alive, healthy, and happy from the beginning of his time to the end, sixteen years later, when the establishment was broken up and the animals were to be shot in their cages. The great secret of his success, he tells me, was caring for their minds as well as for their bodies.

It is a well-known fact that lions and many other animals in traveling circuses are healthier and live longer than those in ordinary menageries. At first one might think that the traveling animals get more fresh air and exercise than the others. Yet this is not the case, for the circus cage is always very small and cramped. While traveling, it is usually shut up, and when showing, it is in a tent, always a drafty, ill-ventilated, foul-smelling place. The great advantage of the circus is the constant change of scene—the varied excitements that give the animals something to think about, and keep them from torpid habits and mental morbidness.

It has long been known that caged animals, especially the highly organized kinds, suffer from a variety of mental diseases. Mr. Ohnimus, the superintendent referred to, informs me that camels and several other species commonly end their cage lives in lunacy. The camels turned loose in Arizona some years ago were reduced at length to one old male. In course of time his solitary life affected his brain. According to local tradition, he went crazy and used to attack every living creature near, until he was killed by a mounted cowboy whom he had pursued with murderous intent.

Captive bears are apt to fall into a sort of sullen despondency. Foxes and cats often go crazy, and no matter how obviously mental the disease, it is usually set down to hydrophobia, and the unanswered question is, How did they get it? Dogs that are constantly chained up commonly become sullen and dangerous. The higher apes and baboons rarely thrive in cages. Soon or late they become abnormally vicious, or else have a complete physical breakdown. All this is so human, and so emphasizes the great truth of evolution, that the wise keeper seizes on the cue, and in his management of his charges treats them like human beings of a lower development than himself.

Many a man shut up in a cell has saved his mind by inventing some trifling amusement. It is recorded that one set a daily watch on the movements of a spider. Another tried how many times he had to toss five pins before they fell in just the same way. Another busied himself inventing new arrangements for the two or three articles of furniture in his cell. Many have paced up and down each day for a number of hours. And whatever they did, all alike were seeking to put in time, to while away the awful tedium of their monotonous lives, to respond to the natural craving for exercise, and to save their minds and bodies from actually withering from disease.

If instead of "human captives" we read "wild animals" in all this, we shall have a very fair portrait of what we may see every day in an ordinary menagerie. Why does the elephant swing to and fro forever from his chain picket? Why does he gather from the floor all the straw he can reach, throw it over his back and over the stable, to be regathered later? Why does the squirrel enter and work for hours the aimless treadwheel, and the marten leap listlessly half a day from point to point—floor, perch, slat, box—again and again, with monotonous sameness day after day? Why does the lone ostrich waltz far more than does his wild kinsman that has many admiring spectators of his own kind, and why do the fox and the wolverine trot miles and miles of cage front every day? Why does the bear roll and tumble for hours over the same old wooden ball as if it were a new-found chum; or, if no ball is supplied, swing back and forth on pivotal hind foot for hours each day? Why does the rhinoceros keep on forever nosing at some projection that his horn can almost fasten under, till it gets more and more elusive through the smoothening of perpetual use? Why do wolves and monkeys put in hours and hours on humble duties that in the wild state were the work of a few minutes at most? To all, the answer is the same as to the similar query about the man prisoner. They are putting in time. They are responding to the natural craving for exercise. They are trying to pass the tedium of their hopeless lives. They are doing anything—everything—their poor brains can suggest to while away the weary drag of dull, eventless days. Their bellies are well cared for, or at least are always plentifully cared for, but how few keepers have learned that in each animal is a mentality, large or small, that ought to be considered!

Here is where Ohnimus scored. He tried to make their lives interesting. The excitement of the chase must necessarily be denied those animals whose nature prompts them that way, but one of his first and most successful moves was made in consideration of their special case. He divided the single meal of all flesh-eating animals in two; the same in quantity each day, but a light morning meal and a light afternoon meal. Thus, he "gave them something more to think about." It made two breaks in the day's monotony, and in time it unquestionably bore good fruit.

Another variation was made by changing them into new cages. An animal soon learns a cage by heart. He knows every bar and bolt, and every trifling roughness in wall or floor. He can walk to and fro without his eyes if need be. But putting him into a new cage is like opening a new life. Everything new and to be learned must naturally create new interests, and be of corresponding benefit, unless it has come too late.

There is a pathetic story of an old tiger that had passed his life in a traveling cage until in a railway accident his car and his cage alike were overturned and broken open. The tiger was unharmed, and he passed through the broken grating, and for the first time since he left India as a cub he was free, standing untrammeled, with the whole world open to him. But all his splendid powers were gone or were dwarfed. He seemed appalled by the new responsibilities. After a moment's hesitation he declined the freedom that had come too late and crawled back again into his narrow cage, realizing that this was the only thing that he was fit for now.

One of the best expedients of all to enliven and brighten the lives of the caged animals is friendship with the keeper. There was no such thing as solitary confinement in Woodward's Gardens. Every prisoner there had at least one powerful friend who was always near and ready to attend to all his wants, including the craving for sympathetic companionship which few animals are entirely without.

But all these allayments are mere expedients. The real plan is to restore the natural conditions. We are slowly grasping the idea, taught by the greatest thinkers in all ages, that the animals have an inalienable, God-given right to the pursuit of happiness in their own way as long as they do not interfere with our happiness. And if we must for good reason keep them in prison, we are bound to make their conditions tolerable, not only for their sakes, but for our own, because all the benefit that we can get out of them in bondage is increased in proportion as we slacken their bonds within the limits of judicious restraint.

If a Chinaman after going through Sing Sing were to say, "I have heard much of the high mentality, the attainments, and the refinement of the white race, but these seem to me merely a lot of sullen, stupid brutes," it would about parallel the case of an ordinary menagerie viewed by an ordinary onlooker. If we wish to enjoy the beauty of the animals, or study their development and learn how it bears on our own, we must see them living their lives. This cannot be done in box cages, is very difficult in the wilds, and is easily possible only in a zoological park.

Occupation and plenty of good food are not the only things needful to a well-rounded life. No matter how cared for, fed, and housed, the occupants of every well-known monkey house were formerly afflicted with coughs, colds, and lung diseases that made their abode like a hospital and carried off the inmates at plague rates, so that but few monkeys saw their second season in confinement. All sorts of remedies were tried, without avail; hothouses with natural accessories, continual medical treatment, and all failed to lower the death rate. At last it occurred to the monkey-keeper of a European zoo that all this coddling would be very bad for a human being, so why not bad for monkeys? He decided to treat them like fellow creatures; he discarded the stuffy hothouses; he gave his monkeys free access to the pure air and sun, in a cage as large as he could get it, large enough to give room for exercise, and the result was that coughs and colds began to disappear. The death rate rapidly fell; each month and year that passed gave fuller indorsement to the idea. In short, he had learned the art of monkey keeping.

Each advance of knowledge has emphasized these great principles that the lower animals are so like ourselves that to keep them in health we must give some thought to their happiness, and in aiming at both we must accept the ordinary principles obtained from study of ourselves.

These are among the considerations that shaped the scheme of the National Zoo at Washington; or, more comprehensively put, the restoration of the natural conditions of each animal was the main thought in Mr. Langley's plan—a plan that, though not yet fully realized, has been more than justified by the results.

In the center of the park is the coon tree. This very tree had undoubtedly been climbed many a time by the wild coons, within a few years, before it was selected to be the center of a little coon kingdom. It is now the abode of over thirty thrifty specimens which live their lives here much as they once did in the woods, and there is no reason to suppose that they suffer in any way, since all their needs—food, shelter, companionship, and amusement—are cared for. They have indeed all the good things that their wild brethren have, excepting only that there is a limit to their liberty.

Usually they may be seen all day sunning themselves in the high crotches, and the sunnier the day the higher the crotch, so that they are a living barometer. When there is a prospect of continued fine weather, the coons climb up as far as they can safely go, and at a distance they look like fruit hanging on the tree. But in doubtful weather they sit lower and nearer the trunk; there they look more like nests, and give the tree the appearance of a rookery; while, in a storm, all descend and huddle together in the great hollow trunk that lies on the ground below and at times serves as the bedroom of the colony.

The scientific name of the coon means "washer," and one of his popular names is "wash bear," from the peculiar trick he has of carefully washing his food. This interestingly Mosaic habit the coons keep up in captivity, no matter how clean the morsel or how doubtful the water may be; and as their tactile paw is busied soaking the next piece of provender, their eyes take in the surroundings as though they were not needed in the supposed purification of the food. These, of course, are habits learned in the woods. The coon feeds along the edges of the creeks and ponds, picking up crawfish, frogs, and other mud dwellers. Then, having secured them, he is careful to clean them off in their native stream, so as not to eat mud with every course. And this being a matter he can very well leave to his sensitive fingers, his eyes are judiciously employed in scanning the woods about, either for more game or to guard against being made game of himself by some powerful enemy.

Those who have seen the little ones when they are old enough to be brought to the water by their mother, and there receive their first lessons in frog hunting, describe them as doing everything just as she does, copying her in all things, dabbing their paws in the mud as their watchful eyes rove about scanning the neighboring woods.

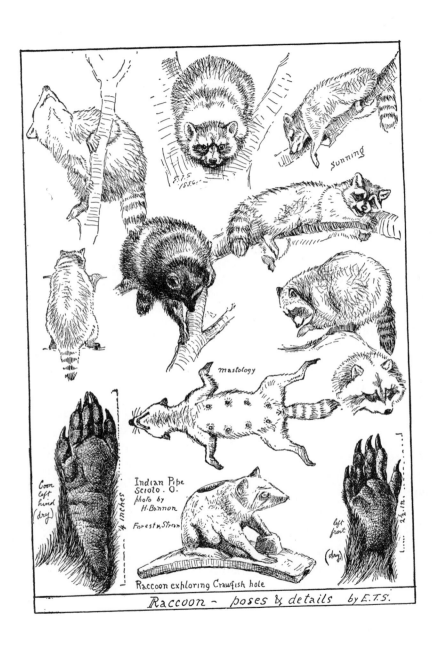

sunning

E.T.S.
1886

mastology

Indian Pipe
Scioto . O.
photo by
H. Bannon

Forest & Stream

Coon
left
hind
(dry)

4 inches

left
front

(dry)

2½ in.

Raccoon exploring Crawfish hole

Raccoon — poses & details   by E.T.S.

Another microcosm, and even more picturesque than that for the coons, is planned for the mountain sheep, but still delayed for lack of means. Mr. Langley proposes to inclose a tract of several acres of rocky, hilly land, more or less covered with timber, and therein establish a miniature of the Rocky Mountains, where the bighorn sheep and his neighbors, the calling hare and the mountain marmot, may live together and show us how they used to live at home.

There may be many obscure problems of life history and environment that might demonstrate themselves in an enclosure of this sort. To illustrate the complexity of such questions: The presence of the pelicans on Pelican Island, Yellowstone Lake, is declared by authority to be essential to the life of the parasites that infest the trout of the same waters, since at one stage the parasite lives in the bird. This case is of a type that is common. No man can say now whether or not the general failure in other zoos to preserve the mountain sheep in confinement is due to the need for any one element of its native environment, but the way to find out is by restoring the proper surroundings, animate, as well as inanimate, as far as possible. Experiments of this sort must increase our knowledge of the laws of life, and in time will solve the problem of successfully maintaining our mountain sheep in captivity.

For the bears also is planned a roomy park with restored environment. Bears are restless, roving animals, much more so than deer, or indeed than most of our large quadrupeds, and they suffer proportionately when shut up. Many carnivorous animals breed in captivity, but bears are among those that do not, not more than two or three cases being on record. This is an evidence of the great pathological disturbance from caging in the ordinary way. The added feature of a geological disturbance in the small bear pen near the south entrance resulted in a little ripple of excitement some years ago. A heavy rainstorm during the night washed down

from the cliff into the unfinished pen such a pile of rocks and sand
that a young grizzly mounting on it was enabled to climb up and
escape into the open. He hid himself in the thickest shrubbery of
the park and for a day or two eluded recapture, to the consterna-
tion of numerous mothers whose children going to school had to
pass near the park. Each one, of course, could in imagination see
her own particular offspring suffering the fate of the naughty children who scoffed at the baldheaded prophet. But those who saw
the grizzly during his brief spell of liberty say that he was so overwhelmed by the novelty of his situation that he was quite the most
timorous of all concerned in the affair.

The buffalo was one of the American animals chiefly in view
when the idea of the park occurred to Mr. Langley. The present
herd is a fine one, but the amount of ground available for them is
not sufficient.

I have heard it said that a little enmity in the life of a caged
animal is better than absolute stagnation; but of course the enmity
must be within limits. The buffalo herd had so far reverted to the
native state that the old bull ruled for several years, much as he
would have done on the plains. He was what the keeper called "not
a bad boss"; that is, he was not malicious in his tyranny. One of
the younger bulls made an attempt to resist him once, and had to
be punished. The youngster never forgot or forgave this, and a
year or so later, feeling himself growing in strength, he decided to
risk it again. He advanced toward the leader, "John L.," and shook
his head up and down two or three times, in the style recognized
among buffalo as a challenge. The big fellow was surprised, no
doubt. He gave a warning shake, but the other would not take
warning. Both charged. But, to the old bull's amazement, the
young one did not go down. What he lacked in weight he more
than made up in agility. Both went at it again, now desperately.
After two or three of these terrific shocks the old one realized that

he had not now his old-time strength and wind. As they pushed and parried, the young bull managed to get under the other, and with a tremendous heave actually pitched his huge body up into the air and dashed him down the hillside. Three times the old bull was thus thrown before he would yield, and then he sought to save his life in flight. But they were not now on the open plains; the pen was limited, and the victor was of a most ferocious temper. The keepers did what they could, but stout ropes and fences interposed were no better than straws. The old bull's body was at last left on the ground with sixty-three gashes, and his son reigned in his stead. This is one of the melancholy sides of animal life—the weak to the wall, the aged downed by the young. It has happened millions of times on the plains, but perhaps was never before so exactly rendered for human eyes to see.

A more peaceful and pastoral side of life is to be seen among the waterfowl ponds. At one time the park waters were a favorite resting place of the gulls and ducks that passed over in the migrating season; a few of the ducks remained to breed. But the encroachment of the city frightened all away, until the establishment of the park resulted in a new arrangement, whereby gulls, swans, ducks, geese, etc., instead of passing over in spring and fall merely, are induced to stay as permanent residents. Food, protection, and cover are provided for them, that they may live their lives before us; and in order that they may not forget their part of the supposed bargain, a deft, slight operation is performed on the tip of one wing. It leaves no sign of mutilation, but it effectually induces them to remain permanently in the park.

Among the birds of prey, many old friends of the woods and plains are to be seen, though not taking to their cage life as do the more cheerful waterfowl.

The familiar red-tailed buzzard is here, but his eye has ever kept the look of untamed savageness; he has no appearance of being even partly at home in his cage. None of his race has ever been known to accept submissively the prisoner's condition, so that the species does not breed in captivity, nor do his relatives and fellow captives, the buzzard hawk and the serpent eagle. Doubtless this is simply another case where it is necessary to restore the wild condition in order to know the perfect bird. Some day we may have a cage large enough to give them a chance really to use their wings, and then they may condescend to show us how their forbears built their nests and reared and trained their offspring for the chase.

The fine collection of wolves, still in small quarters, gives a good opportunity of seeing how near they are to dogs in their general habits and appearance.

Zoologists have long discussed the origin of the dog. Some consider it the descendant of a wolf; others, of an extinct species; and some say that the jackal is the wild stock it came from. There are many good arguments against the second theory. Today it is believed that either the wolf or the jackal was the wild ancestor of the dog. I am convinced that the jackal is the stock parent, though a strain of wolf blood has certainly been infused in some countries.

It long ago struck me that reversion is the best evidence in a discussion of this kind, and my own observations on dogs that have reverted, or gone back, to their ancestral form point very uniformly to one conclusion.

The general color of a wolf is grayish, with a black or dark tail tip, rarely with light-colored spots, or "bees," over its eyes, and with a height at the shoulder of about twenty-six inches.

The general color of a jackal is yellowish, with more or less white hair at the tip of its tail, and invariably with bees over its eyes. Its height is about twenty inches at the shoulder.

All the largest breeds of dogs show signs of overdevelopment, such as faulty teeth, superfluous toes, frail constitutions, etc. All dogs that have any white about them have at least a few white hairs in the tip of the tail; and when allowed to mongrelize freely —that is, to revert—the dog always becomes a small, yellowish animal, with brown bees over its eyes, a white tail tip, and a height at the shoulder of about twenty inches—that is, it resumes the jackal type.

Another argument, which I have not seen in print, is this: although the wolf was abundant in Europe during the old Stone Age, the dog was unknown till it appeared on the scene with the Neoliths, a race that came from the home of the jackal.

My observations on the habits are evidence for the jackal theory. Wolves rarely turn around before lying down; dogs and jackals usually do. Wolves rarely bark, while jackals, as is well known, do frequently bark after the manner of dogs.

While sketching among the jackals in the Jardin des Plantes, Paris, in 1895, I discovered an interesting bit of evidence on the question. Wolves' eyes are set obliquely—and dogs' eyes are set straight. Of the nine jackals then in the menagerie, two had their eyes set wolf fashion, and the remaining seven had them set like those of a dog. Of course, the fact that both styles are found in the same animal takes from its weight as proof, and yet great stress has been laid on this different angle of the eyes as an important difference between dog and wolf. What weight, then, this argument has, is for the jackal.

While making these notes among the animals of the Washington Zoo, I used to go at all hours to see them. Late one evening I sat down with some friends by the wolf cages, in the light of the full moon. I said, "Let us see whether they have forgotten the music of the West." I put my hands to my mouth and howled the hunting song of the pack. The first to respond was a coyote from the plains. He put up his muzzle and *yap-yapped* and howled. Next an old wolf from Colorado came running out, looked and listened earnestly and, raising her snout to the proper angle, she took up the wild strain. Then all the others came running out and joined in, each according to his voice, but all singing that wild-wolf hunting song, howling and yelling, rolling and swelling, high and low, in the cadence of the hills.

> They sang me their song of the West, the West:
>   They set all my feelings aglow;
> They stirred up my heart with their artless art,
>   And their song of the long ago.

Again and again they raised the cry, and sang in chorus till the whole moonlit woods around was ringing with the grim refrain—until the inhabitants in the near city must have thought all the beasts broken loose. But at length their clamor died away, and the wolves returned, slunk back to their dens, sadly I thought, as though they realized that they could indeed join in the hunting song as of old, but their hunting days were forever done.[1]

# 11.

# TWO LIFE HISTORIES:

### *Grizzly Bear and Moose*

THE range of the individual grizzly varies greatly with local conditions. In a rugged mountainous region where food abounds, it will not go half a dozen miles from a central point. In the days when it followed the buffalo herds, it probably went ten times as far, for unlike the black bear, it is, or was, at home on the plains. But a typical grizzly in ordinary mountain country today will ramble over a home region at least twenty-five miles across.

The ideal home of this animal is high, rolling uplands, where dry, open prairies are interspersed with rocky ridges and densely wooded thickets. Here it finds food in abundance as well as sunning places and shady retreats in which he can wallow in mud and coolness, and defy alike the overhot sun, the bot, the gnat, and the relentless mosquito.

Even in the days when it roved the wide plains, it was usually found in the bottom lands and places that had a vestige of cover rather than bold and bull-like on the level open.

It may visit, but it never stays long on bleak mountains above timberline. It is not content on broad, level wastes that are without cover or water. It is not happy in a big swamp where the footing is everywhere wet. Otherwise, it may be, or once might have been, looked for in all parts of its vast range where there was food, water, and shelter.

189

*Polar Bears*
sketches by E.T. Seton 1925

In general, the grizzly's habits resemble those of the black bear. Both are shy, but desperate fighters when cornered. Both are lovers of the twilight, but travel in full day or black night on occasion. They differ in this: the black bear rarely quits the woods; the grizzly often lives permanently in the open country.

Anything that any fourfoot will eat, we are safe to assume that the grizzly will consider food, be it grass, roots, berries, nuts, insects, honey, snakes, frogs, fish, birds, eggs, animals small or large from mice to sheep and cattle—yea, even though they have reached the potent stage called carrion.

Wild as the guesses have been when dealing with the size of a grizzly, they are safe and sane compared with those ventured on his weight. There is no reason to believe that a true grizzly ever weighed 1,500 pounds, or that any but the giants reach 1,000 pounds; 500 pounds is more nearly the average weight of the male and 400 of female.

In the Washington Zoo is the large grizzly from the Yellowstone Park. In September 1894 he weighed 730 pounds, and has since added considerably to his bulk. Of course, he is cage fat.

Each year the number of hunters increases; each year more deadly traps, subtler poisons, and more irresistible guns are out to get the grizzly. He has no chance at all to escape. There is no closed season, no new invulnerability to meet the new peril. He is absolutely at the mercy of those who know no mercy; and before five years more, I expect to learn that there are no more grizzlies left in the United States, except in the Yellowstone Park, that last blessed haven of the fugitive from inevitable and nearly universal destruction.

In Canada and Alaska things are not quite so bad. There has been a shrinkage of range, and there can be no doubt that in extensive areas the grizzly has been exterminated. But there are still enormous stretches of grizzly country in practically primitive condition.

The coming of the white man with his flocks of sheep and herds of cattle have made a far-reaching change in his habits. Sheep and cattle are of slower, stupider breed (than buffalo), and this led in sundry cases and diverse regions to the making of sheep killers and cattle-killing grizzly.

The sheep-killing grizzly was confined to the far Southwest, for the sufficient reason that sheep were not elsewhere introduced, except in unimportant numbers.

I am not a sheep owner and I do not love sheep. My sympathies are all with the forests—and the bear.

The cattle-killing grizzly is the lineal descendant and natural heir of the buffalo killer. But he has an easier job, for a range steer is a light matter compared with an old buffalo bull. Nevertheless, the grizzly could, and did, kill the latter. A cow or yearling heifer of the range breed must be a passing amusement.

Some individuals are much more given to meat diet than others, and such have become veritable nuisances on the cattle range near their headquarters.

Cattle-killing grizzlies are rare now, but undoubtedly they still exist. . . .

About 1880, grizzlies were very numerous in the country some sixty miles south of Helena. They used to come in there for the berries, but would occasionally kill cattle. When a beef was thus killed, Russel used to sit up over it in a tree.

One night a large silvertip came to the carcass. The watcher was ten feet up a small cottonwood. The bear smelt him and came sniffing up the wind to find him, but each time lost the trace as he got near. The scent seemed to go over his head. Several times this happened. Then, in determination to find his foe, he began to

break down the brush around. He would smash down a thicket
with great uproar and then remain still as death to see if the man
was flushed; then another, and again a wait. Sometimes he would
wait for three or four minutes without a move. In this way he
flattened all the brush for an acre about the hunter and the carcass, but the night was so dark that there was no opportunity for
a shot.

Another time a cow was killed by a grizzly, dragged halfway
across the river, and then left lying in the water; fifty yards away
was a high cut-bank covered with brush. It was not on the usual
trail of the bears, and as they could not climb up the face, Russel
decided to hide there and shoot from it. On getting ready to go,
however, he found that he had but one cartridge, and so gave up
the attempt. Next morning he learned that the grizzly had come,
but before feasting was careful to break down all the brush on this
commanding point, so that had the man been there, he would certainly have fallen into the power of the bear.

As a fitting finish to the section on food is a paragraph on the
food cache. Most animals whose food is subject to vast and seasonal
variation develop the thrifty habit of storing up surplus food for
a time of want. The grizzly is one of these, though his notion of
want is rarely more than two or three days ahead.

All animals with the storage habit have some way of marking
their cache, putting on it their property mark.

The wolverine may mark his cache with his anal ointment, the
fox uses his protometric musk for the same purpose, and the mountain lion piles brush on his, but the old grizzly uses fresh, clean
earth. . . .

Grizzlies cough, growl, grunt, roar, and sniff, in expression of
various feelings. If they have a love song, it has not yet been
recorded.

But the grizzly, in common with the black bear, has another

means of sending tidings to others of its race, and that is by the use of bear trees or signposts, also called "registers" and "measuring trees." I never had the luck to see a wild bear using them, but have once or twice seen the act in a zoo.

The bear has fixed pathways through the woods and over difficult places. These it will use for years, till they are deeply worn. In going up a bank, or over logs, it will put its feet into the same tracks each time till they become a kind of stairway.

It is a remarkable fact that although all animals make and use trails more or less, it is only those of the lower order, such as rodents, that take the trouble to repair or improve their trails. If a tree branch falls across a rabbit or beaver trail, it is cut in two; if a twig grows up, it is nipped off. But the bear, the wapiti, and the buffalo take no such trouble. If mere wear will improve their highway, it is improved, but if a tree fall across it or a self-rolled stone should block it, the lazy giant goes around the balk and strikes out a second trail.

Notwithstanding the sinister reputation that has won him the names *horribilis, grisly, ferox,* etc., the grizzly, according to all the best authorities, never attacks man, except when provoked. That is, he is a harmless, peaceful giant, perfectly satisfied to let you alone if you let him alone.

Even in the palmy days of the West, when he was the unquestioned monarch of the range, trapper and cowboy knew right well that they need only exercise a little self-restraint, show some decent courtesy to this big dignified giant in the fur cloak, and they need not fear but what he would respond.

One reads of grizzly bears that had been the terror of such and such a range for thirty or forty years, etc. But on what is the evidence of such great age founded? Little but guesswork.

Usually we find that a mammal normally attains an age which is four or five times the period they need to reach maturity, that is, puberty. A grizzly bear is fully grown and capable of breeding at four, certainly at five, years of age. Therefore, its life term should be about twenty, or not more than twenty-five years. . . .

While the story of Wahb was published as fiction, the incidents in it were from life. The most unusual of these was the last, the death of the old grizzly in the place of the poison gas. How near this is to the truth may be gathered from the following:

Death Gulch is a well-known small and gloomy ravine in the northeast corner of Yellowstone Park. Into this the wild things are tempted by promise of food, water, and shelter. But they are led into a bath of invisible poisonous vapor in which each, in turn, sinks down to sleep his last sleep.

Twice it has been investigated by members of the United States Geological Survey. In 1888 Walter H. Weed visited the place and wrote an account of it for *Science,* February 15, 1899. After commenting on the volcanic origin of the gulch formation, he says: "Although hot water no longer flows from these vents, gaseous emanations are now given off in considerable volume."

Weed says: "The gulch ends, or rather begins, in a scoop or basin about 250 feet above Cache Creek, and just below this was found the fresh body of a large bear, a silvertip grizzly, with the remains of a companion in an advanced stage of decomposition above him. Nearby were the skeletons of four more bears, with the bones of an elk a yard or two above, while in the bottom of the pocket were the fresh remains of several squirrels, rock hares and other small animals, besides numerous dead butterflies and insects. The body of the grizzly was carefully examined for bullet holes or other marks of injury, but showed no traces of violence, the only indication being a few drops of blood under the nose. It was evident that he had met his death but a short time before, as the carcass was still perfectly fresh, though offensive enough at the time of a later visit." . . .

The picture I form of him, with some personal experience, many campfire tales and much reading, is of a grand old monarch —alone, always alone—marching over the mountaintops, dignified and unafraid—Mishe Mokwa, the Great Bear of the Mountains, feeding on every living thing that grows, from mouse to moose, from millet to mushroom; accustomed to deference from every wild thing, unwilling to quarrel with man, but terrible when roused to fury or revenge.

In my story of Wahb, I have aimed to picture this fearless and unaggressive old giant, asking only to be let alone. No home has he. No grown bear has a home; that is, a den where he may always be found. But, like the buffalo and elk, he sleeps wherever night finds him. The mountain range is his home.

Retiring he always was, feeding or traveling chiefly by night and sleeping when the sun was high. A distinct dislike of public notice he always had; but more than ever today. For man, aggressive, brutal, and destructive, has forced him to change many of his ancient habits. The heedless bear that roamed the open and fed by day is gone. His place is taken by bears that feed secretly, silently, by night, in cover—always secretly.

The buffalo killer, usually a rare and sporty individual, is gone; he has given place to the cattle killer.

But the cattle killer, too, is marching on the sundown trail. A great shrinkage of the big bear's range is seen today, and a woeful change in the bear himself. All the old travelers, from Lewis and Clark to those of forty years ago, aver that the grizzly had little fear of man, and ofttimes claimed and received from him the right of way.

We have lived to see another mind in the king of the ranges; we find in him now the exemplar of an ancient law: the beasts are shy in proportion to their bigness, that is really in measure of man's eagerness to add them to his bag. The mouse will let you walk up within a few yards, will even run over your foot if you are still; the moose will flee on the slightest intimation that man is within a mile. And the grizzly, too, accepts the common greed. No longer the arrogant despot of all trails and ranges, he has retreated to secluded fastnesses, to wild and inaccessible regions of thicket and mountainside. He is changed in temper as in life, and the faintest whiff of man scent now is enough to drive him miles away.

And what is it that has made this change—that has turned the heart of the mountain terror and made him shyer than ever fawn or hare? The educating force was *modern guns*. Repeating rifles have instilled the idea that man is master—omnipotent, merciless —therefore, shun the onset that can end in only one way. The fallen monarch is become a fugitive in his own kingdom. In many parts of the country, particularly the South and East, his kind is extinct. In a little while he will have left the United States, or will continue only as a pensioner in the Yellowstone Park. And I, for one, would gladly see the total abolition of all bounty laws on the grizzly's head. I should welcome a movement to prevent his ex-

termination. His day and scepter are gone; right well he knows that; he is harmless now and is, moreover, a magnificent animal, whose extinction would be just such a loss to zoology as the destruction of St. Peter's would be to the world of art.

A fine bull moose shot near Kippewa, Quebec, by Mrs. Ernest Thompson Seton, September 25, 1905, in good condition, was black on forelegs, breast, shoulders, flanks, and hams, shading into rusty brown on the withers, back, neck, and head; palest on nose and lips, and shading into white on the belly; the insides of the ears also were whitish; the legs from the knees to the ground were of pale warm gray or caribou color. The appearance of this animal at a distance was that of a black beast, with brown head and white stockings. This is typical of all eastern moose. The coat fades toward springtime.

The sexes are much alike.

The calf is dull reddish brown without spots; it turns darker at three months. According to the Ottawa guides, the male calf is darker than the female, and less brown. The difference is obvious when there are twins. An ordinary bull moose stands six feet high at the withers.

Charles H. Stonebridge, of New York, tells me that, while hunting at Chesuncook Lake, Maine, in October 1897, he killed a bull moose that was six feet, eight inches at the withers after skinning.

Not many authentic weights of moose have been recorded, because of the difficulties of getting the scales and the moose together. For long, we had nothing but hunters' guesses, which, of course, are of the same order as fishermen's. Now, however we have some trustworthy evidence.

The only moose I ever killed gave 500 pounds (Fairbanks scales) of dressed meat, which, according to butchers' reckoning, would be a live weight of 900 pounds. As he lay, he measured six feet, two inches at the withers, which means about six feet alive. He was of medium size.

A marked peculiarity in the moose is the bell on the throat. I have examined many of these in the newly killed specimens and in the living animal, and could find nothing in them but a long dewlap of skin with appropriate blood vessels. Sometimes it is round; sometimes flat, lying the long way; sometimes flat the cross way of the animal's throat; sometimes simple; sometimes forked; sometimes hanging from the jaw, and sometimes from a long bladelike dewlap, but always without discernible scent glands. I have squeezed and worked them with my hands on the living moose, and have been unable to discover any smell or signs of exudation; or, indeed, any specialization that would afford a hint of their purpose. No one yet has given any satisfactory explanation of this curious dangler.

The "bell," as we have seen, is an extremely variable feature; it is found in the young of both sexes, but tends to disappear with age. Therefore, it may be a character that is being lost because it no longer answers any useful purpose.

The big bull moose shot at Chesuncook Lake by Charles H. Stonebridge had a twenty-inch bell, of which the hair was about four inches. The longest bell I ever heard of, however, was found on a cow moose. Ordinarily, it is eight or ten inches long; fourteen inches would be exceptional for even a bull; but this one was thirty-eight inches long, exclusive of the hair. The moose that wore it was shot by an Indian in eastern Manitoba.

No wild animal roams at random. All have a certain range that they consider home. Some have two—one for summer, the other for winter; these are called migratory animals. The moose has but one home, and to that it keeps the year round. As a general rule, the extent of an animal's range corresponds somewhat with its size. A deer's range is larger than that of a rabbit, because its wants are greater. Flesh eaters are, of course, on a different basis. The moose appears to be the widest ranger of the nonmigratory ruminants.

The Carberry Swamp, Manitoba, was the home of a small band of moose that never left its limits at any time, so far as I could learn; though it was but three miles wide by ten long. The moose that inhabit the east slopes of the Teton Mountains in Jackson Hole, Wyoming, are known to continue all year in a narrow belt about three miles by ten on the east of Jackson Lake.

Fred Reeves, my guide in the Caughawanna region of Quebec, says: "For five years I have known an old gray cow moose on a ridge between Green Lake and Blue Lake. It is a third of a mile broad and seven miles long."

Linklater, Reeves, and Mitigwab all agree that moose will not necessarily go half a mile from one place all summer; may spend their entire life within a ten-mile tract. But when chased in winter, they will travel fifteen or twenty miles and not return to the same place all winter afterward (unlike deer).

While the wolf and fox may greatly extend their home range in winter time, the moose and some others seem to restrict themselves to a smaller locality then than in summer—no doubt on account of the difficulty of traveling in the snow.

In the winter, according to all testimony, the moose is satisfied with so small a range that it is called the winter yard. This may be less even than fifty acres. Indeed, George H. Mearns writes me from Manitoba that he has known a family of four moose to pass all winter within a radius of 300 feet. Having found a suitable place to yard, a family will stay there until the snow is gone, the food fails, or they are driven out by hunters. I should think that ordinarily a moose, especially a cow, passes its life within ten miles of the spot where it was born.

There is one peculiarity of the moose range that is unique, at least among our deer. Many observers state that moose are *now found* in such and such a large region *where formerly they were unknown*. It has always seemed to me more likely that in these cases moose are *now common where formerly rare*. If moose can live there today, why not in primitive times?

What is the explanation of these definite movements? They are not of the nature of migrations, but rather are emigrations; and are not without parallel. Beaver, possum, white fox, red fox, white-tailed deer, and others are known to make similar changes of homeland; and in every case, the chief motive has apparently been the search for better food.

In a small lake on my homeland, the yellow lilies or spatter-docks were overabundant. To get rid of them, I mowed the leaves off as near the root as possible, using a scythe over the stern of the boat. After the first mowing, a second crop of leaves appeared in a month. But after the third mowing, no more came up, and the roots died, I suppose, of suffocation; the bed was destroyed.

In this, we may find one reason for the drift of the moose. Many guides have assured me that lily pads are an essential of moose diet. By overcropping the pads in a given region, the moose have killed the lily beds. Such an occurrence in a wide area might easily send the whole moose population on to another region, till lily beds had time to recuperate.

The antlers' size and shape have even less relation to the age of the animal than with the wapiti. After the third year, no one can tell the age by the antlers.

The young bull moose grows his first pair—two snags a few inches long—in his second summer, shedding them the following spring. Next year he grows his prongs, shedding them late the following winter or in spring. The third pair have a beginning of palmation. Thenceforth, each pair is more palmated and is dropped earlier—usually in January or February; but bulls of exceptional vigor drop their antlers as early as December. As with most male deer, the full development of the horns is attained about the seventh or eighth year; then comes a period of little change, followed, after three or four years, by a decline.

After the moose has grown old, or passed his vigor, the palmation becomes wider and the points shorter until, in very old but still-vigorous specimens, the upper part of the antler is merely scalloped along the edge. The moose killed by Mrs. Seton had the long brow tines displaced by a palmation that joined with the main web. This individual was past his prime, but still lusty. He had several battle scars on his shoulders, and his right ear was badly torn by some recent encounter.

The guides on the Ottawa claim that moose are right- and left-handed. A right-handed moose lies on his right side, and the effect on his growing horns is very marked, giving that one a twist.

The locked horns, so common among wapiti, caribou, whitetail, and blacktail deer, are also found among moose. One may wonder how these big, flat shovels can become entangled; and yet they do.

There are several cases on record, the most wonderful being the antlers of a pair of giants from Alaska. These I saw in Sheard's establishment in Tacoma. The man who found them brought them out at great cost. He thought he had a wonderful prize, yet Sheard remarked: "I will give half as much more to anyone who will unlock these antlers without using a saw. As they stand, they are an unwieldy curiosity which no man wishes to buy, but separated, each will make a fine trophy."

The antlers of the bull moose are developed for battle with his own kind. As soon as the rut is over, they are of little use; and nature, true to her principle of economy, proceeds to get rid of them. The useless lumber is dropped in the depth of winter for, notwithstanding the voice of the people (which is said to be the voice of God), they are *not* used for shoveling snow. As the hunters say, when the sap begins to flow in the trees, the sap begins to run in the antlers of the moose. They sprout afresh in April; earlier if the moose be very vigorous; later if he be a weakling. Yet he has not been by any means disarmed; for his mighty forefeet, armed with a pair of stubby bayonets of horn, are ample protection against any wolf or bear that might dare to assail him or the family in his care.

In three months the antlers are finished and the velvet begins to shed off, showing the white, bony structure beneath. By September the antlers are sunburnt to a deep brown, except the tips, which are white and polished from being rubbed on the brush and trees.

How are we to know there are moose in a swamp, since they rarely give us a chance to see them?

The sure, certain, lasting sign is the "fumet" or dung balls. These resemble in character those of large deer, but their size is distinctive.

Another important sign is the track. "Like the track of a cow, but sharper," is the earliest description I ever heard of it. This sign is soon changed by weather, and tells the observer how much time has elapsed since the moose was here.

While feeding in winter, the moose will chisel the bark off saplings with its front teeth, as indeed do most deer; but the size of the mark and the height from the ground will usually tell if such a mark was made by a moose. It is often remarked that only one side of the bark is taken, and therefore the tree survives.

The nipping of twigs also at a great height is an important moose sign.

Other telltale marks are the scrapings of the trees with the antlers and the deliberate crossing of bogs. In this last respect, the moose is second only to the caribou. An important sign in fall is the wallow. The bull moose makes a wallow—a "soil" or "gross," it is called in the Old World. At a chosen spot in the thicket he digs and paws mud, and irrigates it abundantly till it is a mud bath with every intensified odor that his physical personality can contribute. In this he wallows and plays to his infinite satisfaction; and with results which seem to prove that it does not in the least repel the lady of his choice.

I have seen this wallow or soiling pit many times in America, especially on the Ottawa.

On September 27, 1905, on Caughawanna, forty miles north of Deux Rivières, Quebec, I found and photographed a fine big specimen. It smelled horrible.

All the guides are familiar with the wallows, and do not consider that these have special reference to the mating season.

The food of the moose is browse, twigs, and leaves of many hardwoods, their particular favorite being moosewood or striped maple. Yet they do eat grass, as I have many times witnessed.

They do not kneel for it, as is stated; but often eat like a horse, merely bending their necks if the grass is high, or adopting an inelegant giraffelike straddle if it be low.

Although they feed chiefly on twigs and bark in winter, I observed that about Carberry, they devoured quantities of equisetum, or joint grass, which sticks up through the snow.

In the summer, the favorite food of the moose is the lily pads and lily roots. In pursuit of these, the whole moose population seems to gather along the rivers and ponds. Here they feast; and at the same time, are so much in the water and in the wind that they experience much relief from the pest of mosquitoes.

In winter, the moose gather in small herds of five to twenty-five; and, having found a sheltered part of the woods where birch, willow, poplar, moosewood, grass, equisetum, and pea vine abound, will settle down there; not moving half a mile away until the food supply is eaten out.

The deeper the snow, the more marked are the many intersecting pathways made and the area so marked is known as the "moose yard," discussed elsewhere.

The enemies of the moose are, in order of danger: man, mosquitoes, deer flies, ticks, disease, deep snow, wolves, bears, and cougars. Without doubt, man should stand first, since pump guns have come into use.

Mosquitoes are dangerous only inasmuch as they drive the moose out of the woods into the open or into the water, where they are easily found and destroyed by man, during the summer months. So far as known, the actual drain of blood sucking does not seriously injure the moose.

Little is on record concerning ticks and disease, beyond the fact that moose are subject to these.

## *A Gift of Manitou*

In all the vast region (of the range of the moose) the moose is, or was, the Indians' staff of life. What the buffalo was to the Plains, the whitetail deer to the Southern woods, and the caribou to the Barrens, the moose is to this great Northern belt of swamp and timberland. It stands forever between man and the great, inaccessible world of crude plant nutrients, transmuting them into terms of human food.

It is the creature that enables the native to live. Assisted in warm weather by various fish, it bears practically the burden of their support. Its delicious steaks are their staple food, but its nose or muffle is a delicacy. Its hide furnishes the best clothing and moccasin leather, or provides snowshoes that enable the hunter to kill more moose. Its back sinew is the sewing thread of the country; its horns and bones make tools for cutting ice or dressing hides; its hoofs can be converted into rattles; and its coarse, bristly mane, six inches long, and white except the tips, furnishes raw material for embroidery. When dyed with native dyes, and skillfully worked into leather and birchbark, these bristles are as effective for decoration as porcupine quills—are indeed often mistaken for them by the uninitiated.

The moose-calling hunter is one who, with a birchbark trumpet, imitates the bellow of the cow moose and tempts the bull forth into plain view for an easy shot.

Though the least unsportsmanlike, it is the most popular method of pursuit, because it is the most effectual way of getting a bull moose. Fortunately, it can be practiced only for about a month, at the beginning of the season, and in exactly the right weather and surroundings. Dead calm is essential. If there be wind from the moose to you, he cannot hear your call; if it be from you to the moose, he smells you and flies to far regions. In a calm, the call can be heard for miles—so far, indeed, that even if the moose came directly and quickly, he might be an hour or more getting to you. I once called from a hill at sunset, and learned later that friends four miles away heard me distinctly. Therefore, a moose, with his keener hearing, might have heard it five or six miles off.

The experienced moose caller begins very low, as there is always a possibility of a bull lurking in some near thicket. He calls not more than once in ten minutes; some think every twenty minutes often enough. This is probably so, once the response has come. The bull's answer is a deep, long grunt, varied with the snapping of branches as he plunges forward through the woods, stopping at times to thrash some bush in his course. When at length, in the last dim afterglow, the much-heralded monster heaves his bulk into view, overtopping the shrubbery like an elephant, looming huge and black against the last streak of red light, he affords one of the most impressive sights in the animal world.

No matter how much we may be expecting his coming, it is always a thrilling surprise. We knew how big he was, yet how startlingly huge he looks! And those antlers—a heavy burden for a man—he switches about as easily as an Indian does the eagle feathers in his hair.

By softly modulated squeals, whines, and other sounds suggestive of an amorous female, a skillful caller can decoy the great beast within a few yards; and get the chance to see, shoot, or immortalize the giant, according to the mood and purpose of the party.

## *The Moose I Called*

Some forty miles north of Mattawa, Quebec, it happened; and in the September of 1905. Two good friends, Mr. and Mrs. W. E. Bemis of New York, with my wife and self, were camping in the moose range, rejoicing in the daily small exploits of finding flowers, moss, squirrel doings, bear sign, wolf sign, and in hearing nightly soft, far moaning of the timber wolf.

But our two friends were there to get a moose. Indian, French, and American guides were with us; and our evening talk by the blazing pine knots was of record heads and moose calls.

"Mebbe so you can call?" said the French guide politely.

"Yes," I said. "I can a little." Which was true, for I had learned the moose calling rather as an illustration for my platform work. I had called moose, but never to their death.

The half-breed handed me his birchen horn. I gave a few grunts, then three bellows—the last long and loud—the ringing call of a cow moose in search of a mate. Then I gave the deep *oo-wah, oo-wah* of the bull, and slashed the brush with a piece of thin board that lay at hand.

"Very good," said the Frenchman; but the Indian said: "Too loud—cow call more soft."

"The horn is new to me. Tomorrow I shall make my own horn and do it better," was my reply.

Next day, Will Bemis wounded a moose, but it got away. The guide said it was only scratched; but Will was a dead shot—at target practice, at least—and was certain it was *his* moose. The guide was rebellious, and refused to do the hard trailing that would be entailed by a follow-up.

"Seton, won't you follow that moose for me?"

"Yes," I said, for trailing was one of my specialties, and I was glad to please my friend.

It was straight, hard trailing over granite ridges, bare rocky ground, through swamps and slashings. At first there was a faint splash of blood at long intervals; then, at an alder thicket, I found where the bull had rubbed himself, and I was able to announce a shoulder wound "but so little blood that I think it is only a scratch."

Still I followed, sometimes with great difficulty, where dry leaves were deep or rocks abundant. Sometimes other trails crossed it, but I kept on for a mile and a half. By this time, my friend was played out, for he weighed over 200 pounds, and was desk soft.

"See," I said, "there is no blood at all. The moose is striding along as usual; but I will follow until I am certain," thinking I might sight the bull in some open stretch or burnt land.

So away I went for nearly two miles more, and then I came to an alder swamp, where the moose had settled down comfortably to feed. I never saw him, but now I knew that the guide was right.

On the back trail, I met the guide, and the one low, soft grunt he gave at my report was the equivalent of "I told you so; now you will trust the guide next time." He liked me after that.

By the fire, that night, I fashioned a birchbark horn of my own. It was of regular size, but only one thickness, and sewn with wattap (spruce roots). The Indian watched me and grunted approval. Then I took ink, and on it drew two dancing medicine men, each with a moose's mask and horns. The Indian shook his head and said: "Bad medicine," which means a hoodoo. "No," I said, "good medicine," which means a mascot. Still the Indian shook his head.

Next day, it was my wife's turn to try for a bull. She was not blood athirst, but it seemed her duty to our host. She and I and the youngest guide set out per canoe for Foley's Lake, a small, sedgy pond seven silent miles away. There was but one gun in the party—the carbine that my wife had used in the Rockies with success. I took my hoodoo horn. The guide and I paddled.

The red sun was purpling the tall, black masts of a last-year's forest fire as we reached the silent lake. I put the hoodoo horn to my lips, and gave a short, hankering grunt. Then another, in case a bull might be very near. But the silence was complete.

For fifteen minutes I waited. Then, after a couple of peevish grunts, slowly weaving figures-of-eight in the air with the trumpet mouth, I gave the long, hankering cow call, the love bellow, the plaint of a maiden all forlorn.

"That's all right," said the guide, "only don't do it any louder."

For twenty minutes by the watch I waited. The silence was blank; the forest seemed steeped in it.

Then again I raised the horn, and after three petulant grunts made the magic figure in the air, as I poured out the sad, sad plaint of a cow moose—willing, but unmated.

The sun was gone. The long, low lights of the west were fading when, from a ridge a mile or two away, the first sound came that we had heard from the woods—the scratching of a tree trunk, the smashing of smaller branches.

"Sounds almost like a bear," whispered the guide. Then we heard the slashing of brushwood half a mile away. And finally a deep, grunted *oo-wah, oo-wah.*

"Bull—bull moose," whispered the guide. We waited ten minutes, then I used the horn, giving out softly a whining, hankering *errr-errr.*

After five minutes of anxious waiting, the willows in a swamp

200 yards away were seen to wave. A minute later, out in marvelous silence there strode a huge bull moose.

How big and gray he looked! What a massive neck! And high above was a pair of yellow-brown antlers, fringed with ivory points. They looked like record breakers, and the guide whispered: "A big fellow! A regular buster! Get ready for him!"

We steadied the canoe as the girlish figure in the bow arose and prepared to shoot.

On came the bull, striding and fearless, but silent. On, on, till only sixty yards away.

"Take him now," breathed the guide.

The rifle spoke. The big brute, stung and astonished, wheeled around, then stood again. A second shot, and he trotted into the bushes as though untouched. But a low crash sounded among the alders. A deep *ugh* came from the place.

"He's down," exclaimed the guide.

We landed quickly. From the bushes came a long, low moan, and another. "Oh, let me get another shot! I can't stand to have him tortured," said a female voice.

We pushed cautiously forward. The monster was down, but the big head swung up spasmodically from time to time. A cautious crawl-up, the rifle cracked, and the chapter ended not more than five minutes from the first approach.

That night I heard the guides discussing me. They spoke in French and were not guarded in their speech. The Indian was puzzled over the success of the hoodoo horn. The guide of the wounded-moose episode was frankly for me; but the French half-breed, beaten in his argument against me, said in Quebec patois:

"Well, I don't care. He's not as good as a real guide."

I felt happy. He was praising me with faint damns.

I have never called another moose to his death. Thoughtful men call it foul play.[1]

# 12.

# A HORSE STORY

## The Horse As Mammal

I F *the domestic quadrupeds were ranged in line according to their anatomical affinity, the cat would probably be found at one end and the horse at the other. The cat with eighteen toes, the horse with but four; the cat with a supple form, its manifold muscles, and its infinity of complex movements and positions, the horse with muscles and bones greatly reduced in number and its movements and positions almost limited to those required for mere locomotion.*

*The horse's characteristic external features are so well known that they need not here be enlarged upon.*[1]

## Coaly-bay, the Outlaw Horse

Five years ago in the Bitterroot Mountains of Idaho there was a beautiful little foal. His coat was bright bay; his legs, mane, and tail were glossy black—coal black and bright bay—so they named him "Coaly-bay," which sounds like "Kolibey," which is an Arab title of nobility, and those who saw the handsome colt, and did not know how he came by the name, thought he must be of Arab blood. No doubt he was, in a far-away sense; just as all our best horses have Arab blood, and once in a while it seems to come out strong and show in every part of the creature, in his frame, his power, and his wild, free-roving spirit.

Coaly-bay loved to race like the wind, he gloried in his speed, his tireless legs, and when careering with the herd of colts they met a fence or ditch, it was as natural to Coaly-bay to overleap it as it was for the others to sheer off.

So he grew up strong of limb, restless of spirit, and rebellious at any thought of restraint. Even the kindly curb of the hay yard or the stable was unwelcome, and he soon showed that he would rather stand all night in a driving storm than be locked in a comfortable stall where he had no vestige of liberty he loved so well.

He became very clever at dodging the horse wrangler, whose job it was to bring the horse herd to the corral. The very sight of that man set Coaly-bay agoing. He became what is known as a "quit-the-bunch"—that is, a horse of such independent mind that he will go his own way the moment he does not like the way of the herd.

So each month the colt became more set on living free, and more cunning in the means he took to win his way. Far down in his soul, too, there must have been a streak of cruelty, for he stuck at nothing and spared no one that seemed to stand between him and his one desire.

When he was three years of age, just in the perfection of his young strength and beauty, his real troubles began, for now his owner undertook to break him to ride. He was as tricky and vicious as he was handsome, and the first day's experience was a terrible battle between the horse trainer and the beautiful colt.

But the man was skillful. He knew how to apply his power, and all the wild plunging, bucking, rearing, and rolling of the wild one had no desirable result. With all his strength the horse was hopelessly helpless in the hands of the skilled horseman, and Coaly-bay was so far mastered at length that a good rider could use him. But each time the saddle went on, he made a new fight. After a few months of this the colt seemed to realize that it was useless to resist, it simply won for him lashings and spurrings, so he pretended to reform. For a week he was ridden each day and not once did he buck, but on the last day he came home lame.

His owner turned him out to pasture. Three days later he seemed all right; he was caught and saddled. He did not buck, but within five minutes he went lame as before. Again he was turned out to pasture, and after a week, saddled, only to go lame again.

His owner did not know what to think, whether the horse really had a lame leg or was only shamming, but he took the first chance to get rid of him, and though Coaly-bay was easily worth fifty dollars, he sold him for twenty-five. The new owner felt he had a bargain, but after being ridden half a mile Coaly-bay went lame. The rider got off to examine the foot, whereupon Coaly-bay broke away and galloped back to his old pasture. Here he was caught, and the new owner, being neither gentle nor sweet, applied spur without mercy, so that the next twenty miles was covered in less than two hours and no sign of lameness appeared.

Now they were at the ranch of the new owner. Coaly-bay was led from the door of the house to the pasture, limping all the way, and turned out. He limped over to the other horses. On one side of the pasture was the garden of a neighbor. This man was very proud of his fine vegetables and had put a six-foot fence around the place. Yet the very night after Coaly-bay arrived, certain of the horses got into the garden somehow and did a great deal of damage. But they leaped out before daylight and no one saw them.

The gardener was furious, but the ranchman stoutly maintained that it must have been some other horses, since his were behind a six-foot fence.

Next night it happened again. The ranchman went out very early and saw all his horses in the pasture, with Coaly-bay behind them. His lameness seemed worse now instead of better. In a few days, however, the horse was seen walking all right, so the ranchman's son caught him and tried to ride him. But this seemed too good a chance to lose; all his old wickedness returned to the horse; the boy was bucked off at once and hurt. The ranchman himself now leaped into the saddle; Coaly-bay bucked for ten minutes, but finding he could not throw the man, he tried to crush his leg against a post, but the rider guarded himself well. Coaly-bay reared and threw himself backward; the rider slipped off, the horse fell, jarring heavily, and before he could rise the man was in the saddle again. The horse now ran away, plunging and bucking; he stopped short, but the rider did not go over his head, so Coaly-bay turned, seized the man's foot in his teeth, and but for heavy blows on the nose would have torn him dreadfully. It was quite clear now that Coaly-bay was an "outlaw"—that is, an incurably vicious horse.

The saddle was jerked off, and he was driven, limping, into the pasture.

The raids on the garden continued, and the two men began to quarrel over it. But to prove that his horses were not guilty the ranchman asked the gardener to sit up with him and watch. That night, as the moon was brightly shining, they saw not all the horses, but Coaly-bay, walk straight up to the garden fence—no sign of a limp now—easily leap over it, and proceed to gobble the finest things he could find. After they had made sure of his identity, the men ran forward. Coaly-bay cleared the fence like a deer, lightly raced over the pasture to mix with the horse herd, and when the men came near him he had—oh, such an awful limp.

"That settles it," said the rancher. "He's a fraud, but he's a beauty, and good stuff, too."

"Yes, but it settles who took my garden truck," said the other.

"Wall, I suppose so," was the answer, "but luk a here, neighbor,

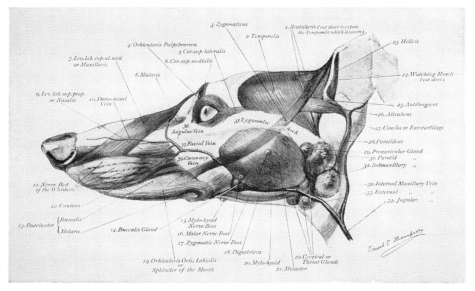

Anatomy of a greyhound's head

Hair pattern of a wolf

*Lobo*

*Sandhill stag*

Sat. Aug. 6.    Among the Bears.

At 9.30 am. a short fat black bear came. He was very nervous, running to a distance at each slight sound — sketch & foto . He was so timid that all nervousness left me .

At 10, a medium sized short haired sleek looking black-bear appeared. + no 1 ran away at once but I got both on one plate . He left at 10.10.

no 2

At 11 an old she-bear with the lame cub known as little Johnny - came I took fots etc . They went away in 5 minutes , frightened by a slight sound that I made

At 11.10 Saw a large black bear in the near woods, but he seemed afraid to come out

At 11.40 A large cinnamon came to the pile. (2 fotos) He stayed 20 minutes .

All these bears came noiselessly as shadows their tread gave out no sound that I could detect . I could hear the squirrels scampering over the dead leaves 300 yards away — But even the great sleepy cinnamon's tread gave no notice of his approach, he simply came

*From the Yellowstone Park diary of 1897*

*Female caribou*

*Bighorn sheep*

*Grouse*

*Identification of birds by pattern rather than by color; a method introduced by Seton*

# Studies in caribou attitudes

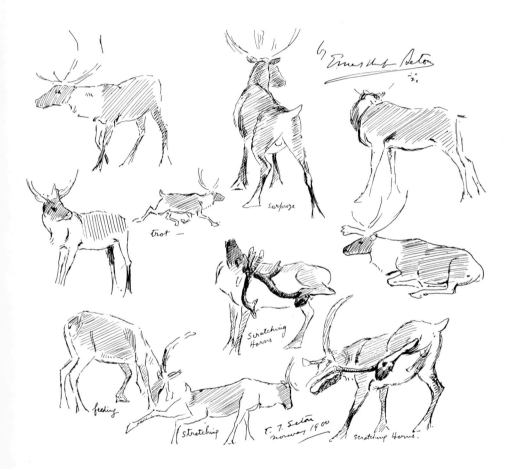

*by Ernest Thompson Seton*

surprise

trot

Scratching
Horns

feeding

Stretching

E. T. Seton
Norway 1900

scratching Horns.

From instantaneous photographs by Muybridge

*Attitudes of a hound running*

you ain't lost more'n ten dollars in truck. That horse is easily worth—a hundred. Give me twenty-five dollars, take the horse, an' call it square."

"Not much I will," said the gardener. "I'm out twenty-five dollars' worth of truck; the horse ain't worth a cent more. I take him and call it even."

And so the thing was settled. The ranchman said nothing about Coaly-bay being vicious as well as cunning, but the gardener found out, the very first time he tried to ride him, that the horse was as bad as he was beautiful.

Next day a sign appeared on the gardener's gate:

FOR SALE

First-class horse, sound and gentle.     $10.00

Now, at this time a band of hunters came riding by. There were three mountaineers, two men from the city, and the writer of this story. The city men were going to hunt bear. They had guns and everything needed for bear hunting, except bait. It is usual to buy some worthless horse or cow, drive it into the mountains where the bears are, and kill it there. So, seeing the sign up, the hunters called to the gardener: "Haven't you got a cheaper horse?"

The gardener replied: "Look at him there, ain't he a beauty? You won't find a cheaper horse if you travel a thousand miles."

"We are looking for an old bear bait, and five dollars is our limit," replied the hunter.

Horses were cheap and plentiful in that country, buyers were scarce. The gardener feared that Coaly-bay would escape. "Wall, if that's the best you can do, he's yourn."

The hunter handed him five dollars, then said: "Now, stranger, bargain's settled. Will you tell me why you sell this fine horse for five dollars?"

"Mighty simple. He can't be rode. He's dead lame when he's going your way and sound as a dollar going his own; no fence in the country can hold him; he's a dangerous outlaw. He's wickeder nor old Nick."

"Well, he's an almighty handsome bear bait," and the hunters rode on.

Coaly-bay was driven with the pack horses, and limped dreadfully on the trail. Once or twice he tried to go back, but he was easily turned by the men behind him. His limp grew worse, and toward night it was painful to see him.

The leading guide remarked: "That thar limp ain't no fake. He's got some deep-seated trouble."

Day after day the hunters rode farther into the mountains, driving the horses along and hobbling them at night. Coaly-bay went with the rest, limping along, tossing his head and his long splendid mane at every step. One hunter tried to ride him and nearly lost his life, for the horse seemed possessed of a demon as soon as the man was on his back.

The road grew harder as it rose. A very bad bog had to be crossed one day. Several horses were mired in it, and as the men rushed to the rescue, Coaly-bay saw his chance to escape. He wheeled in a moment and turned himself from a limping, low-headed, sorry, bad-eyed creature into a high-spirited horse. Head and tail aloft now, shaking their streamers in the wind, he gave a joyous neigh and, without a trace of lameness, dashed for his home 100 miles away, threading each narrow trail with perfect certainty, though he had seen them but once before, and in a few minutes he had steamed away from their sight.

The men were furious, but one of them, saying not a word, leaped on his horse—to do what? Follow that free ranging racer? Sheer folly. Oh, no! he knew a better plan. He knew the country. Two miles around by the trail, half a mile by the rough cut-off that he took, was Panther Gap. The runaway must pass through that, and Coaly-bay raced down the trail to find the guide below awaiting him. Tossing his head with anger, he wheeled on up the trail again, and within a few yards recovered his monotonous limp and evil expression. He was driven into camp, and there he vented his rage by kicking in the ribs of a harmless little packhorse.

This was bear country, and the hunters resolved to end his dangerous pranks and make him useful once. They dared not catch him—it was not really safe to go near him—but two of the guides drove him to a distant glade where bears abounded. A thrill of pity came over me as I saw that beautiful, untamable creature going away with his imitation limp.

"Ain't you coming along?" called the guide.

"No, I don't want to see him die," was the answer. Then, as the tossing head was disappearing, I called: "Say, fellows, I wish you would bring me that mane and tail when you come back!"

Fifteen minutes later a distant rifle crack was heard, and in my mind's eye I saw that proud head and those superb limbs, robbed of their sustaining, indomitable spirit, falling flat and limp—to suffer the unsightly end of fleshy things. Poor Coaly-bay; he would not bear the yoke. Rebellious to the end, he had fought against the fate of all his kind. It seemed to me the spirit of an eagle or a wolf it was that dwelt behind those full, bright eyes—that ordered all his wayward life.

I tried to put the tragic finish out of mind, and had not long to battle with the thought; not even one short hour, for the men came back.

Down the long trail to the west they had driven him; there was no chance for him to turn aside. He must go on, and the men behind felt safe in that.

Farther away from his old home on the Bitterroot River he had gone each time he journeyed. And now he had passed the high divide and was keeping the narrow trail that leads to the valley of bears and on to Salmon River, and away to the open, wild Columbian Plains, limping sadly as though he knew. His glossy hide flashed back the golden sunlight, still richer than it fell, and the men behind followed like hangmen in the death train of a nobleman condemned—down the narrow trail till it opened into a little beaver meadow, with rank rich grass, a lovely mountain stream and winding bear paths up and down the waterside.

"Guess this'll do," said the older man. "Well, here goes for a sure death or a clean miss," said the other confidently and, waiting till the limper was out in the middle of the meadow, he gave a short, sharp whistle. Instantly Coaly-bay was alert. He swung and faced his tormentors, his noble head erect, his nostrils flaring; a picture of horse beauty—yes, of horse perfection.

The rifle was leveled, the very brain its mark, just on the cross line of the eyes and ears, that meant sure, sudden, painless death.

The rifle cracked. The great horse wheeled and dashed away. It was sudden death or miss—and the marksman *missed*.

Away went the wild horse at his famous best, not for his eastern home, but down the unknown western trail, away and away; the pine woods hid him from view, and left behind was the rifleman vainly trying to force the empty cartridge from his gun.

Down the trail with an inborn certainty he went, and on through the pines, then leaped a great bog, and splashed an hour later through the limpid Clearwater and on, responsive to some unknown guide that subtly called him from the farther west. And so he went till the dwindling pines gave place to scrubby cedars and these in turn were mixed with sage, and onward still, till the far-away flat plains of Salmon River were about him, and ever on, tireless as it seemed, he went, and crossed the canyon of the mighty Snake, and up again to the high plains where the wire fence still is not, and on, beyond the Buffalo Hump, till moving specks on the

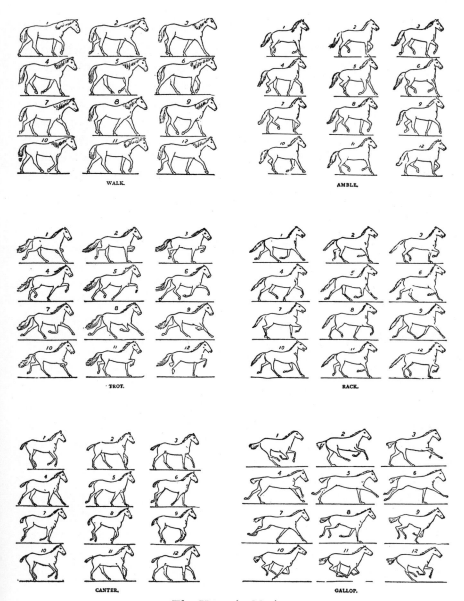

The Horse in Motion

far horizon caught his eager eyes, and coming on and near, they moved and rushed aside to wheel and face about. He lifted up his voice and called to them, the long shrill neigh of his kindred when they bugled to each other on the far Chaldean plains; and back their answer came. This way and that they wheeled and sped and caracoled, and Coaly-bay drew nearer, called and gave the counter-signs his kindred know, till of this they were assured—he was their kind, he was of the wild free blood that man had never tamed. And when the night came down on the purpling plain, his place was in the herd as one who after a long, hard journey in the dark had found his home.

There you may see him yet, for still his strength endures, and his beauty is not less. The riders tell me they have seen him many times by Cedra. He is swift and strong among the swift ones, but it is that flowing mane and tail that mark him from afar.

There on the wild, free plains of sage he lives: the stormwind smites his glossy coat at night and the winter snows are driven hard on him at times; the wolves are there to harry all the weak ones of the herd, and in spring the mighty grizzly, too, may come to claim his toll. There are no luscious pastures made by man, no grain foods; nothing but the wild, hard hay, the wind and the open plains, but here at last he found the thing he craved—the one worth all the rest. Long may he roam—this is my wish, and this— that I may see him once again in all the glory of his speed with his black mane on the wind, the spur galls gone from his flanks, and in his eye the blazing light that grew in his far-off forebears' eyes as they spurned Arabian plains to leave behind the racing wild beast and the fleet gazelle—yes, too, the driving sandstorm that overwhelmed the rest, but strove in vain on the dusty wake of the desert's highest born.[2]

# 13.

# A DOG STORY

### Hank and Jeff

*A group of hunters about the campfire they were—one spoke about swapping dogs, much as he would horses or cows. Then a silent man growled out: "No man ever gave up his dog—if it was really, truly his dog."*

*This struck a chord of memory in my heart, and I told this tale as it came to me long years before.*

It was in the wild, romantic days of eighty years ago, when the Ohio River flowed through unbroken, glorious woods, when Kentucky was one great game field. Here, on the lower Kentucky River, in his lonely cabin, lived Jeff Garvin, a grizzled old hunter, with no company but a big brindled bearhound whose name was Hank.

Very close were Jeff and Hank. Night and day their lives were the same. They shared the same food and the same perils. More than once, when the hunter's arm had failed, it was staunch old Hank that bore the brunt and saved him. Never once had they been apart from the day when first, as a lubberly pup, Garvin carried him from his mother's kennel.

Their living came from the woods and the streams; deer, bear, and wild turkeys abounded. When they wanted meat, all Garvin needed to do was to take down the trusty rifle, call Hank, and within a mile or two their wants were amply supplied.

221

In the winter he trapped a few furs. Those, with bear and buckskins, were swapped at the trading store, twenty miles down the river, for powder, tobacco, tea, and such few things as the forest did not furnish for their needs.

In autumn, when the woods abounded in food and the bears were fat, it was Garvin's custom to kill about twenty fine black fellows, and smoke their hams for a food supply to carry him over next winter, spring, and summer.

He was very expert at smoking hams. Garvin-cured hams were readily accepted by the trader on account. But a bear's ham is heavy, and four times heavy when you must be your own pack horse over twenty miles of rugged trail through heavy woods. The hams, therefore, were used at home, "a specialty of the house," when rare strangers called, or a satisfying staple for himself and dog.

It was in the fall of 1848. Garvin had stocked his smokehouse with twenty hams, mostly small, for these are best. The smoking had taken a month or more; but now that the nights were cool, the meat was safe. Garvin let the fire go out, and enjoyed the vista of smoky hams that greeted the eye as he opened the heavy door. Very heavy was that door of hickory splits, and strong as the walls that made the smokehouse, for there were thieves to be reckoned with—not two-legged; in those days, man was the scarcest animal in the country, except woman—but four-footed robbers—nothing less than bears themselves.

There was no reason to fear them when Hank and Jeff were in the neighborhood, but the hunter and his dog were often away for a week at a time. Therefore the smokehouse was built like a pier dock, with heavy, close logs over, under, and around. On the roof was a smoke hole with a hatch that was hung nearly balanced with a pulley rope. It stayed where placed for a while, but slowly settled down unless propped. It was closed at other times to keep out small marauders; the wall and overhang kept bears away.

It was early in November when Garvin went in to pick a ham for use. He was surprised to see that one peg was empty. He counted the hams—there were nineteen. He looked about carefully. There was no sign of burglary; doors, walls, and roof were all in perfect order. He searched about for tracks, but found none.

He called Hank. The dog was busy chewing an old bear skull, and came slowly.

"Here, Hank, smell him out, sic 'em. Where is he?"

The dog obeyed, sniffed all about the cabin, and circled farther off; then without apparent interest went back to the bear skull. Garvin was puzzled, and asked himself whether there were really twenty hams; maybe he had miscounted. But no—all honest normal bears wear their hams in pairs, and here was an odd ham.

Their cabin door was only loosely closed at night. Hank slept on a bearskin by his master's couch. At the slightest noise he would get up, scratch the door open, and challenge or assail any creature, man or beast, that might on rare occasions come near.

It seemed impossible for a burglar to enter the smokehouse, which was close by. The mystery was unexplained.

Three days later, Garvin entered the place and found another ham gone. Again he sought for clues, again he and the dog searched for tracks. They found none, and so Hank returned to an old bear hide that he had been chewing on behind the cabin.

A few days afterward, Garvin and Hank set out toward the mountains on a preliminary trapping round, making a few deadfalls ready so they would be purged of the man taint by rain, and weathered before the cold winter should come and make trapping profitable.

That night, as they were about to turn in by the campfire, they were aroused by the scream of a panther not far away. They were familiar with these unearthly yells and quite unafraid. But there was a strange new note in this; at times it was like the agonizing scream of a madwoman.

Hank ran off, baying loud defiance to the challenge. And soon the sound of the baying hound and the screaming panther died away.

Hank was gone so long that Garvin fell asleep. In the morning, the dog was back, apparently unharmed, but seeming dull and listless. Jeff offered some venison, part of his own meal, but the dog seemed not hungry. He barely mouthed the juicy steak.

There was something disquieting about the whole affair. Garvin could not help remembering that an Indian devil was said to haunt these hills; and some of these yells were unlike any panther call he had ever heard.

Instead of going farther into the hills, he turned homeward, and by afternoon was back at his cabin. A general inspection showed another ham gone. Garvin was furious now. He scouted about for tracks, without success. He and Hank quartered the ground near and far, but they found nothing unusual. The smoke-house door was untouched, the house intact, and yet another ham was gone. There were no bear tracks or man tracks near, and Hank was much more interested in mauling that old bear skull with gritting teeth and rolling eyes than in searching for an impossible track.

That night Garvin was deeply depressed. He cleaned his rifle and smoked long and idly. He had heard often of spooks and warlocks in the Kentucky Mountains not so far away. He had heard of Indian devils, catamounts and medicine bears. And all these weird creatures for once almost seemed real in the light of the recent doings. For they seemed the only explanation of the continual losses and that uncanny voice.

Hank, too, seemed deeply moved by something of the sort. He

curled his brawny brown form on the bearskin as usual, and slept. But his sleep was broken with short whines and twitchings of his legs. Once or twice he yelped as though in pain. So Garvin muttered at last: "I wonder if that cussed panther hurt him, or maybe he's got spiked."

He examined the dog's body and limbs, but found no injury. Hank responded to this care by licking his master's hand; then curled up again for slumber.

But his sleep was broken and fitful as before. Garvin himself was wakeful. He sat up in his bunk, and something like superstitious fear possessed him as he watched the indomitable old bearhound tremble and whine in his sleep.

As Garvin stared uneasily, a thought came to him. "That old medicine man at Scioto put me up to a dodge that will tell what a dog is dreaming—a way to make you have the same dream."

He reached for his big red bandanna hanging on a pair of deer horns, he softly spread it out on the head of the sleeping hound, left it for five or ten minutes; then, lying flat on his back, he spread the bandanna on his own face.

He fell asleep and dreamed that he was a dog, that indeed he was Hank, the companion of the bear hunter. He dreamed that he rose from his bearskin in the night, went softly to his master's bunk, poked his moist snout in the face of the sleeping man, listened for a time, then softly went to the cabin door. Deftly opening it, he made for the smokehouse.

Six feet away was a tall pine stump. He leaped on this, then with a mighty spring landed on the roof of the smoker. Near the top was the hung hatch. He thrust his nose under the edge and raised it; then reached his long, powerful neck and plucked the nearest ham from its peg, drew it out through the smoke hole, then down and away.

The hatch closed of its own weight. He carried the plunder off

to a cedar swamp some forty rods away, and there feasted to reple-
tion on the meat he loved the most. He could not eat it all; and
what was left, he buried in the black muck, digging a hole with his
paws but rooting the earth back with his nose till the meat was
covered.

Garvin slept late. When he awoke the dog was still on the rug.
The door was a little open, which might mean that the dog had
been out chasing some prowling beast. For, though Hank could
open the door, he never was known to shut it. And oftentimes the
door was left open all night, so that proved nothing.

His dream was strong upon him as Garvin went out. He opened
the smokehouse to find *another ham gone.* His lips were tight, his
jaw set, as he glanced toward the cabin, to note that Hank was
again mauling the old bear skull as though that were to blame.
Garvin went on alone to the cedar swamp. He saw Hank watching,
even while pretending to maul the skull.

Every stump and tree was familiar through his dream, and he
went direct to the cedar bush. There were signs of recent disturbance. He dug fiercely with his fingers. Soon he unearthed a bone—
then another—bear bones—ham bones—then—part of the last
ham!

He stood up straight. He gasped. "My God!" He glanced furiously toward the cabin, and gave a familiar whistle. But no Hank
came joyously bounding. He strode quickly back, to see the dog
disappearing in the bushes.

"Come here, you," he yelled. The dog came cowering and whim-
pering. "Come right along."

He marched back to the swamp hole, Hank slinking behind.
There he turned to the dog and, pointing to the bones, said in a
voice of thunder: "See that? So it was you all the time. You that
was my pard. You that I trusted. Hank, you're a traitor."

The dog groveled at his feet, whined, licked his boot. Jeff spurned him.

"You damned traitor!" Hank raised his big strong head just a little, and howled a very wail of death. He tried to reach his master's feet. The hunter kicked him off, muttering an oath.

"You *traitor!* Now you come and get what's coming to you!" He strode back to the cabin. Hank slunk far behind in an agony of shame and humiliation.

Garvin took the ready-loaded rifle, and came out. Hank was groveling twenty yards away, whining his shame and sorrow.

"Come hyar," yelled the man. The great hound crawled slowly to his feet, and gazed with blinking eyes on the face he had loved so long and deeply.

Jeff leveled the rifle at his partner's brain, right between those bright, brave eyes that had ever greeted him in love, that had never yet feared facing death when his master was in peril. And a deep revulsion seized the hunter as he glared.

"No, I won't," he gasped. "I can't do it. You are my dawg. But I'm through with you."

He flung himself on his fur-rugged couch, and sobbed like a child.

Inch by inch, the old hound crawled in, slowly, belly to earth. Inch by inch his velvet ears trailed the dust, and his hung lips slobbered on the sill. A little, little moan he made, just one. Slowly he reached the old familiar bearskin. His master's hand hung down from the bunk.

The dog reached humbly forward, and ventured to lick the hand. At once it was withdrawn, and the hunter sat up. Growling harshly, "You traitor!" he gave the dog a fierce kick. With no sound but an involuntary gasp, the hound crawled out of the door, then raising his muzzle he howled the mournful death song of a dog that knows he is lost.

Garvin lay in silence for an hour; then glancing at the sun streak on the floor that was his clock, he rose, took his rifle, slipped a bundle of meat into his wallet, and stepped out. Hank was sprawling with his noble head humiliated in the dust. He raised his big brown eyes, and moaned. He did not raise his head or wag his tail.

"Come here, you traitor," said Garvin savagely; and away he marched for two long hours with his humble partner following far behind.

At last they reached the Ohio River, and the steamboat landing. The *General Jackson* was swinging in to get wood. He had counted on this. The Negroes were hard at work, carrying in the cord sticks. On the upper deck were travelers, well-to-do planters and their families. A tall Southerner, leaning on the rail, marked the picturesque group of the skin-clad hunter and the superb dog. He said: "That's a fine dog you got, my friend."

"The best b'arhound in all Kentucky," was the answer.

"Will you sell him?" said the planter.

"No," said the hunter savagely.

"I've taken a fancy to him. I'd give a big price."

"Not for any price," was the answer.

"I'd surely love to have him."

The hunter glared across the river in silence for a time, then abruptly said:

"Would you be good to him?"

"Yes. I'm a sporting man. I love a good dog. What'll you take for him?"

"I won't sell him," growled Garvin with a savage finality. "But —if you'll be good to him, I'll *give* him to you."

The planter was surprised, but the dog was tied and led up the gangplank, the leash was placed in the planter's hand, and Garvin returned to the dock.

"My name is La Pine of New Orleans," said the planter, with an air of one whose name is a guarantee of honorable behavior.

The steamer swung out. High on the upper deck was Hank, near his new master. With his back against a snubbing-post, Garvin gazed as the open water widened between him and his dog. The old hunter's face writhed in an inner struggle, his eyes were blurred with tears so he could not see much; but he could hear; the long, agonizing wail that came from the upper deck went through his very soul.

He waved his arm to sign "Come back." He shouted, "Let him go. That's my dawg." But the steamer sped away.

He turned and traveled now as he seldom had before through the downstream woods. He knew that twenty miles away was another wooding dock. The steamer had to make forty miles to reach this point. He spared himself not at all. He covered that rugged twenty miles in less than three hours.

As he came worn and breathless and feebly shouting down the hill, he was just in time to see the *General Jackson* swing away with all the wood she needed.

The river boys thought him a madman when they heard him. But the familiar explanation, "He missed the boat and got mad about it," was enough.

"Where do she dock next?" was his question when he was calm enough to ask.

"She don't dock till she makes Memphis, now," was all he could find out.

He went back to the cabin, broken-hearted. He tried to think it would blow over in a month or so.

He would get another dog. Then the notion of that was loathsome. "There ain't no other dawg," he told himself, and hid his real feeling in more foul language.

He stuck it out alone for a week. One bright morning, he girded up his thin loins, and set his long hunter legs striding till he came to the trading store. He had brought what furs he could lay hands on, and everything that promised a little ready money. But his plans were vague.

He sat silently smoking by the open fire till Culberson, the trader, was unoccupied and sat down at the other side of the hearth.

"Say, Jack," said Garvin, "when do the *General Jackson* come back this way?"

"Heh," said Jack, "you ain't up to date. She won't come back never."

"What?"

"Ain't you heard? She struck a sawyer the night after she left here, just below Memphis, and was lost with all on board. Not a soul saved but the darky cook."

Garvin stared stupidly. Then, in a cold way, he said: "Wished I'd been aboard her."

His unspoken purpose had been to go to New Orleans to seek his dog, and the blankness and futility of everything was stupefying.

He had no plans. He could not live his hunter life without his dog, "and there ain't no other dawg."

He hated the thought of his desolate shanty. He hung around the "Corner" which, with the trading store, the saloon, and one or two houses, constituted the settlement. After a month his cash was gone and his credit in danger.

He sat about, gloomily silent, or muttering to himself. The men began to avoid him. He was pointed at as "something on his mind —likely killed someone."

It was in the second month of his loafing that Culberson said: "Jeff, why don't you take a job? They want a mail carrier to cover the forty miles between Carrolton and Frankfort."

Tramping the lonely woods with a mail sack was more to his taste than steady labor. Thus it was that Garvin made the weekly trip, and thus he came to hang around Carrolton docks, and at length to hear much about the sinking of the *General Jackson*.

"No, sah," said a voice in his hearing. "They wasn't all drowned. They was one man as had a big dog. That thar dog shur toted 'im ashore."

"What did you call him?"

"Pine or Lavine or something like that."

"And went on to New Orleans?" said Garvin, with interest that almost scared the Negro.

"Ah don' know. Ah s'pose so."

He went as a deck hand, but in two weeks Garvin was in New Orleans. The name La Pine was wholly sufficient. He stood at last in a big house, to be kindly received by the tall planter.

"Where is my dawg?" was the blunt and passionate opening.

Then he heard a simple tale. The sinking of the *General Jackson* was all too true. Every passenger but one was lost. La Pine's big dog had safely borne him down the midnight flood to a friendly shore.

Arriving in New Orleans, he was made much of by the children, and responded to their friendship. But many times they missed him, and found him again on the docks, watching some steamer coming in, watching and sniffing at every man who came down the gangplank; or howling as it sped away.

Two months went by. Hank was an established member of the family, loved by the children. Had he not rescued their father from death?

And less often, now, he went to the dock front to wail.

But one day, a hamper arrived from a friend in the hills. When opened, it disclosed six smoked bear hams.

Hank entered the room as they were being displayed. He sniffed intently, gave a short yelp and dashed away. On the lawn, he stopped and howled a heart-rending howl, then ran. When last they saw him, he was running like mad toward the dock.

La Pine mounted horse and followed. He was too late to see it, but many witnesses there were.

"That big houn' dawg jes' lep in the water when he seen that there steamer. Them men in boat tried to pull him out, but he bit at them. He jes' was plumb bound he'd swim under that steamboat, an' the paddles struck him and dar he is."

Yes, there he was, crushed, still warm, with battered body and a broken skull.

Pointing to the spot under the cypress trees, La Pine continued: "That's where he lies. We all loved him."

The hunter stared his wild-animal stare. Slowly his words rasped out: "He—were—mah—dawg—I didn't—oughter—done—it. I had oughter forguv him—like he would me. He were mah dawg. He—were—mah—dawg."

He turned and was lost sight of.

There is a little white stone in a place of honor under the cypresses and moss of New Orleans. Six months later, there was an unnamed, now-forgotten mound 2,000 miles away on the track of the Forty-niners. But no one knows that their histories were closely bound together. They are the graves of Hank and Jeff.[1]

# 14.

# LIFE HISTORY OF THE
# BIGHORN SHEEP

THE *Genus Ovis* of Linnaeus, to which this animal belongs, are ruminants of the sheep type. They are large animals—most of them larger than the domestic sheep—stoutly built, with medium or short legs; ears, small and pointed, and without a tuft on the end; feet, with four hoofs each; snout, with small naked place between the nostrils; chin, without beard; glands between toes and under the eyes; mammae two; horns in both sexes, those of the ram large and massive, sweeping back, round, and up again in a noble curve, and bearing, besides many wrinkles, a rugged cross ridge for each year of his age. The horns of the ewe much smaller and nearly straight.

When the bighorn is seen in its native surroundings, the first impression is of a deer with ram's horns. In color, it seems all over of a dull, grayish brown, with white nose and stern.

A closer view shows that it has a blackish tail whose color is joined to the brown of the back by a long, dark stripe cutting the rump patch in two; and that it wears white stockings with dark front facings.

The ewe is much smaller than the ram.

The horns are of a dark umber brown; the hoofs black, and the eyes in all adults of a beautiful pale amber or golden yellow. In the lambs, the eyes are brown.

233

Some specimens have the white of the snout expanded so it covers the whole face; and in some, the black stripe does not cross the stern patch of the tail.

Sheep are darkest in late summer and early autumn. The hairs are darkest at the tip, and lighter and grayer toward the base; the bases of those of the head being nearly white. By December, the coat begins to fade a little from exposure. It also becomes brittle as it ages, so that the combined result of fading and wearing off of the dark points is continuously to lighten the animal's color. The face gets much hard rubbing in feeding, so that the white roots of the hair are more or less exposed by the springtime. Many have the face pure white by February; when May comes, the process has gone so far that many sheep look white at a distance and have thus given rise to the report of mountain goats in Colorado. In June, the old hair is shed; and in their new, sleek, short August coats they are once more of a rich brown. This hue, however, is subject to much variation, some specimens being slaty, and some very dark umber.

At this time, the ram looks very slim, sleek, and deerlike; but the general fleshing of his body as the cool weather approaches gives him quite a burly, thick-set, and massive look by early winter.

In color, the ewe is much like the ram, but paler and of less emphatic color pattern. In several examined, the tail stripe did not cross the white stern patch.

Her changes of coat are like his.

The marvelous curling horns of the rams were apparently the first things to catch the eyes and rivet the attention of the early historians. Without exception, they commented on them.

The horns of the ram are the coveted trophy of the sportsman; for they are the creature's peculiar gift and crowning glory, his own distinguishing and imperishable ornament, the record of his size and of his life.

A horn that measures thirty-six inches around the outside curve, from base to tip, and fifteen inches in girth at base, must be considered in the highest class.

A ram's horns should be measured as soon as secured. Horns shrink surprisingly as they dry out. In one year they will shrink an inch to an inch and a half, that is to say, five to ten per cent in girth; somewhat but not so much in length.

The big ram taken by N. Hollister in the Mount Robson region, mid-September, 1911, had a horn girth of seventeen and seven eighths inches in the field, but only sixteen and a half inches when it got to the museum. As these were careful measurements with a steel tape, it shows how much the horns may shrink in seven months.

These facts shed light on some apparent inconsistencies. In perfect good faith, some sportsman announces that he secured a pair of nineteen-inch horns ten years ago; and when the doubting critics apply the tape, and find them seventeen and a half inches, the sportsman is unfairly put in a wrong light.

When one examines the horn rings—the yearly notches on a ram's horns—one is struck by the fact that all the best horns have but seven or eight years' growth. After that, what?

It seems that the apex of vigor is then reached; for thenceforth the mighty masses that commanded success in the battle for wives and descendants are become a burden with nothing to offset their weight. How gladly would the ram shed this useless load of junk if he could; and, like some elk who is past his prime, wear a modest headgear—one reflecting more accurately his powers.

All the ancient records, and all the old-timers that I have consulted, tell that this creature was not originally a cliff dweller. Its feeding grounds were the grassy foothills and bluffs not far from the crags. It would follow along the river bottoms to graze, but was ever ready to fly to the rocks for protection.

It was not gifted with speed, or weapons, or fighting strength; nor could it find shelter underground like so many of the other defenseless. But this it had—the power to bound up a sheer and rugged cliff that was impossible to any other big creature in its range—except, perhaps, a cougar or a white goat.

Today all that is changed; the pressure of new perils has driven the white sheep permanently to the high mountains. It is now a mountaineer. Nevertheless, it does at times set out across the level country to seek better forage. Its keen eye takes in mountains five to ten miles away; and the wise old ewe will strike out with her band, if she must, and make her way to the far, fair pastures she has spied out from some peak.

Some idea of the primitive number of sheep may be formed from the population in Glacier National Park. In 1916 I spent some weeks camping in the park, and after using all sources of information, calculated that the 2,500 square miles of the park contained not less than 1,500 sheep. In the official Report* this estimate of mine was raised to 2,000, or about one sheep to the square mile of this possible territory.

The park is far from ideal range. It contains very little true sheep pasture of the kind that they sought a hundred years ago. One can travel about a whole month, as I proved in 1916, and never see a sheep. In the Bighorn Basin, judging by Lewis and Clark's accounts, and those of later travelers, sheep may have been ten times as numerous as the above park estimate. Offsetting this, however, is the sparse population of the arid desert regions. So that it is very safe to assume the primitive numbers to be between 1,500,000 and 2,000,000. This, of course, does not include the slim-horned sheep of the north, whose numbers may be at least as great.

In Yellowstone Park the sheep, of course, hold their own. When I lived there in 1897, there were about 150 sheep in the park; in

* *Wild Animals of Glacier National Park,* Department of the Interior, 1918.

1914, there were 210; and in 1922 there were supposed to be 300.

When I was in the Glacier National Park in 1916, I concluded from the evidence of the guides there were about 1,000 sheep within the boundaries. As already noted, these have steadily increased, and now number probably 2,500.

The sheep are very clannish. A certain flock roams on a certain upland, and although at some seasons the rams are apart, they are not on a different range. They seem to keep in touch with the herd, which is composed of ewes, lambs, and spike rams; that is, those not yet arrived at full ramhood.

Like all our big game in the snow lands, the bighorns have two ranges—one for summer and one for snow time. The only direct observation I have to fix the extent of these was made in Yellowstone Park, where something like primitive conditions have been restored.

There are two well-marked herds that I observed and followed about—the Washburn herd of about twenty-five and the Mount Everts of about fifty. In the summer, they could always be found within two or three miles of their headquarters, which was the highest part of their not-very-high mountain. In snow time they descended much lower, and sought the sheltered hillsides.

One advantage of this attachment to their range is that the sheep are thoroughly versed in all local conditions. Especially is this true of the old ewe who is their bellwether. She knows all the places of shelter from a storm; she knows where to find choice foods in time of scarcity; she knows every drinking place, as well as the salt licks and semisalt licks. Above all, she knows every trap, every jump-off, every sheep ladder, every shoot that is possible for a sheep, but beyond the powers of wolves, bears, cougars, dogs, or humans. Amply equipped is she, therefore, when pursuit becomes unpleasantly stimulating, to lead the swiftest foe on a fool's errand, to take excellent care of herself, and incidentally of those that have the wit to follow her.

The bighorn is a delicate feeder. When one sets in parallel columns the foodstuffs of elk, deer, and bighorn, one is slightly shocked to see what a variety of crude, rough, woody, or rank-smelling and -tasting things the deer folk will eat. The bighorn, on the other hand, eats nothing but the sweetest and most delicate of hillside or mountain grasses and flowers. This rare combination of niceness with sweetness seems to bear fruit in the delicacy of its flesh.

Most of the close-observing hunters describe the mountain sheep as strictly a grass feeder. A. A. Anderson tells me that in the Big-horn Basin, the sheep never browse; their food the year round is grass, even when they must paw for it under the snow.

There seems to be no doubt that the normal bighorn in its normal range drinks deeply of the best water it can find—once every day, preferably in the evening. On the rugged buttes of the Yellow-stone in August, it was one of the daily pictures to see the wise old ewe leading her band down, down by devious, dangerous paths with many a cautious, peering, sniffing halt, to the familiar drinking place.

In winter, they commonly eat snow, so dispense with drinking.

But on the great desert ranges of the far Southwest, where the sheep still exist in flocks, protected by the climate, the desert sands, and the scarcity of water, what do they drink?

Like the antelope, the kangaroo rat, the jackrabbit—yes, even the cattle of those arid regions—they have learned perforce to do without drinking, wherever there is cactus. These vegetable tanks store up greedily every drop of water that they can seize during the rare showers; and keep bristling array of fearsome spikes that keep most would-be plunderers away. But the sheep have learned to nibble off the spines with fine adroitness, until an opening is made to the fat, green water bag. And so, their thirst is quenched.

Other plants, too, have in less measure a supply of water. Even domestic sheep learn to use them; and nature adapts their constitution, so that these sheep often go for months without any other drink than the juices of plants.

There is an ancient legend that a certain man believed eating to be merely a bad habit, so trained his horse, by degrees, to do with ever less food. Just as he got it down to one straw a day, the unappreciative animal died. The moral of this tale does not apply to the mountain sheep; for it seems actually to have trained down so that it does without drinking, and yet lives.

There is a wide difference between the mountaineering of the white goat and that of the bighorn. The goat is a climber, like the monkey; the sheep is a sure-footed bounder, like the chamois.

At once, since bounding is his great gift and the secret of his power, the question arises: how far can he bound? Not more than six or seven feet straight up; not more than fifteen feet on the broad jump. These limits I have proved in many ways. Those upward leaps, that look sheer jumps of fifteen or twenty feet, are easily explained, as will be seen; while the broad jumps more than three or four times the animal's length are always on the down slant. A perfectly level broad jump is practically unknown.

A proof that this is so is seen in the fact that smooth walls, or walls with an overhang—although only seven feet high—are enough to hold the strongest and wildest bighorn.

In Amsterdam Zoo, 1900, I saw three bighorns confined in a pen that had walls only five feet high, but with two and a half feet inhang, i.e., a total height of about seven feet.

In Washington Zoo, they kept their five superb mountain sheep in a roomy paddock, the walls of which are only seven and a half feet high, without any overhang. All of which is evidence that a height of seven and a half feet is beyond the jumping power of the bighorn, however strong and active.

How, then, are we to account for the amazing feats of high jumping ascribed to the creature by good observers?

In 1886 I saw, at the Smithsonian Institution in Washington, a five-month-old mountain lamb that had been brought from Montana, destined to be the nucleus of the National Zoo. It was confined in a wire netting corral eight feet high, and yet again and again it was found to have leaped out. It was quite tame and easily led back; and at length, its puzzling eight-foot leaps were explained. A horizontal 2″x4″ timber, all around at four feet from the ground, supplied a satisfactory halfway ledge. In a corner of the pen the lamb would take a flying leap to the flat, narrow, two-inch timber of the side; in a flash, he turned, got a new take-off at an angle, and reached the top of the fence in what was the second bound.

In discussing these wonderful feats, one should begin by considering the weapons with which they are done. First, the quick, calm brain—the "strong heart," as the Indian would call it; second, the superb outfit of tireless, tense, life-tingled muscles; third, the tremendously strong and supple feet, equipped each with two great, soft rubber pads that can grip on any surface, hard or soft, rough or slippery. These feet are further armed with two hard, shell-shaped claws that are backed by a pair of emergency brakes which function or not, according as their owner bends or straightens out his limbs. So we see that soft-rubber heels as shock absorbers are not, primarily, a human invention; and hobnails and toe clutches were used by bighorns for unknown ages, while man was still running barefooted.

Many fragmentary observations, put together, have enabled us to detail the method by which bighorn can negotiate an appalling cliff that would be certain death to man, mule, or dog.

First, be it remembered, cliffs that are perfectly smooth and plumb are so rare as to be negligible. No high rock overhangs for any considerable distance; gravity forbids that. And this is law: all cliffs, in some part of their front, lean backward; and are varied with ledges, bumps, and little shelves or crannies. In short, every cliff in the West has somewhere in its front a sheep ladder.

Provided there be two-inch footholds not more than five or six feet apart coming up, or twenty feet apart going down, the bighorn faces the climb without hesitation. A wide crevice with rugged walls is an easy stairway to this mountaineer. A monkey might use it successfully; I doubt if a cougar could; for he has not the right kind of mind. A man might have the mental training, but he is wholly without the necessary physical powers.

Now arises the question—do these wonderful mountaineers *never* fail? Are their muscles tireless, their judgment unerring, and their nerves rattleproof?

In Arizona University Museum at Tucson is a bighorn that evidently had been killed by a fall from a cliff. It was found on Baboquivari Mountain, October 31, 1919.

Enos A. Mills writes: "A few times I have known one or more to be carried down to death by a snowslide."*

June is bright and often cold on the highlands of the Yellowstone; but it is mild and balmy to the wild things in whom the memory of March is yet strong. High on some broad, level bench they are strung along—the bighorn ewes, the lambs of last year, and one or two rams too young to be accounted full-grown, dangerous personages—only in the big-boy stage.

The warm sun in this sheltered nook, the lush, sweet grass, the protection of the cliffs, the absence of insects, make life very pleasant on this high upland. The sheep laze in the sun, they sprawl,

* *Watched by Wild Animals*, Mills, 1922.

and rub their chins on nearby rocks, they nibble their own legs and flanks, or chew their cud.

The bellwether is a portly ewe, the grandmother of most of them, but a "young woman" still. She is less at ease than the rest of the flock. She rises, looks about, changes her couch, stands head down and pensive. She makes a move to go away, and is at once followed by some of her flock. Then she comes back; she does not want them; she wishes to be alone. Maybe more than once she moves off before she can get away unnoticed. When behind the rocks and out of sight, she goes more quickly. A few hundred yards removed, in some quiet hollow she stops, screened by bushes and rocks, from foes and weather; she stands, legs widespread, head down, and listless. Those who know the ways of the wilds could tell you that she was suffering. For half an hour she waits; then, yielding to the pressure of the Allmother's hand and unspoken whisper, she lies down on the soft grass. In half an hour more are born the little ones—two lambs, long-legged, slabsided little things, but bright-eyed, and colored like the mother.

So far as is known, the gestation is the same length as in the common sheep, that is, 150 days. In the Washington Zoo, young have been born on May 20, May 21, May 24, May 27, June 26, July 2. In a wild state, nearly all come in June.

Now comes the important ceremony called "owning the lamb." As is well known in our barnyards, the lamb that the mother does not own is doomed. In the mountains, the ceremony is equally vital. The owning consists in licking it from head to foot and cleaning it; and incidentally the mother supplying herself with a purge. The lamb's coat is fluffed and dried, so he is warm and safe, his circulation is promoted; he and his mother get well acquainted for a start. Observations made on a twin of the mountain goat showed that the owning of the second one came late, so that the blowflies did their deadly work on the tender mucous parts before the mother care had functioned; and by next sunrise hour, the little stranger was dead—dead for lack of the "owning."

The second of the twin lambs is soon cleaned and dried like the first; the owning is complete. Now her maternal instincts are fully aroused; the fond mother absolutely committed to her task.

Then she cuddles over them and rubs her hankering body over their trembling forms; their feeding instinct is aroused, they butt at her twin-peaked udder. Bending, lending herself to them, she cowers low; a few more blind responses to the blind instinct, and the twins are drinking their first drink; the mother's heart is flushed with the joy that is beyond words or understanding.

Maybe she fondles and feeds them for an hour; then, full of food, the lambs lie down under some slight shelter. Sounds from the distance remind the mother that she has social duties and other children.

Glancing apprehensively about, to make sure she is not betraying the crib of her darlings, she saunters quietly but crookedly back to the flock; and life goes on as before. Late that day, she goes again to feed the little ones, and continues to visit them for two or three days.

I find great divergence of opinion as to the length of their hiding time. Some say that the lamb is hidden three or four days and visited by the mother twice a day. Some say that she never leaves it, and that the lambs can follow the mother slowly within an hour, are vigorous in twenty-four hours, and when a week old can easily keep by her side at her best pace.

Late June sees all the lambkins born and skipping. They are reveling in full supplies of mother's milk, and are beginning to nibble the soft, sweet grasses of their happy upland.

Many enemies they have at this time—coyotes, cougars, eagles, etc. But the cliffs are a sure refuge from the coyotes, and partly a safeguard against cougars. Eagles are easily baffled if a few bushes be near; for, once the lamb is in them, the eagles give up the chase.

There is a special circumstance that helps to save the lambs during their period of weakness. That is the fact that all kinds of game are then abundant. The beast of prey that in winter would follow a week to get a chance at a feeble lamb would not waste half an hour on it in June, because it is quite easy at that time to fill his belly with other foods strewn lavishly over the whole country.

They have another protection, too, in mother. Sheep though she be, she has sharp horns and a valiant heart when her little one is menaced.

Perhaps the most perilous of the little journeys imposed on the bighorn is their regular trip for the daily drink; mostly taken in evening, but sometimes at night by the light of the moon.

It seems probable that even when the little one is a month old, it does not follow to a far or dangerous watering place, but holds back, in some safe retreat till mother's return. No one, apparently, has ever seen the old one at a water hole accompanied by her lamb in the wobbly-legged stage.

Nevertheless, a time comes when, having learned to eat and drink, the lambs do follow mother to the spring. How she dreads the risk of it for her charges! But go she must; and those who have seen her give a picture of her consummate watchfulness, alertness, and apprehension. She descends a few yards, sniffing, gazing, listening for signs of foe; then advances farther, followed closely by her lambs, till the spring is reached. Their thirst quenched, quickly they return to the nearest friendly rock to graze, to play, and at last to lie down for the night.

A still more hazardous trip that she must face with them, though less often, is in the search for salt.

Once a month, all summer, it seems necessary for the grown-ups to seek the health resorts known as "salt licks." When the sheep dwelt on the lower levels, where alkali was everywhere found, they seem not to have been in need of seeking licks. But now that they have changed their range to higher, sweeter hills, the salt lick has become a necessity all summer long, at intervals of two or three weeks.

They nurse till two months old, and are then able to live on solid food.

The summer and autumn go by, without the lambs necessarily seeing their fathers.

Now the early snows begin to drive the game down lower, by hiding their food and hampering their movements.

The weather gets colder, and the sheep begin to adopt a kind of cave life.

The sheep and the white goat are the only horned ruminants herein treated [*Lives of Game Animals*] that habitually use caves for shelter. Elk, antelope, and buffalo might seek the lee side of a cliff during a blizzard; but the sheep have well-known selected caves in the rocks, into which they crowd in bad weather. They do not go in very far; that is, not far enough to be in gloom; but only far enough to have shelter from the wind and snow.

In mild weather, when cave shelter is unnecessary, the sheep make beds; not in the same sense that squirrels and chipmunks do, yet they are well known to prepare a resting place by hollowing the ground and scraping away any loose stones that might make the sleeper uncomfortable. This is exactly what hares do, but neither hares nor sheep, as far as I know, do anything in the way of lining their forms with warm or soft material.

Of all our big, hoofed game, the sheep alone are never solitary. Spring, summer, autumn, and winter they go normally in flocks. When one sees a sheep alone, one may rest assured that it is sick or wounded.

There are, then, these two well-marked social groups in the

sheep world—the great flock that is the main body, consisting of ewes, lambs, and young rams, led always by the wise old ewe who is grandmother to many of them; and the second group, composed of half a dozen huge rams, seven or eight years old, in their full-grown prime, with curling horns that would be a crushing load to a weaker beast.

There is a natural aloofness, an instinctive etiquette, that has hitherto kept these groups apart. But this feeling now weakens, as they see each other daily on the range. Often, in late September, they have become so tolerant of each other that they drift about together, still led, however, by the wise old ewe.

December on the northern ranges means deep snow, hard frost, and the mating season of the sheep—mating, as in most animals, and especially among the highly polygamous, is ushered in with deadly combats. Lions roar, elk bugle, cattle paw the earth, deer slash the brush by way of challenge, then close and do their best to win. The mountain ram wastes little time in idle mockery, squanders no breath in bawling.

Sometimes he scratches the gravel as a gesture of defiance, and I think that sometimes he stamps.

But even in the height of the love-and-war season, the ram seems to dispense with the unnecessary embellishment of loud talk. He looks to his enemy, shakes his head, maybe rears for a moment. The other knows exactly what that means, and gets ready. They back off a little for a good start and, from a hundred feet apart, they let loose. With a muzzle velocity of twenty miles an hour, they meet like two pile drivers. The crack of horn against horn can be heard two miles off on a calm day; each a 300-pound projectile hurled with that fearful force. How can skulls and neckbones stand it? Yet they do; and the mighty brutes wheel off, ramping on their hind legs, like heraldic unicorns. Each strives to show the other fellow how fresh and unwinded he is. Then they back up and go at it again—BANG!

But this is rarely the finish. Weight and endurance are what count. They wheel and charge again and again, maybe half a dozen times before they prove the present problem, and show clearly, to the satisfaction of both, that 312 pounds multiplied by twenty miles an hour and backed by ten recuperative kilowatts is better than 340 pounds multiplied by twenty miles an hour and backed by five recuperatives. This is nature's try-out. For this they grew these mighty horns.[1]

# 15.

# A SHEEP STORY

## Krag, The Kootenay Ram

. . . I SEE a broken upland in the far Northwest. Its gray and purple rocks are interpatched with colors rich and warm, the new-born colors of the upland spring, the greatest springtime in the world; for where there is no winter there can be no spring. The gloom is measure of the light. So, in this land of long, long winter night, where nature stints her joys for six hard months, then owns her debt and pays it all at once, the spring is glorious compensation for the past. Six months' arrears of joy are paid in one vast, lavish outpour. And latest May is made the date of payment. Then spring, great, gorgeous, sixfold spring, holds carnival on every ridge.

Even the sullen Gunder Peak, that pierces the north end of the ridge, unsombers just a whit. The upland beams with all the flowers it might have grown in six lost months yet we see only one. Here by our feet, and farther on, and right and left and onward far away, in great, broad acre beds, the purple lupine blooming. Irregular, broken, straggling patches near, but broader, denser, farther on; till on the distant slopes they lie, long, devious belts, like purple clouds at rest.

But late May though it be, the wind is cold; the pools tell yet of frost at night. The white wind blows. Broad clouds come up, and down comes driving snow, over the peaks, over the upland, and over the upland flowers. Hoary, gray, and white the landscape grows in turn; and one by one the flowers are painted out. But the lupines, on their taller, stiffer stems, can fight the snow for long: they bow their whitened heads beneath its load; then, thanks no little to the wind itself, shake free and stand up defiantly straight, as fits their royal purple. And when the snowfall ends as suddenly as it began, the clouds roll by, and the blue sky sees an upland shining white, but streaked and patched with blots and belts of lovely purple bloom.

And wound across, and in and out, are two long trails of track.

Late snow is good trailing, and Scotty MacDougall took down his rifle and climbed the open hills behind his shanty on Tobacco Creek, toward the well-known mountain sheep range. The broad white upland, with its lupine bands and patches, had no claim on Scotty's notice, nor was his interest aroused until he came on the double trail in the new snow. At a glance he read it—two full-grown female mountain sheep wandering here and there across the country, with their noses to the wind. Scotty followed the prints for a short time, and learned that the sheep were uneasy, but not alarmed, and less than an hour ahead. They had wandered from one sheltered place to another; once or twice had lain down for a minute, only to rise and move on, apparently not hungry, as the abundant food was untouched.

Scotty pushed forward cautiously, scanning the distance, and keeping watch on the trail without following it, when, all at once, he swung around a rocky point into view of a little lupine-crowded hollow, and from the middle of it leaped the two sheep.

Up went his rifle, and in a moment one or both would have fallen, had not Scotty's eye, before he pulled, rested on two tiny, new-born lambs, that got up on their long, wobbly legs, in doubt for a moment whether to go to the newcomer or to follow their mothers.

The old sheep bleated a shrill alarm to their young, and circled back. The lambs' moment of indecision was over; they felt that their duty lay with the creatures that looked and smelled like themselves, and coolly turned their uncertain steps to follow their mothers.

Of course Scotty could have shot any or all of the sheep, as he was within twenty yards of the farthest; but there is in man an unreasoning impulse, a wild hankering to "catch alive"; and without thinking of what he could do with them afterward, Scotty, seeing them so easily in his power, leaned his gun in a safe place and ran after the lambs. But the distressed mothers had by now communicated a good deal of their alarm to their young; the little things were no longer in doubt that they should avoid the stranger; and when he rushed forward, his onset added the necessary final touch, and for the first time in their brief lives they knew danger, and instinctively sought to escape it. They were not yet an hour old, but nature had equipped them with a set of valuable instincts. And though the lambs were slow of foot compared with the man, they showed at once a singular aptitude at dodging, and Scotty failed to secure them—as he had expected.

Meanwhile the mothers circled about, bleating piteously and urging the little ones to escape. Scotty, plunging around in his attempt, alarmed them more and more, and they put forth all the strength of their feeble limbs in the effort to go to their mothers. The man slipping and scrambling after them was unable to catch either, although more than once he touched one with his hand. But very soon this serious game of tag was adroitly steered by the timid mothers away from the lupine bed, and once on the smooth, firmer ground, the lambs got an advantage that quite offset the weariness they began to feel; and Scotty, plunging and chasing first this way and then that, did not realize that the whole thing was being managed by the old ones, till they reached the lowest spur of the Gunder Peak, a ragged, broken, rocky cliff, up which the mothers bounded. Then the little ones felt a new power, just as a young duck must when first he drops in the water. Their little black rubber hoofs gripped the slippery rocks as no man's foot can do it, and they soared on their new-found mountain wings, up and away, till led by their mothers out of sight.

It was well for them that Scotty had laid aside his rifle, for a sheep at a hundred yards was as good as dead when he pulled on it. He now rushed back for his weapon, but before he could harm them, a bank of fog from the peak came rolling between. The same white wind that brought the treacherous trailing snow that had betrayed them to their deadliest foe, now brought the fog that screened them from his view.

So Scotty could only stare up the cliff and, half in admiration, mutter: "The little divils, the little divils—too smart for me, and them less'n an hour old."

For now he fully knew the meaning of the uneasy wandering that he had read in the old one's trails.

He spent the rest of the day in bootless hunting, and at night went home hungry, to dine off a lump of fat bacon.

The rugged peaks are not the chosen home, but rather the safe and final refuge, of the sheep. Once there, the mothers felt no fear, and thenceforth, in the weeks that followed, they took care that in feeding they should never wander far on the open away from their haven on the crags.

The lambs were of a sturdy stock, and grew so fast that within a week they were strong enough to keep up with their mothers when the sudden appearance of a mountain lion forced them all to run for their lives.

The snow of the lambs' birthday had gone again within a few hours, and all the hills were now carpeted with grass and flowers. The abundant food for the mothers meant plenty of the best for the young ones, and they waggled their tails in satisfaction as they helped themselves.

One of the lambs, whose distinguishing mark was a very white nose, was stockily built, while his playmate, slightly taller and more graceful, was peculiar in having little nubbins of horns within a few days of his birth.

They were fairly matched, and frisked and raced alongside their mothers or fought together the livelong day. One would dash away, and the other behind him try to butt him; or if they came to an inviting hillock they began at once the world-old, world-wide game of King of the Castle. One would mount and hold his friend at bay. Stamping and shaking his little round head, he would give the other to understand that *he* was King of the Castle; and then back would go their pretty pink ears, the round woolly heads would press together, and the innocent brown eyes roll as they tried to look terribly fierce and push and strive, till one, forced to his knees, would wheel and kick up his heels as though to say: "I didn't want your old castle, anyway," but would straightway give himself the lie by seeking out a hillock for himself and, posing on its top with his fiercest look, would stamp and shake his head, after the way that, in their language, stands for the rhyming challenge in ours, and the combat scene would be repeated.

In these encounters Whitenose generally had the best of it because of his greater weight; but in the races Nubbins was easily first. His activity was tireless; from morning till evening he seemed able to caper and jump.

At night they usually slept close against their mothers, in some sheltered nook where they could see the sunrise, or rather where they could feel it, for that was more important; and Nubbins, always active, was sure to be up first of the lambs. Whitenose was inclined to be lazy, and would stay curled up, the last of the family to begin the day of activity. His snowy nose was matched by a white patch behind, as in all bighorn sheep, only larger and whiter than usual, and this patch afforded so tempting a mark that Nubbins never could resist a good chance to charge at it. He was delighted if, in the morning, he could waken his little friend by what he considered a tremendous butt on his beautiful patch of white.

Mountain sheep usually go in bands; the more in the band, the more eyes for danger. But the hunters had been very active in the Kootenay country; Scotty in particular had been relentless. His shanty roof was littered over with horns of choice rams, and inside it was half filled with a great pile of sheepskins awaiting a market. So the droves of bighorn were reduced to a few scattering bands, the largest of which was less than thirty, and many, like that of which I speak, had but three or four in it.

Once or twice during the first fortnight of June old Scotty had crossed the sheep range, with his rifle ready, for game was always in season for him; but each time, one or the other of the alert mothers saw him afar, and either led quickly away, or, by giving a short, peculiar *sniff*, had warned the others not to move; then all stood still as stones, and so escaped, when a single move might easily have brought sure death. When the enemy was out of sight they quickly changed to some distant part of the range.

But one day, as they rounded a corner of the pine woods, they smelled an unknown smell. They stopped to know what it was, when a large dark animal sprang from a rock and struck White-nose's mother down.

Nubbins and his mother fled in terror, and the wolverine, for that was the enemy, put a quick end to her life; but before he began to feast he sprang on Whitenose, who was standing stupefied, and with merciful mercilessness laid him by his mother.

Nubbins's mother was a medium-sized, well-knit creature. She had horns longer and sharper than usual for a ewe, and they were of the kind called spikehorns, or spikers; she also had plenty of good sheep sense. The regions above Tobacco Creek had been growing more dangerous each month, thanks chiefly to Scotty, and the mother sheep's intention to move out was decided for her by the morning's tragedy.

She careered along the slope of the Gunder Peak at full speed, but before going over each rising ground she stopped and looked over it, ahead and back, remaining still as a lichen-patched roof for a minute or more in each place while she scanned the range around.

Once as she did this she saw a dark, moving figure on a range behind her. It was old Scotty. She was in plain view, but she held as still as could be, and so escaped notice; and when the man was lost behind the rocks she bounded away faster than before, with little Nubbins scampering after. At each ridge she looked out carefully; but seeing no more of either her enemy or her friends, she pushed on quietly all that day, traveling more slowly as the danger field was left behind.

Toward evening, as she mounted the Yak-in-i-kak watershed, she caught a glimpse of moving forms on a ridge ahead. After a long watch she made out that they were in the uniform of sheep—gray, with white-striped stockings and white patches on face and stern. They were going upwind. Keeping out of view, she made so as to cross their back trail, which she soon found, and thus learned that her guess was right: there were the tracks of two large bighorn; but the trail also said that they were rams. According to mountain sheep etiquette, the rams form one community and the ewes and lambs another. They must not mix or seek each other's society, excepting during the early winter, the festal months, the time of love and mating.

Nubbins's mother, or the Spikerdoe, as we may call her, left the trail and went over the watershed, glad to know that this was a sheep region. She rested for the night in a hollow, and next morning she journeyed on, feeding as she went. Presently the mother caught a scent that made her pause. She followed it a little. Others joined on or crisscrossed, and she knew now that she had found the trail of a band of ewes and lambs. She followed steadily, and Nubbins skipped alongside, missing his playmate, but making up as far as possible by doing double work.

Within a very few minutes she sighted the band, over a dozen in all—her own people. The top of her head was just over a rock, so that she saw them first; but when Nubbins poked up his round head to see, the slight movement caught the eye of a watchful mother in the flock. She gave the signal that turned all the band to statues, with heads their way. It was now the Spiker's turn. She walked forth in plain view. The band galloped over the hill, but circled behind it to the left, while Nubbins and his mother went to the right.

In this way their positions in the wind were reversed. Formerly she could smell them; now they could smell her; and having already seen her uniform from afar, they were sure her credentials were right. She came cautiously up to them. A leading ewe walked out to meet her. They sniffed and gazed. The leader stamped her feet, and the Spikerdoe got ready to fight. They advanced; their heads met with a *whack!* then, as they pushed, the Spikerdoe twisted so that one of her sharp points rested on the other ewe's ear. The pressure became very unpleasant. The enemy felt she was getting the worst of it, so she sniffed, turned, and, shaking her head, rejoined her friends. The Spikerdoe walked after her, while little Nubbins, utterly puzzled, stuck close to her side. The flock wheeled and ran, but circled back, and as the Spiker stood her ground, they crowded around her, and she was admitted one of their number. This was the ceremony, so far as she was concerned.

But Nubbins had to establish his own footing. There were some seven or eight lambs in the flock. Most of them were older and bigger than he, and, in common with some other animals, they were ready to persecute the stranger simply because he was strange.

The first taste of this that Nubbins had was an unexpected *bang* behind. It had always seemed very funny to him when he used to give Whitenose a surprise of this kind, but now there seemed nothing funny about it; it was simply annoying. And when he turned to face the enemy, another one charged from another direction; and whichever way he turned, there was a lamb ready to butt at him, till poor Nubbins was driven to take refuge under his mother. Of course she could protect him, but he could not stay there always, and the rest of the day with the herd was an unhappy one for poor Nubbins, but a very amusing one for the others. He was so awed by their numbers, the suddenness of it all, that he did not know what to do. His activity helped but little. Next morning it was clear that the others intended to have some more fun at his expense. One of these, the largest, was a stocky little ram. He had no horns yet, but when they did come they were just like himself, thickset and crooked and rough, so that, reading ahead, we may style him "Krinklehorn." He came over, and just as Nubbins rose, hind legs first, as is sheep fashion, the other hit him square and hard. Nubbins went sprawling, but jumped up again, and in something like a little temper went for the bully. Their small heads came together with about as much noise as two balls of yarn, but they both meant to win. Nubbins was aroused now, and he dashed for that other fellow. Their heads slipped past, and now it was head to shoulder, both pounding away. At first Nubbins was being forced back; but soon his unusual sprouts of horns did good service, and after getting one or two punches in his ribs from them, the bully turned and ran. The others, standing round, realized that the newcomer was fit. They received him as one of their number, and the hazing of Nubbins was ended.

It is quite common to hear conventionality and social rules derided as though they were silly, manmade tyrannies. They are really important laws that, like gravitation, were here before human society began, and shaped it when it came. In all wild animals we see them grown with the mental growth of the species.

When a new hen or cow appears in the barnyard, she must find her level. She must take rank exactly according to the sum of her powers. Those already there have long ago ranged themselves in a scale of precedence; no one can climb in this scale without fighting all those over which she would go. Somewhere in this scale there must be a place for the newcomer, and until this is settled, her life is one of battles.

No doubt strength, courage, and activity fix her standing in most cases, but sometimes wisdom and keenness of sense are of greater importance. Which one is the leader of a band of wild animals? Not necessarily the strongest or fiercest. That one might *drive* the rest, but not lead them. The leader is not formally elected, as with man, but is rather slowly selected, thus, *that individual* who can impress the rest with the idea that he or she is *the best one to follow* becomes the leader, and the government is wholly by consent of the governed. The election is quite unanimous. For if in the herd are some who do not care to follow, they are free to go the other way. In many kinds of animals that go in herds, the leader whose courage and prowess have so often stood all tests, and who has inspired all the rest with confidence in his sagacity, is usually not the strongest male, but an *elderly female*. This is especially the case with elk, buffalo, blacktail, and the summer bands of mountain sheep.

The Gunder Peak band of sheep was made up of six or seven

ewes with their lambs, three or four yearlings, and a promising young rising ram, two years of age, and just beginning to be very proud of his horns, now in what is called the "ibex" stage. He was the largest member of the band, but not by any means the most important. The leader was a sagacious old ewe; not the one that had tried a round with the Spikerdoe, but a smaller one with short, stubby horns, who was none other than the mother of Krinkle-horn, the little bully.

The sheep think of this leader not as one *to be obeyed,* but as the one *safe to follow,* the one who is always wise; and though they do not give one another names, they have this idea; therefore I shall speak of her as the Wise One.

The Spikerdoe was a very active sheep, in her early prime, cool, sagacious, keen of eye, nose, and ear, and forever on the watch. At least once in three steps she raised her head to look around, and if she saw anything strange or anything moving, she did not cease gazing until she had made it out and went on grazing again, or else gave the long *snoof* that made them all stand like stocks. Of course she was only doing what they all did, but happened to do it better than they. The Wise One, however, was rarely far behind her, and sometimes ahead in seeing things, and had the advantage of knowing the country; but they were so nearly matched in gifts that very soon the Wise One felt that in the Spikerdoe she had a dangerous rival for the leadership.

The band was not without its cranks. There was a young ewe that had a lazy fashion of feeding on her front "knees." The others did not copy her methods; they vaguely felt that they were not good. The effect of this original way of feeding was to bring a great callous pad on each knee (in reality the wrist). Then those growing pads and the improper use of her front legs began to rob Miss Kneepads of her suppleness. She could not spring quickly aside and back as the others could. Ordinarily this does not matter much, but there are times when it is very needful. All animals that must save themselves by flight have developed this trick of zigzag bounding. It is the crouching hare's best foil when sprung at by the fox or the hound; it is the sleeping rabbit's only counter to the onset of the wild cat; it is the resting deer's one balk to the leap of a wolf; and it is the plan by which the snipe, springing zigzag from the marsh, can set at naught the skill of the gunner as well as the speed of the hawk, until she herself is under full headway.

Another odd sheep in the band was a nervous little ewe. She obeyed the leader, except in one thing. When the short *snoof* turned all the rest to stone, she would move about, fidgeting nervously, instead of heeding the Wise One's timely order to "freeze."

Some weeks went by in frequent alarms and flights. But the band was ably sentried, and all went well. As summer drew near, a peculiar feverish restlessness came over the sheep. They would stand motionless for a few minutes, neither grazing nor chewing the cud. They showed signs of indigestion, and kept on, seeking for something—they did not know what. As soon as the Wise One herself felt this listlessness and loss of appetite, she rose to the occasion. She led the whole band to a lower level, down among the timber, and lower still. Where was she going? The road was new to most of them. The Spikerdoe was full of distrust; she stopped again and again; she did not like these sinister lower levels. But the leader went calmly on. If any of the band had been disposed to stop and go back with her, the Spikerdoe would certainly have made a split. But all went listlessly after the Wise One, whose calm decision really inspired confidence. When far below the safety line, the leader began to prick up her ears and gaze forward. Those near her also brightened up. They were neither hungry nor thirsty, but their stomachs craved something which

they felt was near at last. A wide slope ahead appeared, and down
it a white streak. Up to the head of this streak the Wise One led
her band. They needed no telling; the bank and all about was
white with something that the sheep eagerly licked up. Oh, it was
the most delicious thing they had ever tasted! It seemed they could
not get enough; and as they licked and licked, the dryness left
their throats, the hotness went from eye and ear, the headache quit
their brains, their fevered, itching skins grew cool and their stomachs sweetened, their listlessness was gone, and all their nature
toned. It was like a most delicious drink of life-giving cordial, but
it was only *common salt.*

This was what they had needed—and this was the great healing
salt lick to which the leader's wisdom had been their guide.

For a young animal there is no better gift than obedience. It is
obedience to the mother that gives him the benefit of all his
mother's experience without the risk of getting it. Courage is
good; speed and strength are good: but his best courage, speed,
and strength are far below those of his mother, and they are at
his service to the uttermost, if only he will obey. Brains are all-
powerful, but among very young bighorn sheep at least, an obedient fool is far better off than the wisest headstrong lamb that ever
drew the breath of life.

When they had lingered an hour or two and licked the salt till
nature was satisfied, the Wise One turned to go back to the range.
The grass in the valley was uncommonly good, rich, rank, and
abundant, and the lambs just beginning to feed were reveling in
the choicest of pasture; but this was down among the timber, with
all its furtive dangers. The Wise One, as well as the Spikerdoe,
wanted to get back to their own safe feeding ground. She led the
way, and the rest, though unwilling, would have followed, but
little Krinklehorn was too much engrossed with the rich food. He

would not follow. His mother missed him, and when he bleated she came back to him. He did not positively refuse to come, but he lingered so that he held his mother back and encouraged the others to do the same. And when night fell the band was still below timberline, and went to sleep in the woods.

A mountain lion does not make much noise as he sneaks up after his prey; he goes like a shadow; and not a sound was made by the great hungry lion of the Yak-in-i-kak until by chance one little pebble touched by his velvet foot rolled down the bank. It was a slight noise, but the Spikerdoe heard it, and blowing the long *snoooof,* she called litle Nubbins, and, in spite of the darkness, dashed up the cliff toward her safe homeland. The others also leaped to their feet, but the lion was among them. The Wise One leaped up, with a sign to Krinklehorn to follow. She also bounded toward safety—was saved; but her lamb, always wilful, thought he saw a better way of escape, and finding himself alone, he bleated, *"Mother";* and she, forgetting her own danger, dashed down again, and in a moment the lion laid her low. Another sheep forged by, and another, in the hurry and uproar of flight. At each of these in turn the lion sprang, but each offset his pounce by a succession of bewildering zigzag jumps, and so escaped, till, last of all, poor Kneepads made past for the rocks, and when the lion leaped she failed to play the only balk. The power that would have saved her she had long ago resigned; so now she fell.

Far up the bench the sheep went bounding after the one that led. One by one they came up as she slacked her speed, and then they saw that the leader now was Spiker. They never saw the Wise One again, and so they knew that she must have fallen.

When they had reunited and turned to look back, they heard from far below a faint *baah* of a lamb. All cocked their ears and waited. It is not wise to answer too quickly; it may be the trick of some enemy. But it came again—the famliar *baah* of one of their own flock; and Spikerdoe answered it.

A rattling of stones, a scrambling up banks, another *baah* for guidance, and there appeared among them little Krinklehorn—an orphan now.

Of course he did not know this yet, any more than the others did. But as the day wore on and no mother came in response to his plaintive calls, and as his little stomach began also to cry out for something more than grass or water, he realized his desolation, and *baahed* more and more plaintively. When night came he was cold as well as hungry; he must snuggle up to someone or freeze. No one took much notice of him, but Spikerdoe, seemingly the new leader, called once or twice in answer to his call, and almost by accident he drifted near her when she lay down and warmed himself against her beside his ancient enemy, young Nubbins.

In the morning he seemed to Mother Spikerdoe to be her own, in a limited sense. Rubbing against Nubbins made him smell like her own. And when Nubbins set about helping himself to a breakfast of warm milk, poor hungry Krinklehorn took the liberty of joining in on the other side. Thus Nubbins found himself nose to nose and dividing his birthright with his old-time enemy. But neither he nor his mother made any objection, and thus it was that Krinklehorn was adopted by his mother's rival.

There was no one of the others that could equal Spikerdoe in sagacity. She knew all the range now, and it was soon understood that she was to lead. It was also understood that Krinklehorn, as well as Nubbins, was her lamb. The two were like brothers in many things. But Krinklehorn had no sense of gratitude to his foster-mother, and he always nursed his old grudge against Nubbins, and now that they drank daily of the same drink, he viewed Nubbins as his rival, and soon showed his feeling by a fresh attempt to master him. But Nubbins was better able to take care of himself now than ever. Krinklehorn got nothing but a few good prods for his pains, and their relative status was settled.

During the rest of the season they grew up side by side: Krinklehorn thickset and sulky, with horns fast growing, but thick and crinkly; and Nubbins—well! it is not fair to call him Nubbins any longer, as his horns were growing fast and long; so that we may henceforth speak of him as Krag, a name that he got years afterward in the country around Gunder Peak, and the name by which he went down to history.

During the summer Krag and Krinklehorn grew in wit as well as in size. They learned all the ordinary rules of life among bighorn. They knew how to give the warning *sniff* when they saw something, and the danger *snoo-of* when they were sure it was dangerous. They were acquainted with all the pathways and could have gone alone to any of the near salt licks when they felt the need of it.

They could do the zigzag bounding that baffles the rush of an enemy, as well as the stiff-legged jumping which carries them safely up glassy, slippery slopes. Krag even excelled his mother in these accomplishments. They were well equipped to get their own living, they could eat grass, and so it was time they were weaned, for Spikerdoe had to lay on her fat to keep warm in the coming winter. The youngsters themselves would have been in no hurry to give up their comforting breakfast, but the supply began to grow short, and the growing horns of the lambs began to interfere with the mother's comfort so much that she proceeded firmly and finally with their weaning, and long before the earliest snow flurry grizzled the upland, she had them quite independent of her for their daily food.

Among the numbers of the band that met their fate that summer was the two-year-old ram. He had no companion of his age and sex, and his sense of superiority developed a cocksureness which resulted in his skin being added to the pile in Scotty's shanty. When the earliest snows of winter came, all the lambs were weaned and doing for themselves, and the ewes were fat and flourishing but, being free from maternal cares, had thoughts for other matters. With the early frosts and the bracing air came the mating season and, determined to find their mates, the sheep traveled about the likeliest parts of the hills.

Several times during the summer they had seen one or two great rams in the distance, but an exchange of signals had made clear to each what the other was, and they had avoided each other's company. But now, when a pair of large sheep were sighted, and the usual signals exchanged, there seemed no sign of a wish to avoid each other. As the two tall strangers came on, their great size, majestic forms, and vast curling horns left no doubt as to their sex, and, proud of their honors and powers, they pranced forward. But the forwardness of Spikerdoe and her band now gave place to a decided bashfulness. They turned as though to avoid the newcomers. This led to pursuit and to much maneuvering before the two rams were permitted to join the herd. Then came the inevitable quarrel. The rams had so far been good friends—were evidently chums; but chumship and love rivalry cannot dwell together. It was the old story—the jealous pang, the seeking for cause, the challenge, and the duel. But these are not always duels to the death. The rams charged at each other; their horns whacked together till the chips flew from them; but after a few rounds one of them, the lighter, of course, was thrown backward, and leaping up, he tried to escape. The other followed for a quarter of a mile, and as he declined a further fight, the victor came proudly back, and was allowed the position and joys of sultan of the band.

Krag and Krinklehorn were ignored. They were in awe of the

great ram who now took charge, and they felt that their safest plan was to keep as far as possible away from the present social activities of the flock, as they were not very sure of their own standing.

During the first part of that winter they were under guidance of the ram. He was a big, handsome fellow, devoted to his female following, but not without a streak of masculine selfishness that made him take care to have the best of the food and to keep a sharp lookout for danger. Food was plentiful, for the ram knew enough to lead them not into the sheltered ravines where the snow was deep, but up on the bleakest ridges of the upland, where the frigid wind lays bare the last year's grass and, furthermore, where no enemy can approach unseen; so all went well.

The springtime came, with its thrilling sounds and feelings. Obedient to their ancient law, the ram and the band of ewes had parted company in midwinter. The feeling had been growing for days. They were less disposed to follow him, and sometimes he lingered far away for hours. One day he did not rejoin them, and thenceforth to the end of the winter they followed the Spikerdoe as of old.

The little ones came about the first of June. Many of the mothers had two each, but Spikerdoe, now the Wise One, had but one, as before, and this little one displaced Krag for good and engrossed all the mother's attention. He even hindered her in her duties as a leader; and one day, as she was feeding him and watching the happy wagging of his tail, another sheep gave an alarm. All froze except Fidgets. She crossed before the Wise One. There was a far-away *crack!* Fidgets dropped dead, and the Spikerdoe fell with a stifled *baah!* But she sprang to her feet, forgetting her own pain, and looking wildly about her for her lamb, she leaped on the ridge to follow the others. *Bang!* went the rifle again, and the old sheep got a first glimpse of the enemy. It was the man who had once so nearly caught the lambs. He was a long way off, but the ball whistled before the sheep's nose. She sprang back and changed her course, thereby leaving the rest, then leaped over the ridge, bleating to her little one to follow—bleating, too, from pain, for she was hard hit. But she leaped headlong down a rocky place, and the high ground came between. Down the gully she bounded, and out along the farther ridge, keeping out of sight so well that, though Scotty ran as fast as he could to the edge, he never saw her again. He chuckled as he noted the spots of blood; but these soon ceased, and after a long attempt to keep the trail, he gave it up, cursed his luck, and went back to the victim he had secured.

Away went Spikerdoe and her lamb, the mother guiding, but the little one ahead. Her instinct told her that upward was the way to safety. Up the Gunder Peak she must go, but keep from being seen. So she went on, in spite of a burning wound, always keeping a ridge between, till round the nearest rocks she paused to look. She saw no sign either of her friends or her foe. She felt she had a deadly wound. She must escape lest her strength give out. She set off again at a run, forging upward, and the little one following or running ahead as he pleased. On they went till the timberline was reached, and upward still her instinct urged her on.

Another lofty bench was scaled, and then she sighted a long, white streak, a snowdrift lingering in a deep ravine. She eagerly made for that. There was a burning pain through her loins, and on each side was a dark stain on her coat. She craved a cooling touch, and on reaching the white patch sank on her side, her wound against the snow.

There could be only one end to such a wound; two hours, three hours at furthest, and then—well, never mind.

And the little one? He stood dumbly gazing at her. He did not understand. He only knew that he was cold and hungry now, and that his mother, to whom he had looked for everything—food, warmth, guidance, and sympathy—was so cold and still!

He did not understand it. He did not know what next. But we do—the lingering misery, and the inevitable finish, soon or late, according to his strength; and the raven on the rock knew, and waited. Better for the lamb, far better, quicker, and more merciful, had the rifle served him as it did his mother.

Krag was a fine young ram now, taller than any of the ewes, and with long scimitars of horns. Krinklehorn also was well grown, as heavy as Krag, but not so tall, and with horns that looked diseased, they were so short, thick, and bumpy.

The autumn came again, with the grand reunion of the families, the readvent of the ram, and also with a readjustment that Krag had not looked for. He was just beginning to realize that he was a ram, and to take an interest in certain ewes in the flock, when the great ram came, with his curling horns and thick bull neck; and the first thing he did was to bundle Krag out of the flock. Krag, Krinklehorn, and three or four more of their age were packed off by themselves, for such is etiquette among sheep. As soon as the young males reach, or nearly reach, maturity they must go off to study life for themselves, just as a boy leaves home for college. And during the four years that followed, Krag led a roving bachelor life with a half-dozen companions. He became the leader, for he inherited his mother's wit, and they traveled into far countries, learning new pastures, new ways, and new wisdom, and fitting themselves to become fathers of large and successful families; for such is the highest ambition of every good mountain ram.

It was not choice that left Krag unmated, but a combination of events against which he vainly chafed, and he was still left with his bachelor crew. It was really better so. It seemed hard at the time, but it proved his making, for he was thus enabled to develop to the full his wonderful powers before being hampered and weakened by the responsibilities and mingled joys of a family. Each year the bachelor rams grew handsomer. Even sulky Krinklehorn became a tall and strong, if not a fine-looking, ram. He had never gotten over his old dislike of Krag. Once or twice he put forth his strength to worst him, and even tried to put him over a cliff; but he got so severely punished for it that thenceforth he kept away from his foster-brother. But Krag was a joy to behold. As he bounded up the jagged cliffs, barely touching each successive point with his clawed and padded hoofs, floating up like a bird, deriding all foes that thought of following afoot, and the sunbeams changing and flashing from his back as the supple muscles working changed the surface form, he was more like a spirit thing, that had no weight and knew no fear of falling, than a great 300-pound ram with five year rings on his horns.

And such horns! The bachelors that owned his guidance had various horns, reflecting each the owner's life and gifts: some rough half-moons, some thick, some thin. But Krag's curled in one great sweep, three quarters of a circle, and the five year marks told, first, beginning at the point, of the year when he was a lamb and grew the straight long spikes that had helped him so well in his early fight; next year the growth thicker and much longer; the next two years told of yet more robust growth with lesser strength; but the last was record of a year of good food, of perfect health, and un-exampled growth, for the span grown then was longer, wider, and cleaner horns than any of the others.

Tucked away under the protecting shadow of each rugged base, like things too precious to expose, were his beautiful eyes. Dark brown when he was a lamb, yellowish brown when a yearling, they were now, in his early prime, great orbs of shining gold, or splen-did amber jewels, with a long, dark, misty depth in each, through which the whole bright world was born and mirrored on his brain.

There is no greater joy to the truly living thing than the joy of being alive, of feeling alive in every part and power. It was a joy to Krag now to stretch his perfect limbs in a shock of playful battle with his friends. It was a joy to press his toes on some thin ledge, then sail an impossible distance across some fearful chasm to another ledge, whose size and distance he gauged with absolute precision. It was a joy to him to set the mountain lions at naught by a supple ricochet from rock to rock, or to turn and drive the bounding blacktail band down pell-mell backward to their own, the lower, levels. There was a subtle pleasure in every move, and a glorying in his glorious strength, which, after all, is beauty. And when to such a being the early winter brought also the fire of love and set him all aglow, he was indeed a noble thing to see. In very wantonness of strength and power, he bounded, ball-like, up or down long, rugged slopes, leaping six feet high where one would have fully answered every end except the pleasure of doing it. But so he went, seeking, searching—for what? He could not have told; but he would know when he found it. Away he careered at the head of his band, till they crossed the trail of another band, and, instinct guided, he followed after. In a mile or two the other band was sighted, a group of ewes. They fled, of course, but being cornered on a rugged bench, they stood, and after due punctilio they allowed the rams to approach.

The bighorn is no monogamist. The finest ram claims all the ewes in the flock, and any question of his claim must be settled on the spot in mortal fight. Hitherto there had been a spirit of good-fellowship among the rams, but now that was changed; and when great Krag bounded forward, snorting out a challenge to all the rest to disprove his right of might, there was none to face him, and strange to tell, with many claimants, there was no fight. There was nothing now for the rest to do but to wheel at his command and leave him to the devotion and admiration of his conquest.

If, as they say, beauty and prowess are winning cards in all walks of animal life, then Krag must have been the idol of his band. For, matched with rams he had seemed a wonder, and among the ewes his strength, his size, and the curling horns must have made of him a demigod, and the winged heart and the brimming cup were his.

But on the second day of joy two rams appeared, and after maneuvering came near. One was a fine big animal, as heavy in the body as Krag, but with smaller horns, and the other was— yes, it surely was—Krinklehorn. The new ram snuffed a challenge as he came near, then struck the ground with his foot, meaning, "I am a better ram than you, and mean to oust you from your present happy position."

Krag's eyes blazed. He curled his massive neck. He threw his chin up and down like a champing horse, shook his great horns as though they were yet mere points, laid back his ears, and charged; and forward sprang the foe. *Choch!* they came together; but the stranger had an advantage of ground, which left the first onset a draw.

The rams backed off, each measuring the other and the distance and, seeking for firm footing, kept on the edge of the great bench; then, with a *whoof!* they came on again. *Whack!* and the splinters flew, for they were both prime. But this time Krag clearly had the best of it. He followed up his advantage at once with a second *whack!* at short range and his left horn twisting around, hooked under the right of his foe, when, to his utter dismay, he received a terrific blow on his flank from an unknown enemy. He was whirled around and would have been dashed over the cliff but that his horn was locked in that of his first foe, and so he was saved; for no ram has weight enough in his hind quarter to oppose the headlong charge of another. Krag scrambled to his feet again, just in time to see the new enemy irresistibly carried by the violence of his own charge over the ledge and down.

It was a long time before a far-away crash told to those on the ledge that Krinklehorn had found the very end he plotted for his foster-brother. Ram fights are supposed to be fair duels. Krinklehorn, failing in fair fight, had tried foul, and had worked his own destruction; for not even a bighorn can drop 200 feet on rock and live.

Krag now turned on his other foe with double fury. One more shock and the stranger was thrown, defeated. He leaped to his feet and bounded off. For a time Krag urged him to further flight by the same means that Krinklehorn once used to persecute him, then returned in triumph to live unmolested with his family.

Scotty had gone from his Tobacco Creek location in 1887. The game was pretty well hunted out. Sheep had become very scarce, news of new gold strikes in Colorado had attracted him southward, and the old shanty was deserted. Five years went by with Krag as the leading ram. It was five years under a good genius, with an evil genius removed—five years of prosperity, then, for the bighorn.

Krag carried further the old ideas that were known to his mother. He taught his band to abjure the lowlands entirely. The forest coverts were full of evil, and the only land of safety was the open, wind-swept peaks, where neither lions nor riflemen could approach unseen. He found more than one upland salt lick where their natural need could be supplied without the dangerous lowland journeys that they once had thought necessary. He taught his band never to walk along the top of a ridge, but always along one side, so as to look down both ways without being conspicuous. And he added one famous invention of his own. This was the "hide." If a hunter chances close to a band of sheep before they see him, the old plan was to make a dash for safety—a good enough plan in the days of bows and arrows or even of muzzle-loading rifles, but the repeating rifle is a different arm. Krag himself learned, and then taught his tribe, to crouch and lie perfectly still when thus surprised. In nine cases out of ten this will baffle a human hunter, as Krag found times without number.

It is always good for a race when a great one arises in it. Krag marked a higher level for the bighorns. His children multiplied on the Yak-in-i-kak around the Gunder Peak, and eastward as far as Kintla Lake at least. They were healthier and much wiser than had been the bighorn of other days, and being so, their numbers steadily increased.

Five years had made some changes in Krag's appearance, but his body was square and round and muscular as ever; his perfect legs seemed unchanged in form or in force; his head was as before, with the heart-shaped white patch on his nose; and his jewel eyes blazed as of old. But his horns, how they had changed! Before, they were uncommon; now they were unique. The massive sweeps—the graven records of his life—were now a circle and a quarter, and they told of years of joy and years of strife, and one year, tallied in a narrow band of dark and wrinkled horn, told of the year when all the mountains were scourged by the epidemic of grippe—when numbers of lambs and their mothers died; when many strong rams succumbed; when Krag himself had been smitten, but recovered, thanks to his stalwart growth and native force, and after a time of misery had shown no traces of those wretched months, except in the yearly growth of horn. For that year, 1889, it was barely an inch in width, plain for those who read such things—a record of a time of want.

At length old Scotty came back. Like all mountaineers, he was a wanderer, and he once more returned alone to his shanty on Tobacco Creek. The sod roof had fallen in, and he hesitated to repair it. Anyhow, he would prospect a while first. He took his rifle and sought the familiar upland. Before he returned he had sighted two large bands of mountain sheep. That decided him. He spent a couple of days repairing the shanty, and the curse of the Yak-in-i-kak returned.

Scotty was now a middle-aged man. His hand was strong and steady, but his eyes had lost some of their power. As a youth he had scorned all aids to sight; but now he carried a field glass. In the weeks that followed he scanned a thousand benches through the glass, and many a time his eyes rested on the form of the Gunder ram. The first time he saw him, he exclaimed, "Heavens, what horns!" then added prophetically, "Them's mine!" and he set out to make them his. But the bighorn of his early days were fools to these, and month after month passed without his ever getting a nearer view of the great ram. The ram had more than once seen him at short range, but Scotty never knew it.

Several times, through the glass, he marked old Krag from afar on a bench; then, after a labor of hours, stalked round to the place only to find him gone. Sometimes he really was gone, but on more than one occasion the ram was close at hand and hidden, watching his foe.

Then came a visitor to Scotty's shanty—a cattleman named Lee, a sportsman by instinct, and a lover of dogs and horses. His horses were of little use in mountain hunting, but his wolfhounds, three beautiful Russian borzois, were his constant companions, and he suggested to Scotty that it would be a good plan to try the dogs on the bighorn.

Scotty grinned. "Guess you're from the plains, pard. Wait till you see the kind of place whar ole Krag hangs around."

Where the Yak-in-i-kak River leaves its parent mountains, south of Gunder Peak, it comes from a tremendous gorge called Skinkler's Gulch. This is a mere crack in the vast granite hill, but is at least 500 feet in depth. Southward from the back of Gunder Peak is a broken upland that runs to a point at this canyon and ends in a long promontory over the raging, walled-in stream.

This upland is good sheep range, and by a strange chance Scotty, coming up there with Lee and the three wolfhounds, got a glimpse of the Gunder ram. The men kept out of sight and hurried along by the hollows toward the spot. But it was the old story. No sign of their quarry. They found his great hoof mark just where they had seen him, so it was no illusion; but the hard rocks about refused further information, and no doubt Scotty would have had another mysterious disappearance to add to his list, but that the dogs, nosing about in all the near hollows and thickets of dwarf birch, broke out suddenly into a loud clamor, and as they did so, up jumped a huge, gray, white-sterned animal—the ram, the wonderful Gunder ram. Over the low bushes, over the broken rocks, bounding, soaring, floating, supple, certain, splendid, he bore the great curling wonders on his head as lightly as a lady might her earrings; and then, from various other coverts, sprang up his band and joined him. Up flew the rifles; but in a moment the three great dogs, closing in, gave unwitting screen to one victim on which every thought was fixed, and not a shot was heard. Away they went, the ram forging quickly to the lead, and the others stringing along after. Over the upland, flying, sailing, leaping, and swerving, they went. Over the level plains the dogs would soon have caught the hindmost or perhaps their noblest prey, but on the rugged rocks it was clear that the sheep were gaining. The men ran, one to the right, the other to the left, the better to keep sight; and Krag, cut off from the peak, dashed southward over the benchland. Now it was a straight race. On it went—on, southward. The dogs gained, and were near catching the hindmost sheep; then it seemed that the ram dropped back and now ran the rearmost. A rugged stretch was reached, and there the sheep gained steadily, though little.

One, two, three miles, and the chase was sweeping along the rocky ridge that ends in the sudden gash of Skinkler's Gulch. A minute more and the crowd of sheep were rounded up and cornered on the final rock. They huddled together in terror, 500 feet of dizzy canyon all around, three fierce dogs and two fiercer men behind. Then, a few seconds later, old Krag dashed up. Cornered at last, he wheeled to fight; for the wild thing never yields.

He was now so far from the bounding dogs that two rifle balls whistled near. Of the dogs he had no fears—them, he could fight; but the rifles were sure death. There was one chance left. The granite walls of the Yak-in-i-kak could prove no harder than the human foe. The dogs were within forty rods now, fine, courageous animals, keen for fight, fearless of death; and behind, the hunters, remorseless and already triumphant. Sure death from them, or doubtful life in the gulch. There was no time to hesitate; he, the leader, must act. He wheeled to the edge, and *leaped*—down— down, not to the bottom, not blindly. Thirty feet downward, across the dizzy chasm, was a little jut of rock, no bigger than his nose— the only one in sight, all the rest smooth, sheer, or overhanging. But Krag landed fairly, poised just a heartbeat. In a flash his blazing eyes took in another point, his only hope, on the other side, hidden under the overhanging rocks he had leaped from. His supple loins and corded limbs bent, pulsed, and floated him across, there got fresh guidance to his flight, then back, sometimes to a mere roughness of the rock, on which his hoofs, of horn and rubber built, gripped for an instant, and took fresh ricochet to another point. Then sidewise fifteen feet, and down, down with modulated impact from point to point, till, with a final drop of twenty feet, he reached a ledge of safety far below.

And the others, inspired by his example, followed fast—a long cascade of sheep. Had he failed at one point all must have failed. But now they came down headlong. It was splendid, it was inspir-

ing! Hop, skip, down they came, one after the other, now ten, now twenty feet, first to last leaping, sailing, bounding from point to ledge, from ledge to point, with masterly command of thew and hoof, with marvelous poise, and absolute success.

But just as the last had reached the second slender, specklike foothold for its life, three white-and-yellow creatures whirled past her in the air, with gurgled gasps of horror, to perish far below. The hounds, impetuous and brave, never hesitated to follow a foe, and never knew how far more gifted was that foe than themselves until it was too late. Down below, almost at the water's edge, Krag paused at length. Far above he heard the yells and whistles of the hunters; below in the boiling Yak-in-i-kak he saw a battered white-and-yellow form being hurried to the sea.

Lee and Scotty stood blankly at the edge. Sheep and dogs had vanished; no possibility of escape for any. Scotty uttered words that had no bearing on the case, only they were harsh, blasphemous

words, and seemed to be necessary. Lee had a choking feeling in
his throat, and he felt as no man can comprehend who has not
lost a noble dog by a sudden, tragic, and untimely end.

"Bran! Rollo! Ida!" he called in lingering hope; but the only
response was from the western wind, that *snoofed* and whistled as
it swept down Skinkler's Gulch.

Lee was a young, warm-hearted, impulsive cattleman. For a day
or two he hung about the shanty. The loss of his three friends was
a sad blow: he had no heart for more mountaineering. But a few
days later a spell of bracing weather helped his spirits, and he
agreed when Scotty suggested a hunt. They reached the upper
level, when Scotty, who had from time to time been scanning the
hills with his glass, suddenly exclaimed:

"H—l! If that ain't the old Gunder ram. Thought he was
smashed in Skinkler's Gulch!" and he sat down in amazement. Lee
took the glass, and he recognized the wonderful ram by his superb
horns. The color rushed to the young man's face. Now was his
chance for glory and revenge at once! "Poor old Bran! good Rollo
and Ida!"

Few animals have cunning enough to meet the combined drive
and ambush. Scotty knew the lay of the land as well as the habits
of the ram.

"He ain't a-goin' to run down the wind, and he ain't a-goin'
to quit the rocks. That means he'll pass up by the Gunder Peak, if
he moves at all, an' he must take one side or the other. He won't
go the west side if I show meself once that ar way. So you take the
east; I'll give you two hours to get placed. I've a notion he'll cross
the spur by that ledge."

Lee set out for his post. Scotty waited two hours, then moved
on to a high ridge and, clear against the sky, he waved his arms

and walked up and down a few times. The ram was not in sight, but Scotty knew he would see.

Then the old mountaineer circled back by hidden ways to the south, and began to walk and cut over the ridges toward the place where the ram had been. He did not expect to see old Krag, but he did expect the ram to see him. Lee was at his post and, after a brief spell, he sighted the great ram himself, bounding lightly down a ridge a mile away, and close behind him were three ewes. They disappeared down a pine-clad hollow, and when they reappeared on the next ridge they were running as though in great alarm, their ears laid back; and from the hollow behind came, not, as Lee expected, the crack of Scotty's rifle or the sound of his yell, but the hunting chorus of timber wolves. Among the rocks the sheep could easily escape, but among the timber or on the level such as now lay ahead, the advantage was with the wolves; and a minute later these swept up in sight—five shaggy, furry brutes. The level open was crossed at whirling speed. The sheep, racing for their lives, soon lengthened out into a procession in order of speed: far ahead the great ram; behind him, with ten-yard gaps between them, the three ewes; and forty yards behind the last, the five grim wolves, closing, gaining at every leap. The benchland narrowed eastward to pass a rocky shoulder. Long years and countless perils had taught the sheep that in the rocks was safety, and that way led the ram. But in the tangled upland birch the last of the ewes was losing ground; she gasped a short *baah* as, thrown by a curling root, she lost a few more precious yards. The wolves were almost within leaping distance when Krag reached the shoulder ledge. But a shoulder above means a ravine below. In a moment, at that call of distress, Krag wheeled on the narrow ledge and faced the foe. He stood to one side, and the three ewes leaped past him and on to safety. Then on came the wolves, with a howl of triumph. Many a sheep had they pulled down, and now they knew they soon would feast. Without a pause they closed, but in such a narrow pass, it was one at time. The leader sprang; but those death-dealing fangs closed only on a solid mass of horn, and back of that was a force that crushed his head against himself, and dashed him at his friend behind with such a fearful vim that both were hurled over the cliff to perish on the rocks. On came the rest. The ram had no time to back up for a charge, but a sweep of that great head was enough. The points, forefronting now, as they did when he was a lamb, speared and hurled the next wolf, and the next; and then Krag found a chance to back up and gather his force. None but a mad wolf could have failed to take warning; but on he came, and Krag, in savage glory of the fight, let loose that living thunderbolt—himself—and met the last of the furry monsters with a shock that crushed him flat against the rock, then picked him up on his horns as he might a rag, and hurled him farthest yet and standing on the edge he watched him whirl and gasp till swallowed in the chasm.

The great ram raised his splendid head, blew a long blast from his nostrils, like a war horse, and gazed a moment to see if more were coming; then turned and lightly bounded after the ewes he had so ably guarded.

From his hiding place young Lee took in the whole scene with eager, sparkling eyes. Only fifty yards away from him it had passed.

He was an easy mark—fifty yards, standing; he was a splendid mark, all far beyond old Scotty's wildest talk. But Lee had seen a deed that day that stirred his blood. He felt no wish to end that life, but sat with brightened eyes, and said with fervor: "You grand old warrior! I do not care if you did kill my dogs. You did it fair. I'll never harm you. For me, you may go in safety."

But the ram never knew; and Scotty never understood.

There was once a wretch who, despairing of other claims to notice, thought to achieve a name by destroying the most beautiful building on earth. This is the mind of the head-hunting sportsman. The nobler the thing that he destroys, the greater the deed, the greater his pleasure, and the greater he considers his claim to fame.

During the years that followed, more than one hunter saw the great ram and feasted his covetous eyes on his unparalleled horns. His fame even reached the cities. Dealers in the wonderful offered fabulous prices for the head that bore them—set blood money on the life that grew them; and many came to try their luck, and failed. Then Scotty, always needy, was fired by a yet larger money offer, and setting out with his partner, they found the ram, with his harem about him. But in three days of hard following they never got a second glimpse; and the partner "reckoned thar was easier money to git," and returned home.

But back of Scotty's sinister gray eyes was the fiber of dogged persistency that has made his race the masters of the world. He returned with Mitchell to the shanty, but only to prepare for a long and obstinate hunt. His rifle, his blanket, his pipe, with matches, tobacco, a pot, a bundle of jerked venison, and three or four pounds of chocolate were all he carried. He returned alone next day to the place where he had left the track of the ram, and followed it fast in the snow, winding about, in and out, and obscured by those of his band, but always distinguishable by its size. Once or twice Scotty came on the spots where the band had been lying down, and from time to time he scanned the distance with his glass. But he saw nothing of them. At night he camped on their trail; next day he took it up again. After following for hours, he came on the place where evidently the ram had stopped to watch him afar, and so knew of his pursuer. Thenceforth the trail of the band for a long time was a single line as they headed for distant pastures.

Scotty followed doggedly behind; all day he followed, and at night, in a little hollow, crouched like a wild beast in his lair, with this difference only: he had a fire, and he smoked a pipe in

very human fashion. In the morning he went on as before. Once
or twice in the far distance he saw the band of sheep traveling
steadily southward. Next day passed, and the sheep were driven to
the south end of the Yak-in-i-kak range, just north of Whitefish
Lake.

South of this was the Half-moon Prairie, east the broken land
that stretched toward the north fork of the Flathead, and north of
them their pertinacious and deadly foe. The sheep were in doubt
now, and as old Krag sought to sneak back by the lower benches
of the east slope, he heard a *crack!* and a stinging something
touched one horn and tore the hair from his shoulder.

The touch of a rifle ball on the horns of a ram has a more or
less stunning effect; and Krag, dazed for a moment, gave the signal
which in our speech is, "Everyone for himself now"; and so the
band was scattered. Some went this way and some that, running
more or less openly.

But Scotty's one thought was old Krag: he heeded no other; and
when the ram made straightaway eastward down the hill, Scotty
again took up the trail, and cursed and gasped as he followed.

The Flathead River was only a few miles away. The ram crossed
on the ice, and keeping the roughest ground, turning when the
wind turned, he traveled all day northeastward, with Scotty steadily behind. On the fifth day they passed near Terry's Lake. Scotty
knew the ground. The ram was going east, and would soon run
into a lot of lumber camps; then turn he must, for the region was
a box canyon; there was only one way out. Scotty quit the trail,
and crossing northward to this one defile, down which the ram
must go, he waited. The west—the Chinook—wind had been rising for an hour or more, the one damp wind of the Rockies, the
snow wind of the hills; and as it rose the flakes began to fly. In
half an hour more it was a blinding snowstorm. Things twenty
yards away were lost to view. But it did not last; the heaviest of it
was over in a few minutes, and in two hours the skies were clear

again. Scotty waited another hour, but seeing nothing, he left his post and searched about for sign; and found it, too—a dimpling row of tracks, much hidden by the recent snow, but clear in one place under a ledge. The ram had passed unseen, had given him the slip, saved by the storm wind and the snow.

Oh, Chinook! Mother West Wind! that brings the showers of spring and the snows of winter; that makes the grass grow on these great rolling uplands; that sustains the grass and all flesh that the grass sustains; that carved these uplands themselves, as well as made all things that live upon them—are you only a puff of air, or are you, as Greek and Indian both alike have taught, a something better, a living, thinking thing, that first creates, then loves and guards its own? Why did you come that day and hold your muffler about the eyes of the wolfish human brute, if it were not that you meant he should not see or harm your splendid dear one as he passed?

And was there not purpose in the meeting of these very two, that you brought about long years ago, the day the ram was born?

Now Scotty thought there must be an object in the ram's bold dash for the east side of the Flathead, and that object must be to reach the hills around Kintla Lake, on which he was well known and had many times been seen. He might keep west all day today, while the Chinook blew, but if the wind changed in the night he would surely turn eastward. So Scotty made no further attempt to keep the trail, or to make the west point of the Kintla Range, but cut straight northward over the divide toward the lake. The wind did change in the night. And next day, as Scotty scanned the vast expanse between him and the lake, he saw a moving speck below. He quickly got out of sight, then ran to intercept the traveler. But when he got to the spot he aimed at, and cautiously peered, there, 500 yards away, on the next ridge, he stood—the famous ram. Each was in plain view of the other.

Scotty stood for a minute and gazed in silence. Then, "Wal, ole Krag, ye kin see the skull and crossbones on my gun. I'm Death on yer track; ye can't shake me off. At any price, I mean to have them horns. And here's for luck." Then he raised the rifle and fired; but the distance was great. The ram stood till he saw the puff of smoke, then moved quickly to one side, and the snow was tossed by the ball not far from his former stand.

The ram turned and made eastward, skirting the rugged southern shore of the lake, making for the main divide; and Scotty, left far behind for a time, trudged steadily, surely, behind him. For added to his tireless strength was the Saxon understreak of brutish grit, of senseless, pig-dogged pertinacity—the inflexible determination that still sticks to its purpose long after sense, reason, and honor have abandoned the attempt, that blinds its owner to his own defeat, and makes him, even when he is downed, still feebly strike—yes, spend his final mite of strength in madly girding at his conqueror, whose quick response, he knows, will be to wipe him out.

It was on, on, all day; then camp for the night, and up again in the morning. Sometimes the trail was easy to follow, sometimes blotted out by new-fallen snow. But day after day they went. Sometimes Scotty was in sight of the prize that he pertinaciously was hunting, but never very near. The ram seemed to have learned that 500 yards was the farthest range of the rifle, and allowed the man to come up to that, the safety limit. After a time it seemed as though he much preferred to have him there, for then he knew where he was. One time Scotty stole a march, and would have had a close shot had not the fateful west wind borne the taint, and Krag was warned in time; but this was in the first month of that dogged, fearful following. After a while the ram was never out of sight.

Why did he not fly far away, and baffle the hunter by his speed? *Because he must feed.* The man had his dried venison and chocolate, enough for many days; and when they were gone he could shoot a hare or a grouse, hastily cook it, and travel all day on that. But the ram required hours to seek the scanty grass under the snow. The long pursuit was telling on him. His eyes were blazing bright as ever, his shapely corded limbs as certain in their stride; but his belly was pinching up, and hunger, weakening hunger, was joining with his other foe.

For five long weeks the chase went on, and the only respite to the Gunder ram was when some snowstorm from the west would interpose its veil.

Then came two weeks when they were daily in sight of each other. In the morning Scotty, rising wolflike from his frosty lair, would call out, "Come, Krag; time we wuz a-movin'." And the ram on the distant ridge would stamp defiantly, then, setting his nose to the wind, move on, now fast, now slow, but keeping ever the safe 500 yards or more ahead. When Scotty sat down to rest, the ram would graze. If Scotty hid, the ram would run in alarm to some place where near approach unseen would be impossible. If Scotty remained still for some time, the ram would watch him intently and as still as himself. Thus they went on, day after day, till ten eventless weeks dragged slowly by. A singular feeling had grown up between the two. The ram became so used to the sleuth-hound on his track that he accepted him as an inevitable, almost a necessary evil; and one day, when Scotty rose and scanned the northern distance for the ram, he heard the long snort far behind, and turning, he saw old Krag impatiently waiting. The wind had changed, and Krag had changed his route to suit. One day after their morning's start Scotty had a difficult two hours in crossing a stream over which old Krag had leaped. When he did reach the other side he heard a snort, and looked around to find that the ram had come back to see what was keeping him.

Oh, Krag! Oh, Gunder ram! Why do you make terms with such a foe implacable? Why play with Death? Have all the hundred warnings of the Mother Wind been sent in vain? Keep on, keep on; do your best, that she may save you yet; but make no terms. Remember that the snow, which ought to save, may yet betray.

Thus in the winter all the Chief Mountain was traversed; the Kootenay Rockies, spur by spur, right up to the Crow's Nest Pass; then westward, in the face of the white wind, the indomitable pair turned their steps, west and south to the McDonald Range; and onward still, till the Galtom Range was reached. Day by day the same old mechanical following—two dark, moving specks on the great expanse of snow. Many a time their trail was crossed by that of other sheep and other game. Once they met a party of miners who knew of Scotty and his hunt, and they chaffed him now; but he stared blankly, heeded them not, and went on. Many a time the ram sought to hide his fateful footprints in the wake of some passing herd. But Scotty was not to be balked; his purpose had become his nature. All puzzles he worked out, and now there were fewer interruptions of the chase, for the snowstorms seemed to cease, the white wind held aloof, and nature offered no rebuke.

On and on, still the same scant half mile apart; and on them both the hands of Time and Death seemed laid. Both were growing hollow-eyed and were gaunter every day. The man's hair had bleached since he set out on this insane pursuit, and the head and shoulders of the ram were grizzling; only his jewel eyes and his splendid sweeping horns were the same, and borne as proudly as when first the chase began.

Each morning the man would rise—stiff, half frozen, and gaunt, but dogged as a very hound infernal—and sneak along, trying for a close shot. But always Krag was warned in time, and springing into view from his own couch, would lead the chase as before. Till in the third month they crossed again from Galtom to Tobacco Range, then eastward back to Gunder Peak—the ram, and the sleuth inexorable upon his trail behind him. Here, on the birthplace of the ram, they sat one morning, at rest—the ram on one ridge, Scotty 600 yards away on the next. For twelve long weeks the ram had led him through the snow, over ten long mountain ranges—500 rugged miles.

And now they were back to their starting point, each with his lifetime wasted by one half in that brief span. Scotty sat down, and lit his pipe. The ram made haste to graze. As long as the man stayed there in view the ram would keep that ridge. Scotty knew this well; a hundred times he had proved it. Then, as he sat and smoked, some evil spirit entered in and sketched a cunning plot. He emptied his pipe deliberately, put it away, then cut some rods of the low-creeping birch behind him; he gathered some stones; and the great ram watched afar. The man moved to the edge of the ridge, and with sticks, some stones, and what clothing he could spare, he made a dummy of himself. Then, keeping exactly behind it, he crawled backward over the ledge and disappeared. After an hour of crawling and stalking he came up on a ridge behind the ram.

There he stood, majestic as a bull, graceful as a deer, with horns that rolled around his brow like thunderclouds about a peak. He was gazing intently on the dummy, wondering why his follower was so long still. Scotty was nearly 300 yards away. Behind the ram were some low rocks, but between was open snow. Scotty lay down and threw snow on his own back till he was all whitened, then set out to crawl 200 yards, watching the great ram's head, and coming on as fast as he dared. Still old Krag stared at the dummy, sometimes impatiently stamping. Once he looked about sharply, and once he would have seen that deadly crawler in the snow, but that his horn itself, his great right horn, must interpose its breadth between his eye and his foe, and so his last small chance of escape was gone. Nearer, nearer to the sheltering rocks crawled the evil one. Then, safely reaching them at last, he rested, a scant half-hundred yards away. For the first time in his life he saw the famous horns quite close. He saw the great, broad shoulders, the curving neck, still massive, though the mark of famine was on all; he saw this splendid fellow creature blow the hot breath of life from his nostrils, vibrant in the sun; and he even got a glimpse of the life light in those glowing amber eyes: but he slowly raised the gun.

Oh, Mother White Wind, only blow! Let not this be. Is all your power offset? Are not a million idle tons of snow on every peak awaiting? And one, just one, will do; a single flying wreath of snow will save him yet. The noblest living thing on all these hills, must he be stricken down to glut the basest lust of man? Because he erred but once, must he be doomed?

But never day was calmer. Sometimes the mountain magpies warn their friends, but not a bird was anywhere in view; and still the Gunder ram was spellbound, watching that enemy, immovable, across the dip.

Up went the gun that never failed—directed by the eye that never erred. But the hand that had never trembled taking twenty human lives now shook as though in fear.

Two natures? Yes.

But the hand grew steady; the hunter's face was calm and hard. The rifle sang, and Scotty—hid his head; for the familiar *crack!* had sounded as it never did before. He heard a rattling on the distant stones, then a long-drawn *snoof!* But he neither looked nor moved. Two minutes later all was still, and he timidly raised his head. Was he gone? or what?

There on the snow lay a great gray-brown form, and at one end, like a twin-necked hydra coiling, were the horns, the wonderful horns, the sculptured record of the splendid life of a splendid creature, his fifteen years of life made visible at once. There were the points, much worn now, that once had won his lamb-days' fight. There were the years of robust growth, each long in measure of that growth. Here was that year of sickness, there the splinter on the fifth year's ring, which notched his first love fight. The points had now come round, and on them, could we but have seen, were the lives of many gray wolves that had sought his life. And so the rings read on, the living record of a life whose very preciousness had brought it to a sudden end.

The golden chain across the web of white was broken for its gold.

Scotty walked slowly over and gazed in sullen silence, not at the dear-won horns, but at the calm yellow eyes, unclosed, and yet undimmed by death. Stone cold was he. He did not understand, himself. He did not know that this was the sudden drop after the long, long slope up which he had been forcing himself for months. He sat down twenty yards away, with his back to the horns. He put a quid of tobacco in his mouth. But his mouth was dry; he spat it out again. He did not know what he himself felt. Words played but little part in his life, and his lips uttered only a torrent of horrid blasphemies, his one emotional outburst.

A long silence; then, "I'd give it back to him if I could."

He stared at the distance. His eyes fell on the coat he had left, and realizing that he was cold, he walked across and gathered up his things. Then he returned to the horns, and over him came the wild, inhuman lusting for his victim's body that he had heard his comrades speak of, but had never before understood—the reactionary lust that makes the panther fondle and caress the deer he has stricken down. He made a fire; then, feeling more like himself, he skinned the ram's neck and cut off the head. This was familiar work, and he followed it up mechanically, cutting meat enough to satisfy his hunger. Then, bowing his shoulders beneath the weight of his massive trophy—a weight he would scarcely have noticed three months ago—he turned from the chase, old, emaciated, grizzled, and haggard, and toiled slowly down to the shanty he had left twelve weeks before.

"No! Money couldn't buy it"; and Scotty turned sullenly away to end discussion. He waited a time till the taxidermist had done his best, then he traversed 300 miles of mountain to his lonely home. He removed the cover, and hung the head where it got the best light. The work was well done: the horns were unchanged; the wonderful golden eyes were there, and when a glint of light gave to them a semblance of regard, the mountaineer felt once more some of the feelings of that day on the ridge. He covered up the head again.

Those who knew him best say he kept it covered and never spoke about it. But one man said: "Yes; I saw him uncover it once, and look kind o' queer." The only remark he ever made about it was: "Them's my horns, but he'll get even with me yet."

Four years went by. Scotty, now known as Old Man Scotty, had never hunted since. He had broken himself down in that long madness. He lived now entirely by his gold-pan, was quite alone, and was believed to have something on his mind. One day, late in the winter, an old partner stopped at his shanty. Their hours of conversation did not amount to as many paragraphs.

"I heared about ye killin' the Gunder ram."

Scotty nodded.

"Let's see him, Scotty."

"Suit yourself"; and the old man jerked his head toward the draped thing on the wall. The stranger pulled off the cloth, and then followed the usual commonplace exclamations of wonder. Scotty received them in silence; but he turned to look. The firelight reflected in the glassy eyes lent a red and angry glare.

"Kivver him up when you're through," said Scotty, and turned to his smoking.

"Say, Scotty, why don't ye sell him if he bothers ye that-a-way? That there New Yorker told me to tell ye that he'd give—"

"To h—l with yer New Yorker! I'll niver sell him—I'll niver part with him. I stayed by him till I done him up, an' he'll stay by me till he gits even. He's been a-gittin' back at me these four years.

He broke me down on that trip. He's made an old man o' me. He's left me half luny. He's sucking my life out now. But he ain't through with me yet. Thar's more o' him round than that head. I tell ye, when that old Chinook comes a-blowin' up the Ter-bak-ker Crik, I've heared noises that the wind don't make. I've heared him just the same as I done that day when he blowed his life out through his nose, an' me a-layin' on my face afore him. I'm up ag'in it, and I'm a-goin' to face it out—right—here—on—Ter-bak-ker—Crik.''

The white wind rose that night, and hissed and wailed about Scotty's shanty. Ordinarily the stranger might not have noticed it; but once or twice there came in over the door a long *snoof* that jarred the latch and rustled violently the drapery of the head. Scotty glanced at his friend with a wild, scared look. No need for a word; the stranger's face was white.

In the morning it was snowing, but the stranger went his way. All that day the white wind blew, and the snow came down harder and harder. Deeper and deeper it piled on everything. All the smaller peaks were rounded off with snow, and all the hollows of the higher ridges leveled. Still it came down, not drifting, but piling up, heavy, soft, adhesive—all day long, deeper, heavier, rounder. As night came on, the Chinook blew yet harder. It skipped from peak to peak like a living thing—no puff of air, but a living thing, as Greek and Indian both alike have taught, a being who creates, then loves and guards its own. It came like a mighty goddess, like an angry angel with a bugle horn, with a dreadful message of war; for it sang a wild, triumphant battle song; and the strain of the song was:

> I am the mothering white wind;
> This is my hour of might.
> The hills and the snow are my children;
> My service they do tonight.

And here and there, at the word received, there were mighty doings among the peaks. Here new effects were carven with a stroke; here lakes were made or unmade; here messengers of life and death despatched. An avalanche from Purcell's Peak went down to gash the sides and show long veins of gold; another hurried, by the white wind sent, to block a stream and turn its wasted waters to a thirsty land—a messenger of mercy. But down the Gunder Peak there whirled a monstrous mass, charged with a mission of revenge. Down, down, down, loud *snoofing* as it went, and sliding on from shoulder, ledge, and long incline, now wiping out a forest that would bar its path, then crashing, leaping, rolling, smashing over cliff and steep descent, still gaining as it sped. Down, down, faster, fiercer, in one fell and fearful rush, and Scotty's shanty, in its track, with all that it contained, was crushed and swiftly blotted out. The hunter had forefelt his doom. The ram's own mother White Wind, from the eastern sea, had come—had long delayed, but still had come at last.

Over the rocky upland dawned the spring, over the level plain of Tobacco Creek. Gently the rains from the westward washed the great white pile of the snowslide. Slowly the broken shanty came to light; and there in the middle, quite unharmed, was the head of the Gunder ram. His amber eyes were gleaming bright as of old, under cover of those wonderful horns; and below him were some broken bones, with rags and grizzled human hair.

Old Scotty is forgotten, but the ram's head hangs enshrined on a palace wall today, a treasure among kingly treasures; and men, when they gaze on those marvelous horns, still talk of the glorious Gunder ram who grew them far away on the heights of the Kootenay.[1]

# 16.

# LIFE HISTORY OF THE GRAY WOLF

THE home region of the individual usually corresponds somewhat with the size of the animal. It is probable that the wolf's home area is larger than any other of our nonmigratory animals, because it is a large animal, therefore compelled to find much food—a flesh eater whose food supply is notoriously uncertain, and a swift-footed animal that can travel great distances.

When I lived at Pine Ridge, South Dakota, in 1902, Dr. James R. Walker and others told me of an enormous white wolf that had been living around there for three years. It was usually seen within fifteen miles of Pine Ridge.

In New Mexico, several wolves were well known by their individual marks and believed to be permanent residents of a region about thirty miles across. In Dakota, near Medora, was a well-known wolf called Mountain Billy; he was so named because he was always found near a certain mountain called Sentinel Butte. This would limit his range to a radius of a dozen miles. . . .

It is the opinion of all hunters whom I have consulted, that the summer range of a gray wolf is less than twenty miles across. In winter, however, it may be doubled by the scarcity of food, but at all times there is a region that it recognizes as home. Yet the great Custer wolf had a known range of forty by sixty-five miles.

Unlike the deer, the wolf, so far as known, does not have two home regions, one for summer and another, entirely distinct, to which it migrates for the winter; i.e., the gray wolf is a wide ranger but nonmigratory.

As one views and considers the vast continental range of the gray wolf, one realizes that it is equally at home in the semitropics of lowland Texas and on the rugged islands of the Polar Sea. It is found everywhere within the territory marked—open plains, dense forests, rolling uplands, or matted canebrakes—competent and triumphant, except in the water, on thirsty, burning desert of the Southwest, and among the wind-swept peaks of Goatland. . . .

In primitive times the wolf ranged over about 7,000,000 square miles, the widest range in North America of any large land mammal. All of Canada and Alaska and all of the United States, except California and Nevada, were all well supplied with wolves; but not in equal distribution. Wolves were certainly most numerous in the region where their food most abounded, that is, the Buffalo Plains of the West, the deer-teeming forests of the Mississippi Valley, and the middle states of the Atlantic seaboard—the central and temperate regions of the range, its great heart. . . .

The wolf is totally extinct today in Nova Scotia, New Brunswick, Quebec south of the St. Lawrence, Ontario south of Lake Simcoe, all of New England, the Middle Atlantic States, the Ohio Valley, the middle Mississippi country, and the lower Missouri region. That is, it is extinct in the part of its range where formerly it was the most numerous. Though this area is barely one fourth of the total, there can be little doubt that it contains at least one half of the wolf population. In the remaining part, the inevitable process reduced the wolves by half; that is, the wolves in the year 1900 were not more than a quarter of their primitive number. Since then they have been very greatly reduced, though in some localities they are holding their own.

The young ones of the Philadelphia Zoo would whine like puppies as soon as they were born, and the mother would answer and call them in the same manner.

As soon as they could see, they began to play together like the young of the domestic dog. All their growth-stimulating exercise comes to them in the form of play.

At from three to four weeks, according to their vigor, all would come out daily, never at night, and sit or play in the sun about the door of the den, but were ever ready to scurry in again at the slightest alarm. According to Lee Hampleman, my Rocky Mountain guide, the young ones in Colorado first began to follow the mother for short distances from the den in June when they were about three months old, though farther north they might not begin this life for another month.

In August the young are so far grown that they begin to follow the mother about in her hunting expeditions, and the den is abandoned. By this time the doorway is littered with the bones, fur, and feathers of the game brought home by the parents.

The education of the cubs now begins in earnest. The chief means is example. Whether consciously or not, on the part of the teacher or of the class, there can be no doubt that it is by seeing the mother do, or not do, that the little ones learn much that is necessary to their success in life. Thus she inspires them with terror of a trap by showing her own terror of it; no matter whether conscious or unconscious, *this is teaching*. The same is true, I suppose, of all the ideas that modern wolves have; that is, the ideas so recent they have not yet had time to become ingrained as instinct.

There can be little doubt that the ordinary wolf pack seen in summer and autumn is merely the family under guidance of the parents, though on rare occasions, two families will unite for a time.

The most I ever saw in a band was five. This was in northern

New Mexico, January 1894. The most I ever heard of in a band was thirty-two. This was in the same region and was doubtless a winter assemblage of four or five families.

The wolf does not breed till it is two years old. Consequently, bands of immature, unmated wolves are sometimes seen in spring and summer. These are known as the bachelor packs.

The fact that these foot-loose, carefree wanderers keep together is an evidence of sociability. Indeed, the wolves are the most sociable beasts of prey. Not only do they gather in bands, but they arrange to render each other assistance, which is the most important test of sociability.

The large packs are apparently formed in winter only. I think, further, that this species is not gregarious in the sense that the antelope and wapiti are. The pack are probably temporary associations of personal acquaintances, for some temporary purpose, or passing reason, such as food question or mating instinct. As soon as this is settled, they scatter. No doubt these same individuals are ready to reunite as soon as a new occasion requires it, and would resent the presence of a total stranger. This I take to be true sociability. . . .

The usual cry of the wolf is a long, smooth howl. It is quite musical, though decidedly eerie when heard in the woods at night. I cannot distinguish it from the howl of a large dog. Its beginning is also much like the hoot of an owl. This is usually the "muster" or "rallying cry"—the intimation of the wolf to his friends that he has found game too strong for him to manage alone. It is the call commonly heard at night about the settlers' cabins and it never fails to affect me personally with a peculiar prickling in the scalp that I doubt not is a racial inheritance from the Stone Age.

A second sound is a high-pitched howl, vibrating on two notes. This may be styled the "hunting song"; it corresponds exactly with the full cry of a pack of hounds on the hot scent.

A third is a combination of a short bark and a howl. It seems to mean the "closing in" for a finish. There are several others that I have often heard, but cannot comprehend. . . .

The speed of the wolf is often exaggerated. My impression is that twenty-one or twenty-two miles an hour would represent the *highest rate* of an average individual *for one mile.* This is much less than the speed of the coyote, jackrabbit, deer, antelope, greyhound, or even foxhound; but the wolf can keep it up longer than most animals.

The diet of this species includes every kind of animal food that he can secure, from mouse to moose. Throughout the summer, mice and "small deer" are doubtless the staples. The coming of winter makes a radical change. First, it puts the small game beyond reach; second, it robs the moose and deer of the same refuge afforded by the lakes and rivers and thus brings these great ruminants into the dietary of the wolves.

When a man goes a-hunting to get food, we call him a pothunter and despise him. When a man goes a-hunting for the pleasure of the chase, and piles up a long list of dead, announcing an incredible bag, we laud him as a sportsman.

When a wolf goes hunting for his food, we hate him for a destroyer, even though he be starving. When he has sufficient food and kills for the love of sport, we have no language strong enough to condemn the destructive monster. . . .

Can we not be honest enough to say that the wolf is a sportsman, swayed not by vulgar appetite or desire for material possession, but by the love of the game, the joy of the chase? He is a real sport.

The gray wolf is one of the shyest of wild animals. I have talked with men who have lived their whole lives in regions where the gray wolves were far from rare, and yet they have never seen one. They hear them at night, they see their trails and their work in the morning, but never see the animals themselves until they have been trapped or poisoned. Their extreme shyness is partly a modern development, as also is the respect for man, which now fully possesses every gray wolf in the cattle country. There are many records that show the wolf to have been a continual danger to mankind in the bow-and-arrow days. There can be no doubt that then man was considered a fair prey—a difficult and wide-awake one, no doubt, but still a creature to be eaten in times of scarcity. Consequently, each winter in America, as in Europe, a number of human beings were killed and devoured by hungry wolves.

During the last 50 years, I cannot find a reliable instance of wolves killing or even attacking human beings. The question then arises, are the old records wrong, relating as they do the frequent destruction of man by wolves; so much so that in the ancient days of Europe, the wolf was the most dreaded of the wild animals? Or are the modern wolves of different species?

The answer is, the modern wolves are the same as the old ones, except in one particular, *viz.,* that they have been educated by gunpowder to let man alone. Man with the modern gun is a different creature from man with the bow and arrow. The wolves have learned this and are now no more a menace to human life than are the prairie wolves or coyotes. Not only do they abstain from harming man, but they have learned that they are likely to be harmed by him; usually they keep out of sight in the daytime. This, I think, is why wolves are so rarely seen, even where comparatively common.

In accounting for these changes, it is not necessary to attribute human intelligence to this animal. Evidently much hard luck and many unpleasant surprises have engendered in it a deep and general distrust of all strange things, as well as a well-founded fear of anything that bears the taint of a human being. This distrust, combined with its exquisite sense of smell, may explain much that looks like profound sagacity in this animal. Nevertheless, this will not explain all, as I have had very good reason to remark again and again, when I have endeavored to trap or poison wolves on the cattle ranges.

Although we must be cautious about receiving accounts on the gray wolf's ferocity, we are sure to be surprised by facts about its strength. I have known a young gray wolf, scarcely six months old, drag off a 100-pound bar of iron to which it was chained, taking it 200 or 300 yards without stopping and a quarter of a mile before discovered. This same cub could almost hold its own against an ordinary man pulling at its chain. I have several times seen a gray wolf in a trap go off with the drag that weighed considerably over 100 pounds; and on one occasion I saw an eighty-pound female that was trapped drag a fifty-two pound beef head over rough ground faster than I could follow on foot, and kept up the flight for one and a half miles.

I have known a gray wolf to go off carrying the head of an ox in his jaws, and take it so far that I gave up following this trail in the dust. I did not weigh the oxhead, but found that a small cow head weighed over fifty pounds, so it must have been at least seventy-five pounds.

The wolf's great strength, indeed, is in his jaws. It is doubtful whether any dog of truly domesticated race has such powerful jaws as the wolf. It is generally believed by the hunters that for this reason no dog has yet been found which, single-handed, could conquer a full-grown wolf.

The rope used for lassos on the Plains is half-inch manila, and yet has often been cut through by a single clip of the wolf's jaws when he has been lassoed.

When the buffalo swarmed over western America from the Alleghenies to the Rockies, and from Great Slave Lake to Central Mexico, their herds were followed by bands of buffalo wolves that preyed on the weak and helpless. As the buffalo disappeared, the wolves were harder put for a living. When the last buffalo herds were destroyed and the wolves were left without their usual support, they naturally turned their attention to the cattle on the ranges.

The ranchmen declared vigorous war against them; traps and poison were imported in vast quantities, a bounty was offered for each wolf scalp, and every inducement was held out to wolf hunters.

In those days the wolves were comparatively unsuspicious, and it was easy to trap or poison them. The result was that enormous numbers were killed in the early days of 1880 to 1888 or 1889; so many, indeed, that the species seemed on the verge of extinction. The remnant of the race continued on the foothills of the Rockies or the Badlands, but they were so rare as to be no longer a factor in the cattle question. Then new knowledge, a better comprehension of the modern dangers, seemed to spread among the wolves. They learned how to detect and defy the traps and poison, and in some way the knowledge was passed from one to another, till all wolves were fully possessed of the information. How this is done is not easy to say. It is easier to prove that it *is* done. Few wolves ever get into a trap, fewer still get into a trap and out again, and thus learn that a steel trap is a thing to be feared. And yet all wolves have that knowledge, as every trapper knows, and since they could not get it at first hand, they must have got it second hand; that is, the information was communicated to them by others of their kind.

It is well known among hunters that a piece of iron is enough to protect any carcass from the wolves. If a deer or antelope has been shot and is to be left overnight, all that is needed for its protection is an old horseshoe, a spur, or even any part of the hunter's dress. No wolf will go near such suspicious-looking or human-tainted things; he will starve rather than approach the carcass so guarded.

With poison, a similar change has come about. Strychnine was considered infallible when first it was introduced. It did vast destruction for a time, then the wolves seemed to discover the danger associated with that particular smell, and will no longer take the poisoned bait, as I know from numberless experiences.

It is thoroughly known among the cattlemen now that the only chance of poisoning wolves is in the late summer and early autumn, when the young are beginning to run with the mother. She cannot watch over all of them the whole time, and there is a chance of some of them finding the bait and taking it before they have been taught to let that sort of smell-thing alone.

The result was that the wolves increased during the late 80's. They returned to many of their old hunting grounds in the cattle countries, and each year they seemed to be more numerous and more widely spread, thanks to their mastery of the new problems forced upon them by civilization.

But the growing extent of the ravages led to higher bounties, so that many men became wolvers, that is, professional wolf hunters. New means of destruction were invented, but by far the most effective of these was the plan of locating the dens.

In the northern cattle ranges, the young are born while yet there is snow on the ground, and it has proved quite easy to backtrack the old wolves, discover the den, destroy the brood, and later the old ones, for they continue to hover about till shot. Thus their parental devotion is made the means of their destruction.

Such methods have resulted in a steady diminution of the wolves, till now the time is in sight when the gray wolf will be extinct on the cattle ranges of the western states.

Just as there are geniuses and heroes among men, so there are extraordinary individuals among wolves. These have always interested me, and I have endeavored to record the lives of such as came to hand.

The pages of European history are picturesquely varied by accounts of wonderful wolves that appeared from time to time, usually specimens that left frightful records of destruction among men and cattle.

One of the most celebrated was *La Bête de Gevaudan,* which lived in central France about 1760 to 1765, during which time he devoured ninety-three persons and mangled some thirty more, before he was destroyed. He stood thirty-five inches at the shoulder and weighed 165 pounds.

In our own country we have no lack of famous wolves—heroes, for they are the unusually gifted individuals that have appeared, bravely fighting with unusual success their own hopeless fight against us. One of the first of them that I met was the Winnipeg Wolf. In March 1882, while coming to Winnipeg from St. Paul, I saw a sight that stirred my blood. As the train flashed through an opening of the poplar woods south of St. Boniface, there stood a great, splendid gray wolf, erect and defiant, surrounded by a motley rabble of town dogs, big and small. A small dog was lying in the snow near him, and a big dog was bounding about doing some magnificent barking, but keeping his safe distance. The train passed and I saw no more.

A dog driver was killed next winter on the ice of the Red River while bound for Fort Alexander. The team was big, fierce huskies, and he was a strange driver. It is thought that he struck at one of them with the whip, it had snapped back, and he, in retreating, had fallen, whereupon the four savage creatures had set on him and ended by devouring him. The counter theory was that he had been killed by a wolf or wolves, of which the dogs are notoriously afraid. The latter explanation found favor only with the dogs' owner, for the reason, people said, that he did not wish to lose his valuable team.

A large wolf was seen several times afterward about the city, and at length was killed near the slaughterhouse, some said, by poison, dogs, guns, or all three. This was a male and weighed 104 pounds. It was mounted by W. R. Hine, the taxidermist, and shown at the Chicago Exposition of 1893. This interesting relic was one of the valuable specimens lost in the Mulvey Grammar School when the building was destroyed by fire in 1896.

I have, of course, no evidence that in each case it was the same wolf, but in writing the story of "The Winnipeg Wolf" I took a writer's liberty in making them so. The other adventures ascribed to him really belonged to other wolves in distant regions.

In the story of "Lobo," I assumed a similar freedom. I ascribed to one wolf the adventures of several, and I selected for him the most heroic exterior I could find. But the final chapter recording his capture and death is given exactly as it happened, and was indeed the inspiring motive of the story.[1]

# 17.

# TWO WOLF STORIES

## *Lobo, the King of Currumpaw*

CURRUMPAW is a vast cattle range in northern New Mexico. It is a land of rich pastures and teeming flocks and herds, a land of rolling mesas and precious running waters that at length unite in the Currumpaw River, from which the whole region is named. And the king whose despotic power was felt over its entire extent was an old gray wolf.

Old Lobo, or the king, as the Mexicans called him, was the gigantic leader of a remarkable pack of gray wolves that had ravaged the Currumpaw Valley for a number of years. All the shepherds and ranchmen knew him well, and wherever he appeared with his trusty band, terror reigned supreme among the cattle, and wrath and despair among their owners. Old Lobo was a giant among wolves, and was cunning and strong in proportion to his size. His voice at night was well known and easily distinguished from that of any of his fellows. An ordinary wolf might howl half the night about the herdsman's bivouac without attracting more than a passing notice, but when the deep roar of the old king came booming down the canyon, the watcher bestirred himself and prepared to learn in the morning that fresh and serious inroads had been made among the herds.

Old Lobo's band was but a small one. This I never quite understood, for usually, when a wolf rises to the position and power that he had, he attracts a numerous following. It may be that he had as many as he desired, or perhaps his ferocious temper prevented the increase of his pack. Certain it is that Lobo had only five followers during the latter part of his reign. Each of these, however, was a wolf of renown, most of them were above the ordinary size, one in particular, the second in command, was a veritable giant, but even he was far below the leader in size and prowess. Several of the band, besides the two leaders, were especially noted. One of these was a beautiful white wolf, that the Mexicans called Blanca; this was supposed to be a female, possibly Lobo's mate. Another was a yellow wolf of remarkable swiftness which, according to current stories, had on several occasions captured an antelope for the pack.

It will be seen, then, that these wolves were thoroughly well known to the cowboys and shepherds. They were frequently seen and oftener heard, and their lives were intimately associated with those of the cattlemen, who would so gladly have destroyed them. There was not a stockman on the Currumpaw who would not readily have given the value of many steers for the scalp of any one of Lobo's band, but they seemed to possess charmed lives, and defied all manner of devices to kill them. They scorned all hunters, derided all poisons, and continued, for at least five years, to exact their tribute from the Currumpaw ranchers to the extent, many said, of a cow each day. According to this estimate, therefore, the band had killed more than two thousand of the finest stock, for, as was only too well known, they selected the best in every instance.

The old idea that a wolf was constantly in a starving state, and therefore ready to eat anything, was as far as possible from the truth in this case, for these freebooters were always sleek and well conditioned, and were in fact most fastidious about what they ate. Any animal that had died from natural causes, or that was diseased or tainted, they would not touch, and they even rejected anything that had been killed by the stockmen. Their choice and daily food was the tenderer part of a freshly killed yearling heifer. An old bull or cow they disdained, and though they occasionally took a young calf or colt, it was quite clear that veal or horseflesh was not their favorite diet. It was also known that they were not fond of mutton, although they often amused themselves by killing sheep. One night in November 1893, Blanca and the yellow wolf killed 250 sheep, apparently for the fun of it, and did not eat an ounce of their flesh.

These are examples of many stories which I might repeat, to show the ravages of this destructive band. Many new devices for their extinction were tried each year, but still they lived and throve in spite of all the efforts of their foes. A great price was set on Lobo's head, and in consequence poison in a score of subtle forms was put out for him, but he never failed to detect and avoid it. One thing only he feared—that was firearms, and knowing full well that all men in this region carried them, he never was known to attack or face a human being. Indeed, the set policy of his band was to take refuge in flight whenever, in the daytime, a man was descried, no matter at what distance. Lobo's habit of permitting the pack to eat only that which they themselves had killed was in numerous cases their salvation, and the keenness of his scent to detect the taint of human hands or the poison itself completed their immunity.

On one occasion, one of the cowboys heard the too-familiar rallying cry of old Lobo, and stealthily approaching, he found the Currumpaw pack in a hollow, where they had rounded up a small herd of cattle. Lobo sat apart on a knoll, while Blanca with the rest was endeavoring to cut out a young cow which they had selected; but the cattle were standing in a compact mass with their heads outward, and presented to the foe a line of horns, unbroken save when some cow, frightened by a fresh onset of the wolves, tried to retreat into the middle of the herd. It was only by taking advantage of these breaks that the wolves had succeeded at all in wounding the selected cow, but she was far from being disabled, and it seemed that Lobo at length lost patience with his followers, for he left his position on the hill and, uttering a deep roar, dashed toward the herd. The terrified rank broke at his charge, and he sprang in among them. Then the cattle scattered like the pieces of a bursting bomb. Away went the chosen victim, but ere she had gone twenty-five yards Lobo was upon her. Seizing her by the neck he suddenly held back with all his force and so threw her heavily to the ground. The shock must have been tremendous, for the heifer was thrown heels over head. Lobo also turned a somersault, but immediately recovered himself, and his followers, falling on the poor cow, killed her in a few seconds. Lobo took no part in the killing—after having thrown the victim, he seemed to say, "Now, why could not some of you have done that at once without wasting so much time?"

The man now rode up shouting, the wolves as usual retired, and he, having a bottle of strychnine, quickly poisoned the carcass in three places, then went away, knowing they would return to feed, as they had killed the animal themselves. But next morning, on going to look for his expected victims, he found that, although the wolves had eaten the heifer, they had carefully cut out and thrown aside all those parts that had been poisoned.

The dread of this great wolf spread yearly among the ranchmen, and each year a larger price was set on his head, until at last it reached $1,000, an unparalleled wolf bounty, surely; many a good man has been hunted down for less. Tempted by the promised reward, a Texan ranger named Tannerey came one day galloping up the canyon of the Currumpaw. He had a superb outfit for wolf hunting—the best of guns and horses, and a pack of enormous wolf hounds. Far out on the plains of the Panhandle, he and his dogs had killed many a wolf, and now he never doubted that, within a few days, old Lobo's scalp would dangle at his saddlebow.

Away they went bravely on their hunt in the gray dawn of a summer morning, and soon the great dogs gave joyous tongue to say that they were already on the track of their quarry. Within two miles, the grizzly band of Currumpaw leaped into view, and the chase grew fast and furious. The part of the wolfhounds was merely to hold the wolves at bay till the hunter could ride up and shoot them, and this usually was easy on the open plains of Texas; but here a new feature of the country came into play, and showed how well Lobo had chosen his range; for the rocky canyons of the Currumpaw and its tributaries intersect the prairies in every direction. The old wolf at once made for the nearest of these and by crossing it got rid of the horsemen. His band then scattered and thereby scattered the dogs, and when they reunited at a distant point of course all of the dogs did not turn up, and the wolves, no longer outnumbered, turned on their pursuers and killed or desperately wounded them all. That night, when Tannerey mustered his dogs, only six of them returned, and of these, two were terribly lacerated. This hunter made two other attempts to capture the royal scalp, but neither of them was more successful than the first, and on the last occasion his best horse met its death by a fall; so he gave up the chase in disgust and went back to Texas, leaving Lobo more than ever the despot of the region.

Next year, two other hunters appeared, determined to win the promised bounty. Each believed he could destroy this noted wolf, the first by means of a newly devised poison, which was to be laid out in an entirely new manner; the other a French Canadian, by poison assisted with certain spells and charms, for he firmly believed that Lobo was a veritable *loup-garou,* and could not be killed by ordinary means. But cunningly compounded poisons, charms, and incantations were all of no avail against this grizzly devastator. He made his weekly rounds and daily banquets as aforetime, and before many weeks had passed, Calone and Laloche gave up in despair and went elsewhere to hunt.

In the spring of 1893, after his unsuccessful attempt to capture Lobo, Joe Calone had a humiliating experience, which seems to show that the big wolf simply scorned his enemies, and had absolute confidence in himself. Calone's farm was on a small tributary of the Currumpaw, in a picturesque canyon, and among the rocks of this very canyon, within a thousand yards of the house, old Lobo and his mate selected their den and raised their family that season. There they lived all summer, and killed Joe's cattle, sheep, and dogs, but laughed at all his poisons and traps, and rested securely among the recesses of the cavernous cliffs, while Joe vainly racked his brain for some method of smoking them out, or of reaching them with dynamite. But they escaped entirely unscathed, and continued their ravages as before. "There's where he lived all last summer," said Joe, pointing to the face of the cliff, "and I couldn't do a thing with him. I was like a fool to him."

This history, gathered so far from the cowboys, I found hard to believe until in the fall of 1893 I made the acquaintance of the wily marauder, and at length came to know him more thoroughly than anyone else. Some years before, in the Bingo days, I had been a wolf hunter, but my occupations since then had been of another sort, chaining me to stool and desk. I was much in need of a change, and when a friend, who was also a ranch owner on the Currumpaw, asked me to come to New Mexico and try if I could do anything with this predatory pack, I accepted the invitation and, eager to make the acquaintance of its king, was as soon as possible among the mesas of that region. I spent some time riding about to learn the country, and at intervals my guide would point

to the skeleton of a cow to which the hide still adhered, and remark, "That's some of his work."

It became quite clear to me that, in this rough country, it was
useless to think of pursuing Lobo with hounds and horses, so that
poison or traps were the only available expedients. At present we
had no traps large enough, so I set to work with poison.

I need not enter into the details of a hundred devices that I
employed to circumvent this *loup-garou;* there was no combination
of strychnine, arsenic, cyanide, or prussic acid that I did not
essay; there was no manner of flesh that I did not try as bait; but
morning after morning, as I rode forth to learn the result, I found
that all my efforts had been useless. The old king was too cunning
for me. A single instance will show his wonderful sagacity. Acting
on the hint of an old trapper, I melted some cheese together with
the kidney fat of a freshly killed heifer, stewing it in a china dish,
and cutting it with a bone knife to avoid the taint of metal. When
the mixture was cool, I cut it into lumps, and making a hole in
one side of each lump, I inserted a large dose of strychnine and
cyanide, contained in a capsule that was impermeable by any odor;
finally I sealed the holes up with pieces of the cheese itself. During
the whole process, I wore a pair of gloves steeped in the hot blood
of the heifer, and even avoided breathing on the baits. When all
was ready, I put them in a rawhide bag rubbed all over with blood,
and rode forth dragging the liver and kidneys of the beef at the
end of a rope. With this I made a ten-mile circuit, dropping a bait
at each quarter of a mile, and taking the utmost care, always, not
to touch any with my hands.

Lobo, generally, came into this part of the range in the early
part of each week, and passed the latter part, it was supposed,
around the base of Sierra Grande. This was Monday, and that
same evening, as we were about to retire, I heard the deep bass

howl of his majesty. On hearing it one of the boys briefly remarked, "There he is, we'll see."

The next morning I went forth, eager to know the result. I soon came on the fresh trail of the robbers, with Lobo in the lead —his track was always easily distinguished. An ordinary wolf's forefoot is four and a half inches long, that of a large wolf four and three quarters, but Lobo's, as measured a number of times, was five and a half inches from claw to heel; I afterward found that his other proportions were commensurate, for he stood three feet high at the shoulder and weighed 150 pounds. His trail, therefore, though obscured by those of his followers, was never difficult to trace. The pack had soon found the track of my drag, and as usual followed it. I could see that Lobo had come to the first bait, sniffed about it, and finally had picked it up.

Then I could not conceal my delight. "I've got him at last," I exclaimed; "I shall find him stark within a mile," and I galloped on with eager eyes fixed on the great broad track in the dust. It led me to the second bait and that also was gone. How I exulted—I surely have him now and perhaps several of his band. But there was the broad paw mark still on the drag; and though I stood in the stirrup and scanned the plain I saw nothing that looked like a dead wolf. Again I followed—to find now that the third bait was gone— and the king wolf's track led on to the fourth, there to learn that he had not really taken a bait at all, but had merely carried them in his mouth. Then having piled the three on the fourth, he scattered filth over them to express his utter contempt for my devices. After this he left my drag and went about his business with the pack he guarded so effectively.

This is only one of many similar experiences which convinced me that poison would never avail to destroy this robber, and though I continued to use it while awaiting the arrival of the traps, it was only because it was meanwhile a sure means of killing many prairie wolves and other destructive vermin.

About this time there came under my observation an incident that will illustrate Lobo's diabolic cunning. These wolves had at least one pursuit which was merely an amusement; it was stampeding and killing sheep, though they rarely ate them. The sheep are usually kept in flocks of from one thousand to three thousand under one or more shepherds. At night they are gathered in the most sheltered place available, and a herdsman sleeps on each side of the flock to give additional protection. Sheep are such senseless creatures that they are liable to be stampeded by the veriest trifle, but they have deeply ingrained in their nature one, and perhaps only one, strong weakness, namely, to follow their leader. And this the shepherds turn to good account by putting half a dozen goats in the flock of sheep. The latter recognize the superior intelligence of their bearded cousins, and when a night alarm occurs they crowd around them, and usually are thus saved from a stampede and are easily protected. But it was not always so. One night late in last November, two Perico shepherds were aroused by an onset of wolves. Their flocks huddled around the goats which, being neither fools nor cowards, stood their ground and were bravely defiant; but alas for them, no common wolf was heading this attack. Old Lobo, the werewolf, knew as well as the shepherds that the goats were the moral force of the flock, so hastily running over the backs of the densely packed sheep, he fell on these leaders, slew them all in a few minutes, and soon had the luckless sheep stampeding in a thousand different directions. For weeks afterward I was almost daily accosted by some anxious shepherd, who asked, "Have you seen any stray OTO sheep lately?" and usually I was obliged to say I had; one day it was, "Yes, I came on some five or six carcasses by Diamond Springs"; or another, it was to the effect that I had seen a small "bunch" running on the Malpai

Mesa; or again, "No, but Juan Meira saw about twenty, freshly killed, on the Cedra Monte two days ago."

At length the wolf traps arrived, and with two men I worked a whole week to get them properly set out. We spared no labor or pains; I adopted every device I could think of that might help to insure success. The second day after the traps arrived, I rode around to inspect, and soon came upon Lobo's trail running from trap to trap. In the dust I could read the whole story of his doings that night. He had trotted along in the darkness, and although the traps were so carefully concealed, he had instantly detected the first one. Stopping the onward march of the pack, he had cautiously scratched around it until he had disclosed the trap, the chain, and the log, then left them wholly exposed to view with the trap still unsprung, and passing on, he treated over a dozen traps in the same fashion. Very soon I noticed that he stopped and turned aside as soon as he detected suspicious signs on the trail, and a new plan to outwit him at once suggested itself. I set the traps in the form of an H; that is, with a row of traps on each side of the trail, and one on the trail for the crossbar of the H. Before long, I had an opportunity to count another failure. Lobo came trotting along the trail, and was fairly between the parallel lines before he detected the single trap in the trail, but he stopped in time, and why or how he knew enough I cannot tell—the Angel of the wild things must have been with him—but without turning an inch to the right or left, he slowly and cautiously backed on his own tracks, putting each paw exactly in its old track until he was off dangerous ground. Then returning at one side he scratched clods and stones with his hind feet till he had sprung every trap. This he did on many other occasions, and although I varied my methods and redoubled my precautions, he was never deceived, his sagacity seemed never at fault, and he might have been pursuing his career of rapine today, but for an unfortunate alliance that proved his ruin and added his name to the long list of heroes who, unassailable when alone, have fallen through the indiscretion of a trusted ally.

Once or twice, I had found indications that everything was not quite right in the Currumpaw pack. There were signs of irregularity, I thought; for instance, there was clearly the trail of a smaller wolf running ahead of the leader, at times, and this I could not understand until a cowboy made a remark which explained the matter.

"I saw them today," he said, "and the wild one that breaks away is Blanca." Then the truth dawned upon me, and I added, "Now, I know that Blanca is a she-wolf, because were a he-wolf to act thus, Lobo would kill him at once."

This suggested a new plan. I killed a heifer, and set one or two rather obvious traps about the carcass. Then, cutting off the head, which is considered useless offal, and quite beneath the notice of a wolf, I set it a little apart and around it placed six powerful steel traps properly deodorized and concealed with the utmost care. During my operations I kept my hands, boots, and implements smeared with fresh blood, and afterward sprinkled the ground with the same, as though it had flowed from the head; and when the traps were buried in the dust I brushed the place over with the skin of a coyote, and with a foot of the same animal made a number of tracks over the traps. The head was so placed that there was a narrow passage between it and some tussocks, and in this passage I buried two of my best traps, fastening them to the head itself.

Wolves have a habit of approaching every carcass they get the wind of, in order to examine it, even when they have no intention of eating of it, and I hoped that this habit would bring the Currumpaw pack within reach of my latest stratagem. I did not doubt

that Lobo would detect my handiwork about the meat, and prevent the pack approaching it, but I did build some hopes on the
head, for it looked as though it had been thrown aside as useless.

Next morning, I sallied forth to inspect the traps, and there, oh,
joy! were the tracks of the pack, and the place where the beef head
and its traps had been was empty. A hasty study of the trail showed
that Lobo had kept the pack from approaching the meat, but one,
a small wolf, had evidently gone on to examine the head as it lay
apart and had walked right into one of the traps.

We set out on the trail, and within a mile discovered that the
hapless wolf was Blanca. Away she went, however, at a gallop, and
although encumbered by the beef head, which weighed over fifty
pounds, she speedily distanced my companion who was on foot.
But we overtook her when she reached the rocks, for the horns of
the cow's head became caught and held her fast. She was the hand-
somest wolf I had ever seen. Her coat was in perfect condition and
nearly white.

She turned to fight, and raising her voice in the rallying cry of
her race, sent a long howl rolling over the canyon. From far away
upon the mesa came a deep response, the cry of old Lobo. That
was her last call, for now we had closed in on her, and all her
energy and breath were devoted to combat.

Then followed the inevitable tragedy, the idea of which I shrank
from afterward more than at the time. We each threw a lasso over
the neck of the doomed wolf, and strained our horses in opposite
directions until the blood burst from her mouth, her eyes glazed,
her limbs stiffened and then fell limp. Homeward then we rode,
carrying the dead wolf and exulting over this, the first deathblow
we had been able to inflict on the Currumpaw pack.

At intervals during the tragedy, and afterward as we rode homeward, we heard the roar of Lobo as he wandered about on the distant mesas, where he seemed to be searching for Blanca. He had

never really deserted her, but knowing that he could not save her, his deep-rooted dread of firearms had been too much for him when he saw us approaching. All that day we heard him wailing as he roamed in his quest, and I remarked at length to one of the boys, "Now, indeed, I truly know that Blanca was his mate."

As evening fell he seemed to be coming toward the home can-yon, for his voice sounded continually nearer. There was an un-mistakable note of sorrow in it now. It was no longer the loud, defiant howl, but a long, plaintive wail; "Blanca! Blanca!" he seemed to call. And as night came down, I noticed that he was not far from the place where we had overtaken her. At length he seemed to find the trail, and when he came to the spot where we had killed her, his heart-broken wailing was piteous to hear. It was sadder than I could possibly have believed. Even the stolid cow-boys noticed it, and said they had "never heard a wolf carry on like that before." He seemed to know exactly what had taken place, for her blood had stained the place of her death.

Then he took up the trail of the horses and followed it to the ranch house. Whether in hopes of finding her there, or in quest of revenge, I know not, but the latter was what he found, for he sur-prised our unfortunate watchdog outside and tore him to little bits within fifty yards of the door. He evidently came alone this time, for I found but one trail next morning, and he had galloped about in a reckless manner that was very unusual with him. I had half expected this, and had set a number of additional traps about the pasture. Afterward I found that he had indeed fallen into one of these, but such was his strength, he had torn himself loose and cast it aside.

I believed that he would continue in the neighborhood until he found her body at least, so I concentrated all my energies on this one enterprise of catching him before he left the region, and while yet in this reckless mood. Then I realized what a mistake I had made in killing Blanca, for by using her as a decoy I might have secured him the next night.

I gathered in all the traps I could command, 130 strong steel wolf traps, and set them in fours in every trail that led into the canyon; each trap was separately fastened to a log, and each log was separately buried. In burying them, I carefully removed the sod and every particle of earth that was lifted we put in blankets, so that after the sod was replaced and all was finished the eye could detect no trace of human handiwork. When the traps were concealed I trailed the body of poor Blanca over each place, and made of it a drag that circled all about the ranch, and finally I took off one of her paws and made with it a line of tracks over each trap. Every precaution and device known to me I used, and retired at a late hour to await the result.

Once during the night I thought I heard old Lobo, but was not sure of it. Next day I rode around, but darkness came on before I completed the circuit of the north canyon, and I had nothing to report. At supper one of the cowboys said, "There was a great row among the cattle in the north canyon this morning, maybe there is something in the traps there." It was afternoon of the next day before I got to the place referred to, and as I drew near, a great grizzly form arose from the ground, vainly endeavoring to escape, and there revealed before me stood Lobo, King of the Currumpaw, firmly held in the traps. Poor old hero, he had never ceased to search for his darling, and when he found the trail her body had made he followed it recklessly, and so fell into the snare prepared for him. There he lay in the iron grasp of all four traps, perfectly helpless, and all around him were numerous tracks showing how the cattle had gathered about him to insult the fallen despot, without daring to approach within his reach. For two days and nights he had lain there, and now was worn out with struggling. Yet, when I went near him, he rose up with bristling mane and raised his voice, and for the last time made the canyon reverberate with his deep bass roar, a call for help, the muster call of his band. But there was none to answer him, and left alone in his extremity, he whirled about with all his strength and made a desperate effort to get at me. All in vain; each trap was a dead drag of over 300 pounds, and in their relentless fourfold grasp, with great steel jaws on every foot, and the heavy logs and chains all entangled together, he was absolutely powerless. How his huge ivory tusks did grind on those cruel chains, and when I ventured to touch him with my rifle barrel he left grooves on it which are there to this day. His eyes glared green with hate and fury, and his jaws snapped with a hollow *chop,* as he vainly endeavored to reach me and my trembling horse. But he was worn out with hunger and struggling and loss of blood, and he soon sank exhausted to the ground.

Something like compunction came over me, as I prepared to deal out to him that which so many had suffered at his hands.

"Grand old outlaw, hero of a thousand lawless raids, in a few minutes you will be but a great load of carrion. It cannot be otherwise." Then I swung my lasso and sent it whistling over his head. But not so fast; he was yet far from being subdued, and before the supple coils had fallen on his neck, he seized the noose and, with one fierce chop, cut through its hard thick strands and dropped it in two pieces at his feet.

Of course I had my rifle as a last resource, but I did not wish to spoil his royal hide, so I galloped back to the camp and returned with a cowboy and a fresh lasso. We threw to our victim a stick of wood which he seized in his teeth, and before he could relinquish it our lassoes whistled through the air and tightened on his neck.

Yet, before the light had died from his fierce eyes, I cried, "Stay, we will not kill him; let us take him alive to the camp." He was so completely powerless now that it was easy to put a stout stick through his mouth, behind his tusks, and then lash his jaws with a heavy cord which was also fastened to the stick. The stick kept the cord in, and the cord kept the stick in, so he was harmless. As soon as he felt his jaws were tied he made no further resistance, and uttered no sound, but looked calmly at us and seemed to say, "Well, you have got me at last, so do as you please with me." And from that time he took no more notice of us.

We tied his feet securely, but he never groaned, nor growled, nor turned his head. Then with our united strength we were just able to put him on my horse. His breath came evenly as though sleeping, and his eyes were bright and clear again, but did not rest on us. Afar on the great rolling mesas they were fixed, his passing kingdom, where his famous band was now scattered. And he gazed till the pony descended the pathway into the canyon, and the rocks cut off the view.

By traveling slowly we reached the ranch in safety, and after securing him with a collar and a strong chain, we staked him out in the pasture and removed the cords. Then for the first time I could examine him closely, and proved how unreliable is vulgar report when a living hero or tyrant is concerned. He had *not* a collar of gold about his neck, nor was there on his shoulders an inverted cross to denote that he had leagued himself with Satan. But I did find on one haunch a great broad scar, that tradition says was the fang mark of Juno, the leader of Tannerey's wolf-hounds—a mark which she gave him the moment before he stretched her lifeless on the sand of the canyon.

I set meat and water beside him, but he paid no heed. He lay calmly on his breast, and gazed with those steadfast yellow eyes away past me down through the gateway of the canyon, over the open plains—his plains—nor moved a muscle when I touched him. When the sun went down he was still gazing fixedly across the prairie. I expected he would call up his band when night came, and prepared for them, but he had called once in his extremity, and none had come; he would never call again.

A lion shorn of his strength, an eagle robbed of his freedom, or a dove bereft of his mate, all die, it is said, of a broken heart; and who will aver that this grim bandit could bear the threefold brunt, heart-whole? This only I know, that when the morning dawned, he was lying there still in his position of calm repose, but his spirit was gone—the old king wolf was dead.

I took the chain from his neck, a cowboy helped me to carry him to the shed where lay the remains of Blanca, as we laid him beside her, the cattleman exclaimed: "There, you *would* come to her, now you are together again."[1]

## Badlands Billy—the Wolf That Won

Do you know the three calls of the hunting wolf: the long-drawn, deep howl, the muster, that tells of game discovered but too strong for the finder to manage alone; and the higher ululation that ringing and swelling is the cry of the pack on a hot scent; and the sharp bark coupled with a short howl that, seeming least of all, is yet a gong of doom, for this is the cry *"Close in"*—this is the finish?

We were riding the Badland Buttes, King and I, with a pack of various hunting dogs stringing behind or trotting alongside. The sun had gone from the sky, and a blood streak marked the spot where he died, away over Sentinel Butte. The hills were dim, the valleys dark, when from the nearest gloom there rolled a long-drawn cry that all men recognize instinctively—melodious, yet with a tone in it that sends a shudder up the spine, though now it has lost all menace for mankind. We listened for a moment. It was the wolf hunter who broke silence: "That's Badlands Billy; ain't it a voice? He's out for his beef tonight."

In pristine days the buffalo herds were followed by bands of wolves that preyed on the sick, the weak, and the wounded. When the buffalo were exterminated the wolves were hard put for support, but the cattle came and solved the question for them by taking the buffalos' place. This caused the wolf war. The ranchmen offered a bounty for each wolf killed, and every cowboy out of work was supplied with traps and poison for wolf killing. The very expert made this their sole business and became known as wolvers. King Ryder was one of these. He was a quiet, gentle-spoken fellow, with a keen eye and an insight into animal life that gave him especial power over broncos and dogs, as well as wolves and bears, though in the last two cases it was power merely to surmise where they were and how best to get at them. He had been a wolver for years, and greatly surprised me by saying that "never in all my experience have I known a gray wolf to attack a human being."

We had many campfire talks while the other men were sleeping, and then it was I learned the little that he knew about Badlands Billy. "Six times have I seem him and the seventh will be Sunday, you bet. He takes his long rest then." And thus on the very ground where it all fell out, to the noise of the night wind and the yapping of the coyote, interrupted sometimes by the deep-drawn howl of the hero himself, I heard chapters of this history which, with others gleaned in many fields, gave me the story of the Big Dark Wolf of Sentinel Butte.

Away back in the spring of '92 a wolver was "wolving" on the east side of the Sentinel Mountain that so long was a principal landmark of the old Plainsmen. Pelts were not good in May, but the bounties were high, five dollars a head, and double for she-wolves. As he went down to the creek one morning he saw a wolf coming to drink on the other side. He had an easy shot, and on killing it found it was a nursing she-wolf. Evidently her family were somewhere near, so he spent two or three days searching in all the likely places, but found no clue to the den.

Two weeks afterward, as the wolver rode down an adjoining canyon, he saw a wolf come out of a hole. The ever-ready rifle came up, and another ten-dollar scalp was added to his string. Now he dug into the den and found the litter, a most surprising one indeed, for it consisted not of the usual five or six wolf pups, but of eleven, and these, strange to say, were of two sizes, five of them larger and older than the other six. Here were two distinct families with one mother, and as he added their scalps to his string of trophies, the truth dawned on the hunter. One lot was surely the family of the she-wolf he had killed two weeks before. The case was clear: the little ones awaiting the mother that was never to come, had whined piteously and more loudly as their hunger pangs increased; the other mother passing had heard the cubs; her heart was tender now, her own little ones had so recently come, and she cared for the orphans, carried them to her own den, and was providing for the double family when the rifleman had cut the gentle chapter short.

Many a wolver has dug into a wolf den to find nothing. The old wolves, or possibly the cubs themselves, often dig little side pockets and off galleries, and when an enemy is breaking in they hide in these. The loose earth conceals the small pocket and thus the cubs escape. When the wolver retired with his scalps he did not know that the biggest of all the cubs was still in the den, and even had he waited about for two hours, he might have been no wiser. Three hours later the sun went down and there was a slight scratching afar in the hole; first two little gray paws, then a small black nose appeared in a soft sand pile to one side of the den. At length the cub came forth from his hiding. He had been frightened by the attack on the den; now he was perplexed by its condition.

It was thrice as large as it had been and open at the top now. Lying near were things that smelled like his brothers and sisters, but they were repellent to him. He was filled with fear as he sniffed at them, and sneaked aside into a thicket of grass as a night-hawk boomed over his head. He crouched all night in that thicket. He did not dare to go near the den, and knew not where else he could go. The next morning, when two vultures came swooping down on the bodies, the wolf cub ran off in the thicket and, seek-ing its deepest cover, was led down a ravine to a wide valley. Sud-denly there arose from the grass a big she-wolf, like his mother, yet different, a stranger, and instinctively the stray cub sank to the earth, as the old wolf bounded on him. No doubt the cub had been taken for some lawful prey, but a whiff set that right. She stood over him for an instant. He groveled at her feet. The impulse to kill him or at least give him a shake died away. He had the smell of a young cub. Her own were about his age, her heart was touched, and when he found courage enough to put his nose up and smell her nose, she made no angry demonstration except a short, half-hearted growl. Now, however, he had smelled some-thing that he sorely needed. He had not fed since the day before, and when the old wolf turned to leave him, he tumbled after her on clumsy puppy legs. Had the mother wolf been far from home he must soon have been left behind, but the nearest hollow was the chosen place, and the cub arrived at the den's mouth soon after the mother wolf.

A stranger is an enemy, and the old one, rushing forth to the defense, met the cub again, and again was restrained by something that rose in her responsive to the smell. The cub had thrown him-self on his back in utter submission, but that did not prevent his nose reporting to him the good thing almost within reach. The she-wolf went into the den and curled herself about her brood; the cub persisted in following. She snarled as he approached her own little ones, but disarming wrath each time by submission and his very cubhood, he was presently among her brood, helping him-self to what he wanted so greatly, and thus he adopted himself into her family. In a few days he was so much one of them that the mother forgot about his being a stranger. Yet he was different from them in several ways—older by two weeks, stronger, and marked on the neck and shoulders with what afterward grew to be a dark mane.

Little Duskymane could not have been happier in his choice of a foster-mother, for the yellow wolf was not only a good hunter with a fund of cunning, but she was a wolf of modern ideas as well. The old tricks of tolling a prairie dog, relaying for antelope, houghing a bronco or flanking a steer, she had learned partly from instinct and partly from the example of her more experienced relatives, when they joined to form the winter bands. But, just as necessary nowadays, she had learned that all men carry guns, that guns are irresistible, that the only way to avoid them is by keeping out of sight while the sun is up, and yet that at night they are harmless. She had a fair comprehension of traps, indeed she had been in one once, and though she left a toe behind in pulling free, it was a toe most advantageously disposed of; thenceforth, though not comprehending the nature of the trap, she was thoroughly imbued with the horror of it, with the idea indeed that iron is dangerous, and at any price it should be avoided.

On one occasion, when she and five others were planning to raid a sheep yard, she held back at the last minute because some new-strung wires appeared. The others rushed in to find the sheep beyond their reach, themselves in a death trap.

Thus she had learned the newer dangers, and while it is unlikely that she had any clear mental conception of them she had acquired a wholesome distrust of all things strange, and a horror of one or two in particular that proved her lasting safeguard. Each year she raised her brood successfully and the number of yellow wolves increased in the country. Guns, traps, men, and the new animals they brought had been learned, but there was yet another lesson before her—a terrible one indeed.

About the time Duskymane's brothers were a month old his

foster-mother returned in a strange condition. She was frothing at the mouth, her legs trembled, and she fell in a convulsion near the doorway of the den, but recovering, she came in. Her jaws quivered, her teeth rattled a little as she tried to lick the little ones; she seized her own front leg and bit it so as not to bite them, but at length she grew quieter and calmer. The cubs had retreated in fear to a far pocket, but now they returned and crowded about her to seek their usual food. The mother recovered, but was very ill for two or three days, and those days with the poison in her system worked disaster for the brood. They were terribly sick; only the strongest could survive, and when the trial of strength was over, the den contained only the old one and the black-maned cub, the one she had adopted. Thus little Duskymane became her sole charge, all her strength was devoted to feeding him, and he thrived apace.

Wolves are quick to learn certain things. The reactions of smell are the greatest that a wolf can feel, and thenceforth both cub and foster-mother experienced a quick, unreasoning sense of fear and hate the moment the smell of strychnine reached them.

With the sustenance of seven at his service, the little wolf had every reason to grow, and when in the autumn he began to follow his mother on her hunting trips he was as tall as she was. Now a change of region was forced on them, for numbers of little wolves were growing up. Sentinel Butte, the rocky fastness of the plains, was claimed by many that were big and strong; the weaker must move out, and with them Yellow Wolf and the Dusky Cub.

Wolves have no language in the sense that man has; their vocabulary is probably limited to a dozen howls, barks, and grunts expressing the simplest emotions; but they have several other modes of conveying ideas, and one very special method of spreading information—the wolf telephone. Scattered over their range are a number of recognized "centrals." Sometimes these are stones, sometimes the angle of cross trails, sometimes a buffalo skull—indeed, any conspicuous object near a main trail is used. A wolf calling here, as a dog does at a telegraph post, or a muskrat at a certain mud-pie point, leaves his body scent and learns what other visitors have been there recently to do the same. He learns also whence they came and where they went, as well as something about their condition, whether hunted, hungry, gorged, or sick. By this system of registration a wolf knows where his friends, as well as his foes, are to be found. And Duskymane, following after the Yellow Wolf, was taught the places and uses of the many signal stations without any conscious attempt at teaching on the part of his foster-mother. Example backed by his native instincts was indeed the chief teacher, but on one occasion at least there was something very like the effort of a human parent to guard her child in danger.

The Dark Cub had learned the rudiments of wolf life: that the way to fight dogs is to run, and to fight as you run, never grapple, but snap, snap, snap, and make for the rough country where horses cannot bring their riders.

He learned not to bother about the coyotes that follow for the pickings when you hunt; you cannot catch them and they do you no harm.

He knew he must not waste time dashing after birds that alight on the ground; and that he must keep away from the little black-and-white animal with the bushy tail. It is not very good to eat, and it is very, very bad to smell.

Poison! Oh, he never forgot that smell from the day when the den was cleared of all his foster-brothers.

He now knew that the first move in attacking sheep was to scatter them; a lone sheep is a foolish and easy prey; that the way to round up a band of cattle was to frighten a calf.

He learned that he must always attack a steer from behind, a sheep in front, and a horse in the middle, that is, on the flank, and never, never attack a man at all, never even face him. But an important lesson was added to these, one in which the mother consciously taught him of a secret foe.

A calf had died in branding time and now, two weeks later, was in its best state for perfect taste, not too fresh, not overripe— that is, in a wolf's opinion—and the wind carried this information afar. The Yellow Wolf and Duskymane were out for supper, though not yet knowing where, when the tiding of veal arrived, and they trotted up the wind. The calf was in an open place, and plain to be seen in the moonlight. A dog would have trotted right up to the carcass, an old-time wolf might have done so, but constant war had developed constant vigilance in the Yellow Wolf, and trusting nothing and no one but her nose, she slacked her speed to a walk. On coming in easy view she stopped, and for long swung her nose, submitting the wind to the closest possible chemical analysis. She tried it with her finest tests, blew all the membranes clean again, and tried it once more; and this was the report of the trusty nostrils, yes, the unanimous report. First, rich and racy smell of calf, seventy percent; smells of grass, bugs, wood, flowers, trees, sand, and other uninteresting negations, fifteen percent; smell of her cub and herself, positive but ignorable, ten percent; smell of human tracks, two percent; smell of smoke, one percent; of sweaty-leather smell, one percent; of human-body scent (not discernible in some samples), one-half percent; smell of iron, a trace.

The old wolf crouched a little but sniffed hard with swinging nose; the young wolf imitatively did the same. She backed off to a greater distance; the cub stood. She gave a low whine; he followed unwillingly. She circled around the tempting carcass; a new smell was recorded—coyote trail scent, soon followed by coyote body scent. Yes, there they were sneaking along a near ridge, and now as she passed to one side the samples changed, the wind had lost nearly every trace of calf; miscellaneous, commonplace, and uninteresting smells were there instead. The human-track scent was as before, the trace of leather was gone, but fully one-half percent of iron odor, and body smell of man raised to nearly two percent.

Fully alarmed, she conveyed her fear to the cub, by her rigid pose, her air intent, and her slightly bristling mane.

She continued her round. At one time on a high place the human-body scent was doubly strong, then as she dropped it faded. Then the wind brought the full calf odor with several track scents of coyotes and sundry birds. Her suspicions were lulling as in a smalling circle she neared the tempting feast from the windward side. She had even advanced straight toward it for a few steps when the sweaty leather sang loud and strong again, and smoke and iron mingled like two strands of a parti-colored yarn. Centering all her attention on this, she advanced within two leaps of the calf. There on the ground was a scrap of leather, telling also of a human touch, close at hand the calf, and now the iron and smoke on the full vast smell of calf were like a snake trail across the trail of a whole beef herd. It was so slight that the cub, with the appetite and impatience of youth, pressed up against his mother's shoulder to go past and eat without delay. She seized him by the neck and flung him back. A stone struck by his feet rolled forward and stopped with a peculiar clink. The danger smell was greatly increased at this, and the Yellow Wolf backed slowly from the feast, the cub unwillingly following.

As he looked wistfully he saw the coyotes drawing nearer, mindful chiefly to avoid the wolves. He watched their really cautious advance; it seemed like heedless rushing compared with his mother's approach. The calf smell rolled forth in exquisite and overpowering excellence now, for they were tearing the meat, when a sharp clank was heard and a yelp from a coyote. At the same time the quiet was shocked with a roar and a flash of fire. Heavy shots spattered calf and coyotes, and yelping like beaten dogs they scattered, excepting one that was killed and a second struggling in the trap set here by the ever-active wolvers. The air was charged with the hateful smells redoubled now, and horrid smells additional. The Yellow Wolf glided down a hollow and led her cub away in flight, but as they went, they saw a man rush from the bank near where the mother's nose had warned her of the human scent. They saw him kill the caught coyote and set the traps for more.

The life game is a hard game, for we may win ten thousand times, and if we fail but once our gain is gone. How many hundred times had the Yellow Wolf scorned the traps; how many cubs she had trained to do the same! Of all the dangers to her life she best knew traps.

October had come; the cub was now much taller than the mother. The wolver had seen them once—a Yellow Wolf followed by another, whose long, awkward legs, big, soft feet, thin neck, and skimpy tail proclaimed him this year's cub. The record of the dust and sand said that the old one had lost a right front toe, and that the young one was of giant size.

It was the wolver that thought to turn the carcass of the calf to profit, but he was disappointed in getting coyotes instead of wolves. It was the beginning of the trapping season, for this month fur is prime. A young trapper often fastens the bait on the trap, an experienced one does not. A good trapper will even put the bait at one place and the trap ten or twenty feet away, but at a spot that the wolf is likely to cross in circling. A favorite plan is to hide three or four traps around an open place, and scatter some scraps of meat in the middle. The traps are buried out of sight after being smoked to hide the taint of hands and iron. Sometimes no bait is used except a little piece of cotton or a tuft of feathers that may catch the wolf's eye or pique its curiosity and tempt it to circle on the fateful, treacherous ground. A good trapper varies his methods continually so that the wolves cannot learn his ways. Their only safeguards are perpetual vigilance and distrust of all smells that are known to be of man.

The wolver, with a load of the strongest steel traps, had begun his autumn work on the "Cottonwood."

An old buffalo trail crossing the river followed a little draw that climbed the hills to the level upland. All animals use these trails, wolves and foxes as well as cattle and deer: they are the main thoroughfares. A cottonwood stump not far from where it plunged to the gravelly stream was marked with wolf signs that told the wolver of its use. Here was an excellent place for traps; not on the trail, for cattle were here in numbers, but twenty yards away on a level, sandy spot he set four traps in a twelve-foot square. Near each he scattered two or three scraps of meat; three or four white feathers on a spear of grass in the middle completed the setting. No human eye, few animal noses, could have detected the hidden danger of that sandy ground, when the sun and wind and the sand itself had dissipated the man-track taint.

The Yellow Wolf had seen and passed, and taught her giant son to pass, such traps a thousand times before.

The cattle came to water in the heat of the day. They strung down the buffalo path as once the buffalo did. The little vesper birds flitted before them, the cowbirds rode on them, and the prairie dogs chattered at them, just as they once did at the buffalo.

Down from the gray-green mesa with its green-gray rocks, they marched with imposing solemnity, importance, and directness of purpose. Some frolicsome calves, playing alongside the trail, grew sober and walked behind their mothers as the river flat was reached. The old cow that headed the procession sniffed suspiciously as she passed the "trap set," but it was far away, otherwise she would have pawed and bellowed over the scraps of bloody beef till every trap was sprung and harmless.

But she led to the river. After all had drunk their fill they lay down on the nearest bank till late afternoon. Then their unheard dinner gong aroused them, and started them on the backward march to where the richest pastures grew.

One or two small birds had picked at the scraps of meat, some bluebottle flies buzzed about, but the sinking sun saw the sandy mask untouched.

A brown marsh hawk came skimming over the river flat as the sun began his color play. Blackbirds dashed into thickets and easily avoided his clumsy pounce. It was too early for the mice, but as he skimmed the ground, his keen eye caught the flutter of feathers by the trap and turned his flight. The feathers in their uninteresting emptiness were exposed before he was near, but now he saw the scraps of meat. Guileless of cunning, he alighted and was devouring a second lump when—*clank*—the dust was flirted high and the marsh hawk was held by his toes, struggling vainly in the jaws of a powerful wolf trap. He was not much hurt. His ample wings winnowed from time to time, in efforts to be free, but he was helpless, even as a sparrow might be in a rattrap, and when the sun had played his fierce chromatic scale, his swan song sung, and died as he dies only in the blazing west, and the shades had fallen on the melodramatic scene of the mouse in the elephant trap, there was a deep, rich sound on the high flat butte, answered by another, neither very long, neither repeated, and both instinctive rather than necessary. One was the muster call of an ordinary wolf, the other the answer of a very big male, not a pair in this case, but mother and son—Yellow Wolf and Duskymane. They came trotting together down the buffalo trail. They paused at the telephone box on the hill and again at the old cottonwood root, and were making for the river when the hawk in the trap fluttered his wings. The old wolf turned toward him—a wounded bird on the ground surely, and she rushed forward. Sun and sand soon burn all trail scents; there was nothing to warn her. She sprang on the flopping bird and a chop of her jaws ended his troubles, but a horrid sound—the gritting of her teeth on steel—told her of peril. She dropped the hawk and sprang backward from the dangerous ground, but landed in the second trap. High on her foot its death grip closed, and leaping with all her strength to escape, she set her fore foot in another of the lurking grips of steel. Never had a trap been so baited before. Never was she so unsuspicious. Never was catch more sure. Fear and fury filled the old wolf's heart; she tugged and strained, she chewed the chains, she snarled and foamed. One trap with its buried log, she might have dragged; with two, she was helpless. Struggle as she might, it only worked those relentless jaws more deeply into her feet. She snapped wildly at the air; she tore the dead hawk into shreds; she roared the short, barking roar of a crazy wolf. She bit at the traps, at her cub, at herself. She tore her legs that were held; she gnawed in frenzy at her flank, she chopped off her tail in her madness; she splintered all her teeth on the steel, and filled her bleeding, foaming jaws with clay and sand.

She struggled till she fell, and writhed about or lay like dead, till strong enough to rise and grind the chains again with her teeth.

And so the night passed by.

And Duskymane? Where was he? The feeling of the time when his foster-mother had come home poisoned, now returned; but he was even more afraid of her. She seemed filled with fighting hate. He held away and whined a little; he slunk off and came back when she lay still, only to retreat again, as she sprang forward, raging at him, and then renewed her efforts at the traps. He did not understand it, but he knew this much, she was in terrible trouble, and the cause seemed to be the same as that which had scared them the night they had ventured near the calf.

Duskymane hung about all night, fearing to go near, not knowing what to do, and helpless as his mother.

At dawn the next day a sheepherder seeking lost sheep discovered her from a neighborhood hill. A signal mirror called the wolver from his camp. Duskymane saw the new danger. He was a mere cub, though so tall; he could not face the man, and fled at his approach.

The wolver rode up to the sorry, tattered, bleeding she-wolf in the trap. He raised his rifle and soon the struggling stopped.

The wolver read the trail and the signs about, and remembering those he had read before, he divined that this was the wolf with the great cub—the she-wolf of Sentinel Butte.

Duskymane heard the *crack* as he scurried off into cover. He could scarcely know what it meant, but he never saw his kind old foster-mother again. Thenceforth he must face the world alone.

Instinct is no doubt a wolf's first and best guide, but gifted parents are a great start in life. The dusky-maned cub had had a mother of rare excellence and he reaped the advantage of all her cleverness. He had inherited an exquisite nose and had absolute confidence in its admonitions. Mankind has difficulty in recognizing the power of nostrils. A gray wolf can glance over the morning wind as a man does over his newspaper, and get all the latest news. He can swing over the ground and have the minutest information of every living creature that has walked there within many hours. His nose even tells which way it ran, and in a word renders a statement of every animal that recently crossed his trail, whence it came, and whither it went.

That power had Duskymane in the highest degree; his broad, moist nose was evidence of it to all who are judges of such things. Added to this, his frame was of unusual power and endurance, and last, he had early learned a deep distrust of everything strange, and, call it what we will, shyness, wariness, or suspicion, it was worth more to him than all his cleverness. It was this as much as his physical powers that made a success of his life. Might is right in wolf land, and Duskymane and his mother had been driven out of Sentinel Butte. But it was a very delectable land and he kept drifting back to his native mountain. One or two big wolves there resented his coming. They drove him off several times, yet each time he returned he was better able to face them; and before he was eighteen months old he had defeated all rivals and established himself again on his native ground; where he lived like a robber baron, levying tribute on the rich lands about him and finding safety in the rocky fastness.

Wolver Ryder often hunted in that country, and before long he came across a five-and-one-half-inch track, the footprint of a giant wolf. Roughly reckoned, twenty to twenty-five pounds of weight or six inches of stature is a fair allowance for each inch of a wolf's foot; this wolf therefore stood thirty-three inches at the shoulder and weighed about 140 pounds, by far the largest wolf he had ever met. King had lived in goat country, and now in goat language he exclaimed: "You bet, ain't that an old Billy?" Thus by trivial chance it was that Duskymane was known to his foe as "Badlands Billy."

Ryder was familiar with the muster call of the wolves, the long, smooth cry, but Billy's had a singular feature, a slurring that was always distinctive. Ryder had heard this before, in the Cottonwood Canyon, and when at length he got a sight of the big wolf with the black mane, it struck him that this was also the cub of the old yellow fury that he had trapped.

These were among the things he told me as we sat by the fire at night. I knew of the early days when anyone could trap or poison wolves, of the passing of those days, with the passing of the simple wolves; of the new race of wolves with new cunning that were defying the methods of the ranchmen and increasing steadily in numbers. Now the wolver told me of the various ventures that Penroof had made with different kinds of hounds: of foxhounds too thin skinned to fight; of greyhounds that were useless when the animal was out of sight; of danes too heavy for the rough country, and, last, of the composite pack with some of all kinds, including at times a bull terrier to lead them in the final fight.

He told of hunts after coyotes, which usually were successful because the coyotes sought the plains, and were easily caught by the greyhounds. He told of killing some small gray wolves with this very pack, usually at the cost of the one that led them; but above all he dwelt on the wonderful prowess of "that thar cussed old black wolf of Sentinel Butte," and related the many attempts to run him down or corner him—an unbroken array of failures. For the big wolf, with exasperating persistence, continued to live on the finest stock of the Penroof brand, and each year was teaching more wolves how to do the same with perfect impunity.

I listened even as gold hunters listen to stories of treasure trove, for these were the things of my world. These things indeed were uppermost in all our minds, for the Penroof pack was lying around our campfire now. We were out after Badlands Billy.

One night late in September, after the last streak of light was gone from the west and the coyotes had begun their yapping chorus, a deep, booming sound was heard. King took out his pipe, turned his head and said: "That's him—that's old Billy. He's been watching us all day from some high place, and now when the guns are useless he's here to have a little fun with us."

Two or three dogs arose, with bristling manes, for they clearly recognized that this was no coyote. They rushed out into the night, but did not go far; their brawling sounds were suddenly varied by loud yelps, and they came running back to the shelter of the fire.

One was so badly cut in the shoulder that he was useless for the rest of the hunt. Another was hurt in the flank—it seemed the less serious wound, and yet next morning the hunters buried that second dog.

The men were furious. They vowed speedy vengeance, and at dawn were off on the trail. The coyotes yelped their dawning song, but they melted into the hills when the light was strong. The hunters searched about for the big wolf's tracks, hoping that the hounds would be able to take it up and find them, but they either could not or would not.

They found a coyote, however, and within a few hundred yards they killed him. It was a victory, I suppose, for coyotes kill calves and sheep, but somehow I felt the common thought of all: "Mighty brave dogs for a little coyote, but they could not face the big wolf last night."

Young Penroof, as though in answer to one of the unput questions, said:

"Say, boys, I believe old Billy had a hull bunch of wolves with him last night."

"Didn't see but one track," said King gruffly.

In this way the whole of October slipped by; all day hard riding after doubtful trails, following the dogs, who either could not keep the big trail or feared to do so, and again and again we had news of damage done by the wolf; sometimes a cowboy would report it to us; and sometimes we found the carcasses ourselves. A few of these we poisoned, though it is considered a very dangerous thing to do while running dogs. The end of the month found us a weather-beaten, dispirited lot of men, with a worn-out lot of horses, and a footsore pack, reduced in numbers from ten to seven. So far we had killed only one gray wolf and three coyotes; Badlands Billy had killed at least a dozen cows and dogs at fifty dollars a head. Some of the boys decided to give it up and go home, so

King took advantage of their going, to send a letter asking for re-inforcements, including all the spare dogs at the ranch.

During the two-days' wait we rested our horses, shot some game, and prepared for a harder hunt. Late on the second day the new dogs arrived—eight beauties—and raised the working pack to fifteen.

The weather now turned much cooler, and in the morning, to the joy of the wolvers, the ground was white with snow. This surely meant success. With cool weather for the dogs and horses to run; with the big wolf not far away, for he had been heard the night before; and with tracking snow, so that once found he could not baffle us—escape for him was impossible.

We were up at dawn, but before we could get away, three men came riding into camp. They were the Penroof boys back again. The change of weather had changed their minds; they knew that with snow we might have luck.

"Remember now," said King, as all were mounting, "we don't want any but Badlands Billy this trip. Get him an' we kin bust up the hull combination. It is a five-and-a-half-inch track."

And each measured off on his quirt handle, or on his glove, the exact five and a half inches that was to be used in testing the tracks he might find.

Not more than an hour elapsed before we got a signal from the rider who had gone westward. One shot: that means "attention," a pause while counting ten, then two shots: that means "come on."

King gathered the dogs and rode direct to the distant figure on the hill. All hearts beat high with hope, and we were not dis-appointed. Some small wolf tracks had been found, but here at last was the big track, nearly six inches long. Young Penroof wanted to yell and set out at full gallop. It was like hunting a lion; it was like finding happiness long deferred. The hunter knows nothing more inspiring than the clean-cut line of fresh tracks that is leading to a wonderful animal he has long been hunting in vain. How King's eyes gleamed as he gloated over the sign!

It was the roughest of all rough riding. It was a far longer hunt than we had expected, and was full of little incidents, for that endless line of marks was a minute history of all that the big wolf had done the night before. Here he had circled at the telephone box and looked for news; there he had paused to examine an old skull; here he had shied off and swung cautiously upwind to examine something that proved to be an old tin can; there at length he had mounted a low hill and sat down, probably giving the muster howl, for two wolves had come to him from different directions, and they then had descended to the river flat where the cattle would seek shelter during the storm. Here all three had visited a buffalo skull; there they trotted in line; and yonder they separated, going three different way, to meet—yes—here—oh, what a sight, a fine cow ripped open, left dead and *uneaten*. Not to their taste, it seems, for see! within a mile is another killed by them. Not six hours ago, they had feasted. Here their trails scatter again, but not far, and the snow tells plainly how each had lain down to sleep. The hound's manes bristled as they sniffed those places. King had held the dogs well in hand, but now they were greatly excited. We came to a hill whereon the wolves had turned and faced our way, then fled at full speed—so said the trail—and now it was clear that they had watched us from that hill, and were not far away.

The pack kept well together, because the greyhounds, seeing no quarry, were merely puttering about among the other dogs, or running back with the horses. We went as fast as we could, for the wolves were speeding. Up mesas and down coulees we rode, sticking closely to the dogs, though it was the roughest country that could be picked. One gully after another, an hour and another hour, and still the threefold track went bounding on; another

hour and no change, but interminable climbing, sliding, struggling, through brush and over boulders, guided by the far-away
yelping of the dogs.

Now the chase led downward to the low valley of the river,
where there was scarcely any snow. Jumping and scrambling down
hills, recklessly leaping dangerous gullies and slippery rocks, we
felt that we could not hold out much longer; when on the lowest,
driest level the pack split, some went up, some went down, and
others straight on. Oh, how King did swear! He knew at once
what it meant. The wolves had scattered, and so had divided the
pack. Three dogs after a wolf would have no chance, four could
not kill him, two would certainly be killed. And yet this was the
first encouraging sign we had seen, for it meant that the wolves
were hard pressed. We spurred ahead to stop the dogs, to pick
for them the only trail. But that was not so easy. Without snow
here and with countless dog tracks, we were foiled. All we could
do was let the dogs choose, but keep them to a single choice. Away
we went as before, hoping, yet fearing that we were not on the
right track. The dogs ran well, very fast indeed. This was a bad
sign, King said, but we could not get sight of the track because
the dogs overran it before we came.

After a two-mile run the chase led upward again in snow country; the wolf was sighted, but to our disgust, we were on the track
of the smallest one.

"I thought so," growled young Penroof. "Dogs was altogether
too keen for a serious proposition. Kind o' surprised it ain't turned
out a jackrabbit."

Within another mile he had turned to bay in a willow thicket.
We heard him howl the long-drawn howl for help, and before we
could reach the place King saw the dogs recoil and scatter. A
minute later there sped from the far side of the thicket a small
gray wolf and a black one of very much greater size.

"By golly, if he didn't yell for help, and Billy come back to help him; that's great!" exclaimed the wolver. And my heart went out to the brave old wolf that refused to escape by abandoning his friend.

The next hour was a hard repetition of the gully riding, but it was on the highlands where there was snow, and when again the pack was split, we strained every power and succeeded in keeping them on the big "five-fifty track," that already was wearing for me the glamour of romance.

Evidently the dogs preferred either of the others, but we got them going at last. Another half hour's hard work and far ahead, as I rose to a broad flat plain, I had my first glimpse of the big black wolf of Sentinel Butte.

"Hurrah! Badlands Billy! Hurrah! Badlands Billy!" I shouted in salute, and the others took up the cry.

We were on his track at last, thanks to himself. The dogs joined in with a louder baying, the greyhounds yelped and made straight for him, and the horses sniffed and sprang more gamely as they caught the thrill. The only silent one was the black-maned wolf, and as I marked his size and power, and above all his long and massive jaws, I knew why the dogs preferred some other trail.

With head and tail low he was bounding over the snow. His tongue was lolling long; plainly he was hard pressed. The wolvers' hands flew to their revolvers, though he was 300 yards ahead; they were out for blood, not sport. But an instant later he had sunk from view in the nearest sheltered canyon.

Now which way would he go, up or down the canyon? Up was toward his mountain, down was better cover. King and I thought "up," so pressed westward along the ridge. But the others rode eastward, watching for a chance to shoot.

Soon we had ridden out of hearing. We were wrong—the wolf had gone down, but we heard no shooting. The canyon was crossable here; we reached the other side and then turned back at a gallop, scanning the snow for a trail, the hills for a moving form, or the wind for a sound of life.

*Squeak, squeak,* went our saddle leathers, *puff—puff* our horses, and their feet *ka-ka-lump, ka-ka-lump.*

We were back opposite to where the wolf had plunged but saw no sign. We rode at an easy gallop, on eastward, a mile, and still on, when King gasped out, "Look at that!" A dark spot was moving on the snow ahead. We put on speed. Another dark spot appeared, and another, but they were not going fast. In five minutes we were near them, to find—three of our own greyhounds. They had lost sight of the game, and with that their interest waned. Now they were seeking us. We saw nothing there of the chase or of the other hunters. But hastening to the next ridge we stumbled on the trail we sought and followed as hard as though in view. Another canyon came in our path, and as we rode and looked for a place to cross, a wild din of hounds came from its brushy depth. The clamor grew and passed up the middle.

We raced along the rim, hoping to see the game. The dogs appeared near the farther side, not in a pack, but a long, straggling line. In five minutes more they rose to the edge, and ahead of them was the great black wolf. He was loping as before, head and tail low. Power was plain in every limb, and double power in his jaws and neck, but I thought his bounds were shorter now, and that they had lost their spring. The dogs slowly reached the upper level, and sighting him they broke into a feeble cry; they, too, were nearly spent. The greyhounds saw the chase, and leaving us they scrambled down the canyon and up the other side at impetuous speed that would surely break them down, while we rode, vainly seeking means of crossing.

How the wolver raved to see the pack lead off in the climax of the chase, and himself held up behind. But he rode and wrathed and still rode, up to where the canyon dwindled—rough land and a hard ride. As we neared the great flat mountain, the feeble cry of the pack was heard again from the south, then toward the high butte's side, and just a trifle louder now. We reined in on a hillock and scanned the snow. A moving speck appeared, then others, not bunched, but in a straggling train, and at times there was a far faint cry. They were headed toward us, coming on, yes! coming, but so slowly, for not one was really running now. There was the grim old cow killer limping over the ground, and far behind a greyhound, and another, and farther still, the other dogs in order of their speed, slowly, gamely, dragging themselves on that pursuit. Many hours of hardest toil had done their work. The wolf had vainly sought to fling them off. Now was his hour of doom, for he was spent; they still had some reserve. Straight to us for a time they came, skirting the base of the mountain, crawling.

We could not cross to join them, so held out breath and gazed with ravenous eyes. They were nearer now, the wind brought feeble notes from the hounds. The big wolf turned to the steep ascent, up a well-known trail, it seemed, for he made no slip. My heart went with him, for he had come back to rescue his friend, and a momentary thrill of pity came over us both, as we saw him glance around and drag himself up the sloping way, to die on his mountain. There was no escape for him, beset by fifteen dogs with men to back them. He was not walking, but tottering upward; the dogs, behind in line, were now doing a little better, were nearing him. We could hear them gasping; we scarcely heard them bay— they had no breath for that; upward the grim procession went, circling a spur of the butte and along a ledge that climbed and narrowed, then dropped for a few yards to a shelf that reared above the canyon. The foremost dogs were closing, fearless of a foe so nearly spent.

Here in the narrowest place, where one wrong step meant death, the great wolf turned and faced them. With fore feet braced, with head low and tail a little raised, his dusky mane a-bristling, his glittering tusks laid bare, but uttering no sound that we could hear, he faced the crew. His legs were weak with toil, but his neck, his jaws, and his heart were strong, and—now all you who love the dogs had better close the book—on—up and down—fifteen to one, they came, the swiftest first, and how it was done, the eye could scarcely see, but even as a stream of water pours on a rock to be splashed in broken jets aside, that stream of dogs came pouring down the path, in single file perforce, and Duskymane received them as they came. A feeble spring, a counterlunge, a gash, and "Fango's down," has lost his foothold and is gone. Dander and Coalie close and try to clinch; a rush, a heave, and they are fallen from that narrow path. Blue Spot then, backed by mighty Oscar and fearless Tige—but the wolf is next the rock and the flash of combat clears to show him there alone, the big dogs gone; the rest close in, the hindmost force the foremost on—down—to their death. Slash, chop and heave, from the swiftest to the biggest, to the last, down—down—he sent them whirling from the ledge to the gaping gulch below, where rocks and snags of trunks were sharp to do their work.

In fifty seconds it was done. The rock had splashed the stream aside—the Penroof pack was all wiped out; and Badlands Billy stood there, alone again on his mountain.

A moment he waited to look for more to come. There were no more, the pack was dead; but waiting, he got his breath, then raising his voice for the first time in that fatal scene, he feebly gave a long yell of triumph, and scaling the next low bank, was screened from view in a canyon of Sentinel Butte.

We stared like men of stone. The guns in our hands were forgotten. It was all so quick, so final. We made no move till the wolf was gone. It was not far to the place: we went on foot to see

if any had escaped. Not one was left alive. We could do nothing—
we could say nothing.

A week later we were riding the upper trail back of the Chimney
Pot, King and I. "The old man is pretty sick of it," he said. "He'd
sell out if he could. He don't know what's the next move."

The sun went down beyond Sentinel Butte. It was dusk as we
reached the turn that led to Dumont's place, and a deep-toned
rolling howl came from the river flat below, followed by a number of higher pitched howls in answering chorus. We could see
nothing, but we listened hard. The song was repeated, the hunting
cry of the wolves. It faded, the night was stirred by another, the
sharp bark and the short howl, the signal "close in"; a bellow came
up, very short, for it was cut short.

And King as he touched his horse said grimly: "That's him, he
is out with the pack, an' thar goes another beef."[2]

# 18.

# THE RISE OF
# THE WOODCRAFT INDIANS*

In the year 1900 A.D. I found myself in a position to realize the dream of my life—a dream that is common to nine men out of ten. I was blessed with means and opportunity to buy a few small, abandoned farms not far from New York City. I was now absolute owner of a tract of tangled woodland, with hills, rocks, and trees in abundance, a few little meadows, and a beautiful brook that spread into an alder swamp. The swamp was easily turned into a lake, and furnished the central beauty spot to a little paradise of birds and wildlife.

I built an inexpensive cabin, and around the place put an impassable mesh-wire fence ten feet high and finished at the top with barbed-wire entanglements.

Here I proposed to live most of the time. Here I meant to try many experiments at conservation and restocking. Every native kind of wildlife was to be encouraged. I rejoiced in my dream come true. I gloried in my wild wood. I thought I owned it.

But the boys in the neighborhood thought otherwise. I was an outsider, an interloper. I had fenced in the land on which for generations they had gathered nuts, picnicked, levied firewood and pasturage. I had shut off all the public from shooting privi-

* A true story of the birth of the Woodcraft League, a forerunner of other American youth programs.—Ed.

leges, for squirrels and an occasional woodcock in season were found on the place.

The boys declared war. They decided to freeze me out; and their method of freezing me out was making it hot for me. They destroyed my fence, they shot my animals, they painted wicked pictures on my gate.

All summer long, I kept on repairing the fence, replacing the animals, and repainting the gate. I thought that patient nonresistance would surely win. But it had no visible effect. The nightly depredations continued.

One Saturday morning, late in the summer, I was busied painting out a dreadful array of pictures, when a gang of the boys went by. I turned to them and said: "Now, boys, I don't know who has painted this gate, and I don't wish to know. But if you know, I wish you would ask him to stop. It doesn't do him any good. I merely have to paint the gate over again, and it has as many coats now as are any good for it."

The boys giggled, snickered, whistled with much significance, and passed on.

The next morning, the gate, the posts, and the adjoining trees and rocks were decorated with a new array of the most shockingly improper pictures, with inscriptions to give them personal point, all showing the same object, the same modes of thought, and the same masterhand. Such pictures, such inscriptions, not even a Sunday paper would have dared to print.

Thus it was brought home to me that nonresistance was a failure.

Now, I had a number of city friends who owned country places. One of them, a man of experience, counseled me thus: "There is just one simple thing to do: arrest the whole gang; some will turn State's evidence. Then send the worst of them to jail."

The advice gave me a little shock. I replied: "Put the stamp of crime on a boyish prank! Make jailbirds of a lot of boys for doing something that I probably did myself at that age! No," I said. "I have tried nonresistance and personal appeal without success. Now I shall try something else. I shall try a little hypnotism.

"I know something of boys; in fact, I am much of a boy myself. The boy is a caveman till he is sixteen or seventeen. At this time, he is in the clan period. Loyalty to his clan or gang is his real religion, far overpowering any loyalty he may feel to church or state. The British in India, and the Romans everywhere, used to handle their savage tributary races simply and inexpensively by dealing through their own chiefs. This is the plan I shall follow."

So, on a morning soon afterward, I went to the village school and asked the teacher if I might talk to the boys for five minutes. She said: "Certainly."

Then I said: "Will all the boys twelve years old and upward please stand?" A dozen stood.

"Are all here today?" I asked

"No." There were three absentees.

"Good! That is about the right number. Now, boys," I continued, "I invite you standing and the three not here today, to come to the Indian Village on my place, next Friday after school, to camp with me there from Friday after school till Monday before school. I shall have boats, canoes, tents and tepees in good shape, ticks full of straw, plenty of firewood, and all the grub you can eat. All I ask you to bring is two blankets each; and remember I will not have any firearms, any matches, any tobacco, or any whiskey. Now, will you come?"

The answer was a most eloquent burst of—*dead silence;* not a hint of reply.

This was puzzling. I knew that they had been in my Indian Village, because it was forbidden. Perhaps they did not understand the invitation, so I repeated: "Remember, you do not have to pay anything. You come as my guests. We are going to have a jolly camp-out together."

Still no sign, even of comprehension. The dozen boys looked variously stolid, sulky, or suspicious. I repeated my invitation. "Don't any of you care to come into the woods for a camping trip, with everything provided, and nothing to do but have a good time?"

Still no response; not even an intelligent look. I was stumped. Had they said, "No," or perhaps asked a question, I could have faced the situation. But a stone wall of silence was baffling. In my perplexity, I selected a tall, good-looking, bright-eyed boy who stood near me, and put it up to himself personally:

"Don't you care to come for a trip in the woods—everything provided, nothing to do but have fun?"

His only answer was a nod. Now I addressed a second and a third. In each case, I got nothing but a more or less cautious nod. So I let it go at that, assuming these to represent the crowd. Then, with a final, "Now, remember, next Friday after school," I departed to make my preparations.

All tents, tepees, boats, and canoes were put in perfect shape. Beds with straw ticks, plenty of firewood were provided, various apparatus for games and an abundance of good food were secured —not merely for the dozen boys I had seen, but a possible eighteen or twenty. Last of all, I secured a man for cook and general aide.

All was ready at 4 p.m. on Friday. The cook and I were waiting, but no boys came; 4:15 and no boys; 4:30—no boys. Now the cook, who did not relish his job, said: "I told you you wouldn't get any satisfaction out of those fellows. The only thing that'll do them any good is a rawhide well laid on in the right place."

"No," I said, "I've seen that tried many times, and never saw it do any good."

So I waited, getting more and more nervous and uncomfortable. I could not help remembering the old nursery rhyme:

"Mr. Smarty gave a party
And nobody came."

About five o'clock there was a sudden and increasing racket and riot on the main drive, and in came the boys all together—not the twelve I had seen, not the fifteen I had invited, not the eighteen I provided for—*but forty-two,* each and every one carrying his two old blankets. I thought they would never stop pouring into that council ring.

Being Yankee boys, they got over their trifling bashfulness in about five seconds, and the first question they asked was: "Say, mister, kin we holler?"

"Holler. Yes, blow your lungs out if you like." And they tried. The neighbors told me afterward that they heard them two miles off.

The next was: "Say, kin we take our clothes off?" "Surely, every rag." And I was thankful to see them peel off and jump into the lake, for there they could do but little harm, whereas tearing through the wood, I did not know what might be the result.

It looked as though I had imported and turned loose a Frankenstein; but naked boys can't set the woods afire, or smash property to any great extent. It was only part of a process. I wanted the animal energy worked off first.

By six o'clock, it was getting dark. The boys were tired and hungry. A blazing campfire was going. The cook called in the savages, with a loud cry of "Grub-Grub."

The boys came trooping into camp, dressed, and went at the provisions. In the language of Scripture, "They came and they did eat." Oh, how they did eat! Such a chance was not to be neglected;

the quality was better than the home stuff. They gorged themselves like forty-two boa constrictors, clearing up that night all the food provided to last till Monday. Fortunately, next day was Saturday, and we could stock up again.

The camp stuffed itself from six to seven; then, tired, gorged, and happy, they lay around in the firelight, ready for some new and quieter amusement. I know something of savages, and boys are precisely the same. So I said: "Now, shall I tell you a story?"

Their reply had more of force than of politeness, but was obviously sincere. "You bet, go ahead."

Thus graciously permitted, I went ahead. I told them of Indians and Plains life, gauging my stories in a steady crescendo till I had renewed the Fenimore Cooper glamor of romance, and heightened it to a blaze of glory about the red man. Meanwhile, I was watching my material. I wanted them all interested and subdued, but not sleepy.

Near eight o'clock, the bickerings and rude practical jokes of the bigger boys had ceased; the little fellows near me were far from sleepy. The group had tightened up about me. The eyes of those nearby, I could see had that tense magnetized look when I told the dramatic story of the spy in the enemy's camp, and how he covered himself with glory by his exploits. As I finished the tale, I could feel the thrill of intense interest; I could feel their regret that the noble red man had departed before their day. Their resentment of me, a stranger, was gone.

In my judgment, the right psychological moment had come. After the proper pause that follows a good climax, I said reflectively: "Say, fellows, how are we going to do this camp-out—just tumble around any way, or shall we do it in the real Indian fashion?"

There was, of course, only one reply possible in view of the atmosphere I had conjured up. "Oh, Injun, bet your life, we're Injuns."

"Good, that will suit me," I said. "Now, remember, we are the tribe. Each warrior has one vote. First, we must elect a Head War Chief."

Then they gave their first sign of politeness. "Well, I reckon we'll take you," was the quick response, born, no doubt, of the recently established bond of sympathy.

But I promptly crushed it. "No, you don't," I replied. "I am not a Chief. I am a Medicine Man. For Chief, I want one of yourselves."

Now there were forty-two claimants for the job, and each had the most convincing reasons why he was the only possible choice. The wrangle grew into a riot, till I said: "Hold on, we can soon settle this another way. What boy here can lick all the others?"

"Oh, that ain't fair," came an aggrieved chorus. "Hank Martin can. He's older and bigger and stronger nor any of us."

"Well, if Hank can lick everything in sight, it is fair. But maybe there is some fellow here who thinks he can lick Hank."

"Yes, I can. I kin do it right now," and up got another athletic boy, another stripling lad, but of different cut.

"Very good," I said. "I am glad to know it. We won't try it now, but may have to some other time."

Now I put these two up for popular election. Martin got it quite easily; his leadership was beyond question.

Oh, how my heart sank at the mention of Hank Martin. He was a square-shouldered, square-jawed, gray-eyed boy of sixteen, strong as a young bull, energetic, self-reliant, and fearless—he could have licked me in one round. But he was "the worst boy in the county." He was into every kind of mischief, his exploits were already past being merely funny boyish pranks, they were developing into crime. Hank was surely pointing toward the penitentiary, and leading a score of boys behind him. His father kept cows, and Hank's morning job was to go round with the milk. This gave him many opportunities for mischief which he failed not to utilize. I knew quite well that Hank was the artist of the gate. I was afraid of Hank Martin. Still, he was unquestionably the leader of the gang. He ruled by his divine right, and his equally celestial left. So, in strict pursuance of my policy, I must win him.

It generally happens that bad boys are simply overenergetic or misdirected good boys, profoundly disguised, and if you can get hold of them, you can probably persuade them to drop their mask.

Hoping it might be so in this case, I took Hank aside, and said: "See here, Hank, the fellows have elected you Head Chief of the tribe, and remember, it isn't simply for today and tomorrow and the next day. We are going to keep this up the year round, indoors and outdoors, in a sort of club, as long as the fellows take any interest in it. Remember, then, you are going to lead all these little boys. I hope you are too much of a man to get them into trouble!"

He replied: "Naw, I wouldn't do nuthin' like that."

These were words, maybe nothing more. I could not tell. However, his mother told me long after, that it did mean something. Hank had never before been appealed to by grown-ups as a person of importance; and it came like a new and delightful experience. He braced up and faced his new responsibilities like a man.

This, however, was years later. We were meanwhile busy with our election. An extraordinarily fat boy now caught my eye. He was evidently about fourteen, but weighted some 220 pounds. I turned to the boy next me, and asked: "Who is that?" He replied: "That's Tom Sewit." I thought: "That's a name I'll remember with such a shape behind it."

Now I called for nominations for Second War Chief. At once there were loud cries of " Tom Sewit, Tom Sewit."

We certainly did not want the fat boy. We needed an athlete, so I took no notice until a feeble voice near me said: "Tom Barney." Tom Barney wasn't much, but he was better than the fat boy—"any port in a storm."

I said: "Now you are talking. Tom Barney is the fellow for the post. Now all in favor of Tam Barney, hands up." Five hands went up. "All in favor of Tom Sewit"—thirty-eight hands appeared—a perfect forest. I counted them carefully, and in some perplexity. Then I discovered one boy holding up two hands. "Here," I said, "you are cheating, stuffing the ballot box. You have queered this whole election. Now we must try over."

I made a strong speech for Tom Barney, giving all the reasons I could think of or invent for his election, but of course could not denounce the enemy as he sat there. I then put my own candidate first, to catch the independents.

"Now," I said, "fair voting. All in favor of Tom Barney for Second War Chief, hands up." To my amazement, only two hands went up—Barney's and his brother's. "All in favor of Tom Sewit." Forty hands appeared now. Not the least doubt of it. Very unwillingly I announced that Sewit was elected. "Tom Sewit, come forward, and take the oath of office as Second War Chief." Tom stepped out. To my amazement, it was not the fat boy at all. That was an error that I fell into by chance. Sewit was the sturdy young chap who was willing to lick the Head Chief if need be, and just the right one for the post.

We now elected a Third Chief, and a Council of Twelve. Among them, we selected one for Chief of the Council Fire, who alone kindles a fire, a Chief of the Tally (Secretary), and Chief of the Wampum (Treasurer). Finally I got myself in as Medicine Man. The rest, of course, were mere braves.

With the organization complete, I now gave them a code of laws and a constitution—impromptu—yes, just as impromptu as most impromptus are, carefully prepared previously with the help of an expert lawyer. In this, I provided for all things not covered by the law of the land. Our code forbade rebellion against the Council, firearms in camp, wildfire, smoking, whiskey, destruction of songbirds or squirrels, breach of game laws, pointing of weapons at anyone; and made chivalry, kindness, courage, and honor the cardinal virtues.

And now we set out on what was destined to be an epoch-making outing for the village boys, for myself, and for thousands of boys elsewhere.

Our motto was: "The best things of the best Indians." Whatever is picturesque, good and safe in Indian life, that we used.

The boys wanted to wear feathers. I said: "Certainly; but remember, after the manner of the Indians. The good old Indians did not want just any feather he could steal and stick in his hair; each feather was conferred by the Council as the decoration for an exploit. I will give you a hundred exploits, each of which will entitle the doer to a feather."

It was essential that my standards should be *national* and *absolute*, not competitive. So, taking the interscholastic athlete for my standard, I allowed a feather for all who were obviously in the highest class, thus: All who could walk four miles in an hour, or run 100 yards in eleven seconds. The only cheap one was for swimming. All who could swim 100 yards, no matter how slowly, got the swimming feather. This for athletics.

In a second department, called Campercraft, I allowed honors to all who could light a campfire with rubbing sticks; could measure the width of a river without crossing it, etc.

The third department was nature study, and honors were allowed to all who could name correctly twenty-five trees, fifty flowers, fifty birds, etc.

I had already invented a game called deer hunting, in which a dummy was pursued by its tracks or paper or corn (or later with a steel tracking iron on the foot) and shot with arrows; a hostile-spy hunt, a bear hunt, a rabbit hunt, a man hunt, spearing the big beaver, trials of quicksight and farsight. These were all prepared and lying in wait with their insidious appeal to the primitive part of these very primitive young persons. There was sanity in every part of the scheme, because it had *picturesqueness;* it made the boys *govern themselves,* and it gave them definite *things to do;* but, above all, it never failed to play on the master power of the savages, the love of glory—that was always kept in mind. It was used as the lure, the lash and the motive power to get these boys into different ways of life and thought.

Its success far exceeded my highest expectations. Rough and wild boys may defy the teacher, and scoff at the opinions of their elders, but they cannot scoff at the public opinion of their gang, nor defy the playmates who are able and ready to inflict condign corporal punishment.

Along this line, we played the game together, and when Monday morning came, instead of forty-two little reprobates, doing all the mischief they could to me and mine, I had forty-two staunch friends. *And I have them all yet*—except four who left their bones in France.

In the final outcome, there was not one of these a bad boy. All turned out well, and are high-class citizens today. Hank Martin is owner of a large garage and bus line. The young rascal who embezzled the funds is now treasurer of the local chapter of a nation-wide organization. The little sneak who carried tales and trouble is attorney-general for the town. The fat boy who could do nothing but swim is manager of a big rubber concern in a nearby city. And the boy who stole the pie is now President of the Board of Trade.

Not one went wrong. All have made good. What would have happened had I tried the compulsory—the military—method, instead of the developmental, the Woodcraft Way?[1]

# 19.

# THREE CAMPFIRE STORIES*

## *Gorm, the Giant of the Club*


THERE once was held a Great Convention of the Church Fathers to settle once for all a multitude of minute, hair-splitting doctrines that some thought fundamental and that others held to be of little account; for example, "How many angels can at one time dance on the point of a needle?" Or, "If a portion of a man's soul is contained in each hair of his head, what happens when a man cuts his hair, or when he becomes bald?"

After some weeks of stormy debate, a monk from the North Country rose up, and made his contribution in the form of a story.

This story Seton has given so many times to American audiences that the language has acquired an American flavor, but the sense of the story is as it was in the first telling.

In the North Country was a farmer of large holdings. He tilled a wide acreage and had many flocks and many dependents. He was a widower whose family consisted of only himself and his son Gorm.

Gorm was a boy of remarkable stature and strength. At ten years of age, he looked like twenty; at twelve, he was over six feet high, and stronger than any man in the region.

* As told by Seton and recorded by Julia M. Seton.

He was tremendously proud of his strength, but his great joy was in his father. His father was the master of the whole farm. His father was the boss of all there was, and he rejoiced in the thought that he was the son of the "big boss," and next to him in authority. Nothing pleased him more than to have his father say: "Gorm, the men over there are idling. Go and stir them up; and if any of them is impudent, give him a crack on the jaw."

But it was seldom necessary to rough-handle the men, for they knew that Gorm was well able to beat any of them.

He kept on growing and developing till, at sixteen, he was over seven feet tall, and built for strength.

One day he came on his father in distress over something. With ready sympathy he asked: "What's the matter, Dad? Have the men been misbehaving? Don't you want me to hand someone a jaw wallop?"

"Oh, son," replied his father, "I wish that was all it was. I'm afraid I am in wrong with the King."

"The King?" cried Gorm. "Who is he? You are not afraid of him?"

"Why, yes, I am. You see he owns the whole country and he could put me off this farm."

"Why, Dad, I thought you were the big boss, and afraid of no one."

"Alas, no!" said the father. "I am afraid of the King—everyone is."

"Then, Dad, he is the big boss. I am the biggest, strongest man in the country, and I won't work for any but the biggest boss. I am off to work for the King."

They could not stop him. Away he went, striding over the hills until he came to the palace of the King.

At the gate, he was halted by the guard. "What do you want?"

"Is this the palace of the King?"

"Yes."

"Then tell him I want to work for him."

They sent word to the King. "Here's a big giant who says he wants to work for you."

"Show him in," said the King, "but guard him carefully."

So between two long rows of drawn pikes, the giant was ushered in.

"Are you the big boss of this country?" said the giant, as he towered over the King.

"I surely am."

"Then I want to work for you."

"Very well," said the King, and they made him one of the guards.

Here he had a fine time. He had little to do but eat and grow, and grow and eat; so that after three years, he was twelve feet tall and tremendously muscular.

Then, one day, a runner came flying up to the King's palace, shouting: "Pirates! Pirates are coming! They have anchored out in the bay, and are landing in small boats to sack the town."

"Send for Gorm!" ordered the King. As the giant strode into the King's presence the monarch cried: "Gorm, what shall we do? How many regiments do you want to meet this bloodthirsty horde?"

"Regiments? None at all!" said the giant. "Just let me at them with my club."

So, clad in armor that could defy their arrows, Gorm strode out to meet the pirates. The water, which was overhead for the common man, was only midthigh for him.

He met the pirate boats, one by one. Splash! Dash! Crash! and down they went. Then, with his club, he cleaned up the pirates swarming in the water. Not one was left.

This done, he waded out to the ships riding at anchor, and

jabbed them with his club deep under water, so that all went down, google, google down, and every one of them was destroyed.

Now Gorm stalked back to shore in triumph.

All the country was crazy with joy. "Hurrah for Gorm! Good old Gorm with the club!" they cried. There was nothing too good for him. They were so wild in their cheers for Gorm that they quite forgot the King, and he was just a little bit peeved.

"They might hand me some credit," said his Majesty, "and a couple of cheers once in a while."

But no. Gorm was their glorious hero and their protector.

One morning some months later, Gorm went to the King, for orders. He found him pacing up and down, tearing his hair and raving.

"What's the matter, your Majesty?" asked Gorm. "Any more pirates coming?"

"Oh, Gorm, I wish that was all," said the King. "This is something you would not understand."

"Can't you make me understand?" said Gorm.

"Well, this is the trouble," exclaimed the King. "I am hard up. I don't know which way to turn for money. Our treasury is empty, our army hasn't been paid for six months, and the men are getting into furious rebellion. I dare not add one cent to the taxes, and the whole bally kingdom is just going to the Devil, *the Devil,* THE DEVIL!" shouted the King.

"The who?" asked Gorm, bewildered.

"The Devil," replied the King.

"Who is he?" said the giant in surprise.

"Oh, Gorm, I hope you never meet him."

"Why, are you afraid of him?"

"Certainly I am, everyone is," said the King.

"Well, then, he is your boss," growled the giant. "I thought you were the big boss, but you are not, the Devil is your boss. I am going to work for the Devil."

They could not stop him. He seized his club and went off in a rage, to seek for the biggest boss.

But he had no information; he knew not which way to go. Nor could he ask anyone; all the people fled when they saw the great giant, realizing he was in a bad temper.

So he strode away over the hills far into the country. As he went, there came slowly along the road a small man dressed in black, with a shovel-board hat on his head, deeply engrossed in a book he was reading as he walked.

The giant stood still. The little man almost bumped into him, and looked up in surprise to see the great towering monster in front of him.

The little man smiled instead of running away as did most. This pleased the giant.

Looking down on him, Gorm said: "Friend, can you tell me where I can find the Devil?"

"Yes, indeed," was the reply. "But you are going the wrong way. The Devil doesn't live in the country, he lives in town. Go right back to the city, up along the docks to the red-light district. There, at the far end, you will find a house where they sell strong drink. That's his headquarters, his office. If you look in the door, you will see the Devil sitting at the table. When you look in his eyes, you will know that you have found him."

"Thank you," said the giant. Back he went to the town, sought out the red lights and the drink house. There, sitting at a table near the door, was a strange-looking man, a skullcap on his head with two little horns peeping through. Around the leg of his chair was something coiled that looked like a black snake.

"Are you the Devil?" asked the giant as he stooped low to peer in.

"That's what they call me," said the one at the table. He looked up at the giant; and when Gorm looked down into his face, he *knew* he had found the Devil. There could be no mistaking those awful eyes.

"Are you the fellow that scares the King?"

"I scare everybody," was the answer.

"Then," said the giant, "you are the big boss, and I want to work for you."

"Good," said the Devil, "I guess I've a job for a fellow your size. Come on."

So they went and smashed up the town. Then they went over the hills to another town and smashed that to ruins.

"Come on," said the Devil, "there's another town just over the ridge."

As they marched, they came to a curious low house by the roadside. It had a long, sloping roof; and at one end, a short square tower. On the top of the tower, there was a stick which stood erect, and across it at right angles another shorter stick.

"Look at this," said the giant. "Here's a new one. Watch me wipe that off the road with one sweep of my club."

"No! no! no!" gasped the Devil. "You must not touch that."

"Why not?" growled the giant. "Does that belong to the King?"

"No," said the Devil, now trembling with fear. "That belongs to the King of Kings. Come on, let's hurry away."

"Why, you are shivering. You are afraid," exclaimed the giant.

"Well, yes, I am; everyone is afraid of the King of Kings."

"Then he is the big boss, not you. You are afraid like the rest of them, and I won't work for any but the biggest boss. Good-bye."

And again the giant strode angrily away. He had been deceived again.

On he went, swinging his club in a rage. In blind fury, he

swiftly tramped over hill after hill, following the high road. He could get no directions, for all fled at his approach.

But at last, going down a long slope toward a river, he met a little child.

The child looked up at Gorm, and smiled. The giant was pleased. He bent forward, and gently said: "Little one, can you tell me where I can find the King of Kings?"

"Oh, yes," said the child. "He crossed this river at the ford there, not long ago, and said He was coming back. If you wait there, you will surely find Him."

"Thank you," said the giant and sat down on the bank of the river to wait for the King to come.

All day the giant sat on the bank. Then, toward evening, an old woman with a market basket on her arm came down the other shore. She wanted to cross, but the flood looked so dangerous, she was afraid.

"Is there no one here to help an old woman across the ford?" she called.

The giant rose up from the grass where he lay and said: "Yes, Mother, I'll help you."

When the old woman saw the size of the monster, she was panic-stricken. But the giant said: "Never fear, Mother, I'll take you safely over."

He lifted her as one might lift a baby, and set her on the other shore.

"Thank you, good giant," she said. "I have no money to offer you; but if a dozen eggs are any use, I'd gladly give them to you."

"Sure," said the giant, and the eggs were his rations for the day.

He slept on the bank until sunrise, when he was awakened by a shouting on the other shore. Here was a teamster driving a wagon loaded with grain. He came lumbering down the bank into the water, intending to ford the stream. But in the middle he struck a quicksand. His horses, wagon, and all began to sink. In vain swinging his whip, the teamster yelled: "Get up! Get up!"

But they were helpless; all were soon sinking down.

The teamster in his terror shouted: "Is there no one here to help me? Oh, help! help!"

The giant rose from the grass and said cheerfully: "Sure, I'll help you, brother."

The teamster, like the old woman, was scared by the size of the giant. But quickly Gorm came out, took horses, wagon, load and all, and easily pulled them onto the safe bank.

"Thank you, good giant. I have no money to offer you, but here's a bag of oatmeal I'll willingly give you."

"Glad to get it," said Gorm, and the oatmeal kept him for some days.

All day long the giant sat on the bank. Others came, and he helped them. Day after day, he sat there still, waiting for the King of Kings. More and more persons passed that way, for it was soon noised abroad that a kindly giant was there, ready to help those who wished to cross.

All summer and autumn Gorm waited. Then came the cold weather. The giant had to build a little cabin to sleep in. He built it close to the ford, and never did he refuse when a traveler came knocking, saying: "Good giant, won't you help me across?" He demanded no pay, but took what they offered. Often he asked about the King of Kings. Some had never heard of Him, but some few said: "Yes. He crossed here once and is surely coming back."

So passed a year—and another year. Five years, ten years, twenty-five years, sixty years went by. And still the giant was at the ford, waiting, waiting for the King of Kings. Thousands he helped across, and still he was vainly waiting for the King to come.

Then came the most terrible winter ever known in that country.

Intense frost prevailed for months, fierce blizzards of blinding snow, raging floods on the streams.

In the midst of the hardest time, in mid-February, when deadly ice and driving snow were menacing all life, there came during the darkest hour of the night someone knocking at the giant's door. "Good giant, won't you help me to cross? I *must* get across."

The giant rose from his cold hard couch. He had never refused; the habit of a lifetime was on him. But he was no longer the big strong giant he had once been. Seventy years of toil and hardship had robbed him of his strength. His shoulders were bowed with labor, his back was bent, his knees were tottering. His immense stature, too, was reduced.

But he arose; and, leaning on his famous club, he tottered feebly to the door. He opened it, and there stood *a little child.* There was something familiar in the child's face and voice, as he said pleadingly: "Good giant, won't you take me across? I *must* get across."

With trembling, palsied hands, the giant reached down. In the days of his strength, the weight of a full-grown man was a trifle to him, but now he could barely lift that little one to his shoulders. This finally done, he faced the blizzard storm, the blackness of the midnight, and groped his way to the ford. He staggered through the snow, almost crushed by his burden. When he reached the river bank, he found there a great flood on the stream, and shore ice had formed. The giant had to break the ice with his club before he could step into the flood; and when he had done so, the deadly chill of the ice water sent the very pangs of death up into his trembling rheumatic limbs and stabbed to his very heart.

But he staggered on. Never before had the water been above his knees. Now it rose as he entered the deep channel till it was up to his throat. The little one had to stand on the giant's shoulders and clutch his hair to avoid being swept away.

Great blocks of ice came surging down and sent the giant almost off his feet. But he braced himself with his club and waited.

The poor old giant's strength was ebbing fast. He was nearly done for when he crossed the deeper channel. But the child encouraged him: "Keep on, good giant, we are nearly out. I can see the other shore."

They reached the edge of the shore ice, and again the giant had to break it with his club. He slowly dragged his old legs through, but the weight of the child seemed crushing. Finally, with the last of his strength, he was just able to seize hold on the willows and drag himself up on the shore.

As he did so, the child stepped from his once mighty shoulders on to the bank above, then turned and faced him.

The giant lifted up his sick and wearied eyes and saw—*what?* A little child? No! A tall and wonderful man, with a crown of light about His head, and eyes that there could be no mistaking.

In a flash, the giant knew that at last he had found the King of Kings.

He flung himself at the Master's feet, and cried aloud in agony: "My King and my God! Have I found Thee? Have I found Thee at last? All my life have I hungered to enter Thy service, and to give my life and my strength to Thee. But now, my life is gone and my strength is gone. I have nothing to give. I find Thee, alas, too late."

The giant was convulsed with the agony of his sorrow.

But the King laid hands on him in blessing and said: "Not so, not so, my beloved. On the day that you took your stand by this ford to wait My coming, and to help those who had need of your great strength, you did enter My service. Whensoever you carried over the old, the sick, the helpless, the poor, the little ones, you carried Me. Ten thousand times have you carried Me over this dangerous flood. I have been watching you, I have been loving you,

I have been preparing blessings for you. And I have come now to give back your mighty strength and your glorious youth, that you one time did consecrate to Me.

"And I will give you a new name. Men shall remember you no more as 'Gorm of the Club,' nor even as 'The Giant of the Ford,' but as 'Christofero,' Saint Christopher, the giant who carried the Christ Child. I will set your name on the heaven of heavens, a beacon for all time, as that of one who found the only true religion, which is this: TO HELP THOSE WHO HAVE NEED OF HELP. Come now, you shall dwell with Me in peace and glory and honor forever in the Palace of the King."

## *Little Burnt-All-Over*

Long ago, before the white man came, there was an Indian village at the south end of Lake Otsego, and in it there dwelt a young brave and his wife and little daughter, their only child. He was a good hunter, she was a good woman, and their little girl, then twelve years old, made their happiness complete.

The child was well educated, as her people understood education. She could make a fish net; she could set in the lake and catch an abundance of fish; she could split and dry the fish for winter use; she could gum and paddle a canoe; she could follow the broken twigs to where her father had killed a deer; she could skin the deer, cut it up, and bring it home; she could tan the hide into buckskin; she could make of this war shirts and moccasins; she could embroider these garments with porcupine quills dyed red with miscawa and yellow with puccoon; she could make vessels of birchbark; she could keep the lodge in order; she could dance, she could sing, she knew the legends of her people; and last—but by no means least—she was a good cook.

The child was very happy in her home life, especially in the summer evenings, when the mother would take her to sit on the western ridge to watch the wonder of the sunset. There, with His power and glory before them, the mother would tell of the Great Spirit, and of His unfailing care for all His children. The little girl listened with all the reverent intensity of her nature, gazing at the skies, while both her small hands rested in her mother's; silent, but sometimes asking some childish question to which the mother replied with a legend of the older folk.

As they sat one night, there was a sunset of such splendor that both were hushed and awed.

"Why is it so wonderful tonight, Mother?"

"It is a sign of great happenings soon to come, my child."

Long they gazed in silence; then, as the brightness faded, there came on the east a great veil of purple across the sky.

"What is that, Mother?" said the child as she looked.

"That, my child, is the purple robe of the Great Spirit."

Then, after a pause, the little one, both childlike and woman-like, said: "Mother, shall I ever have a purple robe?"

"Yes, my child, when your spirit is great, then indeed you shall have a purple robe."

As the color grew deeper and hid the light, the stars came out like points of white fire.

"What are those, Mother?" she asked.

"Those, my little one, are the wampum beads on the robe of the Great Spirit."

She gazed for a little while; then, harking back to her childlike thought, said: "Mother, shall I have wampum beads on my purple robe, when it comes?"

"Yes," said the mother gravely, "I think you will have many, many big bright beads of wampum on your robe."

As the child pondered these sayings, the mother continued:

"Listen, dear one, the Voices have made it plain to me that I am to be taken away from you very soon. You are going to be left alone, and such sorrows and trials will be yours as never woman of our people has known. But remember this, you must meet them in a spirit of patience and fortitude, that they may pass away. If you meet them in anger and rebellion, they will come again and again, till the hard lesson is learned. Then indeed you shall overcome them, and you shall see them no more, except that each will become a bead of wampum upon your robe. And then such honor and joy shall be yours as woman of our tribe never before has known."

There were tears in the mother's eyes as she silently watched the last bars of splendor dying in the west. Both were silent for a long time, then they rose in the twilight, and went back to make ready the evening meal at the lodge.

Just a few days after this, the mother went out in a canoe to haul the nets; the north wind rose suddenly on that long, treacherous, ice-cold lake—and Mother never came back.

Now the little girl was left alone with her father. After the first sharpness of their grief was past, they settled down and were not uncomfortable, for the girl could do all things well. The lodge was clean, her father's clothes in good order, his war bonnet beautifully decked, and the food well cooked.

But he was a young man. He did not wish to live alone. He desired a wife.

Now it chanced that in the village was a young widow who had two daughters. She was comely, and so the young warrior went to her and said:

"I have no woman; you have no man. Will you be my woman? I will be your man."

And the widow said, "Yes."

So they were married, and she came with her two daughters to live in the lodge of the hunter with his own little girl.

Now these two stepsisters were well trained, as indeed were all Indian girls. They were not bad, but the older one was a little fat and lazy, the younger one a little thin and acid. They soon discovered that the little one was a better cook than either of them, so they let her do the cooking. She could make better moccasins than they could, so they got her to make their moccasins. Little by little, all the work was shifted to the hunter's child. And having begun to give way to it, they became more lazy and unkind. The father did not see what was going on in his lodge; indeed, he was much away, and the stepmother was careful, while he was at home, to keep him from seeing that his own child was little more than a drudge.

One day the father went with a great war party against the Hurons in Canada—and he never came back.

Now, indeed, this family was in hard case, with their hunter gone and none near of kin to help them. One might have thought that the sorrows would bring the family together in closer ties of real affection. But it had the opposite effect; they became bitter with each other, and especially with the little girl. Formerly, they had done some of the work, the second stepsister helping a little with the meals. But now they became lazier as well as bitter. They made the little one do all the work of the lodge, and if she was at all slow, or did not please them, they thought little of beating her with a stick. Sometimes the handiest stick was one already burning in the fire. Yet they would beat her with that, so that she was covered with little burns on her face, head, neck, and arms.

Oftentimes she could not help screaming in pain, and the neighbors would come to ask what it was about. Then the cruel stepmother would say: "Oh, it's that little fool. She has no sense at all; she has fallen into the fire again. Look at her. She is a disgrace, with all her little scarburns. She is burnt—burnt all over." And from this she got the only name she ever heard now—*Little Burnt-All-Over.*

Sometimes the neighbors gave them a haunch of venison, but nearly all that they ate now was fish hard won by Little Burnt-All-Over from the lake, corn from a tiny patch, and berries and roots that she gathered in the woods. She knew nothing of kindness or joy. Her life was one long slavery repaid with cruel unkindness.

She had but one solace in it all. At sundown, she would sometimes slip away from the lodge and sit on the ridge, as she used to sit with her mother, and watch the symbol of the Great Spirit go down in gold and glory, and remember that in that was proof that the brightness would come again. And when the purple robe was laid across the sky and the wampum beads were shining, her mother's words came back: "Such sorrows and trials will be yours as never woman of our people has known. But remember this, you must meet them in a spirit of patience and fortitude, that they may pass away. You shall see them no more, except that each will become a bead of wampum upon your robe. And then such honor and joy shall be yours as woman of our tribe never before has known."

This thought strengthened her, and she went back to her life of cruel drudgery without complaint.

And so four years went by. She was now sixteen, a marriageable woman, according to the custom of her tribe. Her silent fortitude had filled her great eyes with a lustrous splendor, and her mouth, always beautiful, had now a gentleness and a strength that told of the tried and proven soul within. Her figure, always supple, was womanly and graceful now.

But the sisters had eaten up their beauty with their evil thoughts and repinings, and their girlish forms were grown ugly with idleness. The stepmother was hideous.

Then there came into the village a rumor that set all astir with eager curiosity. It was said, yes, openly told in council, that the King of the Snow Peaks was coming, the greatest chief on all the earth was coming, coming in all his power. He was coming into the village to seek a wife.

Now every marriageable woman, maid or widow, wondered what she might do to win for herself this coveted position, the honor of being wife to the greatest chief on earth.

And many lay awake at night planning and hoping, and yet knowing nothing but the rumor.

But one morning when they arose, behold a wonderful sight. At the end of the lake, there was a new lodge that had not been there before. It was of great size and dazzling whiteness, and the symbols thereon told that this was surely the lodge of the King of the Snow Peaks.

Then the stepmother said to her elder daughter: "Now is your chance." She took her to the spring where they made their toilets. They put on her all the best clothing they had. With the help of the young stepsister, they hung on her dress all the elk's teeth and shell beads they could get. They greased her hair till it shone, and painted her cheeks each with a bright spot of red; then on the parting of hair the mother painted a bright red streak. She looked at her, and said: "Oh, my child, you are beautiful; if he sees you, you will surely win his heart."

So, full of hope and pride, the big fat daughter went waddling round the lake to the shining white lodge. On the door flap she scratched with her long fingernail, for one does not knock at a lodge. It was opened by an old, old woman with a very wrinkled face, but very kind eyes.

The girl said: "Mother, is this the lodge of the King of the Snow Peaks?"

"Yes, my child," was the answer. "This is my son's lodge."

"Is he in, Mother?"

"No, my child, but he is coming. I expect him any moment. He is coming into the village to seek a wife, and that woman shall be his wife who first shall see him as he really is."

"What way does he come, Mother?"

"Over those hills in the east, down that little trail," said the old woman.

"Mother, I am going to meet him."

"Go," said the mother.

Away went the girl, and as she began to climb the trail, she saw at the top against the sky a tall young hunter striding along. He had an eagle feather in his hair which waved in the wind. In one hand he carried the bow and arrows of a hunter, and in the other he had a thong by which he led two dogs.

The girl gazed till he was so close that it was rude to stare into his face; then she slipped aside and looked on the ground. As soon as he had passed, she turned quickly, but he had disappeared.

She ran swiftly to the lodge, and when the old woman opened the flap, she said: "Mother, I saw your son."

"Did you? And what did he look like?"

"Oh, Mother, a tall, splendid young chief with an eagle feather in his hair that fluttered in the wind."

"What did he have in his hand, daughter?"

"The bow and arrows of a hunter."

"And in the other hand?"

"Why, Mother, he led two great hunting dogs."

"What did he lead them with?"

"I think it was a rawhide thong, Mother."

The old woman said in disdain, "No, that was not my son, you didn't see my son." And she flapped back the lodge flap.

The girl went away weeping bitterly, for she knew that she had failed.

Her mother heard the story, and said: "Well, it may be that that great honor is reserved for your sister."

So the next morning they took the sister to the spring and put all the best clothes on her. They spangled her skirts with elk's teeth and shells; they painted her cheeks with two great red spots, and on her chin they drew three red lines as well as the line down her head between the plaits of hair. They hung a bunch of white shells on the end of each long braid; then they greased her hair till it shone. The mother looked on her with pride and said: "My child, you are wonderfully beautiful. If only he sees you, you are sure to win."

The thin girl went to the white lodge and scratched with her fingernail. When the old woman came, she said: "Mother, is this the lodge of the great King of the Snow Peaks?"

"Yes, my child, this is my son's lodge."

"Is he in?"

"No, but he is coming soon. He comes down that trail on the eastern hills."

"Mother, I am going to meet him."

"Go."

So the thin girl began to climb up the trail on the eastern hills. Suddenly, at the top she saw a tall chief come walking. He had three eagle feathers in his hair, and he led two great hunting dogs as he strode in the full vigor of manhood. She gazed at him as he came toward her. She knew it was he. She took in all the details of his dress till he was so near that it was rude to look. Then she stepped aside and gazed at the ground. As soon as he had passed, she turned to see, but he had disappeared. However, the lodge seemed to glisten in the rays of the sun.

She ran down the hill, and when the old woman came to the door, she said eagerly: "Mother, I saw your son. I saw the King of the Snow Peaks."

"Did you? And what did he look like?"

"Oh, Mother, a tall, splendid war chief with three eagle feathers in his hair, and they waved in the wind as he strode along."

"What was in his hand?"

"He was leading two great black hunting dogs, Mother."

"What did he lead them with?"

"I think, Mother, it was a twisted bark rope."

"What had he on his brow, daughter?"

"Mother, it was a wampum band. I noticed it carefully."

Then the old woman said gruffly and shortly: "No, it was not my son, you never saw my son at all." And she flapped the door flap in her face.

The thin sister went home bitterly weeping, to tell her mother that she also had failed. So the mother and her two daughters wept together.

Suddenly, they chanced to see Little Burnt-All-Over, who was busy preparing the next meal. They did not want her to know or see their humiliation, so they shrieked at her furiously: "Get out of this, you good-for-nothing," and reached for a big stick.

The child dodged under the side of the lodge and escaped. There was one place to go. She went up on the ridge where alone she was at peace; where she so often had talked with her mother in the happy days gone by.

As she sat there, the sun went down in all the glory of the Great Spirit. Never before had she seen so glorious a sunset. And when the purple robe was drawn across, it had never seemed so wonderful as now. The wampum beads came out brighter, more beautiful and nearer than she had seen them; it was as if she could reach them with her uplifted hands.

Thoughts of her mother came as blessing and strength, and her mother's last words of promise: "When you have overcome your sorrows, when your time of trial is past, such honor and joy shall be yours as woman of our tribe never before has known." As she gazed, the purple robe seemed to be coming closer, and then into her heart came the thought: "Maybe that time is now."

She rose up in the morning before the others were astir and went down to the spring. She had no paint to put on her face, but she washed it clean. She had no elk's teeth for her robe, but the robe was neatly mended. She knew she would look better with shell dangles, but they had been taken from her.

She gathered some white flowers and made of them a border for her robe. She looked at herself in the spring and knew that she needed more, so she made a white garland and put it around her head. Again she looked and thought she needed something else, so she hung one flower on the end of each long braid of hair. Then she looked in the spring, and she knew that she was beautiful. Her beauty was not that of externals, but of a strong and valiant soul shining from her eyes, illuminating her face.

She went down to the Great White Lodge and timidly scratched with her fingernail. The flap was opened by the old woman with the wrinkled face and the kind eyes.

Little Burnt-All-Over said: "Mother, is this the lodge of the King of the Snow Peaks?"

"Yes, child, this is my son's lodge. I am his Mother Earth."

"Mother, is he in?"

"No, my little one, not yet, but I expect him very soon. He is coming into the village to seek a wife; and that woman shall be his who first shall see him as he really is."

"Mother, which way does he come?"

"Over those eastern hills, little one, down the trail you see."

"Mother," she almost whispered, "may I go to meet him?"

"Yes, my child; go, and bless you."

Away went Little Burnt-All-Over, and began to climb the trail. Almost at once there was a blaze of light against the sky at the top, and down there came striding the most wonderful being she had ever seen. She knew it was he; she had seen him in her dreams. Around his head were many eagle feathers shimmering against the sky, and she gazed at the weapons in his right hand and the wonder across his brow and the great hunting dogs that he led on his left.

She looked till he was so near that it was rude to stare, so she moved off into the bushes and covered her face with her hands and waited.

When she was sure he had passed, she turned slowly with sinking heart to look after him. He was gone, but the white lodge shone with new splendor, and blue smoke was curling out at the top.

She went quickly to it. The old woman came. The girl began eagerly: "Mother, I saw your son. Oh, mother, the tallest, most glorious war chief I ever dreamed of. Around his head were what at first I thought were eagle feathers. But when I looked, I knew they were beams of the morning light."

"What did he have in his right hand, daughter?"

"Mother, he carried the lightning. I saw it, red and crooked and forked and moving."

"And what in the other hand?"

"He was leading two great hunting dogs, Mother, white and strong. They were strange dogs, Mother. They had but one eye each, in the middle of their foreheads. I have seen those dogs in the winter sky, Mother, in the lull when the white wind makes ready for a storm."

"And what had he on his brow, my child?"

"The rainbow, Mother—red, blue, and yellow, and shining in splendor."

"With what did he lead the dogs?"

"He led them, Mother, with a beam of light."

"Come into the lodge, my little one! You have surely seen my son."

She stepped aside. From the back of the lodge came the great Chief the girl had seen. In one hand, he held a purple robe spangled over with beads of shining wampum; the other hand he held out to her, as he said: "My own Little Burnt-All-Over, I have been waiting for you. I have been waiting till your years of trial and burning were over; till you had overcome your sorrows with patient fortitude. I have come now to claim you as my bride. Here is the purple robe you have won, for your spirit is great. On it are the wampum beads of your victories. Come now and dwell with me forever in the honor and glory that are truly yours. Men know me as the King of the Day. You they shall know as the Queen of the Night. And when they see your beautiful face in the sky, and your purple robe, they shall indeed see the scars of your sorrows and of your burning. But they shall in no wise mar your beauty, but be there forever to remind men that the way to perfect honor, glory, and joy is through the dark valley of sorrows overcome."

## The Mackenzie River Ghost

More than fifty years ago, some eminent scientists headed by Sir Oliver Lodge founded a Society of Psychical Research to ascertain if there was such a thing as a ghost in the ordinary sense of the word. They offered to investigate every supposed ghost and to do it in the calm cold way of exact science.

Hundreds of instances were sent them; and at least 99 percent of the ghosts were totally dissipated under the disintegrating white light of the scientific approach. But a few there were that would not dissipate, that defied all attempts to explain them away. Among them was the ghost of the Mackenzie River.

In his early days—that is, in the eighties—Seton lived in the Northwest and knew many employees of the Hudson's Bay Company. Among them was one bluff old Scotsman, Roderick MacFarlane. After many years, MacFarlane was retired, and lived in Winnipeg on a small pension. Each time Seton was in that city—about once a year—Mac and he would have a pleasant reunion over a good dinner.

About 1904, shortly after the Research Society had recorded a ghost that defied all ordinary explanation, they were dining together.

"Mac," Seton asked, "did you ever hear anything about the Mackenzie River ghost?"

"What ghost?" said he.

"A ghost that came in broad daylight to some men on the ice of the Mackenzie River. The story was told by a Hudson's Bay Company factor."

"Humph," said Mac, "that factor was me. But Lodge and his group didn't tell it right, nor at full length. I'll give you the facts right now if you like. You can do as you please with it after I'm gone. Do you want to hear it?"

"I sure do," said Seton. "Go on. Tell it as long as you please." And this is the tale as MacFarlane told it that night:

Away back in the sixties, the Company thought there was a good chance of a successful trading post at the mouth of the Mackenzie, since this was Eskimo as well as Indian country and there was no post within 400 miles in any direction. So, with Sandy MacDonald for a helper, I was outfitted for the job. When the summer came, we went to the Mackenzie Delta; and then, turning west, we selected the mouth of Peel River, where we built a couple of log houses, gathered a great pile of driftwood, and were ready for any fur trade that came along.

Next spring, when the river opened, we had a visitor by canoe—
a young fellow named Middleton, about twenty-two years of age,
a graduate of Oxford. He came equipped with letters from the
High Council of our Company. He was filled with missionary zeal,
his one hope and dream being to preach the Gospel to the Eskimos.
He had no knowledge of the Eskimos or of their language; but he
was undaunted by these difficulties, for he felt he was the chosen
vessel to bring them the tidings of salvation.

He was the most impractical, helpless creature I ever saw in the
wilds. He knew nothing but his Oxford and his Bible. He seemed
to us something like a madman. But he came with letters from the
boss, so we had to take him into our family.

Yes, we received him first only on the strength of the letters; but
after a month or two, we were ready to accept him on account of
his personal worth and charm. Far from strong, and troubled with
a hacking cough, he was nevertheless always ready to do his share,
and more than his share, of the work. He was the one who got up
first in the morning to light the fire and start the breakfast. He
was the one to wash the dishes or scrub the dirty floor. It might
be a zero blizzard outdoors, but he was the one who volunteered
first to go after more firewood.

He had brought his fiddle with him. He played well and had a
string of good songs, and many a long, dreary winter night he
whiled away for us, with his music and fun. I tell you we learned
to love that poor fellow like a brother.

But there was something sad in it all—that cough. It grew worse, and in spite of his bright spirits and cheerful soul, he was plainly fading away. Toward the end of the winter, he was so thin and weak that he couldn't go out of the door without getting frostbite. His cough was terrible, and he was spitting blood. Still he was bright, cheerful, and hopeful, and worked steadily on his Eskimo Grammar.

Then came the days when he couldn't leave his bunk. One night he called us to him and said to me: "Mac, you know I'm not long for this world; I've felt my Savior calling me home. You fellows have been so good to me I want to ask one last favor."

"There isn't anything in our power you can't ask," I said for both.

"When my soul goes on," he says, "I don't want my poor body to be thrust into a hole in the ground like some animal. Won't you please bury me in consecrated ground?"

"If it costs my last dollar and my life, I give you my word as a man that I will carry out your wishes," was my answer, and Sandy and I took his poor thin hands in ours, and we gave our solemn promise.

I tell you we were blubbering like two babies. But he wasn't; he was bright and happy.

A month later, the end came. He passed away, happy and peaceful.

The nearest consecrated burying ground was at Fort Resolution,

400 miles up the Mackenzie River and fully 500 from our post. We had no right to leave our post now, so we wrapped the corpse in caribou hides; then with our axes we chopped a grave three feet deep in the ice that never melts on the Mackenzie Mouth.

When he was laid in it, we filled it level with water; and within a few hours, it was one solid mass of ice, level with the rest.

We put a little marker at each end of the place, which was all we could do at that time. I tell you living with that kind brave soul had done more than any book or sermon ever did. And Sandy and I just prayed for a way to carry out our promise.

Well, sir, it was full two years we had to wait, and we surely felt bad about it. But the chance came. The High Council of our Company sent orders to close up the post and travel at once with all books and records to Fort Resolution, where we were to report to the Superintendent of the District.

This gave us the chance we had looked for. We had two sleds, each with a team of fine big husky dogs. On one sled we loaded the books and records of the post, our camping outfit, and grub for ourselves and dogs. On the other we loaded the corpse which we were able to dig out after a couple of hours of chopping. Sandy drove one team; an Indian who had been working for us drove the other. I, the boss, trotted ahead to break the trail.

I tell you it was a funeral like nothing else before—a double funeral. First, it was the end of Peel Post. You see, we knew there was no chance of rival traders by land; but we hadn't reckoned on the whalers, who came by sea and wintered not far away. They had some whaling, but their best trade was in fur with the Eskimos.

So we left a lot of valuable stuff in the cabins and nailed them up to keep off the bears. We knew no Eskimo or Indian would steal anything—they never do—and when summer came, the boat brigade would salvage all.

But our big thought was the other sled. We must keep faith with

the dead man. And away we went in easy stages to cover 500 miles of ice and snow.

The Mackenzie River is two miles wide at the mouth. It has gravel banks and runs through a wide plain with only level snow till the black line of forest begins, three to ten miles away on each side.

The best traveling for the sleds is up the middle of the ice, for there the wind has blown the snow away, and the ice is clear and firm for the runners.

So each morning we set out up the middle of the river ice, trotting along for maybe twenty miles. Then we made our noon halt. Driving to the nearest gravel bank, we hauled up on the level plain. But there was no wood short of the pine forest, miles away across the deep soft snow; so, in order to avoid this hard trip, we always carried on the front of the sled enough firewood to melt snow and boil it for our tea, and then a little more to cook our bacon.

After an hour's rest, we set out again for twenty miles more.

Then at night we would leave the river, and break our way to the forest, where we made a comfortable camp with plenty of wood. And I tell you, I always kept the funeral sled by my bed, for I felt under a solemn vow to protect that. In the morning we gathered our new bundle of wood for the noon and set out again on the ice.

This was our daily routine for about a week. Then, one day at noon, after we had driven up on the gravel bank ten feet above the river, I found we had lost some of our firewood. There wasn't enough to melt a kettle of snow and then cook our meal. So I said to the Indian: "Take the ax and chop through the river ice. If we can get to the water, that will save half the wood we need."

The Indian chopped and chopped till he was down level with

the ax handle. But still he was not through the ice. He called, and Sandy went down to see if there was any show of the water.

Soon he shouted back: "No good." I said: "Then look for an air hole," and went down to help the search.

All of a sudden, we heard loud cries from a human voice on the river bank ten feet above us.

"*Allez! Allez! Allez!*" it shouted. Then "*Marchez! Marchez!*"

We did not suppose there was a human being within hundreds of miles of us. But again came the ringing "*Allez! Allez! Allez!*"— the French that one always uses in ordering and driving the dogs harnessed before the sled.

In haste and amazement, we rushed up the bank and into view of our outfit. Here was the wide level expanse of snow bright in the winter sun, and *not a sign of a human being in sight except ourselves*. But there, lying in a groveling heap, were the ten big fierce husky dogs, growling and rumbling, their eyes glowing, their hair bristling. The tracks showed plainly that, taking advantage of our absence, the very first time they were left alone with the corpse, those hungry, half-tame wolves decided to attack and devour the body. But the moment they touched it, that ringing voice of command was heard driving them back in terror.

"Who spoke?" I almost whispered.

Sandy replied, also in a whisper: "Well, it was a white man s voice, for an Indian can't say '*Marchez*'; he says 'Mush.'"

"Who spoke?" I said to the Indian. He pointed with emphasis to the corpse and added in a low tone: "His voice."

I tell you we never took any chances after that—night or day some one of us always was next the body.

Day after day and night after night we went on with the same routine, some days making forty miles, but on many days of blizzard and storm making little or nothing.

Finally we arrived at the upper reaches of the Mackenzie, where timber was plentiful, and where islands with trees were right in the river; so we had no trouble finding good camp sites.

One evening we came on an island covered with timber, right handy, and decided to camp there. Its shores were clay cut-banks about ten feet high. We left our two sleds on the ice, but Sandy and I climbed up. The Indian caught the dogs one by one, and we hauled them up onto the level top. Here we turned them loose, for I knew they would not leave the fire, and that ten-foot drop was as good as a fence all around.

About nine o'clock, I was smoking my pipe before turning in, when I heard a strange, far-away call on the wooded shore.

*"Ye-hoo-ooo-ooo!"*

I started up, for it was repeated.

*"Ye-hoo-ooo-ooo!"*

At first I thought it was a horned owl, or maybe a wolf call. But again it came with human intonation.

*"Ye-hoo-ooo-ooo!"*

"Say, Sandy, there's someone out there, a lost traveler." So I went to the edge of the island, and shouted back.

"Hallo! Hallo! there, who are you?" There was no answer, even to a second call, and I went back to the fire. Very soon again there came:

*"Ye-hoo-ooo-ooo!"*

I went to the edge of the timber, and shouted: "Who are you? Why don't you come on? Can't you see the fire?"

There was no answer to this, and I said to my pal: "Say, Sandy, I don't feel comfortable about leaving our charge on the ice. The dogs can't get near it; but anyway, let's put it up a tree."

So we three went down in the darkness; and after much trouble, got our burden safe up a thick, bushy tree. We heard no more calls in the night.

Next morning, as my helper was packing and making ready for a start, I prowled around in the snow and on the ice. There I learned from the tracks that all the previous evening, and maybe for a couple of days before, we had been followed by a wolverine. Our charge would have been unprotected by the dogs and exposed to the wolverine, which certainly would have found and disfigured it, had we not acted on the weird warning that came in time.

After that, our journey continued with little incident till near Christmas, when we reached Fort Resolution.

There I turned over my charge to the Archbishop, who laid it by the altar in the church, promising to attend to all proper ceremonies as soon as feasible—which meant as soon as the springtime made it possible to dig a grave.

That night we three travelers slept in the ram pasture, which is the name of the bunk house in a Hudson Bay fort.

The moon was full, shining on the snow, and through the window lighted up the place well. About ten o'clock I was awakened with a sudden feeling of alertness. I sat up as unsleepy as could be, and there right opposite to me were Sandy and the Indian both sitting up.

Then there came on me an overwhelming feeling of bliss, of happiness complete; and in the gloom, I thought I saw on Sandy's face the same expression of rapture. I do not know any word to describe the sensation but "ecstasy." It gradually faded away.

We gazed at each other and at the door and at nowhere.

I said: "Sandy, did you see anything?"

"No," he whispered.

"Did you?" I asked the Indian.

He shook his head.

"Did you feel anything, Sandy?"

"I did," he said. "I was filled with joy."

"What was it?" I asked.

In a low but certain voice, he said, "He came in gratitude to us for carrying out our promise. Thank God we didn't fail him! We have surely had our reward."[1]

# 20.

# THE GOSPEL OF THE RED MAN

## *The Teachings of Wabasha**

So live your life that the fear of death can never enter your heart.

When you arise in the morning, give thanks for the morning light.† Give thanks for your life and strength. Give thanks for your food and give thanks for the joy of living. And if perchance you see no reason for giving thanks, rest assured the fault is in yourself.‡

Thank the Great Spirit for each meal; cast a morsel of meat into the fire and pray: "Great Spirit, partake with us."

Sin is trespass against the laws of the Great Spirit; it brings its own punishment. Crime is trespass against the laws of the tribe; and may be punished by the tribe.

No man shall suffer for the sin of another. No man can take the punishment of another, and so make the sinner guiltless.

It is unjust that a wicked man should escape the punishment of his crime. It is tenfold more unjust that an innocent man be punished in his place. God is not a hungry wild beast, demanding only a victim, it matters not who or what, so He be fed. Therefore,

---

* Also ascribed to Tecumseh, Sitting Bull, Crazy Horse, and Wovoka.

† "The white man's creed is the fear of dying; the Indian's creed is the joy of living."—Indian comment.

‡ J. J. Matthews says this was always chanted as an orison among his people, the Osages.

beware of the liars, that offer to secure for you an innocent, to bear the penalty of your sin, while you go free.

Be merciful to those who are in your power. It is the part of a coward to torture a prisoner or ill-treat those that are helpless before you. It is the part of a Chief to take care of the weak, the sick, the old and the helpless.

Only a coward ends his life by suicide; a brave man dies fighting.

Every village should have its Holy Place, its Medicine Lodge, where men may meet to dance the dance, smoke the good smoke, make medicine.

And every man should have his own Holy Place where he keeps lonely vigil, harkens for the Voices, and offers prayer and praise.

If by training, and a right life, and the gift of the Great Spirit, you have made your body beautiful, it is well to have your beauty seen by all, for an example and to give them pleasure. The veil of shame is well for those who are diseased or misshapen or unclean, and so made ugly.

If a wild beast attack your child, your wife, your house, your friend, or yourself, it is your duty as a man to fight with all your strength and with whatever weapons be at hand, and to destroy it as soon as possible or drive it off; and it is none the less your duty if that beast be in the form of a man.

Show respect to all men, but grovel to none.

It is more honorable to give than to receive.

Pray that the smell of your own people be a pleasant smell to you.

I have seen many men whose religion, judging by their lives, is the "love of money and the fear of death." But these were not red men of the old faith.*

---

* We are taught that the love of money is the root of all evil. If this be true, then was the Indian saved from much, for money was unknown among his tribes till brought by the white man. Carver says that to the love of money the

Do not speak of the dead except to recall their good deeds.

Do not speak to your mother-in-law at any time, or allow her to talk to you. If she be in the lodge when the son-in-law enters, she should drop her eyes, and leave in silence. This is the wisdom of the Ancients.

When you arrive at a strange camp or village, first pay your respects to the Chief before you call on your friends or acquaintances of lesser rank. It may be the Chief does not wish you to be received at all.

When you leave camp in the morning, clean up all your rubbish, burn or bury it. Do not go about polluting the land or destroying its beauty.

Do not stare at strangers; drop your eyes if they stare hard at you; and this, above all, for women.

Always give a word or sign of salute when meeting or passing a friend, or even a stranger, if in a lonely place.

A man is bound by his promise with a bond that cannot be broken except by permission of the other party. If that promise is on paper, that is merely to prove that he did give his word. It is not therefore more or less binding.

A Minisino (a man tried and proven) is at all times clean, courteous, and master of himself.

If a man be given over to sex appetite, he is harboring a rattlesnake, whose sting is rottenness and sure death.

## Laws of the Lodge

Be hospitable. Be kind. Always assume that your guest is tired, cold, and hungry. If even a hungry dog enters your lodge, you must feed him.

---

Indians "attribute all the mischiefs that are prevalent among the Europeans, such as treachery, plundering, devastation and murder" (*Travels*, p. 158); therefore, would none of it.

Always give your guest the place of honor in the lodge, and at the feast, and serve him in reasonable ways. Never sit while your guest stands.

Go hungry rather than stint your guest. If he refuses certain food, say nothing; he may be under vow.

Protect your guest as one of the family; feed his horse, and beat your dogs if they harm his dog.

Do not trouble your guest with many questions about himself; he will tell you what he wishes you to know.*

In another man's lodge, follow his customs, not your own.

Never worry your host with your troubles.

Always repay calls of courtesy; do not delay.

Give your host a little present on leaving; little presents are little courtesies and never give offence.

Say "Thank you" for every gift, however small.

Compliment your host, even if you must strain the facts to do so.

Never come between anyone and the fire.

Never walk between persons talking. Never interrupt persons talking.

In council, listen attentively to the other man's words as though they were words of wisdom, however much they may be otherwise.

Let not the young speak among those much older, unless asked.

When you address the council, carry a green bough in your hand, that yours may be living words.

Always give place to your seniors in entering or leaving the lodge. Never sit while your seniors stand.

Never force your conversation on anyone.

Let silence be your motto till duty bids you speak.

Speak softly, especially before your elders or in presence of strangers.

---

* Oskenonton said that his father taught him: Do not even ask him his name. He may be a fugitive from justice, and that is none of your affair.

Do not touch live coals with a steel knife or any sharp steel.

Do not break a marrow bone in the lodge; it is unlucky.

The women of the lodge are the keepers of the fire, but the men should help with the heavier sticks.

When setting up the tepees, keep the camp circle with its opening to the east, the door of each tepee to the sunrise.

Let each tepee be in its place, as long ago pointed by the old men—the wise ones—the nigh kin near each other, and the clans of different totems facing across the circle. In this wise the young men shall see that they must marry across the circle of the camp, never with their close kin in the nearer lodges.

## The Daily Worship

"In the life of the Indian," says Ohiyesa, the Sioux, "there was only one inevitable duty—the duty of prayer, the daily recognition of the Unseen and Eternal. His daily devotions were more necessary to him than daily food. He wakes at daybreak, puts on his moccasins, and steps down to the water's edge. Here he throws handfuls of clear, cold water into his face, or plunges in bodily. After the bath, he stands erect before the advancing dawn, facing the sun as it dances upon the horizon, and offers his unspoken orison. His mate may precede or follow him in his devotions, but never accompanies him. Each soul must meet the morning sun, the new sweet earth, and the Great Silence alone!"

So also their other prophets:

"When you arise in the morning, give thanks for the morning light. Give thanks for your life and strength. Give thanks for your food and give thanks for the joy of living. And if perchance you see no reason for giving thanks, rest assured the fault is in yourself."

Then, continuing the daily round, Ohiyesa says:

"When food is taken, the woman murmurs a 'grace' as she lowers the kettle, an act so softly and unobtrusively performed that one who does not know the custom usually fails to catch the whisper: 'Spirit, partake!' As her husband receives the bowl or plate, he likewise murmurs his invocation to the Spirit. When he becomes an old man, he loves to make a notable effort to prove his gratitude. He cuts off the choicest morsel of the meat and casts it into the fire—the purest and most ethereal element."

When ye are assembled in council, fail not to light in the midst the Fire which is the symbol of the Great Spirit and the sign of His presence.

And light the Sacred Pipe, which is the symbol of Peace, Brotherhood, Council and Prayer, and smoke first to the Great Spirit in Heaven above, then to the Four Winds, His messengers, and to Mother Earth, through whom He furnishes us our food.

And let each councilor smoke, passing the pipe in a circle like that of the Sun from east southward to the west.

At the opening of council, let the Chief arise, light the pipe, and pray: *"Wakan Tanka Wakan na kay chin, Chandee eeya paya wo."* That is, "Great Spirit, by this pipe, the symbol of Peace, Council, and Brotherhood, we ask Thee to be with us and bless us tonight."

## *Indian Prayers*

### I

"O great Spirit of my fathers, this is my prayer.

"Help me to feel Thine urge and Thy message.

"Help me to be just even to those who hate me; and at all times help me to be kind.

"If mine enemy is weak and faltering, help me to the good

thought that I forgive him.

"If he surrender, move me to help him as a weak and needy brother."

## II

"O great Spirit of my fathers, help me to wholly void my heart of fear.

"And above all things, O God of my people and of my soul, help me to be a man."

## III

"O God, show me the way of wisdom, and give me strength to follow it without fear."

## IV

"O Great Spirit, this is my prayer! Grant that fear may never enter into my heart to be the guide of my feet."

## V

"O Great Spirit, make me sufficient to mine own occasions.

"Give to me to mind my own business at all times, and to lose no good opportunity for holding my tongue.

"When it is appointed for me to suffer, let me take example from the dear well-bred beasts and go away in solitude to bear my suffering by myself, not troubling others with my complaints.

"Help me to win, if win I may, but—and this especially, O Great Spirit—if it be not ordained that I may win, make me at least a good loser."*

* This prayer, in brief, was inscribed on the wall of King George's study, Buckingham Palace, London.

## The Omaha Tribal Prayer

*"Wa-kon-da dhe dhu*
*Wapa-dhin a-ton-he."*

Translated into our tongue: "Father, a needy one stands before Thee. I that sing am he."

This noble prayer to God was sung on the Missouri River, we believe, long before Columbus landed, and with the music, words, and attitude just as we of the Woodcraft Way use them today.

During the prayer those assembled stand in a great circle about the fire, with faces and hands raised to heaven. As the final words are sung, hands and heads are bowed to the symbolic fire, and the Chief announces: "With this our council is ended."

## Death Songs

Every Indian in the old days had a Death Song prepared for the time when he knew he was facing the end.

One Indian Chief confided to me that his Death Song was the same as that of the thirty-seven Sioux patriots who were executed at Mankato, Minnesota, in 1862 for seeking to drive the invaders from their country:

"I, Chaska, do sing:
I care not where my body lies,
My soul goes marching on.
I care not where my body lies,
My soul goes marching on."

When Nanni Chaddi and his four Apache warriors, after four days of starvation, thirst, and agony, decided to face and fight rather than surrender to the white regiment that had them cornered in a cave, they sang to God:

> "Father, we are going out to die.
> For ourselves we grieve not,
> But for those who are left behind.
> Let not fear enter into our hearts.
> We are going out to die."

Then, armed only with arrows and lances, they dashed into the fire of a hundred rifles, and were shot to rags.[1]

# 21.

# THE BUFFALO WIND

**I** was only a child when first I heard it. My brother had made an Aeolian harp and set it in the window under the raised sash. It was silent for a time, and then began a soft low strain. This rose and fell with the wind, chimed in weird harmonies. But the wind arose, and it sang, and shrieked; then dropped to a moaning song that wrung my young soul, brought tears to my eyes. I know not why, for music was not in my gift. It gripped me with a sweet agony; it reached my inmost being. I had no words but "I want to go! I want to go!"

Little waftings far away I got. Once or twice I got them from the wind in the trees when, as a boy, I made my cabin in Glenyan; and I flung myself on the leafy ground, and bit the twigs in a craze of longing and inexpression.

Then I went to live in London to study art. I was much alone; and, by force of poverty, lived the life of a desert hermit. My body was purged with simple life and fasting. I was dreaming dreams; and, after two years of discipline, purgation, and absolute domination by the things of the spirit, I began to hear the Voices. I heard them in the ecstatic time that comes near sunrise, when my body seemed to float in the peace that passeth all understanding. I heard the Voices, and I heard the Strain again. It sang or moaned: "The Buffalo Wind, the Buffalo Wind!"

A friend loaned me a book, *The Shades of Shasta,* much of good picture and much of sordid meanness in it. But always when the writer told of Shasta, it was noble. In the end, the Indians of Shasta were massacred—massacred by the Christians—all their love and dreams of the Great Mountain were forgotten. And the writer stood alone on the high shoulder, to look before leaving it all. There was no human sound—the quail whistled in the grass, and the wind moaned in the cedars and the grass, and moaned farewell. My eyes blurred. I knew that he had heard it. The book dropped from my hand, for "The Buffalo Wind was blowing!"

Then I heard the Call of the West—and went. Three Years I roamed and lived, and truly lived—alone, nearly always, alone but rejoicing—until I heard another, the summons back to everything I hated. The glory of the August sun was on the gold and bloom-lit plains when it came in a letter. I went outside the shanty, and gazed away at a line of red willows across the level green—it marked the brook line. It was alive with loved and lovable things; it had held my happy thoughts for three years. And the Wind came whistling across, bending the grass tops, bending the early golden-rods, and carried a burst of song that meant but little till it struck the mosquito screen, and whistled, screamed, then dropped to a low moaning sound. And through my brain and soul it went: "The Buffalo Wind! The Buffalo Wind is blowing!"

Driven by what I called my fate, I went to—I don't know what. But I went to Paris to study with the great French painters—was there for two years when my Vision came. I know not was it a dream, a screaming wind, or a ranting in the street. But I heard it in my sleep; and as I woke, the song was in my ears, a song that clutched and wracked me—a thrilling song that hurt me more than ever I can tell: "The Wind, the Wind, the Buffalo Wind! The Buffalo Wind is blowing!"

So I packed my little all, and went to the Prairies. I halted in Winnipeg. Down by the river below the great railway bridge was an old French half-breed whom I knew; his cabin a relic of the long-ago. He talked of the good old days, or smoked in silence. He gazed across the river with dull far gaze. "They are gone—they are gone—but soon I too will go. I have heard the Buffalo Wind; the good old Buffalo Wind," he said, "that blew from the South in April, and told us that the buffalo were coming, that brought the buffalo, the sustenance of the Plains, the Medicine Beast, the red man's dream of joy."

When I left the Plains that fall to go again to the sordid East, I sat on the rear platform of the train, and gazed at the last great landmark hill as it faded in the evening light. I heard it, but oh, so faintly now. I could not look—I had no eyes.

It was ten years after that it came with new overwhelm. In the hills of Santa Barbara I met her—a strange woman from India. She had sent for me. She looked thirty or ninety, I could not tell which. Her eyes had the far, veiled look of another world. She talked softly of food and coffee, of weather, cats, and common things till I was leaving; then, on me turned her strange blank gaze, with a new light gleaming in her eye, and in other tone, of message and command:

You are not of this people. Why do you not open your ears and your heart? Know you not you are a Red Soul sent back to deliver The Message—to show forth the red-man way? Hear it now—for the Buffalo Wind is blowing!"

I went away, dazed—and tormented.

Oh, God! Give me the strength to know and rise in time! To rise ere yet it is too late.

The swift years have gone—the urge becomes a lash. I am going now—I am going with all my strength. So have I sought a home-land under the white Snow Peaks—where Trail meets Trail—and far away, flashing and bright, the Red Man's River seeks the open Sea.

The Buffalo Wind is blowing![1]

# APPENDIX

## Sources of Selections Used in This Book

### Chapter 1  BOYHOOD DAYS IN CANADA
1. Trail of an Artist-Naturalist.

### Chapter 2  ACROSS CANADA BY RAIL
1. Trail of an Artist-Naturalist.

### Chapter 3  THE MANITOBA PRAIRIES
1. Trail of an Artist-Naturalist.
2. Proceedings of the United States National Museum, 1890.
3. Trail of an Artist-Naturalist.

### Chapter 4  BIRDS OF MANITOBA
1. The Auk, 1885, Vol. 2.
2. Trail of an Artist-Naturalist.
3. Proceedings of the United States National Museum, 1890.

### Chapter 5  TWO BIRD STORIES
1. Lives of the Hunted.
2. Wild Animal Ways.

### Chapter 6  MAMMALS OF MANITOBA
1. Transactions of the Manitoba Scientific and Historical Society, No. 23, 1886. Signed Ernest E. Thompson.

### Chapter 7  BISON AND CARIBOU HERDS
1. Arctic Prairies.

*Chapter 8*   STUDIES IN THE ART ANATOMY OF ANIMALS

1. Trail of an Artist-Naturalist.
2. Studies in the Art Anatomy of Animals.

*Chapter 9*   TRACKING AND TRAILING

1. St. Nicholas Magazine, March 1888. Signed Ernest E. Thompson.
2. Country Life in America, 1909.

*Chapter 10*   CAN ZOO ANIMALS LEAD A NORMAL LIFE?

1. Annual Report of the Smithsonian Institution, 1901: "The National Zoo at Washington; a Study of Its Animals in Relation to Their Natural Environment."

*Chapter 11*   TWO LIFE HISTORIES

1. Lives of Game Animals.

*Chapter 12*   THE HORSE

1. Studies in the Art Anatomy of Animals.
2. Wild Animal Ways.

*Chapter 13*   HANK AND JEFF

1. Great Historic Animals.

*Chapter 14*   LIFE HISTORY OF THE BIGHORN SHEEP

1. Lives of Game Animals.

*Chapter 15*   KRAG, THE KOOTENAY RAM

1. Lives of the Hunted.

*Chapter 16*   LIFE HISTORY OF THE GRAY WOLF

1. Lives of Game Animals.

*Chapter 17*   TWO WOLF STORIES

1. Wild Animals I Have Known.
2. Animal Heroes.

*Chapter 18*   THE RISE OF THE WOODCRAFT INDIANS

1. A privately published pamphlet by Seton.

*Chapter 19*  Stories for the Campfire

1. Trail and Campfire Stories, by Julia M. Seton.

*Chapter 20*  Indians Real and Make-believe

1. The Gospel of the Red Man.

*Chapter 21*  The Buffalo Wind

1. The Buffalo Wind, a privately printed leaflet by Seton, commemorating his seventy-eighth birthday.

# Books by Ernest Thompson Seton

Studies in the Art Anatomy of
Animals, Macmillan Co., 1889

Wild Animals I Have Known,
Scribners, 1898

The Trail of the Sandhill Stag,
Scribners, 1899

The Biography of a Grizzly,
Century, 1900

Lives of the Hunted,
Scribners, 1901

Two Little Savages,
Doubleday, 1903

Monarch, The Big Bear of
Tallac, Scribners, 1904

Woodmyth and Fable,
Century, 1905

Animal Heroes, Scribners, 1905

The Natural History of the Ten
Commandments,
Scribners, 1907

The Birch-Bark Roll of the
Woodcraft Indians,*
Doubleday, 1906

Life Histories of North American Game Animals,
Scribners, 1909

The Biography of a Silver Fox,
Century, 1909

Fauna of Manitoba, British
Assn. Handbook, Winnipeg,
1909

Boy Scouts of America Handbook, Doubleday, 1910

Rolf in the Woods, Doubleday,
1911

Arctic Prairies, Scribners,
1911

The Book of Woodcraft and Indian Lore, Doubleday
(eleventh revision), 1912

The Foresters' Manual, Doubleday, 1912

Wild Animals at Home, Doubleday, 1913

Wild Animal Ways, Houghton
Mifflin Co., 1916

The Preacher of Cedar Mountain, Doubleday, 1917

Sign Talk, Doubleday, 1918

Woodland Tales, Doubleday,
1921

* The Birch-Bark Roll was revised through some 20 editions that appeared
almost yearly up to 1925.

*Bannertail, the Story of a Gray-squirrel,* Scribners, 1922
*Lives of Game Animals,* Doubleday, 1925
*Great Historic Animals,* Scribners, 1937
*The Biography of an Arctic Fox,* Appleton-Century, 1937

*The Gospel of the Red Man,* Doubleday, 1938
*Trail of an Artist Naturalist, Autobiography,* Scribners, 1940
*Santana, the Hero Dog of France,* Phoenix Press, Los Angeles, 1945

Note: *For his hundreds of magazine articles and other publications see* Ernest Thompson Seton, A Biographical Sketch Done by Various Hands, *Doubleday, 1925, to which is attached a complete (up to 1925) Bibliography of the Works of this Author.*

# INDEX